THE 'LABOUR HERCULES'

Jeffrey Leddin was awarded a PhD by the University of Limerick in 2017. He was editor of volume 15 of *History Studies*, Ireland's oldest post-graduate history journal.

THE 'LABOUR HERCULES'

THE IRISH CITIZEN ARMY
AND IRISH REPUBLICANISM
1913–23

Jeffrey Leddin

IRISH ACADEMIC PRESS

First published in 2019 by
Irish Academic Press
10 George's Street
Newbridge
Co. Kildare
Ireland

www.iap.ie

© Jeffrey Leddin, 2019

9781788550741 (Paper)
9781788550758 (Kindle)
9781788550765 (Epub)
9781788550772 (PDF)

British Library Cataloguing in Publication Data
An entry can be found on request

Library of Congress Cataloging in Publication Data
An entry can be found on request

Typeset in Minion Pro 11/14 pt

Cover front: Irish Citizen Army on the roof of Liberty Hall
(Camerapress.com 00209741).
Cover back: James Connolly, *c.*1916 (NPA POLI10).

CONTENTS

ICA Drill circa 1915

Source: Irish Citizen Army Notebook, 1914–15, WOBP, MS 34,937, NLI.

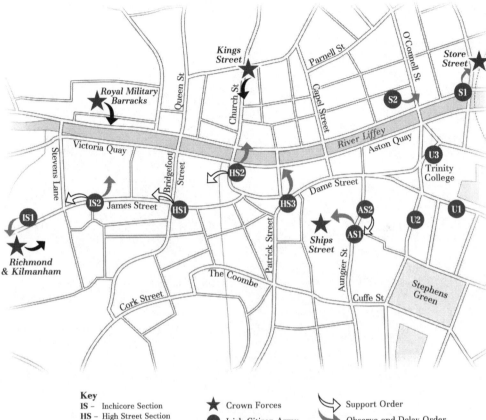

Key
- **IS** – Inchicore Section
- **HS** – High Street Section
- **AS** – Aungier Street Section
- **U** – Unnamed Section
- **S** – 'Strong' Section

★ Crown Forces
● Irish Citizen Army

⇨ Support Order
⇨ Observe and Delay Order
⮩ British Force Movement

Inchicore Section

Section 1: Back James Street to observe and delay all movement form Richmond Military Barracks and Kilmainham Police Barracks.

Section 2: James Street fountain to observe all movements from Royal Military Barracks and support No.1 section.

High Street Section

Section 1: Thomas Street to support section in James Street taking up a position between Meath Street and Francis Street.

Section 2: To take up position at bottom of Bridge Street to observe and delay all members of troops from Royal Barracks along quays. If necessary fall back on section one in Thomas Street.

Section 3: back of Church Palace to observe all movements of police coming from King Street; to hold on until sections from James Street and Thomas Street fall back.

Aungier Street Section

Section 1: Stephen Street to observe and delay movements of troops from Ship Street.

Section 2: South Great George Street to support section in Stephens Street.

Unnamed Section

Section 1: Nassau Street.

Section 2: Griffin Street.

Section 3: College Street.

'Strong' Section

Strong section at Liberty Hall to observe Store Street.

Strong section at Abbey Street midway to O'Connell Street to observe Store Street.

Population Distribution of ICA circa 1916

Source: Three notebooks containing names of ICA members, 1915–1916, WOBP, MS 15,672, NLI.

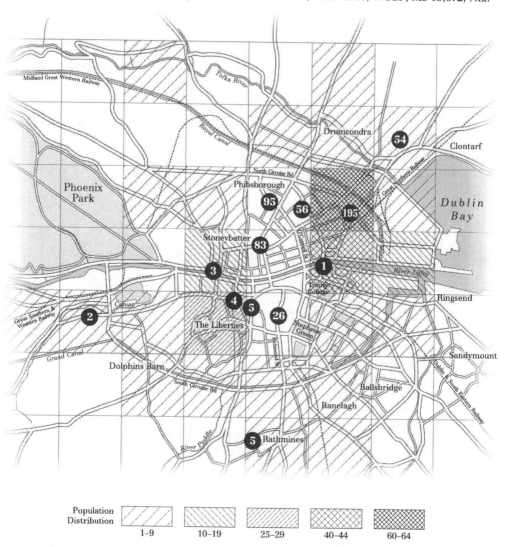

ICA Officers in 1916

(compiled by Christopher Poole)

General **James Connolly**	Army No.1	**Blake, Charles** in Moynetown, Baldoyle	**Kennedy, William** in 13 Sutton
Commandant **Michael Mallin**	Army No.2	**Blake, John** in Moynetown, Baldoyle	Cottages, Baldoyle
Staff Capt. **Christopher Poole**	Army No.195	**Boylan, John** in 23 St Michaels Terrace	**McCormick, James** in 13 Sutton
Capt. **Sean Connolly**	Army No.54	**Chaney, William** in 5 Northcote Avenue	Cottages, Baldoyle
Capt. **Richard McCormack**	Army No.83	**Clements, W.** in Parnell Cottages	**McDonnagh, Joseph** in 18 Cottages
Capt. **John O'Neill**	Army No.56	**Doherty, Patrick** in 5 Sutton	Sutton Rd, Baldoyle
Lieutenant **Michael Kelly**	Army No.5	Terrace, Sutton	**O'Neill, James** in St.Catherine's Lucan
Lieutenant **Thomas Kain**	Army No.3	**Dunn, Mick** in 25 Nortcote Ave	**Roche, Joseph** in Moynetown, Baldoyle
Lieutenant **Robert De Cour**	Army No.26	**Fox, Patrick** in 9 Station Rd, New	**Roche, Patrick** in Moynetown, Baldoyle
Lieutenant **Thomas Donoghue**	Army No.95	Cooatges, Baldoyle	**Roche, Philip** in New Road, Baldoyle
Lieutenant **P. Jackson**	Army No.4	**Gough, Joseph** in Kilbarrack, Sutton	**Rooney, J.** in Borough, Sutton
Lieutenant **Countess Markievicz**	Army No.55		**Rooney, James** in Borough, Sutton

While the map shows the distribution of the vast majority of ICA members (and all its officers) in 1916, some members lived further out in the city's environs which the map does not highlight.

Dublin Castle Bases, Easter 1916

Source: William Oman, BMH WS 421, p. 3.

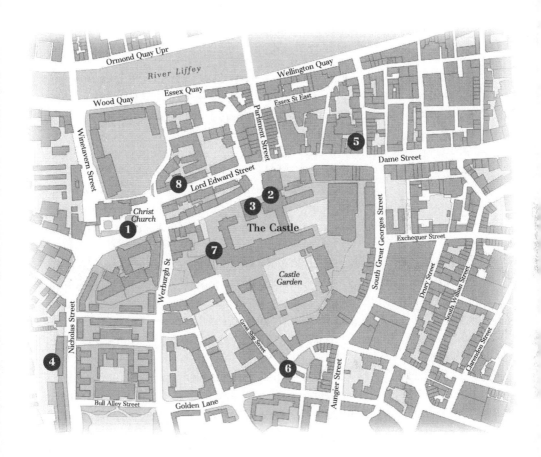

Key

1 Synod Hall
2 City Hall
3 Castle Yard Entrance
4 Churchyard
5 *Daily Mail* office & Henry and James' Tailors
6 Stephen's Street unit
7 Ship Street viaduct
8 Engineering Post

Acknowledgements

This book could not have been undertaken without the generous and immeasurable help of numerous people. I wish to thank Dr Ruán O'Donnell, who has provided constant and incalculable guidance and support.

I also wish to acknowledge the assistance and encouragement given to me by the History Department of the University of Limerick. Thank you to Professor Anthony McElligott, Professor Bernadette Whelan, Dr David Fleming, Dr Richard Kirwan, Dr John Logan, Dr John O'Callaghan, Dr Alistair Malcolm, Dr Odette Clarke, Dr Niamh O'Sullivan and Dr Gavin Wilk.

I thank my friends and colleagues who provided constant comradeship through the years. Thanks to Dr Patrick McMahon, Dr Gearóid Ó Faoleán, Dr Aileen Marron, Dr Stephen Ryan, Dr Niamh Lenahan, Dr Martin Walsh, Seán McKillen, Paul Hayes, Ger Maher, Patrick Miller, Lorraine Barron, and to anyone I have forgotten. My thanks also to all my friends outside of academia.

My thanks go to the staff at the libraries and archives I have visited while undertaking this research: National Archives of Ireland, Irish Labour History Society Museum and Archives, National Archives London, Dublin City Library, Military History Archives, National Library of Ireland and University College Dublin Archives. I also wish to thank the staff of the Glucksman Library, University of Limerick.

To my family, Ger, Ann, Steven, my grandmother and to my other late grandparents who have taught me a love of history and knowledge, and who have supported me in not just my education but all my work throughout the years. I could not have written this without you. Lastly, thanks and love to Sinéad not just for your help with this project but for your never-ending support in all my aspirations.

ABBREVIATIONS

AAA	Anti-Austerity Alliance
AOH	Ancient Order of Hibernians
ASU	Active Service Unit
BSP	British Socialist Party
CA	Connolly Association
CGT	Confédération Génerale du Travail
CMO	Chief Mobilising Officer
CWC	Clyde Workers' Committee
DBC	Dublin Bread Company
DMP	Dublin Metropolitan Police
DORA	Defence of the Realm Act
DUTCLL	Dublin United Trades Council and Labour League
FFF	Farmers' Freedom Force
FGCM	Field General Court Martial
GHQ	General Headquarters
GOC	General Officer Commanding
GPO	General Post Office
ICA	Irish Citizen Army
ILP	Independent Labour Party
ILPTUC	Irish Labour Party and Trades Union Congress
INAAVDF	Irish National Aid Association and Volunteers' Dependents Fund
INL	Irish Neutrality League
INLA	Irish National Liberation Army
IPP	Irish Parliamentary Party
IRA	Irish Republican Army
IRB	Irish Republican Brotherhood
ISRP	Irish Socialist Republican Party

ITGWU	Irish Transport and General Workers' Union
ITUC	Irish Trades Union Congress
ITUCLP	Irish Trades Union Congress and Labour Party
IWG	Irish Workers Group
MO	Mobilising Officer
NUDL	National Union of Dock Labourers
NUR	National Union of Railwaymen
OGCM	Ordinary General Court Martial
OIRA	Official Irish Republican Army
QM	Quartermaster
PIRA	Provisional Irish Republican Army
POW	Prisoner of War
RCSI	Royal College of Surgeons in Ireland
RIC	Royal Irish Constabulary
SDF	Social Democratic Federation
SLP	Socialist Labour Party
SPI	Socialist Party of Ireland
TUC	British Trades Union Congress
UIL	United Irish League
UVF	Ulster Volunteer Force

1

'THE ARMED NATION': EUROPEAN CITIZEN ARMY THEORIES AND THE IRISH REPUBLICAN NEXUS, 1866–1913

Variously referred to as the Transport Union Citizen Army, the Citizen Army, and Árm Lucta Oibre na h-Éireann (Army of the Working Class of Ireland), the Irish Citizen Army (ICA) was the most distinctly leftist element of Dublin's revolutionary republicans between 1913 and 1923.[1] This book explores the ideological and military development of the ICA, and identifies the extent to which the army can be understood as having been a bridging point between the ideologies and aspirations of militant trade unionism and militant nationalism and republicanism. Neither of these political spheres were homogenous groupings throughout this period, and this work examines whether the force, at various points, was best defined as a workers' defence corps or as a republican extra-parliamentary unit. Given this, the relationship it held with organs such as the Irish Transport and General Workers' Union (ITGWU), the Irish Trades Union Congress (ITUC), the Irish Republican Brotherhood (IRB), and Óglaigh na hÉireann (which manifested itself as both the Irish Volunteers and the Irish Republican Army (IRA)) acts as a central thread within the study. Concurrently, the militia has previously been referred to as a 'vanguard'[2] of the rebellion in 1916. Its *bona fides* as a revolutionary body over the ten years are also assessed. Areas such as the use of military terminology; development of martial structure; the use of practices such as drill, recruitment, and arms procurement, as well as active engagement in live warfare are also key. This period has been understood as an Irish revolution.[3]

R.F. Foster argued for an understanding of the role of the 'tipping point' in revolutions: 'the moment when substantive change becomes possible, building on an alteration of "hearts and minds" as well as the "presenting problem" of an immediate crisis.[4] In essence, these are moments which make possible radical changes in the behaviour of a group. In order to assert these 'tipping points' this book presents a periodisation of the force which centres on moments of either significant change or rapid escalation. The collapse of the 1913 strike and lockout and the promotion of James Connolly to the commander of the ICA are examples of these. Similarly, theorists such as James D. Fearon and David D. Laitin, as well as James Ron reasoned that the example of 'weak central governments' or 'indiscriminate state responses' create grievances and 'escalatory tipping points'.[5] Under this theoretical framework, the importance of events such as the Home Rule crisis and the Bachelor's Walk shootings are assessed. However, these moments must also be contextualised within the long gestation of the currents which they helped to escalate. For Foster, Ireland experienced a pre-revolutionary period between the death of Charles Stewart Parnell in 1891 and the week-long rebellion in 1916.[6] He posited that during this phase extremism flourished in a variety of seedbeds, such as feminism and socialism.[7]

The nascent radicalisation of nationalism was a key factor in the evolution of Árm Lucta Oibre na h-Éireann. However, other contexts were also important. The force was defined by the two labour titans, James Larkin and James Connolly. Both lived and worked in Britain and America, and were 'international' men. Wider pan-national socialist and syndicalist thought must be understood in order to properly assess the force in which they were so influential. A key component of this was the development of an 'armed nation' theory which began to be expressed by European socialists and social democrats from the 1860s.[8]

In 1925, J.D. Clarkson described the force as 'the first "red army" in modern Europe'.[9] Given the prevalence of Spartacus and Bolshevik revolutionaries, this was distinguished company. Historians also connected the ICA with socialist expositions on the 'armed nation'. In 1975, Bernard Campbell Ransom argued that the title Citizen Army paid deference to Harry Quelch's pamphlet *Social Democracy and the Armed Nation* (1900).[10] Likewise, D.R. O'Connor Lysaght viewed the Irish militia as rooted in the theories of the French thinker Jean Jaurés and his work on *L'armée Nouvelle* (1911).[11] The theory of the 'nation in arms' began earlier than these two works. From the middle of the nineteenth century onwards there developed within the European left a vocal criticism of the militarism which manifested itself in standing armies. This led to an attempt to formulate and implement an alternative system that did not incorporate the often-seen impracticable pacifism. For example, in an article for the 1896 International Workers' Congress, Professor Albert Russell argued that while preferring passive resistance 'it is not, however necessary or advisable to refuse military training'.[12]

Naturally, the first manifestation of this occurred in the Socialist International gatherings. The International in Geneva in 1866 discussed the French delegates' submission that 'an armed people' should be implemented by the world's countries instead of professional troops. The proposal was carried.[13] While resolutions at the congress in Brussels in 1868 did not mention such theories of citizen-led armed forces, a plethora of writings appeared over the following half-century discussing the merits of the notion.[14] For instance, in 1869 the *Advocate of Peace* published Andrew P. Peabody's polemic 'Standing Armies: Unnecessary' which described that particular military system as a 'vampire-drain made on the vitals of a nation'.[15]

The majority of writing on the theory was disseminated from the First and Second International, and other bodies closely linked with those socialist organisations. The immediate question which faced the various bodies of the International was that of their attitude to the military arrangements of their respective countries as well as the question of the best means in which war could be avoided. There was no simple answer arrived at because the majority of countries had followed Prussia's example and implemented universal compulsory military service, something from which Quelch was at pains to dissociate his 'armed nation' concept.[16] However, as Joll argued, while the 'socialists may have disapproved of whole system, they could not remain indifferent to the conditions under which they themselves, their sons, brothers and comrades passed some two years of their life; any more than they could remain indifferent to the conditions which they were working in factories'.[17]

On 9 April 1872, the First International's general council listened to a translation of the address of the Parisian delegates 'Ferré' which drew upon the collapse of the Paris Commune, a forbearer to the socialist utopian ideals which Lysaght connected to the ICA. The address brimmed with vivid imagery of citizen forces: 'citizens, the proletarian army, scattered by late events, must rally and reorganise itself ... among the soldiers of our cause ...'[18] Furthermore, in 1896, the war commission of the International Socialist Congress argued for the establishment of the 'armed nation'. The

International Workers' Congress in London in 1896 published the war commission's report on the 'standing armies':

> Standing armies, whose maintenance even in times of peace exhausts the nation, and the cost of which is borne by the working class, increase the danger of war between nations, and at the same time favour the brutal oppression of the proletariat of the world. This is why the cry 'lay down your arms' is no more listened to than other appeals to humanitarian sentiments raised by the capitalist classes. The working class alone have the serious desire, and they alone possess the power to realise universal peace. They demand:
>
> a. The simultaneous abolition of standing armies and the establishment of a national citizen force.
> b. The establishment of tribunals of arbitration, to regulate peaceably disputes between nations.
> c. The final decision on the question of war or peace to be vested directly in the people in cases where the governments refuse to accept the decision of the tribunal of arbitration.[19]

Even after the formation of the so-called 'first red army', the Citizen Army in Ireland in 1913, and the outbreak of World War I in Europe in 1914, the terminology continued to be used. In 1916, Granville Fortescue published *Fore-Armed: How to Build a Citizen Army* and argued that the regular army of the United States of America was a 'mercenary force'.[20] In 1915, Harry Hyndman, the founder of the Social Democratic Federation, referenced 'the democratic citizen army' and wrote how 'at international congress after international congress, continental socialists who know well what conscription means, and who are thoroughly versed in the English voluntary system, have voted in favour of a democratic national citizen army'.[21]

Ó'Catháin has stated that debates on the value of a citizen army had long been part of Glasgow's socialist circles.[22] He contended that both Jack White and James Connolly had important contacts in the city which increased the potential for such a force to be created there. It is also true that after the rebellion in 1916 some within wider Irish labour connected Connolly's soldiers to this wider philosophy. During the twenty-second annual Irish Trades Union Congress in 1916 the president of the congress stated that the events of Easter Week had cured him of 'the ideal of a "nation in arms"'.[23]

Clearly, leading ICA figures were not isolated from the wider debate in Europe.

The Easter Rising should be viewed not solely as a national insurgent movement against a colonial power but should also be read within a wider international framework of decades of social unrest and revolution.[24] The belief that 'national liberation movements could contribute to the overthrow of capitalism' was central to Connolly's thought.[25] He was most clear on the relationship between the national struggle and the international situation when he wrote in 1914 'Ireland may yet set the torch to a European conflagration that will not burn out until the last throne and the last capitalist debenture are shrivelled in the war pyre of the last warlord.'[26] He viewed the Citizen Army as a potential catalyst for a trans-national workers' revolt. Indeed, in 1887, Engels discussed the possible effects of a world war on Europe and its working class:

> eight to ten million soldiers will swallow each other up and in doing so eat all Europe more bare than any swarm of locusts ... crowns will roll by dozens in the gutter and no one be found to pick them up ... only one result is absolutely certain: general exhaustion and the establishment of the conditions for the final victory of the working class.[27]

There was a clear similarity of thought between Connolly and Engels. However, as Emmet O'Connor contended, from the outbreak of the war until the Easter Rising, Connolly was consumed by revolutionary pessimism. Connolly was brought to a sense of near fatalism as the Westminster Government's failure to adequately respond to Edward Carson's threats of revolt, combined with the failure of the European socialists to criticise the outbreak of the war.[28] He argued, in August 1914, that through the continuation of the war 'civilisation [was] being destroyed before our eyes'.[29] This attitude is studied within the context of the Second International's treatises on how global war was to be opposed by the working class, such as the report on the International's 1907 congress in Stuttgart.[30] Focus is placed on the question of whether the Citizen Army's involvement in the 1916 revolt was not just a part of a nationalist movement but was in tune with previously established international socialist policies. Examining this question tests Owen Dudley Edwards's claim that while the rebellion was the climax of ambition for Thomas Clarke and Pádraig Pearse, for Connolly the ICA's involvement was the result of the loss of the dreams of syndicalism and the workers' republic.[31]

During the Stuttgart Socialist International Conference in 1907, figures such as Jaurés and Édouard Vaillant introduced the policy that if a continental war broke out it was the duty of both the working class and their parliamentary representatives to do everything within their means to use the conflict to bring about the fall of capitalism.[32] At the time the conference was viewed as turning the socialist movement away from purely 'theoretical discussions' and towards a 'policy of action'.[33] This policy sought the organisation of youth into anti-militarist bodies which were to work alongside trade unions in the battle against the ruling class.[34] While the resolution did not attempt to create a homogenous policy for all European countries it also argued for the use of citizen armies instead of the standing army as a tool in the prevention of 'aggressive wars'.[35] During World War I, Connolly's writings revealed his perception of the importance of the trade union and the militia in the battle against state militarism. In July 1915, he reasserted the connection between the ICA and the Irish Transport and General Workers' Union when he used the title: 'Transport Union Citizen Army', the first time it had been used since the strike and lockout.[36] The relationship between the European working class, the ITGWU, and the ICA was made even more clear in August 1914 when he wrote 'Our Duty In This Crisis':

> Should the working class of Europe, rather than slaughter each other for the benefit of kings and financiers, proceed tomorrow to erect barricades all over Europe ... we should be perfectly justified in following such a glorious example and contributing our aid to the final dethronement of the vulture classes that rule and rob the world ... This may mean more than a transport strike, it may mean armed battling in the streets.[37]

Despite the commonality of this sentiment across Europe, once the war broke out the majority of socialist parties supported their national governments.[38] The French trade union Confédération Génerale du Travail (CGT), Europe's largest syndicalist labour organisation, also embraced 'khaki fever'. This exposed a primary allegiance to nationalism and the state rather than to internationalism and the class.[39] However, within a colonial nation such as Ireland a different set of allegiances existed. For some republicans, allegiance to the Irish nation did not awaken a patriotic support for a war effort. Furthermore, for the ICA the cause of the worker was intertwined with an anti-imperial movement for self-determination. Yet, socialist opposition to the war effort was also found in various non-colonial nations. Research by Wayne Thorpe and Ralph Darlington revealed that the case of the CGT in France was an anomaly as revolutionary syndicalist organisations were the largest block of bodies which opposed the war.[40] The ICA was born out of the Irish syndicalist movement and this thread must be considered when their history is assessed.

Darlington examined the movement in three geographical spaces: Spain and Ireland, France and Italy, and America and Britain. He argued that syndicalists in each area responded differently to the outbreak of war. Responses were dependent on factors such as their country's level of engagement in the conflict, the economic and political situation in the home front, and the state of the syndicalist movement in their particular nations.[41] Within the first region Spain's neutrality and Ireland's colonial history allowed for a political space where syndicalist revolutionary ideologies could flourish as they were able to both contribute to and benefit from the 'broader political issues'.[42]

The varying conditions of the Irish syndicalists and the British syndicalists also helps explain why the ICA flourished during the war while British armed-nation theories were transformed into support for Secretary of State for War Richard Haldane's Territorial Forces. By the outbreak of the war in 1914, the arguments for militia put forward by Harry Quelch, the Social Democratic Federation's leading thinker on the subject, had 'converged with, and was exploited by, the wider "national service" lobby that emerged in the same period'.[43] In contrast to developments in Ireland, even the citizen army bill – a counter proposal to Haldane's policies proposed by SDF politician Will Thorne – was far more acquiescent to the state's military machinery. Its provisions stated that every 18 to 29-year-old male would have annual military training and then pass into the reserves; the force would elect its officers and have full authority over them. Mobilisation would only occur in the face of an invasion while the city or borough council of each district would administer the act. According to Crick, the bill received no support from other labour bodies and was ridiculed by the Independent Labour Party (ILP).[44]

Such derision suggests common themes developed within British and Irish socialist circles, though in a more moderate form in Britain. Under both Connolly and James O'Neill, the ICA was continuously used as a barrier to the implementation of conscription. In Britain no militias did the same. However, political parties and civic action committees such as the ILP, the British Socialist Party (BSP) and the Clyde Workers' Committee (CWC) also agitated against conscription. As early as 1913, figures such as Keir Hardie (a close confidant of Connolly during his days in Scotland) and G.H. Roberts agitated against the attempt to make service in the Territorial Forces compulsory. The left-wing 'autumn campaign' began its focus on impeding conscription in November 1914.[45] However, the campaign was brought to a close the following month.[46]

By summer 1914, opposition to the conflict was voiced in more general terms. The BSP and the ILP held a peace demonstration in Glasgow on 9 August 1914.[47] In 1915, one of the BSP's leading figures, John Maclean, was arrested under the Defence of the Realm Act for anti-war propaganda. Another BSP member, Willie Gallagher, was a key organiser for the CWC, an industrial action group which sought the use of the strike in opposition to the Munitions Act, 1915. However, the CWC's policies extended beyond the singular issue of workers' conditions. It took a distinctly internationalist and an anti-war attitude which tied together strands of the BSP, the ILP and the Socialist Labour Party (SLP).[48]

Opposition to the 1915 Munitions Act, which sought the regulation of wages and employment conditions, also appeared during the docks strike in Dublin throughout 1915. The pervasiveness of the idea of a militia in Ireland meant a more radical opposition to this act could be taken by the Citizen Army. Connolly appreciated that the ICA was able to both act as a defensive unit while also using the dispute as an opportunity for recruitment. The radicalism over the Irish question meant that these disputes operated as an incubator for the revolutionary movement. The trend was described eloquently by Connolly 'when each dispute is settled then a squad of men goes back to work, and some other squad gets locked out, and we get a chance to train them'.[49]

Árm Lucta Oibre na h-Éireann existed within a wider European base of socialist unrest. However, the development of Irish radical politics was also a key component for the emergence of the workers' militia. Pre-revolutionary conduits for the diffusion of revolutionary socialist ideals have been easily forgotten.[50] Despite this, they were central to the creation of the force that went 'out' in Easter 1916. For Ann Matthews, the 'origin of the ICA lies with the Irish Transport and General Workers' Union (ITGWU)', while R.M. Fox contended the 'seed-bed' of the unit was the industrial turbulence that began with the dock strikes in Belfast in 1907 and 1908.[51] This book asserts that the gestation of socialist republican beliefs began earlier through the establishment of the Irish

Socialist Republican Party (ISRP) in 1896. Founded by Connolly, the party was 'recognised both by contemporaries of the period and by those working in the Irish labour movement in the decades following' as the foundation stone on which the convergence of modern Irish socialism and republicanism was built.[52] Grant argued that the ISRP did not represent the socialist republican tendency that followed, however, the similarity between the programme of the ISRP and the constitution of the ICA is notable.[53] According to its 1896 programme, the ISRP's objective was the 'establishment of an Irish socialist republic based upon the public ownership by the Irish people of the land, and instruments of production, distribution and exchange'.[54] Eighteen years later in 1914, the Citizen Army vowed 'that the ownership of Ireland, moral and material is vested of right in the people of Ireland'.[55] In the aftermath of the rebellion, James Larkin further highlighted this similarity of purpose. He contended that the object of the 1916 insurrection was to 'set up a co-operative commonwealth in Ireland, based on industrial democracy'.[56] While this was a general philosophy it was important that the primary aspirations of both labour organs were the same. Although the industrial conflict in Dublin during winter 1913 mobilised the workers of Dublin, the ISRP brought the concept of revolution into the consciousness of the city's proletariat. The ICA, therefore, was energised from the increased 'tempo of labour unrest' which began with Connolly's nationalist political party.[57]

The establishment of James Larkin in the Irish trade union scene was particularly important to the development of a radical, Irish, working-class consciousness. He arrived in Ireland in 1907 as a member of the National Union of Dock Labourers (NUDL) and found a polarised society in terms of Irish class.[58] Over the succeeding years, he led a series of strikes. The most significant of these were in Belfast in 1907, Cork in 1909, and Dublin in 1913. It was not just the strikes but the strategies and ethos behind them which helped arouse the Irish working class. Larkin emboldened them with his own brand of syndicalism: Larkinism. However, definitions of Larkinism have remained vague. It has been defined as representing combativeness, agitation and aggression.[59] More simply, it has been used as the term for the Irish form of syndicalism that had the ultimate aim of establishing 'one big union'.[60] It has also been characterised as 'distrustful of government' and of 'legislative experiments'.[61] While no uniform definition exists, Yeates and Emmet Larkin depicted it as an aspiration for improvement beyond mere material issues such as wages but for the revolution of the prevailing economic system.[62]

Larkin and Larkinism were too militant for the National Union of Dock Labourers. His tactics, in particular the use of the sympathetic strike, were too controversial for the NUDL's secretary, James Sexton. Their relationship quickly became hostile and Larkin was suspended from the union on 7 December 1908.[63] Without a union, Larkin took one of the key decisions in the radicalisation of the mentality of the Irish worker: the establishment of the ITGWU in 1909. This union was seen as particularly dangerous to the employer class due to its attempt to organise more extensively than the craft unions and to agitate for the unskilled worker.[64] The effect this union had on Dublin's working class was seen in Frank Robbins's recollection: 'I was just fifteen when I joined the Irish Transport and General Workers' Union ... the most interesting and exciting period of my early life was that leading up to the 1913 strike and lockout. All through the years from 1909 to 1913 there was an increasing trade union activity.'[65] Guided by the fiery Larkin, and soon to be led by the advanced socialist thinker Connolly, the ITGWU offered a vehicle for a much wider labour unrest than what had previously been possible.

It was in Cork during the strikes of 1908–9 when the role of the labour militia began to be utilised. In June 1909, inter-union hostility caused a number of ITGWU affiliated coal-porters to strike over the employment of men belonging to the Great British and Irish Workers' Union – there were fears amongst the Cork labourers that the Irish Workers' Union men were brought in to help facilitate the mechanism of steam-winches. The coal-porters were quickly joined by carters and storemen before a further 140 ITGWU men belonging to the City of Cork Steam Packet Company came out in support of the strike.[66] On 16 June, the Cork Employers' Federation was created and on 6 July it published its opposition to unionisation as well as its plans for the use of mechanised steam-winches.[67] While the strike ended in July, the significance of the unrest was its parallels with the Dublin strike and lockout of 1913.

William Martin Murphy, a leading Dublin businessman, was aware of the value of a tool such as the Cork Employers Federation when he created the Dublin Employers' Federation. Most relevant to the ICA's development is that when faced with baton charges, labour organisers James Larkin and James Fearon armed workers with armlets and sticks. The Irish Citizen Army began its life primarily as a workers' defence corps and had learnt from the Cork labourers. The intrinsic connection between both events was stressed by Larkin. He contended that 'the Citizen Army was organised in 1908, in

Cork city. It was driven out of existence by persecution and the jailing of its members, including myself, in 1909. It was reborn during the big transport strike in England in 1911 … our first adjutant was Captain White.'[68] Árm Lucta Oibre na h-Éireann was not only rooted in Second International theories on the 'armed nation' but was part of a tradition which stretched beyond Dublin, of workers' defence forces.

Given the pre-existing tradition of the use of protective militias during industrial conflicts in Ireland, it is important to understand what made the Irish Citizen Army different in a way that allowed it to exist for such a prolonged period. The evolution of radical nationalist politics between 1913 and 1923 created a context in which the ICA was able to develop as a largely republican unit. It must be asked why the force was able to survive long after the 1913 strike and lockout while the bodyguard in Cork dissipated as quickly as the effort of the strike. The ICA's republican philosophy may explain this difference in longevity. Furthermore, while the political space was obviously central to the ICA's creation, the geographical space must also be considered, particularly as the ICA did not extend its remit outside of Dublin. This was despite repeated attempts. Foster noted that 'the changes that convulse society do not appear from nowhere, they happen first in people's minds … there is also the important factor of geographical concentration, notably in Dublin'.[69] Also observed in Foster's *Vivid Faces* was Kevin O'Sheil's contention of 'five different Dublins'. These included the 'studentdom', 'castle Dublin', the commercial world, the bohemian space for the intelligentsia, and the slums of the proletariat.[70]

The small workers' enclave which existed in these slums provided a vital incubator for the development of the armed labour tradition and for its socialist republican principles. The *Irish Worker* newspaper, edited by Larkin for most of its existence, was one particular tool for the diffusion of such ideology into this local community. Its first issue, published on 27 May 1911, sold 5,000 copies. The second and third editions sold 8,000 and 15,000 copies respectively, while during its existence it had an average weekly readership of 20,000 people.[71] As the paper's readership never significantly extended outside of Dublin, these figures reveal how Connolly and Larkin's philosophies were widely read around working-class areas such as Beresford Place and Inchicore. The paper was adamant about its purpose of pervading the consciousness of Dublin's working class in order to instil a revolutionary ethic:

the written word is the most potent force in our modern world. The *Irish Worker* will be a lamp to guide your feet in the dark hours of the impending struggle; a well of truth reflecting the purity of your motives, and a weekly banquet from which you will rise strengthened in purpose to emulate the deed of your forefathers, who died in dungeon and on scaffold in the hopes of a glorious resurrection for our beloved country.[72]

It is noteworthy that Captain Frank Robbins stated that from the year of the *Irish Worker*'s first publication 'myself and my union friends found ourselves in the midst of the turmoil leading up to the great lockout of 1913'.[73] During the first years of the ICA's existence a column entitled 'By the campfire' was devoted to potential recruits who read the *Irish Worker*. The paper carried the call for new members and told them to contact the ICA's secretary if they wished to join. One particular edition published Connolly's words 'we know our duties as we know our rights and we shall stand by one another through thick and thin, prepared if necessary to arm and achieve by force our place in the world, and also to maintain it by force'.[74] It also presented the ideology of Árm Lucta Oibre na h-Éireann as it published its constitution on three separate occasions.[75] 'Streams of printers' ink' were important channels for the communication between revolutionaries and potential radicals.[76] The *Irish Worker* and subsequently the *Workers' Republic* were vital in creating the cultural consciousness that allowed for the creation of the Irish Citizen Army.

Outside of the written word, proximity to leaders Larkin and Connolly was also important in inculcating that ethos. A mapping of the addresses contained in Chief Mobilising Officer Thomas Kain's membership book reveals that a significant proportion of the militia lived close to Beresford Place, the hub of Dublin's trade union activity.[77] Remembering the James Fintan Lalor Pipers' Band – the bodyguard of which was subsumed into the ICA – John Hanratty recalled that this period was 'the days when it was a simple matter to contact the general secretary of the union – if he was in the building you just called into him and that was all'.[78] Despite the importance of their roles, figures such as Larkin and Connolly were not isolated from the environs in which the men and women of the ICA lived. They were also men who favoured rhetoric. Numerous rallies were held around Liberty Hall when the force was being formed in 1913. As the succeeding chapter highlights, at these events the two labour titans called for the use of the armed picket.[79] They also repeatedly connected the creation of such a militia with the ensuing national question. It was no coincidence then that these calls had the greatest effect in the areas closest to Liberty Hall. For the geographically larger militias, such as the Irish Volunteers and the Ulster Volunteer Force, variance of regional upheaval, social composition, and entrepreneurial leadership were important to the construct of different units. However, for the almost singularly spaced Irish Citizen Army, proximity to Liberty Hall was central to the diffusion of their ideals.

The value of the social base that was Croydon Park must also be commented upon. This recreational hub in suburban Clontarf was leased to the ITGWU in August 1913. It was here where the majority of ICA training took place. For instance, the estate's house provided the bases where the army practised its defensive manoeuvres. However, regarding the development of a radical mentality, the park was equally important. Matthews contended that 'it soon became central to the development of camaraderie within the union and it was a haven away from the crowded world of the squalid tenements'.[80] The memoirs of Frank Robbins and Jack White reveal how it also played a key social role for the militia. White's autobiography, *Misfit*, detailed that the drilling in Croydon Park was conducted not purely for military training but also to 'put new heart into [the ICA's volunteers]'.[81] Robbins commented on the importance of the *aeriodit* that were held there.[82] It not only offered a respite from the grinding poverty and daily struggle found in Dublin's slums but the setting granted an opportunity for the discussion of ideas that were being put forward by Connolly and Larkin. Here men and women were able to formulate their opinions on the topics that they had read about in the *Irish Worker* and heard discussed in speeches at Beresford Place. It was a forum for political discourse.

It was these formal and informal links that allowed for the development of a collective consciousness of socialist republicanism, but it is also important to understand how this energising labour movement connected with the burgeoning separatist movement. Moran credited pre-rebellion Liberty Hall as 'one of the places where thespian excitement mingled with revolutionary zeal'.[83] Certainly, Connolly's play *Under Which Flag* was one method of diffusion of ideology which was echoed in pan-nationalist Ireland. It was not uncommon for early-twentieth-century Irish playwrights to grant politics eminence over the art form and to use the stage as the place where the nation thought 'in front of itself'.[84] ICA members Countess Markievicz and Helena Molony, alongside revolutionaries such as Pádraig Pearse, have been identified as figures who 'saw their theatrical activities as an integral part of nationalist consciousness-raising'.[85] Works by Pádraig Pearse, Thomas MacDonagh and James Connolly were politically charged texts which sought the radicalisation of culture.[86] However, the importance of these works extended beyond the argument that these revolutionaries adopted a similar cultural mechanism for their ideology. The crossing over into the world of bohemia also allowed for the wider proliferation of socialist republican ideals. This was most evident during the call for the formation of the Citizen Army during winter 1913. During this period, leading figures of the intelligentsia led the call for an armed workers' force. George Bernard Shaw spoke of the necessity for such action.[87] It is also noteworthy that the militia was not created solely in Beresford Place. Rather, it was granted a degree of respectability when Captain Jack White's proposal for the force was accepted at a meeting of the Civic League in the academic enclave that was Trinity College.[88]

Connections were also developing between the soon-to-be republican comrades in arms. Foster presented the Irish nationalist tradition of theatrical funerals as the playing out of politics on the stage. He specifically referred to the burial of the Terence Bellew MacManus in 1861; however, the burial of Jeremiah O'Donovan Rossa on 1 August 1915 can also be considered as part of this pattern.[89] While Pádraig Yeates does not give enough significance to events such as the Bachelor's Walk funerals – during which the Irish Citizen Army and the Irish Volunteers marched together – there was credence to his claim that the O'Donovan Rossa burial was 'the first major manifestation of this new unity of purpose'.[90] Such public theatrics demonstrated the shared mindset of individuals in bodies such as the IRB and Árm Lucta Oibre na h-Éireann. Performances such as Larkin's appearance on the balcony of the Imperial Hotel in Sackville Street, Dublin on Bloody Sunday in 1913 or James Connolly's symbolic dumping of a coffin into the River Liffey during Queen Victoria's Jubilee Day in 1897 were all part of a visible tableau of pageantry. This had a long tradition which both enabled and displayed the connectivity of the different shades of Irish republicanism.[91]

Equally related to the spectacle at Rossa's graveside was the act of remembrance. These moments of veneration not only displayed the interconnectedness of the republican society but also provided the context within which the ICA and the Irish Volunteers began their path to formal unison. For these two forces, events such as the Wolfe Tone commemorations in 1914 and 1915 as well as the Parnell anniversary in 1914 were of importance. However, this trend began much earlier. The turn of the nineteenth century was marked by events such as Queen Victoria's Diamond Jubilee in 1897, the Boer War from 1899 to 1902, and the Queen's royal visits respectively in 1900 and 1903. The centenary of the 1798 rebellion offered an opportunity for republicans of all guises to propagandise and display their hopes for political change.[92] '1798 Committees' were established to oversee the commemorative events and allowed for the coming together of the ISRP with radical nationalists such as Maud Gonne and Arthur Griffith.[93] While the presence of moderate 'Home Rule' nationalists eventually split the movement, the committees both afforded Connolly the opportunity to propagate republican ideology and displayed the nexus in which Dublin's radicals of all hues operated. Metscher contended that through these commemorations Connolly 'had managed to create a closer bond between republican socialists and the younger nationalists by organising and participating in joint activities'.[94] The gradual coalescing of both republican militias throughout 1914 and 1915 was part of this trend.

The use of radical newspapers was a common mode of expressing revolutionary principles. The *Irish Worker* took its place alongside a series of other politically driven newspapers, such as *Irish Freedom, Fianna, The Irish Volunteer, Sinn Féin* and *The Leader*. While these publications never reached the same level of readership as the main stream media, they constructed an imagined Ireland which revolutionaries could strive for.[95] In this way, the sale of the papers acted as both a method of funding for revolutionary organisations as well as a forum for the expression of subversive policies. Again, this was part of a long tradition, evidenced by publications such as the original *Workers' Republic* and *Shan Van Vocht* which were both published during the nineteenth century. However, by the second decade of the twentieth century, the papers allowed for an active dialogue between the members of organisations such as the ICA and the Irish Volunteers. The *Fianna*'s advert for James Connolly's *The Re-Conquest of Ireland* best revealed this cross-communal discourse.[96] While *Irish Freedom* printed criticism of RIC and DMP action on Bloody Sunday, 1913, the *Irish Worker* also congratulated the Irish Volunteers on their first convention in 1914.[97] Visible in the various articles was a commonality of aspirations which helped create a comradeship and enabled joint military action. Newspapers, as with other modes of public performance, revealed a co-existence between socialist republicans and advanced nationalists who shared the same belief in the potential for militant agitation to achieve revolutionary goals.

These modes of expression were not the complete picture of the nexus of such shades of nationalism. No study of one particular militia during the 1913–23 revolutionary situation could present such a holistic analysis of this development. However, an outline of such methods of dissemination does begin to unravel the threads which connected figures such as Connolly to other revolutionaries such as Pearse and MacDonagh. The expressions and ideologies espoused by Connolly and other nationalists from 1913 and 1916 had a long gestation. Such mentalities were developing since the 1890s and for some of Dublin's trade-unionists and nationalists reached a tipping point with the outbreak of the strike and lockout in August 1913.[98]

2

'GLORIOUS TIMES': THE FORMATION OF THE PRE-CONSTITUTIONAL CITIZEN ARMY

On 9 May 1962, Seán O'Casey, by then a famed Irish playwright, wrote to an old and sick friend, Barney Conway. O'Casey wrote of the tumultuous events of winter 1913, of the strike and lockout, and asked Conway to remember 'the glorious times when the workers of Ireland first declared themselves me[n], struck out and shook the bosses ... [when] we, the workers were on the march'.[1] The year 1913 was a tumultuous year in Ireland. Not only were three volunteer military forces formed but the year also saw the highest incidents of non-agrarian offences since the turn of the century.[2] The final months of 1913 saw not only a collision between the Irish Transport and General Workers' Union and Dublin's capitalist class, but also the birth of Irish labour's first long-lasting urban working-class militia: the Citizen Army. Undoubtedly, radical socialist republicanism had begun to develop in the consciousness of the Irish working class since the formation of the ISRP in 1896. However, the scale of the unrest in Dublin in winter 1913 escalated the speed at which this militarism was disseminated to Dublin's workers. While the Citizen Army was part of a long developing culture of working-class unrest and socialist republicanism, the militant culture which pervaded Ireland in 1913 in a way that it did not beforehand was also key to the creation of Árm Lucta Oibre na h-Éireann.

It is true that Whiteboyism had been the most extensive form of labour defence in pre-famine Ireland but this was an agrarian rather than urbanised manifestation.[3] The Citizen Army was part of the same linage as Whiteboyism and was the twentieth-century manifestation of labour defence. By 1913, syndicalist ideas meant that the unskilled worker rather than the agrarian labourer was the most radicalised member of the Irish working class. Given this, it was not surprising that the strike and lockout acted as the primary cause for the creation of Árm Lucta Oibre na h-Éireann. However, Larkinism was also a core characteristic in strikes in Belfast in 1907, Cork in 1908 and Wexford in 1911. Likewise, citizen forces had mobilised in defence of striking workers in these incidents. Yet, in contrast to the Irish Citizen Army, these militias dissipated quickly. In order to understand what separated the labour militia formed in 1913 from its predecessors, the intensification of the Home Rule crisis must also be considered. By the end of 1913, labour and nationalist radicalism were developing at a peace far quicker than previously. It was this doubly defined militancy that formed the over-arching context of the early months of the Citizen Army's existence. Certainly, according to Nora Connolly O'Brien, martial rhetoric and military ideas had seeped into the working-class consciousness before the formation of the force itself. She recalled the day when her father, James Connolly was released after his hunger strike, 13 September 1913:

> He had wired Nelly Gordon to arrange a suitable non-sectarian demonstration as a gesture of labour solidarity. When I arrived therefore in Great Victoria Street, where the station then was, from our home at Glenalina Terrace, I found a great throng ... Finally a man led the way for me. 'We are all here' he said 'to welcome General Connolly.' That was the first time I had heard him referred to in that way. It may have arisen from the now widely proclaimed desire to 'arm the workers', though that had not yet been responded to.[4]

While Dermot Keogh has argued against the idea that a 'significant section' of the ITGWU 'were either politicised revolutionary socialists or syndicalists', it is true that the major catalyst for the arming and subsequent militarisation of the workers was that union's strike in winter 1913.[5] However, this was not the effect of any bellicose nature of 'Larkinism', the particular Irish manifestation of syndicalism, but rather the perception of overt brutality by the DMP against the city's working class. This combined with the workers' belief that the country's officialdom had sided with the employers in the labour dispute and furthered the belief that the workers required a defensive organisation. Indeed, it was events such as the Bloody Sunday police attack in Sackville Street, 31 August 1913, which led to the dissolution of the Dublin Industrial Peace Committee on 11 November 1913 and the establishment of the Civic League on 18 November. The Civic League oversaw the Citizen Army's creation. Concurrently, the conditions which those on strike and those locked out faced also dictated the formation of the army. In Dublin in 1913, 45 per cent of the working-class population lived in tenement houses.[6] The belief in a need for a social element to labour activity had been prevalent from at least 1913 when the union officially opened Croydon Park.[7]

Historians such as Kevin Morley, John Boyle, Donal Nevin and D.R. O'Connor Lysaght asserted that the actions of both the Dublin Metropolitan Police and the Royal Irish Constabulary (RIC) were the initial driving forces for the formation of the ICA. Morley wrote 'the [ICA's] initial role, at its inception during November 1913 was that of a workers' defence force to counter the bosses' hired thugs of the DMP and RIC and their excessive measures of violence on behalf of the employers'.[8] Boyle argued that the force developed with a two-fold purpose: firstly, to protect the workers against blackleg labour and secondly, to boost the workers' fitness and morale.[9] Nevin and Lysaght contended that the formation of the Citizen Army was a response to the tactics of intimidation employed by the DMP and strike breakers during that industrial dispute.[10]

Furthermore, it must be noted that this view of the role of police actions as instrumental to the creation of the Citizen Army was not restricted to the historian. Rather, those involved in the wider contemporary political *milieu* also spoke of this importance. On 11 October 1913, the *Irish Worker* read that 'the future Irish historian … should not fail to chronicle the brutalities of the police'.[11] On 19 April 1924, Seán McLaughlin wrote that the Irish Citizen Army was the result of the battening of unarmed workers and that it was founded by Jim Larkin to prevent the reoccurrence of such events.[12] White argued that the purpose of drill was that it would mean 'drilled and disciplined men [would] not allow themselves, and still lest their women to be battened by the police like clubbed seals'.[13] Likewise, Frank Henderson, the Irish Volunteer and veteran of both the 1916 rebellion and the Anglo-Irish War of Independence, argued that:

Shortly before the formation of the Irish Volunteers, the Irish Citizen Army was formed in 1913, following attacks on strikers in Dublin by the police. That was the famous strike of 1913, when there were a few men killed. Following that, the Irish Citizen Army was started by Jim Larkin, Captain White, and probably in the background at the time was James Connolly. He was outwardly at that time a minor figure, but he was probably the driving force. The Irish Citizen Army was formed primarily to protect the working men in Dublin in view of what happened in the

1913 strike, but no doubt Connolly had revolution in his mind all the time.[14]

In his history of the force, O'Casey recorded Larkin as having stated 'that every conceivable combination had united its forces against the worker'.[15] For Hanratty, the police were motivated by political factors and this intensified the bitterness felt by Dublin's workers.[16] Seamus O'Brien contended that 'it was evident very early in the lockout that the representatives of Dublin Castle were willing to take a hand on the side of the employers'.[17] This sentiment was echoed by the labour figure William O'Brien, who was often at the forefront of the dispute. Writing on the importance of the 1913 industrial conflict, he stated:

> Throughout the whole struggle the combination of Dublin employers had the valuable support of the British government in Ireland, armed and un-armed, law, police, military and prison. From time to time one or other sections of these forces was brought into action against the workers. The police not only protected black-legs but as well forcibly broke up meetings, raided the working class quarters and batoned [sic] two workers to death – James Nolan and James Byrne – and imprisoned leaders of the Irish Transport and General Workers' Union and of other unions and hundreds of workers.[18]

Between August and September 1913, Dublin experienced fifteen distinct riots.[19] As a result of this violence, both of Dublin's police bodies had high levels of involvement in the industrial dispute. Of a total of 1,360 men on-beat during the dispute, 910 of these were placed on strike duty (500 of which were DMP men and 410 of which were RIC men).[20] It is true that such involvement in what was obstinately a dispute between a trade union and an employer does not, in and of itself, constitute convincing evidence that these civic forces were responsible for the organisation of the so-called 'Labour Hercules'. However, many Irish Transport and General Workers' Union members believed that the capitalist society had thrown its lot in behind Murphy, the Dublin Employers' Federation and the 'scab' worker. This furthered the belief in the necessity for a socialist/syndicalist army. Nearly fifty years after the dispute, the ITGWU, celebrating its golden jubilee, recollected how severe they thought the actions of the police were. Its celebratory publication, *Fifty Years of Liberty Hall the Golden Jubilee of* the *Irish Transport and General Workers' Union 1909–59*, contended that the most brutal incidents during the first week of the industrial war in 1913 occurred during Saturday afternoon and evening of the weekend of 30 and 31 August. While the city had previously seen incidents such as the breaking up of political demonstrations, there had been 'never anything like that Saturday's street battles from Ringsend to Inchicore'.[21]

Certainly, it would be inaccurate to say that Dublin's working-class consciousness had an *a priori* disposition against the city's civic defence forces. Only three days before the outbreak of the strike and lockout on 26 August, the *Irish Worker* argued in support of members of the DMP and the RIC. The police have 'a right to organise' it proclaimed, 'and there is no power under the sun to stop them from striking against tyrannical methods to satisfy [he] who owns the trams and runs the *Independent* and the *Herald*'.[22] It is also important to note that this was written within the context of the upcoming class struggle: 'but murder will out and whilst Dublin sleeps something is happening that will surprise the citizens'.[23]

What can be gleaned from this is that a change of opinion occurred during the lockout, and most particularly after the events of Bloody Sunday, where, as Dukova claimed, 'the policemen were inadvertently made into accomplices in this war'.[24] The attack by the police on those who attended Larkin's protest in Sackville Street on 31 August and the deaths of James Nolan and James Byrne, as a result of the DMP's actions, had a deep impact upon the consciousness of those who would later join the Citizen Army. Bloody Sunday has been framed in labour memory as a manifestation of class conflict and made clear in the minds of the 1913 labourer the distinction of class.[25] The day convinced many workers of the necessity to arm. In his memoir *Casement's Last Adventure*, the Irish Volunteer Captain Monteith claimed that it was the attack on Nolan and Byrne that convinced him of the need for the formation of a citizen army in order to protect the citizens of Dublin.[26] James Larkin Jr also described Bloody Sunday as the cause for the ferment of the Citizen Army. He wrote 'in the three days from the 30 August to 1 September no less than thirty battles took place between the workers and the police. It was out of these battles and turmoil that the Irish Citizen Army was born.'[27] For Hanratty, on 31 August 1913 'the Citizen Army had yet to be born but it was in the womb'.[28] *Disturbed Dublin* described in detail the violence that was suffered by the city's workers during the baton charge: 'individuals fled in all directions in their attempt to escape the blows which were dealt with fierce intensity by the infuriated members of the police force.

Innocent sightseers along with rowdy demonstrators shared in the terrible punishment.'[29]

It is true that the Dublin Disturbances Commission which reported on, amongst other events, 'the riot in Sackville Street', blamed the outbreak of the baton charge on both Larkin and the crowd. The report stated that 'a warrant was issued for the re-arrest of Larkin, and it became necessary for the police authorities to take steps for the purpose of preventing and dispersing the meeting if an attempt were made to hold it in Sackville Street on the Sunday'.[30] The report continued:

> Fearing that the object of the crowd who were shouting, brandishing sticks, and throwing stones was to rescue the prisoner, orders were given by Inspector Barrett and other responsible officers to the police to put back and disperse the crowd. In our opinion these orders and the baton charge by which they were carried out were justified by the circumstances.[31]

The information that these findings were based on came from Assistant Commissioner of the Dublin Metropolitan Police W.V. Harrel. On Tuesday, 27 January 1914, he stated that prior to the events of 31 August 1913 had Larkin made good his threats of violence there would have been attacks on the police.[32] His evidence also claimed that no member of the police force that he encountered that day appeared to be intoxicated or showed any signs of 'unwanted excitement'.[33] This account runs contrary to the accounts presented in the *Irish Worker* and the wider left-wing *milieu*. Newsinger wrote that the manner in which both the courts and the police 'threw their weight' behind Murphy transformed the dispute.[34] Certainly, from September onwards the social commentary against such perceived injustice began to be couched in arguments calling for a citizens' defence force.

It is noteworthy that two of the three front-page cartoons that were published in the *Irish Worker* between 31 August and the formation of the Citizen Army on 18 November depicted drunken policemen with bloodied batons.[35] The cartoon on 13 September, by Ernest Kavanagh entitled 'His Majesty in Blue', was described as an 'almost simian depiction' of a policeman.[36] The *Freeman's Journal* also began publishing vitriolic attacks against the Dublin Castle authorities. In an article that is responsible for terming the day as Ireland's first Bloody Sunday, the paper published Count Casimir Markievicz's description of the events. He described the authorities as 'bloodthirsty' and the citizens as 'terror-stricken'.[37] A vivid image of the callousness and violence shown towards the working class appeared in the *Irish Worker* the following month where it told how "'the cossaks', both metropolitan and RIC, showed their consideration for the men who pay them by bludgeoning right, left and centre. No attempt was made to give citizens an opportunity of escaping. In fact, all precaution was taken to prevent them getting away'.[38]

Such condemnation turned into violent rhetoric which argued for the need of a workers' defence force. On 13 September, 'T.B' wrote that 'it matters not to us whether we die as a result of micro bite or baton blow but we must take precautions against both'.[39] A month later, the *Irish Worker* argued for the necessity of workers to arm themselves with sticks.[40] By this point, labour leaders and the more 'respectable' bohemians of the city had begun to call for a defensive force at public meetings and rallies. Hanratty recalled being present at a meeting which Larkin addressed in early October 1913 where he spoke about the need for workers to organise to protect themselves against the 'savage attacks' by the police. As an example, Hanratty recalled instances where 'the right of picketing was denied to the strikers by the police although granted to them by the Trades Disputes Act, 1906. Members picketing, including myself, were assaulted by the police without provocation'.[41] In his memoir, Captain Frank Robbins recalled:

> One night during October 1913 I attended a meeting in Beresford Place and heard Connolly, speaking from the central window of Liberty Hall, say that as a result of the brutalities of the Royal Irish Constabulary and the Dublin Metropolitan Police, it was intended to organise and discipline a force to protect workers' meetings and to prevent such activities – by armed thugs – occurring in the future.[42]

In November, Under-Secretary for Ireland James Brown Dougherty received a confidential report from the Dublin Metropolitan Police which noted that 'to meet the situation it has been found necessary to employ a large extra force of police'.[43] By this point, labour leaders, the city's working class, and some of its artisans had become disillusioned with police action. A natural consequence to this was that the calls for the creation of a defensive unit were turning into plans for the organisation of such a force. On 1 November, in what is perhaps the most famous speech against police brutality that occurred during the lockout, the Irish playwright George Bernard Shaw argued for the citizens of Dublin to take up arms: 'now, if you put the policeman on the footing of a mad dog, it can only end in one way that all respectable men will have to arm themselves'.[44] Six days later, two future ICA leaders, Captain Jack White and James Connolly, appeared publicly together. Standing on the same platform in Liberty Hall, White spoke out against the denial of the right of the individual picket to which Hanratty had referred.[45] This was White's first public appearance where he was associated with the Dublin labour movement and it occurred less than a month before he attended one of the ITGWU's Sunday meetings in Croydon Park to argue for the role of the Citizen Army.[46]

At the same time the Industrial Peace Committee foresaw the organisation of such a force stating that 'the man beaten into a corner may, of course grovel. But he may also act upon the other impulse of despair: he may kill.'[47] An article written by its president Thomas Kettle stated that while the workers have 'talked widely', they acted with calm and reasonable measures while the opposite was true of the employer.[48] This certainly seems to add further credence to Yeates' claim that the committee left no one in doubt on the matter of who they blamed for the struggle.[49] It also explains why the Peace Committee's descendant, the Civic League, was to be receptive to White's calls on 18 November for the formation of the ICA after it had asked the British Government to discontinue 'immediately' the additional police protection for free labour.[50]

The Citizen Army was not the first defence force established during the strike and lockout. During the lockout, Robert de Coeur called a meeting to organise a corps armed with hurleys, whose purpose was to defend the Fintan Lalor Pipers' Band that would often go on marches as a means of uplifting the spirits of those on strike. Charlie Armstrong, a reservist in the Royal Irish Fusiliers, was appointed by the band to drill and train the men, and the bodyguard was established. Thomas O'Donoghue stated that while this organ was soon subsumed into the ICA, the establishment of the two armed units at the same time was coincidental.[51] According to Matthews, this group acted as 'a bodyguard' to be used by the band 'whenever necessary' and that 'these men had effectively organised a defence corps that accompanied striker demonstrations and marches'.[52] Hanratty remembered that 'it preceded the birth of the Citizen Army by a short head. It was absorbed into and marched with that body through the turbulent days of 1913 up to 1916.'[53]

Lorcan Collins wrote that 'the story of who founded [the ICA]' is difficult to piece together.[54] This is because it was the coming together of both trade union and socialist radicalism along with the perception of injustice held by the civic intelligentsia; an organic evolution as much as a concocted design. This merging of ideas occurred over a five-day period between 12 and 18 November 1913. Both Morley and Newsinger claimed that the formation occurred between 12 and 13 November.[55] Matthews has also argued that Connolly 'instigated the creation of the Citizen Army' on 13 November.[56] While the army did not officially form or have its first drilling session until later in the month, these historians referenced a speech by Connolly at Liberty Hall on 13 November 1913. During the speech he proclaimed 'I am going to talk sedition' and argued that the next time the workers were marching they should be accompanied by 'four battalions of trained men' and how every man 'who was willing to enlist in the labour army should give his name when he draws his strike-pay'.[57] It is important to note a matter of terminology: the absence of the term 'Citizen Army'. The exact title would not be used for another five days. While this may appear trivial, the synchronised announcement of the 'Citizen Army' on 18 November revealed that the birth of the force was marked by the coming together of the radical left (as defined by Connolly) and Dublin's sympathetic figures (as defined by White and the Civic League).

On 11 November 1913, the Industrial Peace Committee disbanded. According to the *Irish Times*, this was because of the committee's belief 'that the employers feel that their duty to themselves makes it impossible for them to pay any attention to the claims of the Irish workers or to public opinion in Dublin'.[58] On 18 November 1913, the Civic League convened in Trinity College to protest not only against the intransigent attitude of the employers but also against the postponement of a civic inquiry into police conduct since August 1913.[59] It was at this meeting in Trinity College that White's proposal to form a 'citizen army' was considered and accepted. Simultaneously, across the Liffey and away from high society, Connolly announced the army's formation. He informed the workers that they had been promised the services of a competent military office, White, and he asked the men who were 'willing to join the Citizen Army' to sign up for 'drilling and training'.[60]

This, as suggested by Keohane, can be understood to be the official formation of the ICA.[61] The concurrent announcement should not, however, be considered as evidence of a uniformity in philosophy between Connolly and the Civic League. In response to an inquiry by R.M. Fox, Rev. R.M. Gwynn, whose room was used by the Civic League to discuss the matter, wrote that 'I may add that the title Army was then not intended to suggest military action, but merely drill on military lines to keep the men fit and self-respecting.[62] White also recorded that at the time he had no aspirations for either a national or social revolution.[63] At this time White was beginning to follow a path of radicalisation. Keohane argued 'it was during this time that White's innate questioning of conventional society and the authority it governed developed into a radical critique of capitalism and imperialism as the main impediments to the just society to which he aspired'.[64] However, in November 1913 such a process was only beginning; White the anarchist had yet to reveal himself.

The *Irish Times* recorded a much more radical attitude. 'They [the ICA] were out,' the paper recorded Connolly saying, 'for victory, for the freedom of their country, and his and their grand ideal of a self-centred and a self-governing Ireland [as] a republic amongst the nations.'[65] It is fair to say that the Civic League gave birth to a force which had machinations of which it was entirely unaware.[66] Morley argued that the extra-parliamentary body developed in three distinct stages: the birth of an idea of simply a workers' defence force within the confines of the Industrial Peace Committee, radicalisation undertaken by Jim Larkin through the inspiration of Carsonism, and a stage of fruition under Connolly.[67] However, it is the contention of this book that the latter two strands occurred simultaneously.

Thus, 18 November can be dated as the official announcement of the establishment of an armed labour wing. However, it is far more difficult to be precise regarding the date of the first drilling session. O'Casey contended that Larkin and White announced the formation of the force together and that the drilling was to take place the next day in Croydon Park.[68] Such a tale was corroborated years later by Hanratty, who stated:

> Larkin addressed the meeting ... and in referring to the savagery of the police, he spoke of the need for a disciplined force to protect the workers and signified his intention of forming a citizen army. He introduced Captain Jack White ... All those desirous of joining the new Citizen Army were to attend at Croydon Park the following night. This was the beginning of the Citizen Army. [69]

Collins argued that the date this meeting could have occurred on was 22 November.[70] On 24 November, the *Freeman's Journal* reported that on the previous day, in Croydon Park, 'initial steps to establish' to form the ICA occurred and while there was no drilling about a thousand people were present.[71] All of this would seem to conform to O'Casey's story except that Collins notes Larkin was in London speaking in Albert Hall on 22 November, and could not have been in Dublin.[72] Given this, one might be inclined to follow Collins's reading that 'O'Casey's blanket refusal to acknowledge James Connolly's role as a co-founder of the Citizen Army can only be attributed to his personal dislike for the labour leader' and that 'nearly every account of the birth of the ICA uses O'Casey's account'.[73] The *Irish Times* reported that drilling began to be carried out in Croydon Park on 24 November and that the first public display was held between 20:00 and 21:00 on 27 November. This seems to have been the most likely occurrence.[74]

However, White also stated that he 'inaugurated' the army alongside James Larkin, though he did not record the date of this meeting. Thus, it seems likely that a drilling session with Larkin present did occur on some date in either November or early December 1913.[75] However, some discrepancies between the various narratives about the creation of the Citizen Army must be noted. For instance, in *Misfit* White claimed that this launch occurred in front of between 5,000–10,000 people (most likely a gross exaggeration of the *Freeman's Journal*'s numbers). However, Hanratty argued that only forty people attended and that neither White nor Larkin were present.[76] It is possible that he was actually referring to Connolly's speech on 18 November and that his memory was confused by reading O'Casey's source or that he attended an 'unofficial' drill on 19 November. It is also possible that there was a series of drilling sessions before the official mustering occurred when Larkin had returned from his campaign in Britain. Certainly, on 29 November, White wrote to his mother saying that the men were 'a pleasure to work with' and that he expected the following day to have 'the biggest muster yet'.[77]

3

'SO ARM AND I WILL ARM':
THE PRE-CONSTITUTIONAL CITIZEN ARMY

In 1970, during the height of the political conflict in Northern Ireland, Robbins spoke to the Old Dublin Society about the rank-and-file men and women of the Citizen Army, the struggle for the formation of an Irish republic, and Edward Carson. While this campaign remained active in Northern Ireland, Robbins made a new claim that Carson, the unionist leader during the 1913–21 period, was an 'unwitting ally' to the soon-to-be socialist revolutionaries.[1] Robbins sought to highlight a historical paragon of nationalist–labour armed protest. That the formation of the armed labour body coincided with the outbreak of the more overtly territorial extra-parliamentary forces and the Home Rule crisis was no coincidence. Not only was the Citizen Army deeply affected by the developing culture of radicalism but the formation of the Ulster Volunteers at the beginning of 1913 was consistently used as an example and a tool for the arming of labour in winter 1913. Much like the Irish Volunteers drew inspiration from the UVF, so too did the Citizen Army's earliest members. O'Casey recalled that Larkin told a crowd assembled in Liberty Hall that:

> Labour in its own defence must begin to train itself to act with disciplined courage and with organised and concentrated force. How could they accomplish this? By taking a leaf out of the book of Carson. If Carson had permission to train his braves of the North to fight against the aspirations of the Irish people, then it was legitimate and fair for labour to organise in the same militant way to preserve their rights.[2]

At an epistemological level, it can be understood that the Home Rule crisis had both a direct and indirect effect on the militant labour force. By direct, what is meant is the manner in which armed labour responded to the actual issues upon which the events in Ulster revolved around; most particularly, the threat of partition. By indirect, what is meant is the subsequent emergence of extra-parliamentary organisations, i.e. the Irish Volunteers and the UVF, and their role in the emergence of the ICA. Timothy Bowman stated that 'Ulster led the way of constitutionalism, resistance and rebellion.'[3] The history of the Irish Volunteers is often read through the prism of such an understanding. It is important to view the emergence of the labour militia within the same historical context.

It appears the first reference to a connection between Carson's army and the possibility of a workers' militia occurred on the commencement of the general strike, 26 August 1913. Outside of Liberty Hall, Larkin drew a correlation between the unionists' response to political pressure in Ulster and how he believed the Dublin workers should react to the actions of the DMP. He argued that:

> Police brutality has been shown tonight. I would advise the friends and supporters of this cause to take Sir Edward Carson's advice to the men of Ulster. If he says it is right and legal for the men of Ulster to arm, why should it not be right and legal for the men of Dublin to arm themselves so as to protect themselves ... so arm and I will arm.[4]

Significantly, such rhetoric was still prevalent in the days immediately preceding the army's formation. On 14 November, Larkin argued for drilling 'a la Carson.'[5] Even after the implementation of the Suspension of the Operation of the Government of Ireland Act, 1914 received royal assent on 18 September 1914 he continued to be a proponent of such a theory and carried it with him to America.[6] Given the prevalence of these expressions after Westminster had put the Home Rule question on hold it can, therefore, be extrapolated that this oratory was a rhetorical device used to garner support for the growing labour militarism.

Larkin's talk of Carsonism and the UVF did this in three ways. Firstly, by drawing the attention of the Dublin workers to the UVF's success in asserting its will over Crown authorities, Larkin presented a more convincing argument for the workers to organise along similar lines. As Fox wrote, the Dublin workers had 'the example of Carson arming his volunteers ... to teach them the wisdom of relying on their own strength.'[7] Secondly, as can be seen through Larkin's continuation of this practice in the United States in 1914, this argument justified the arming of labour and enabled a greater degree of support from those who would have been largely sympathetic to the movement as a whole.

Thirdly, highlighting the issue of sedition revealed a degree of hypocrisy within the British forces in Ireland. White stated as much in December when he wrote 'the workers have as much right to drill for the defence of themselves and their country as any other section of the community'.[8] Importantly, at this time the government used the concept of sedition to repeatedly arrest figures such as Larkin and Connolly. These arrests not only jeopardised the on-going strike but were also the biggest danger to the progress and stability of the Citizen Army.[9] However, at the same time, the more outwardly seditious and at times, nearly treasonous actions of the Ulster unionists were being dealt with by the Liberal government with 'general timidity'.[10] This apparent contradiction in the British government's treatment of the two movements was most forcefully noted in the *Irish Worker* which read 'King Ned Carson, k.c, a man who has acted as law advisor to the government can preach armed resistance to the forces of the British crown openly and without restraint. Jim Larkin, a docker – a man they would not accept as an authority on any question of the law – is prosecuted and imprisoned for barely quoting Carson's speeches.'[11] The effect of arguments like that printed in the *Irish Worker* was seen in the *New York Times* on 13 November 1913. In this edition a journalist wrote that Larkin's rhetoric was far less 'obviously and dangerously seditious' than that of those in the Ulster unionist movement.[12] Hanratty remembered Larkin's speeches as 'indoctrinated with the separatist concept of nationalism blended with that of social revolutionarism'.[13]

Connolly also referred to the 'Carson example'. On 13 November 1913, he spoke to a crowd in Beresford Place and asked: 'why should we not train and drill our men in Dublin as they are doing in Ulster?'[14] Furthermore, the Dublin Metropolitan Police referred to the meeting of the Civic League during which White officially proposed the formation of the Citizen Army as 'Captain White's Home Rule Meeting'. This further highlighted the role of the Home Rule crises, and the development of UVF in the formation of labour's armed wing.[15]

An international perspective came from the *Christian Science Monitor* on 2 December 1913. The paper noted 'the formation of the Ulster Volunteers by Sir Edward Carson has been followed by the formation of at least two other bodies, the Citizen Volunteers [sic] and the Irish Volunteers, both of which have been organised as an offset against the Carson army, though not necessarily to fight them'.[16] While it cannot be claimed that the workers who joined White's ranks did so primarily as a counterweight to Carsonism, it seems such a possibility was countenanced. In order to assess the effect of the Ulster question on the formation of the Citizen Army and the resulting arming of the wider labour movement, it is important to understand the degree to which the crises and Ulster Volunteer Force were significant to the leadership of Labour's armed wing. In essence, the question is whether the issue was just a mere justification for a workers' militia needed in a city in the midst of its biggest and most severe labour dispute or if opposition to Carsonism constituted some part of the ideological essence of the ICA.

Police brutality was the main driving force for the formation of the labour militia. However, it would be inaccurate to presume that this emphasis on the protection of striking workers impeded its volunteers, leadership and supporters from expressing concern and responding to the crisis in Ulster. Certainly, all of the three leading figures of the time, White, Connolly and Larkin, appeared to either have a degree of Home Rule sympathises or could be defined as somewhat anti-Carsonist. In October 1913, White, alongside Roger Casement and Alice Stopford Green, attended a pro-Home Rule and anti-Carson meeting at Ballymoney where he protested against Carsonism. He stated that Home Rule was a question of human rights and he read aloud a covenant which argued that 'being convinced in our conscience that Home Rule would not be disastrous to the national well-being of Ulster, and that, moreover, the responsibility of self-government would strengthen the popular forces in other provinces ... we hereunto subscribe our names'.[17] According to White's biographer, Leo Keohane, this 'bravely stood against the coercion' that was characteristic of Carsonist tactics.[18] In 1912, Connolly drafted a resolution which stated 'that this meeting of working men and women of Belfast welcomes the project of the establishment of an Irish parliament, the way for much needed social reform and the reunion of the Irish democracy hitherto divided upon antiquated sectarian lines'.[19] In October 1913, Larkin was reported to have argued that it would be through the avenue of Home Rule that the workers would obtain their 'ultimate emancipation'.[20] Furthermore, at a speech in the Albert Hall in November 1913, Larkin stated that 'important as it for us to win the Dublin strike, it is a thousand times more important that the government of Ireland act goes through your commons'.[21]

The presence of such sympathies brings forth the question of whether or not the three leading figures of the force envisaged that one day the Citizen

Army might be used as a quasi-nationalist counterweight to the UVF. Helena Molony argued that 'James Connolly and Captain Jack White really made the Citizen Army into the national body that it subsequently became.'[22] Certainly, in his Albert Hall speech, Larkin made no reference to the use of the Citizen Army despite referring to Carson as 'that cadaverous lawyer, who finds himself conveniently sick at the psychological moment.'[23] Yet, it must be noted that he made a slight connection between the two forces when he stated to the workers gathered outside Beresford Place that they had nothing to fear from Carson and he responded to the query that the ICA was not armed by saying they would be armed in time.[24]

It is clear that of all the three leading figures of the Citizen Army in 1913 Connolly had the clearest vision in delineating the possibility of ICA involvement in national as well as labour issues. Any empirically based historical understanding of the Citizen Army must lend itself to Morley's claim that 'Connolly had an even more advanced role in mind for the Citizen Army in so far as to what it would eventually become. He looked further and deeper than Larkin's perception as to what was taking place in Ulster.'[25] Or as Molony suggested 'Connolly always had a national wide vision.'[26] Even White wrote 'Connolly was, of course, more definitely revolutionary than I, and more prepared for violent methods.'[27] On the day of the ICA's birth, Connolly was reported to have drawn a direct parallel between the Citizen Army and the Ancient Order of Hibernians (AOH).[28] According to the *Irish Times*, he believed that the Dublin force could eventually supplant the role of the AOH in its opposition to the UVF. The journalist reported him as saying 'we will not leave the whole of that work to the Ancient Order of Hibernians' and that 'they [the Citizen Army] will be able to handle a rifle, and when King Carson comes along here we will be able to line our own ditches.'[29] He continued that the working class of Dublin were out for 'their grand ideal of a self-centred and a self-governing Ireland [which] was a republic amongst the nations.'[30] This is not to say that Connolly was contemplating the events of Easter 1916 but that the possibility of using the Citizen Army as a national weapon had already occurred to him.

Of the three totem poles of the ICA's earliest days, White's attitude towards the possibility of involvement with the Ulster question appears to have been the most complex and often contradictory. In his memoir he asserted 'I was unconsciously sitting on the fence. In moments I saw the clear revolutionary principle; at others I was repelled by the bitterness of a philosophy fighting against the whole established order.'[31]

In an article entitled 'Some Thoughts on Discipline' he likened Carson to Murphy and he expressed to his readership his desire that Dublin's locked out workers had 'knowledge of some elementary military evolutions' in order to deal with both.[32] Furthermore, in December 1913, he wrote an article for the Larkin-edited trade union paper, the *Irish Worker*, and spoke of this duality of labour and nationalist goals. Drawing a direct correlation between the two movements and arguing that neither Ireland nor its workers could be free without the other, he asked the paper's readers to prepare for the so called 'double task' of achieving both.[33] In his memoir he stated clearly that the two ideological forces were tied together by the common aspiration of ridding the country of the British 'crown and government'.[34] White recollected 'the almost simultaneous occurrences' of the outbreak of both the labour and the national question and he outlined his perception of 'the synchronisation [as being] (Keohane's brackets) symbolic of a deep connection which is not visible on the surface. Time, the invisible dimension, brought out the hidden link between the ultimate forces warring respectively to sever and maintain Ireland's connection with the British Empire.'[35] According to Keohane, by writing 'synchronisation' here, White was using the terminology of the Swiss psychologist Carl Jung which suggested that White viewed the two concepts through the prism of acausal parallelism.

White's interpretation makes sense when the strike and lockout is viewed not merely as a dispute over trade unionism but as a 'naked class conflict' and part of the wider syndicalist attempt, then at its height, to seize control of the state.[36] Unlike their contemporary social democrats, for syndicalism the main weapon to achieve this was not the 'armed nation' but the sympathetic strike. Such a difference in strategy may explain why White also recorded that the Citizen Army, at this point, was defined as having a 'pacific purpose'.[37] Furthermore, while he expressed the opinion that 'the Citizen Army, after teaching the police manners, could be the nucleus of industrial organisation in the new era', White simultaneously outlined that he 'certainly had no clear goal of violent revolution'.[38]

Donal Nevin stated that 'it is clear that Captain White's idea at the start was merely to drill workers and make them a disciplined labour force ... Larkin and Connolly, however, had other ideas for the new force.'[39] However, as the above shows, the delineation between the three is not as simple as presented by Nevin. The reductionist argument that both trade union figures had revolutionary goals while the army's drilling instructor viewed the Citizen Army as merely a product of the strike and lockout does not present its early history essential as it was. Rather, the subject of nationalism and the Ulster question's importance to the force existed on a spectrum. In reality, the issue remained constant at a leadership level, though at this point the concept of involvement seemed to be confined to a reactive response rather than a proactive action. Yet, there did remain a divergence of opinion amongst the three figures. Despite burgeoning anarchist tendencies, White seemed hesitant to bring the ICA into such a political quagmire. Larkin appeared aware of this possibility but was far more preoccupied with the ensuing labour crisis. Connolly appears to have been the most advanced in this line of thinking and there remains a sense from his writings and rhetoric of 'when' and not 'if' the 'Labour Hercules' was to become involved in the wider national turmoil. Naturally, such a question, and the class issues connected with it, shaped and defined the ICA's relationship with the Irish Volunteers up until the Easter Rising. Furthermore, the divergence of opinion present at this point explains the complexity of the relationship between the two militias during their infant stages.

In 1913, the nature of the relationship between the labour army and its nationalist cohort was often divisive. The issue of the class discrepancy between both nationalist militias caused acrimony between both forces and within Árm Lucta Oibre na h-Éireann itself. The concept of the Volunteers as a rival force also appears to have been a cause for distrust for some of the socialist soldiers. However, at their nucleus both militias shared a foundational belief within not only the growing militarisation of the early 1910s but also within the culture of advanced nationalism/republicanism that arose out of events such as the Boer War and the centenaries of both the 1798 and 1803 rebellions. Ruán O'Donnell noted that 'by 1907 … Tom Clarke, the mentor of Seán MacDiarmada and later, P. H. Pearse … the famous anti-imperialist Roger Casement, republican feminist Countess Markievicz, educator Eoin MacNeill and Hiberno-Scot militant socialist James Connolly began to move in a common radical milieu from which the revolutionary talent of their generation could be harnessed'.[40] It is noteworthy that Connolly and Markievicz were included.

It is apparent that there were separatist ideas within labour circles in the early twentieth century. For Agnes Newman, the sister of Roger Casement, James Connolly in 1916 was no different from the socialist agitator before he left for America in September 1903.[41] Given that Connolly's political party from 1896 to 1904, the ISRP, proclaimed itself for a 'workers' republic' in much the same vein as the republic he declared on 24 April 1916, there is credibility to this claim.[42] Indeed, in 1909 he drew a correlation between his old political party and some of the politics espoused by Sinn Féin:

> That part of Sinn Féin which teaches that Ireland must rely upon itself, respect her own traditions, know her own history, preserve her own language and literature without prejudice to, or denial of, the worth in the language or literature of other people, stand erect in her own worth and claim to be appraised for her own intrinsic value, and not as part of the wheels and cogs of the imperial system of another people – with that side of Sinn Féin socialists may sympathise; and, indeed, as a cold matter of fact, those doctrines were preached in Dublin by the Irish Socialist Republican Party from 1896 onward …[43]

Likewise, Newsinger wrote that from the outset of the formation of the ITGWU and the *Irish Worker*, that that paper reflected the republican nature of the union.[44] This was evidenced by the *Irish Worker*'s continued use of a James Finton Lalor quote as a masthead. 'The principle that I mean to stand upon,' the front-page of each edition read 'is – that the entire ownership of Ireland, moral and material … is vested of right in the people of Ireland.'[45] This sentiment contained a similar philosophy to the Irish Republican Brotherhood's document that was the Easter proclamation. Furthermore, on 27 May 1913, the *Irish Worker* outlined a platform and a principle of separatism as it argued that it was time the working class awoke to the need to strike a blow for a free Ireland led by Irish people.[46] As the paper was founded by Larkin, edited by Larkin, and that many of the articles were written by Larkin, this evidenced a certain level of affinity on behalf of the Citizen Army's leaders with the political theories held by the IRB. Additionally, given that the paper held an average readership of 20,000 people a week, mainly in Dublin, it can be argued that such a belief system was common amongst Dublin's 'third estate'.[47]

Throughout 1913, the paper published many of O'Casey's references to republican figureheads and struggles. In February, he criticised the absence of pikes (a reference to the 1798 rebellion) within the labour movement.[48] Later that month, he issued a polemic that would have appealed to Tom Clarke and the IRB's burgeoning revolutionary machinations: 'a revolution of votes will be a tame one' he stated, 'the votes of our volunteers were useless when they handed up their arms'.[49] In May, he was even clearer about the symbiotic political philosophy of the two republican spheres and the potential for a union between the radical worker and the radical nationalist within the separatist movement:

> Will the Union Jack flutter over Dublin Castle, unhurtful to the republican eyes, so long as even one of Ireland's knightly sons elects to find joy in the presence of an English viceregal agent, even though a combination of democratic forces might bring that felon flag down with a run never to rise again in Ireland? If a union of labour and republican forces would result in the achievement of an independent Ireland, or even bring that happy consummation appreciably nearer, would we hesitate and say, 'not yet, not yet; wait for the aristocrats' … it is up to us now to turn away from the self-satisfied gentry and the soulless controllers of commerce, and to unite the separatists ranks with the forces of labour for a free Ireland and the social advancement of the people.[50]

Clarke's secret society was also publicly welcoming of their socialist brethren. By the time of 'the great strike' there was a growing divergence between the Irish Parliamentary Party and the labour movement. However, the IRB and its newspaper, *Irish Freedom*, were far more sympathetic towards left-wing political philosophy.[51] In January 1913, *Irish Freedom* published an article which echoed the ideals espoused by the Irish socialist republicans. 'Do you merely want to add a new government to the numerous governments of the world?' it asked, 'is not the Irish question also an economic question? … Ireland can never be socially free until England's grip is loosened, but merely to loosen England's grip is to leave the work unfinished.'[52] Undoubtedly, such an argument endorsed the theory famously promoted by Connolly which stated that 'if you remove the English army tomorrow and hoist the green flag over Dublin Castle, unless you set about the organisation of the socialist republic your efforts would be in vain.'[53]

Outside of this symmetry of beliefs, the article went as far as arguing for the unity of the two political forces in order to further the separatist cause:

> The time approaches when a new understanding must arise, to band together all who love and work for the nation's welfare in different ways and along different paths into one great army, whose aim shall be the disorganisation and destruction of the British government in Ireland and the leaving of a foundation for a fairer and more beautiful Ireland

– a worthy monument to all who have fought and fallen to preserve her soul and identity.[54]

The publication of such a polemic in a paper managed by Seán MacDermott, an IRB man and future signatory of the 1916 proclamation, indicated at least a growing acceptance on behalf of the nation's most advanced republicans of the ideals that were beginning to grow within Dublin's working-class consciousness. It is also noteworthy that this was not just a singular instance of the publication of such principles. In the same issue of *Irish Freedom*, another article argued that there was an inherent correlation between the two movements in that they rested upon 'the same foundations'.[55]

While this evidenced that the founders of the Citizen Army could be placed beside the Irish Republican Brotherhood in Ireland's political spectrum, it must also be noted that by this time the IRB had little organisational strength and had launched few initiatives outside of the continued publication of *Irish Freedom*.[56] Thus, the IRB's embracing of socialist republicanism must be seen within the context of its purpose of building up a republican political consciousness within Ireland and the desire to spread its sphere of influence through the use of the new militant circles which were developing in the country. Grant correctly asserted that 'while the search for national unity was all important, Clarke and the IRB's support for the workers in 1913 was consistent with the strategy of creating a mass separatist movement. There could be no mass movement without working class support'.[57] This must be taken countenance of when Clarke, when describing the DMP in *Irish Freedom*, borrowed the derogatory term Cossack – first used by Casimir Markievicz as a reference to Moscow's 1901 Bloody Sunday. Clarke also advised the city's 'third estate' that they 'after deep consideration and thought, must act' with an army.[58] As Grant stated, this focus on industrial unrest was typical of the IRB's 'espousal of co-operation at the time'.[59] However, this is not to deny the presence of a symbiosis of political outlook within the two political movements.

Even away from the separatist republican organisation, some other future revolutionaries were supportive of both the involvement of labour within the national question as well as the militarisation of the Irish working class. Indeed, at the Bodenstown Wolfe Tone commemoration in June 1913, Pádraig Pearse, not yet a member of the IRB, seemed to welcome the 'large numbers' of transport union men clothed in red hand badges, claiming that there were 'no strangers here'.[60] Furthermore, in November 1913, when the call for the arming of the trade union body was at its zenith, Pearse echoed such rhetoric claiming 'I should like to see the transport workers and I should like to see any and every body of Irish citizens armed.'[61] More importantly such a process of arming was connected with a growing spirit of violent rebellion and a growing lack of faith in parliamentary governance. He stated 'we must accustom ourselves to the thought of arms, to the sight of arms, to the use of arms'. He continued 'bloodshed is a cleansing and sanctifying thing, and the nation which regards it as the final horror has lost its manhood. There are many things more horrible than bloodshed; and slavery is one of them.'[62] It is important to note two things here. Firstly, the subtle implication of parliamentary impotence would not have been lost upon an army which was so intimately connected with the syndicalist ITGWU. Secondly, it highlighted the placement of the militarisation of labour within the context of the wider arming of Irish politics by those who were to play substantial roles within the coming revolution over the next decade. Upon the birth of the Citizen Army, Roger Casement also expressed approval and volunteered to 'aid the wider national movement to drill and discipline'.[63]

Despite such an underlying concurrent of philosophies and sympathies between the Citizen Army and the IRB, the relationship between the labour radicals and the Irish Volunteers began in a hostile fashion.[64] Somewhat ironically, given his history within the Irish Republican Brotherhood and his use of republican militant rhetoric, it was Seán O'Casey who led the anti-volunteer attack on the national militia.[65] The main reasoning for this hostility was twofold: firstly, the class differences between the two forces and secondly, the belief that nationalists had betrayed their Wolfe Tone-based political heritage.[66] In *Drums*, he eloquently described the class divergence between the two nationalist forces:

> Now there were two Cathleen ni Houlihans running round Dublin: one, like the traditional, in green dress, shamrocks in her hair, a little Brian Boru harp under her oxster, chanting her share of song, for the rights and liberties common to all Irishmen; they who fight for me shall be rulers in the land; they shall be settled for ever, in good jobs shall they be, for ever, for ever; the other Cathleen coarsely dressed, hair a little tousled, caught roughly together by a pin, barefooted, sometimes with a whiff of whiskey off her breath; brave and brawny; at ease in the smell of sweat and the sound of bad language, vital and asurge with immortality.[67]

The issue of class and landlordism erupted immediately upon the formation of Óglaigh na hÉireann. The composition of Óglaigh's committee was typically lower middle-class intelligentsia and represented three shades of nationalist opinion: firstly, members of Redmond's party; secondly, senior figures in the Irish Republican Brotherhood; and thirdly, Sinn Féin members who were not part of the IRB.[68] Despite the ICA's symmetry with the policies of the secret brotherhood, and the rather eclectic response from Sinn Féin to the lockout, the presence of the Home Rule politicians on the Volunteers' committee acted as a point of angst for O'Casey and some other Citizen Army members from November 1913 onwards.

During the official formation of the Volunteers at the Rotunda Dublin on 25 November 1913, Laurence Kettle acted as the secretary. Kettle was the son of the Parnellite Land League leader Andrew Kettle, a prominent member of the United Irish League and most importantly, with regard to the Citizen Army, a known strike breaker.[69] It was because of his presence that a group of the labour soldiers began to heckle and harass the meeting: 'cheers for Larkin' and the singing of 'God save Larkin' could also be heard.[70] At a cursory level, this confronting of Kettle seems to have had little impact on those who joined the Volunteers. Both Bulmer Hobson, who had attended *a priori* IRB meetings in Wynn's Hotel to discuss the establishment of the force, and Joseph O'Connor, who enrolled at the Rotunda, seemed to recollect it as a mere insignificant footnote in the wider context of the establishment of the force. Both almost dismissively referred to it as 'a local labour dispute' and 'some family connection with labour trouble', respectively.[71] However, Frank Robbins argued that the Kettle incident at the Rotunda left the Volunteers with a degree of resentment towards Larkin.[72] Certainly, as will be shown later in the chapter, leading figures in the Irish revolutionary movement in America did not see Larkin as a comrade.

The union's paper, the *Irish Worker* published a similar view to that of Robbins. It devoted almost an entire section to the Kettle incident. The paper read:

A regrettable incident happened at the Volunteer meeting held in the Dublin Rotunda Skating Rink on Tuesday. One of the persons chosen to take a leading part – indeed the leading part, as he was to read the manifesto of the new organisation was a Mr L.J. Kettle, who has been notorious of late as an active enemy of the working class's effort to combine for its own benefit. Naturally, his attempt to pose as a friend of freedom was actively resented by the major part of the audience, and a most stormy scene marred as a consequence the proceedings. It might as well be understood once and for all that this union is unqualified in favour of any movement that makes for a greater national freedom but we believe that it is of paramount importance to be clear as to the means by which that freedom is achieved. Hence we cannot tolerate the presence on a platform sacred to freedom men who are actively engaged in an attempt to reduce their fellow-countrymen of the Irish working class to slavery ... the only hope for freedom is an upright and self-respecting working class.[73]

O'Brien recalled that the leaders of the Citizen Army showed 'considerable hostility to the Irish Volunteers' from this point onwards, until Connolly became the ICA's commandant in October 1914.[74] It must be noted that at a time of excessive political policing, there was a genuine fear that the Volunteers could have been used as strike breakers. Furthermore, as O'Casey outlined in the *Irish Worker*, the absence of an invitation to the ITGWU to attend the meeting in the Rotunda would also have increased their sense of isolation and defensive orientation.[75] Such an invitation was not granted because it was believed the presence of the radical syndicalist ITGWU would have resulted in the absence of the moderate 'respectable' nationalists. Larkin, distrusted in parliamentarian and advanced nationalist circles, could not have been allowed a voice as it simply would have been counter-productive to the harmony that was being created. As Newsinger wrote, 'with the conditions of class war prevailing in Dublin in November 1913, the IRB had to choose between the ITGWU and the home rulers of the United Irish League, and they choose the latter.'[76]

By dissecting the above polemic, the reasoning for this antagonism can be illustrated. The *Irish Worker's* argument made clear that the opposition to Volunteers seen in the Rotunda was not the product of a divergence in the political aspirations of both movements. Both sought 'a greater national freedom'. Rather, the Citizen Army's actions in the Rotunda were a result of the presence of Home Rulers who belonged to the constitutionalist petty-bourgoise class of large farmers, landlords and employers. It must be noted that despite the hidden hand of the IRB, the secret society only comprised eleven of the thirty members of the Irish Volunteers' provisional committee; five of its members were affiliated to the United Irish League (UIL) and Irish Parliamentary Party (IPP), four came from the Ancient Order of

Hibernians, and ten were not connected to any party.[77] It is fair to say that the Volunteers represented the broad umbrella of nationalism rather than just the republicanism espoused by the Irish Republican Brotherhood. For the socialist-centric Citizen Army, embroiled in a trade-union and class war with a Home Ruler in the guise of William Martin Murphy, many of the politicians who joined the Volunteers appeared as enemies to the working-class army. Indeed, in a handbill arguing why workers should not join Óglaigh, published by the ICA in April 1914, the first three points dealt with the attitude of such politicians to the labour struggle: 'because many members of the [Volunteers'] executive are hostile to workers. Because it is controlled by forces that have always opposed labour. Because many of its officials have locked out their workers for asserting their right to join the trade union of their choice.'[78]

Prior to the outbreak of the industrial dispute in August 1913, relations between labour and the IPP were frail. The opinion typical of constitutional nationalists that 'long before the existence of the labour party, the cause of the workers in the House of Commons found constant, enthusiastic support from the Irish Party' had begun to tire in the working-class consciousness. This was because of the growing radicalisation of the labour movement which resulted from the emergence of Larkinism.[79] Such attitudes became even more negative after the outbreak of the trade union conflict and Larkin defined the attitude of the 'home rule party' to the crisis as 'utter indifference'.[80] It is noteworthy that Stephen Gwynn was the only sitting Member of Parliament of the IPP to publicly voice his support of the workers' cause throughout the strike and lockout.[81] While McConnel correctly argued that such silence did not necessarily indicate opposition to the union's cause, for Larkin it was 'proof that they [the IPP] acquiesced in all the horrible atrocities and unsavoury doings of our declared enemies'.[82] Keohane argued that in a speech on 28 September 1913 Redmond made his opinion loud and clear by avoiding the issue entirely.[83] When the ITGWU, under the leadership of Edward Byrne in the 1950s, looked back at the lockout they pointed to 'some of Ireland's leading intellectuals' who were the most outspoken in appreciation for the workers' resistance in 1913, namely W.B. Yeats, P.H. Pearse, James Stephens, Seamus O'Sullivan, Padraic Column, Joseph Plunkett, Thomas MacDonagh and Susan Mitchell.[84] Pearse, Plunkett and MacDonagh were, like ICA men Connolly and Mallin, executed for their part in the 1916 rebellion, while the others were representative of the intellectual lobby which threw its weight behind the Dublin Industrial Peace Committee and the Civic League. Within these circles there was a clear isolation of moderate nationalists and the Redmond-led party.

Given this context, it is clear that Kettle's presence, in particular, and the parliamentarians, in general, on the Volunteers' committee provoked not only the derision of Citizen Army members but also the belief amongst the ICA that 'the only hope for freedom is an upright self-respecting intelligent working class ... scabs and the employers of scabs by working for our degradation as individuals and our enslavement as a class' were working against that which would enable the freedom of the workers.[85] The Volunteers' leadership profile explains why the coming together of the ICA and Óglaigh na hÉireann began in earnest after Redmond's Woodenbridge speech in 1914 and the subsequent split in the nationalist militia.

Negative attitudes towards leadership were not restricted to the left. Rather, it appears such opinions were often mutual. As John White has contended 'many advanced nationalists were also hesitant as regards Larkin's methods.'[86] On 12 December 1913, the future 1916 revolutionary Seán MacDermott wrote 'Larkin is not a nationalist. He talks nationalism, but only in so far as he thinks it is likely to help along his socialist programme. We are friendly with Larkin and some of his lieutenants but then he has men about him who have a very bad record.' He continued that 'since the trouble began we had some little difficulty with some of our friends who became Larkin maniacs.'[87] While written after the adoption of the Citizen Army's constitution in March 1914, Clarke, despite previously showing sympathies for the working class, also expressed dissatisfaction with Larkin and the actions of his cohorts during the Citizen Army's pre-constitutional phase. On 14 May 1914, he wrote to the American-based republican Joe McGarrity and argued 'Larkin's people for some time past have been making war on the Irish Volunteers ... by this attitude they have antagonised the sympathy of all sections of the country and none more so than the advanced section. Liberty Hall is now a negligible quantity.'[88]

The presence of conservative nationalists within the Irish Volunteers was not the only cause of antagonism for the radical socialists and syndicalists of the Citizen Army. Undoubtedly part of the enmity towards Óglaigh was the belief that they offered a threat to the survival of such a small socialist organisation. The Volunteers' manifesto made particular reference to its desire to appeal to the 'widest basis.'[89] O'Casey described them as 'catching the light' from the socialist army. According to O'Casey, 'the creation of the National Volunteers was one of the most effective blows which the Irish

Citizen Army received. Thousands that had originally attached themselves to the Citizen Army passed over into the more attractive and better organised camp of the Volunteers.'[90] The *Irish Worker* displayed such a claim when it printed O'Casey's 'Open Letter to the Irish Volunteers' which stated 'the Irish Volunteers … hopes to build its battalions from flank to flank and front to rear with massed bodies of workers'.[91] Almost forty years later, he continued such an argument and told how that force put all 'possible obstacles' in the way of armed labour.[92]

It is clear that the criticism of the Volunteers predominately came from Seán O'Casey, who left the ICA in summer 1914 under acrimonious circumstances. This raises the question of whether his attitude to the issue was heterodoxical in comparison to the wider body or if it was typical of the general attitude of the Citizen Army. It appears that the opposition to Kettle's presence in the Rotunda was not felt amongst all Citizen Army members. James O'Shea recalled trying to diffuse the antagonistic atmosphere in the Rotunda and trying to calm some of the labourers: 'I was at this meeting and it was very near a wreck when some of the farmer employers who had locked out their men appeared on the platform. I helped to quiet some of the element by asking that they be given a chance and showing them my strike card.'[93] Furthermore, O'Casey's attitude to the Volunteers was met with criticism. Between January and February 1914, he engaged in a debate with the ICA's future director of munitions, Seamus McGowan.[94]

In O'Casey's 'An open letter to the Irish Volunteers', written on 24 January, he criticised Óglaigh. He drew a parallel between it and Grattan's Volunteers and he referred to its members as 'a crowd of chattering well-fed aristocrats'.[95] This drew a response from McGowan, who just over a month later was placed on the committee of the ICA's army council. McGowan favoured interaction with the nationalist militia and argued that 'the intermingling of Protestant and Catholic, Home Ruler and republican, Larkinite and Hibernian can only have a healthy impact on the nation as a whole'. He continued that there was something wrong with a republican, such as O'Casey, who attempted to wean workers away from a nationalist body.[96] This debate between the two men continued for the next month. Certainly, such opposition to the Volunteers was not unanimous amongst the ICA. However, the last months of 1913 and the first months of 1914 were the low ebb of the Citizen Army's relationship with republican military forces in the years until the formation of *Soarstát na hÉireann* and the outbreak of the Irish Civil War.

4

'CHANGED FROM AN AIRY NOTHING':
THE ARMY REVITALISED

Defined by O'Casey as an 'airy nothing', the pre-constitutional Citizen Army lacked any consciously established concrete form.[1] It stood for the defence of Dublin's strikers, in particular; and for the Irish working class, in general, and held budding socialist republican beliefs. However, by winter 1914, the labour force had adopted two constitutions, incorporated the prefix 'Irish' into their title, and experienced two leadership changes. Examining the history of the force under White and Larkin, this chapter assesses the process in which the body was 'made solid'.[2] While the cessation of the strike and lockout removed the primary purpose of the Citizen Army, the culture of working-class agitation remained. The collapse of the industrial effort also allowed for the space where the militia could establish a set of political ideals and purposes that extended beyond protecting striking workers. The constitution adopted in March, the army's April manifesto, and the adoption of an army flag (the starry plough) resonated with the prioritisation of republican and revolutionary goals, paid various homages to Ireland's revolutionary past, and represented the beginning of a gradual movement away from the country's biggest trade union, the Irish Transport and General Workers' Union. This new rebellious ethos was echoed by a desire to not only formalise but also to increase the martial strength of the army.

By the first months of 1914 the collapse of the workers' effort during the industrial struggle of the previous year had a dramatic effect on the fortunes of Árm Lucta Oibre na h-Éireann. Recalling these early days, Hanratty wrote 'the strike was finished; we didn't realise it. Our morale was high. We were fighting, and, as long as we were fighting we were winning.'[3] While White was still drilling members on 15 January 1914,[4] that month saw 'the great return to work'.[5] On Monday 12 January, nearly 1,000 returned to work.[6] On

18 January, the ITGWU finally capitulated to the fierce pressure it had been facing and instructed its members to return to their employment under any conditions that they could get. This often meant signing a prerequisite form renouncing the union (still the ICA's parent organisation).[7] Fox described the effect of this:

> When the long dispute ended, every worker was left to make his own terms about reinstatement. Attempts to secure an agreement preventing victimisation failed. In consequence the meaner-spirited of their opponents were able to take their revenge. Liberty Hall and Emmet Hall, from being crowded centres of struggle, became empty shells. Members were afraid to be seen paying their union dues, and as for marching with the Citizen Army this, in many cases, would have been to invite dismissal. Bitterness must have filled the hearts of the few labour enthusiasts who remained when they saw their empty union halls.[8]

Robbins's account confirmed Fox's description. He wrote 'many of the former members were gone. Those who had been reservists in the British army were called up. Others, who were not being imbued by the change taking place within the ranks, had fallen away. There was no longer any flamboyance.'[9] Many of the soldiers, including Hanratty, did not go back to work and chose to migrate to places like Glasgow.[10] Workers involved in the strike and lockout were often blacklisted after its culmination. As unemployment was high and job availability was low in Dublin in the early months of 1914, the Irish Trades Union Congress provided one-way tickets for those who wished to seek employment in Britain which made it increasingly difficult for the ICA to maintain its numerical position.[11] In March 1914 White informed the British Labour leader Con Lehane, who was debating forming his own martial body, and James Larkin that less than fifty members were left in the ICA.[12] The effects of the failed industrial protest were felt not only at a numerical level but at an ideological level. The Citizen Army's primary goal during its pre-constitutional phase was the protection of striking workers from 'political society'. By the time of White's meeting with Lehane, it had lost its main *raison d'etre*.[13] Steps needed to be taken in order to ensure its survival.

On Sunday 22 March 1914, a general meeting of the Citizen Army was held in Liberty Hall with the business set out as '(a) acceptance and amendment of proposed constitution; (b) election of provisional executive'.[14] The body was formally reorganised under its first constitution and set about not only becoming a more corporal force but also a stronger body numerically, geographically, and militarily within the well-developed physical force spectrum of Irish politics. This brought to a close its pre-constitutional phase and it became primarily a nationalist force distinguished from the Volunteers only by the working-class nature of its members and its publicly more advanced republican aspirations.[15] Matthews argued that it was 'Captain Jack White and James Larkin [who] decided to keep it going and quickly set in motion the second phase of this army's existence'.[16] Certainly, they were key leaders at the time, yet no former member questioned Seán O'Casey's 1919 claim that it was he who 'suggested that definite steps should be taken to form the Citizen Army into a systematic unit of labour' and he wrote the constitution.[17] On 22 March 1914, O'Casey was elected to the position of hon. secretary to the Citizen Army. He also began writing the Citizen Army notes for the *Irish Worker* on 18 April.[18] O'Casey, therefore, held control of the force's pulpit in the early days of its new phase. This had important implications for its involvement within nationalist Ireland.

Importantly, the army's first constitution not only gave it a more concrete form but the wording and placement of its policies both granted the national question eminence and began a gradual movement away from the ITGWU. As a preamble to the 1916 proclamation, the first article of the document decreed 'that the first and last principle of the Citizen Army is the avowal that the ownership of Ireland, moral and material, is vested of the right in the people of Ireland'.[19] The use of the phrase 'first and last principle' makes it clear that separatism had become the primary goal for the Citizen Army. Furthermore, not only does the similarity of this wording to the proclamation of the Easter Rising suggest, with hindsight, the particular republican manifestation of such separatist aspirations but the terminology also operated as a homage to both the *Irish Worker* (in which the constitution was published) and the old Irish republican, James Fintan Lalor.[20] In particular, the first clause of the constitution indicated a movement away from a singularly labour viewpoint to an outlook that would attract not only the trade unionist but also the more republican-minded nationalist.[21] Through such a deference to the Young Irelander, the force was linking itself with physical force separatism, the causes of the working class (the tithe in Lalor's case), and to the idea of political potential of linking the causes of the worker (land reform in Lalor's case) to the question of independence.

Like clause one, the fourth article was also echoed in the 1916 proclamation. It stated 'that the Citizen Army shall be open to all who accept the principle of equal rights and opportunities for the Irish people'.[22] However, what is of greater interest here is the final fifth clause of the constitution which read 'before being enrolled, every applicant must, if eligible be a member of his trade union, such a union to be recognised by the Irish Trades Council'.[23] At first glance this may appear to be asserting the close connection with trade unionism, in general, and the ITGWU, in particular. Certainly, of the five vice-chairmen elected to the ICA's council on 22 March, four were members of the ITGWU: Larkin, P.T. Daly, William Partridge and Thomas Foran.[24] Lysaght read this as the most important aspect of the constitution, and contended that the force, at this point, was a labour body. It was, for him, neither socialist nor nationalist, and while many of its members were sophisticated socialist thinkers, the training of the Citizen Army was military but not political.[25]

However, a deeper understanding of the relationship between the union and the force in its initial phase reveals an unconscious step away from the syndicalist body. Despite the lack of a consciously constructed form for the army during the lockout, the terminology used during the period suggested a clearly delineated supportive role under the auspices of the union. It is true that barely a month after the ratification of the force's constitution White resigned as chairman and Larkin assumed its leadership role. This marked the beginning of a two-year period where both the ITGWU and the ICA was headed by the same person, first Larkin and then Connolly. However, this did not indicate a merging of the two forces. For instance, Connolly was 'compelled' in 1916 to separate his union duties with his martial ones.[26] Rather, the relationship between the two bodies was most intimate not during that two-year timeframe but during the pre-constitutional phase of the 1913 era. This is due to both the direct connection with Larkin's union, in particular, as opposed to trade unionism, in general, as well as the ICA's movement towards autonomy after March 1914.

While in May 1914 Connolly wrote that the martial body was formed in connection with the transport union, the documents, actions and terminology which pre-date the constitution suggest that the relationship was more than a connection but rather that martial labour played a direct subsidiary role to the ITGWU.[27] Before adopting the prefix 'Irish' into their name in April 1914 the force was generally referred to as the Citizen Army. However, it was initially termed the Transport and General Workers' Citizen

Army which highlights the possessive nature of the union's relationship with the militia. Furthermore, on 18 November 1913, Connolly explicitly stated that the organ was being formed 'under the Transport Workers' Union'.[28] Certainly, an *Irish Times* report on 24 November implied that it was, at least nominally, restricted to ITGWU men rather than being open to all unions or any worker. The paper reported that 'except for wearers of the red hand badge [the emblem of the Larkinite union] and those accompanying them' the meeting was private.[29] By April, members of the militia were to wear a blue armlet with the initials ICA rather than the union symbol; a subtle shift of authority.[30]

Furthermore, on the same day as the *Irish Times*'s piece, the *Evening Telegraph* reported that the army operated under the auspices of Larkin's union.[31] The following month, the ITGWU's own paper used the possessive title referring to the force as the 'Transport and General Workers' Union Citizen Army' and wrote of how it 'proposed to organise and drill a citizen army of its own'.[32] Indeed, on both 24 and 26 January, the *Daily Herald* referred to the force as the 'Transport Union Citizen Army'.[33] The necessity of belonging to any ITUC trade union and not specifically the transport union was therefore, at an official level, an incremental weakening of the relationship between the union and martial labour. It is also noteworthy that Hanratty believed that the ITGWU 'dislike[d]' clause four of the ICA's constitution, that 'the Citizen Army shall be open to all who accept the principle of equal rights and opportunities for the Irish people'.[34] The clause did contradict the statement in clause five that all ICA members had to belong to a trade union. Therefore, it was further evidence of a weakening relationship between the ITGWU and the ICA. It is likely that it was a natural by-product of the increasing nationalisation of the army's goals. Certainly, this was a major trend within the history of the relationship. Indeed, the mid-to-late 1914 period saw further divergence.

At this time Connolly was growing impatient with the tortoise pace of the evolution of the trade congress's labour party while the division between moderate labour and the more radical ICA was becoming clearer. The inability of the militia to garner more than a few hundred members was indicative of its inability to attract a significant body of union men. The course of events in Europe would only serve to further cement this. By 1916 over half of the ITGWU's membership had joined the British war effort, though it should be said that their class background would have made them more in need of the proverbial king's shilling.[35] The controversy regarding the hoisting of a green flag over Liberty Hall in March 1916 and the union's nervousness over the radical nature of the Citizen Army in post-1916 Ireland were examples of this. Certainly, O'Casey contended that Citizen Army often had to 'passively submit' to the 'indifferent' union.[36]

In May 1914, a revised edition of the constitution was printed. This sought to make 'in a clear and unmistakable manner our attitude nationally and towards organised labour'.[37] The only significant change from the previous document was that the newer version stated in clause 2 (a) that its object was 'to arm and train all Irishmen capable of bearing arms to enforce and defend its first principle'.[38] As Matthews asserted 'the ICA was now firmly in the republican camp'.[39] In a repeat publication of the constitution on 22 August 1914, the notes above the publication stated 'the lines are cast inflexibly; it is simply labour and republican ... the soldier of the Citizen Army is a soldier of the Irish Labour Army of Republicanism'.[40] The revision was a result of the ICA's military development as well its antagonism towards the Irish Volunteers and was published below a sustained critique of the Volunteers.[41] The use of the word 'nationally' at a time when the force was attempting to become an all-Ireland body evidenced this. Furthermore, an advertising bill of the revised edition contained language similar to their competitive April 1914 manifesto to Irish trades bodies: 'this is the time for action. All political organisations are preparing for the future. Shall labour remain apathetic?'[42] The process of placing nationalist/republican goals as its primary objective was echoed by a process of creating a more formal military structure. In essence, as the force was driven more by ideas of national defence rather than workers' defence it needed a clearer military structure to match the development of its rival extra-parliamentary forces.

Certainly, the republican and revolutionary nature of the body's constitution was echoed less than a month after the adoption of the first constitution, when on 4 April 1914, the *Irish Worker* published a new Citizen Army manifesto which read, in full:

To the people of Ireland
our freedom must be had at all times
–Wolfe Tone

The time has come to practice the advice of Fintan Lalor, namely:
to train our hands and our sons' hands for the day will come when
they will have to use them.

The workers must be disciplined and alert if they are to equal the just proceeds of their labour. It has been well said:–

The price of liberty is eternal vigilance

The methods of discipline and alertness and the means of power to train our hands are provided by the Irish Citizen Army.

This organisation embraces the full principle of republican democracy; its aim is to sink the differences of birth, privilege and creed under the common name of the Irish people [this was a Marxist take of Wolfe Tone's philosophy]. It stands for a union of progressive nationalism with the democratic forces of Ireland, and its policy is to achieve that for which Theobald Wolfe Tone died and John Mitchel suffered – an independent Ireland.

Irishmen! Join the Citizen Army now and help us to realise the ideal of an Irish co-operative commonwealth.[43]

Again, the March 1914 constitution can be understood as the first step of this process. Not only did the constitution set out new policies but it also established and delineated a new officer corps. While Larkin presided over the meeting (suggesting that while the ITGWU and the Citizen Army had begun their gradual movement apart, the union still played a significant role), White was made chairman; Markievicz and Richard Brannigan were elected joint treasurers and O'Casey was elected secretary. An army executive was also created, the members of which were P.J. Fox, J. Bohan, Patrick Coady, T. Fogerty, Seamus McGowan, P. Morgan, F. Moss, Christy Poole, P. O'Brien, M. Mullin, T. Blair, T. Bourke, T. Healy, T. Kennedy and J. Shelly.[44] During the lockout, Connolly had stated that the body intended to have 'a regular establishment – majors, captains, sergeants, corporals'.[45] However, during the conflict such a demarcation of rank never occurred. While White was clearly the leading drill master during the pre-constitutional phase, it appears that British ex-service men like Kearns and Armstrong who drilled the Aungier Street section were not given any grade.[46] Connolly referred to these men as 'other officers', however, given the use of White's previously obtained title of captain, Connolly's terminology was not an indication of the incorporation of military ranks into the force.[47]

Clearly then the establishment of a committee and the election of officers was indicative of the re-structuring of the force into an increasingly more concrete martial body in order, in O'Casey's words, to 'consolidate and improve the conditions of the army so that it might become an influential fighting force in the ranks of labour'.[48] However, such militarisation was only at its early stages. There was a clear dichotomy between Connolly's use of martial terminology; 'major, captains, sergeants' and the constitutions' titles; 'chairman,' 'secretary,' 'treasurer'. Furthermore, the fifth vice-chairman, Francis Sheehy-Skeffington had been described by his contemporaries as a 'well known pacifist'.[49] His presence on the committee ensured that there was at least one voice not in favour of armed politics. Indeed, White argued as much in his own biography sixteen years later.[50] Finally, it must be noted that of the twenty-four officers elected in March 1914 only two (Staff Capt. Christopher Poole and Lieut. Countess Markievicz) remained on the officer list in 1916.[51] Many of the members of that council were elected not due to their military skills but due to the influence they could exert on the wider Irish society; indicative of the desire to expand the army's confines. This was almost certainly the case for the president of the ITGWU, Thomas Foran, and for Sheehy-Skeffington.[52] While Seamus McGowan was a member of the army's committee in 1914 and acted as its director of munitions after 1916, the officers of 1914 were not the officers who led the ICA from Liberty Hall to their various stations during the Easter Rising.[53]

From March 1914 onwards, steps were quickly taken to turn the Citizen Army into a proper army. Hanratty noted that it was the post-lockout period that saw the 'beginning of [the] army as a military force'.[54] This was done through the incorporation of uniforms and a flag as well as the focus on training and the attempt to broaden the force's base through recruitment drives. The Citizen Army Women's Ambulance Corps was established and had begun fundraising by July 1914.[55] Running concurrently with the creation and revision of the army's constitutions was a discourse around the adoption of a uniform for the force. According to O'Casey, the debate over uniforms centred on the idea of war with Britain and concepts of international law.[56]

Markievicz was in favour of the adoption of uniforms while O'Casey was against the idea. This was not simply a question of stylistic differences and mutual animosity (though the latter may certainly have played a part) but, rather, it had serious tactical and political implications. Markievicz argued for the wearing of a brassard, blue for the men and red for the officers. She argued the theory that these brassards would classify the men as belligerents and would grant them, under international law, certain protections and rights as prisoners of war. O'Casey, on the other hand, was more focused on the practical elements of any warfare in which the army might engage. He felt the army should employ the use of guerrilla tactics and, thus, argued that the force should have been able to blend in with regular citizens seamlessly; something which the brassards would have rendered impossible.[57] In his autobiography, the playwright wrote 'the words brassard, The Hague, belligerent, took wings' while he argued that 'they [the Citizen Army's soldiers] would be safer in ordinary clothes'.[58] For him it was not a question of belligerency because the British Army would not recognise such a claim; the Citizen Army would be seen as rebels and traitors.[59]

However, sources more contemporary than O'Casey's autobiography reveal a greater acceptance of uniforms on his part than his account portrayed. In his history of the army he avoided negative criticism of their adoption.[60] Furthermore, on 17 July 1914, O'Casey, along with J. Byrne, signed a report regarding a recruitment drive in Kingstown on 1 July. The report argued that the use of uniforms 'would aid in gathering recruits'.[61] Another reason, therefore, for the adoption of uniforms may have been merely to improve their standing as a *bona fide* militia. Robbins wrote of how when he joined the force he suffered from 'many sly smiles and witty remarks' and was asked 'why not join the Volunteers'.[62] Likewise, Prendergast stated that the ICA, prior to their use of uniforms, did not look 'like soldiers with their ordinary working class attires and carrying wooden broom handles'.[63] This period marked the high point of the rivalry between the ICA and the Irish Volunteers. The desire to be seen as a credible competitor to their nationalist brethren may have been a reason to adopt such attire. However, it is right to conclude that the adoption of brassards (blue for the regulars and crimson for the officers) was an echo of the body's ideological positioning. Indeed, such colours were also used when the force's flag, the starry plough, was adopted in April 1914. Before the flag was realised with a green background (a turn towards nationalism/republicanism in its own right), the colour in the design was Saint Patrick's blue, the traditional colour of Ireland, and red with its obvious socialist implications.[64]

On 5 April 1914, in Sackville Street, Dublin, the first battalion of the Citizen Army paraded under the flag for the first time.[65] In the forefront of the flag were the seven stars of the constellation the Ursa Major, 'the Plough, Merak and Dubhe marking the coulter and the Bentnasch the handle'.[66] Like

CHANGED FROM AN AIRY NOTHING

the colour of the flag, its design also reflected the republicanism and socialism that was growing within the force. The use of 'the plough' constellation and the name of the flag can be understood as a homage to Fintan Lalor's demand 'Ireland her own from the sod to the sky' or it may have been a reference to John Mitchel's quote 'the land and the sea and the air of Ireland for the people of Ireland. That is the gospel, the heavens and earth are proclaiming; and that is the gospel every Irish heart is secretly burning to embrace' which was printed on membership cards belonging to the force.[67] Either way, it reflected the separatist elements of the constitution's first clause.[68] Alongside this, the flag seemed to represent the aspirations of a better future for the Irish worker and the desire for societal revolution. In O'Casey's words, 'to plough is to pray, to plant is to prophesy. Again, as in the age gone by, the plough will with a wreath be crowned, and wise men will twine be garland; and the stars will last, and those who have loved them fondly will never be fearful of the night.'[69]

While the force was adopting methods that gave it a more rigidly defined construct and martial appearance, simultaneously it began to attempt to increase its military strength. In April 1914, O'Casey wrote 'steps are being rapidly taken to extend the army everywhere a worker bends his back. Who knows but soon the plough and the harrow may be beaten into the sword.'[70] Structurally, the army was divided into three sections of half companies: the first City Battalion, the second North County Battalion, and the third South County Battalion.[71] Interestingly, despite the period of decline that occurred in February, White and William Partridge opened a new branch in Emmet Hall, Inchicore on 1 February.[72] By 1916, this became the main ICA centre for the members who lived in the more western part of the city.[73] When the leaders sought to establish the South County Battalion, a series of recruitment drives took place in the one day: Chapelizod at 13:00, Lucan at 14:30 and Clondalkin at 16:30. O'Casey wrote that after this, they would look to the rest of Ireland.[74] In June, the *Christian Science Monitor* commented that 'the Irish Citizens [*sic*] Army movement grows'.[75] On 29 August 1914, Larkin claimed that the army was nearing 1,000 members.[76]

O'Casey corroborated Larkin. He wrote that the roll book for the city and county numbered 1,000.[77] However, the only contemporary book uncovered by historians was the 1916 one which placed the numerical strength of the force at 339.[78] Furthermore, it can be garnered from the records of the various recruitment drives that took place during the period that they were typically unsuccessful. The weak size of the Citizen Army was seen in a march to

53

Swords on 14 March 1914. Only thirty-two men, armed with hurleys, took part in this rally from Liberty Hall. The meeting also took place two hours late, at 16:00 rather than 14:00. Furthermore, it is noteworthy that there was no effort made to establish a local corps in the region (though the absence of White was credited as the reason for this).[79] Likewise, the ICA's visit to Kingstown in July, mentioned earlier, led to the enlistment of only twenty-two new members.[80]

Finally, in summer 1914, a manifesto was sent to various trades bodies in Cork, Belfast Derry, Sligo, Limerick, Kilkenny, Waterford, Dundalk, Galway and Wexford.[81] The manifesto was a propaganda piece which aimed to arouse countrywide support and argued 'would it not be a shame if the forces of labour alone were content to believe all things, suffer all things, endure all; to starve rather than take, to be stricken and not to strike back?' It then stated 'the Irish Citizen Army is the only suitable organisation for the workers of Ireland'.[82] Alongside this, Larkin devised a plan which never came to fruition to design a caravan which consisted of a living room and two small bedrooms so as to enable members to travel around the country and establish new units.[83] One of the reasons for the army's failure to recruit outside of the capital was because the Irish Volunteers had already established the structures necessary to garner widespread support and there was simply not enough room for the ICA.[84] This helps explain why the early stage of the revitalised Citizen Army was marked by resentment of the Volunteers. During the first half of 1914, both bodies fought each other for both membership and for the ideological claim of the 'Irish' militia. On 4 April 1914, the Citizen Army began to use the word 'Irish' in their title.[85] This adoption was symbolically important in two ways; firstly, it expressed their desire to expand their base into an all-Ireland organisation; secondly, it articulated the prioritisation of socialist republican, separatist goals.

The sense of revolutionary socialism and the desire to 'be a movement', in O'Casey's terms, was echoed by a drive for armament and a drive for drilling.[86] O'Casey argued that at that point an 'intensive campaign' began and that the force garnered 'stocks of belts, haversacks, French and Italian bayonets, long, lithe, dangerous looking weapons, a number of revolvers, and about a dozen rifles'.[87] Rifles were also gained during the Howth gunrunning. There was a tradition of buying guns from 'sympathetic' British service men, as was used by Michael Mallin to some success in 1915 and this may have been another avenue explored by White and Larkin.[88] By July 1914, the force had spent a sufficient amount of money on uniforms and 'other equipment' that it applied to the ITGWU to hold a display in Croydon Park to pay for the expenses incurred 'in connection with the equipment of [the] army'.[89] The logical next step after garnering a cache was training the soldiers in their use and in October the process of building rifle ranges began. Regarding the force's development of these, Robbins wrote 'along with others I busied myself in perfecting a rifle range in Croydon Park, which was then leased to the Irish Transport and General Workers' Union ... a miniature rifle range was also constructed in a large room in Liberty Hall and was used extensively during the winter nights by those who could afford the charge of three shots per one penny'.[90]

The development of an arms stash was also matched by a renewed zeal for drill. Under the first two leaders drilling took place twice a week in Croydon Park and was conducted by Sergeant Major Fogarty and Captain MacDowell.[91] With an eye towards the social aspect of the army, the organisation of *aeriochtai* in Croydon Park also occurred. On 22 April 1914, O'Casey applied to Branch No. 1 of the ITGWU for permission to hold such an event.[92] On 8 July, the secretary of the Citizen Army Women's Ambulance Corps also applied to hold such open-air functions.[93] Another application for an ICA *aeriocht* was discussed by the ITGWU on 20 August.[94] Each *aeriocht* always finished with the exercise of a mock attack on 'a lonely post'.[95] The gatherings were, Robbins wrote, 'an excellent means of training for the men and an encouragement to those who were not participating to join our ranks'.[96]

By summer 1914, the ICA had begun to receive attention from the intelligence division of the DMP and other 'repressive bodies'. Two detectives, referred to as 'G-men' in Irish republican tradition, Johnny Barton (known by the ICA as 'Calf's Head') and another named Kirwan (nicknamed 'Sheep's Eyes') began compiling intelligence on the army.[97] In March, DMP agents were following the labour force in relatively large numbers. Certainly, the thirty-two volunteers who marched to Swords on 16 March 1914 were followed by fifty men under Inspector Dowling.[98] However, it was not until October of that year that the DMP's 'reports on Irish secret societies' referred to any member of the ICA committee: W.P. Partridge and J. Larkin in this case. Furthermore, the ICA was not mentioned specifically in the report. Rather, Partridge was defined as a 'socialist and pro-German' while Larkin was termed a 'labour organiser'. Likewise, Connolly (also the first time he was mentioned in these reports) was defined as a 'socialist and pro-German'.[99] In contrast, in May 1914 the reports began to devote an entire section to the Irish Volunteers (totalling five pages in that month).[100] As succeeding chapters make clear, it was under Connolly's leadership that the army began to feel the force of the government through actions such as DMP raids on Liberty Hall. It can, therefore, be concluded that while the period from the adoption of the constitution in March 1914 to the departure of Larkin to the United States in November 1914, saw an increased primacy of the republican agenda as well as the development of a martial structure, the ICA, at least in the eyes of some DMP agents, had yet to become a revolutionary threat to the British Empire in the same vein as the Irish Volunteers. This was most probably a result of the relative strength of the two forces.

The ITGWU retrospectively admitted that it was the political crisis caused by the national question rather than 'industrial strife' that was the primary discourse in Ireland in 1914.[101] While the culmination of the strike and lockout meant a collapse in the strength and purpose of the workers' corps, issues over the national question were an important cause of the ICA's movement towards republicanism. Two major watersheds took place in 1914 which pulled the ICA further into the question of Irish sovereignty and separatism: the uncertainty over the third Home Rule bill, and the conflagration on the European continent. The crisis over the creation of an Irish parliament saw a militarisation of politics and the threat of the division of the Irish nation. The controversy bore witness to the increased militarism of the time. According to Eoin MacNeill, Carson brought out one of the most influential consequences of the Irish revolution by founding the UVF.[102] In essence, the crisis further enabled the process of restructuring Árm Lucta Oibre na h-Éireann as it threatened principles core to the army's nationalist ethos, and provided evidence of the impotency of 'Redmondite' parliamentary politics (affected in August by the outbreak of the World War I). Connolly summed up the attitude of both the ICA and labour to the Ulster question in 1914, writing:

> Here in Ireland the proposal of the government to consent to the partition of Ireland – the exclusion of certain counties in Ulster – is causing a new line of cleavage. Not one of the supporters of home rule accepts this proposal with anything like equanimity but rather we are already hearing in North-East Ulster rumours of a determination to resist it by all means. It is felt that the proposal to leave the home rule minority at the mercy of an ignorant majority with the evil record of the Orange party is a proposal that should never have been made, and that

the establishment of such a scheme should be met with armed force if necessary. Personally I entirely agree with those who think so; Belfast is bad enough as it is; what it would be under such rule the wildest imagination cannot conceive. Filled with the belief that they were after defeating the imperial government and the nationalists combined, the Orangemen would have scant regards for the rights of the minority left at their mercy. Such a scheme would destroy the labour movement by disrupting it. It would perpetuate in a form aggravated in evil the discords now prevalent, and help the home rule and Orange capitalists and clerics to keep their rallying cries before the public as the political watchwords of the day. In short, it would make division more intense and confusion of ideas and parties more confounded.[103]

The second principle of the ICA's constitution adopted in March 1914 read 'that the Citizen Army shall stand for the absolute unity of Irish nationhood and shall support the rights and liberties of the democracies of all nations'.[104] The relevance that this clause had to both World War I and to the Home Rule crisis is clear. Indeed, it was reiterated the following month when O'Casey told his readership that the 'workers' army ... stand[s] for the people of Ireland, not for half of the nation'. This was further indicated by the use of the phrase 'the rights and liberties of all Irishmen'.[105] Certainly, it was no coincidence that martial labour's focus on the spectre of partition coincided with the development of the Amendment Bill on 9 March 1914 which, in Prime Minister Asquith's words, was 'to allow the Ulster counties themselves to determine, in the first instance, whether or not they desire[d] to be excluded ... [for] a term of six years', in other words the partition of Ireland. [106] On 1 April 1914, the ITUC's labour party met and discussed the issue of the island's division and expressed its stance against such a cleavage.[107] Furthermore, even after the outbreak of World War I, the Irish Neutrality League (INL), founded in October 1914, stated that the Amendment Bill meant that Home Rule would have been dictated by the unionist leader Edward Carson and would have resulted in the partition of Ireland.[108] Importantly, Connolly presided over the INL and Citizen Army committee member, Countess Markievicz was one of its treasures. In May, the ITUC met for their twenty-first annual congress where Thomas Johnson, the body's vice-chairman, stated that the crisis in Ulster was 'uppermost in their minds'.[109] In April, Belfast's trades council read out a report by the Irish Trades Union Council and Labour Party which stated:

that this committee, representing the trade union and labour movement of all Ireland, views with dismay and anger the attempt to divide Ulster from the rest of Ireland under the proposed amendments to the home rule bill. We declare our belief that the suggested exclusion of Ulster (or any part thereof) will intensify the divisions at present existing and destroy all our hopes of uniting the workers of Ulster with those of Munster, Leinster, and Connaught on the basis of their industrial and economic interest. We call all those who profess to have the well-being of the workers of Ireland at heart to vigorously oppose any form of 'exclusion', either temporary or permanent, and to insist that whatever measures may be enacted concerning Ireland's political future must apply to the country as a whole.[110]

In the months following the Amendment Bill a noticeable increase occurred in Connolly's writing on the issue of partition. In March and April, articles entitled 'Labour and the Proposed Partition of Ireland', 'The First Hint of Partition' and 'The Exclusion of Ulster' appeared in various papers.[111] Connolly wrote that 'it [was] the trusted leaders of Ireland that in secret conclave with the enemies of Ireland have agreed to see Ireland as a nation disrupted politically and her children divided under separate political governments with warring interest'.[112] Firstly, the term 'her children' meant that this article, like the March 1914 constitution, found echoes in the 1916 proclamation. Secondly, it was evident that Connolly believed that the abilities of Redmond, Devlin (both mentioned specifically in this article), and the Irish Parliamentary Party to prevent the division of the country were, at best, feeble.

Certainly, Connolly was thinking about the use of armed force in order to prevent the 'amputation' of Ulster. In the same article he argued that labour in Ulster should 'fight even to the death, if necessary, as our fathers fought before us'.[113] It is noted that the fight was to be expanded out of the narrow confines of Ulster's boundaries. In a public meeting in Swords, on 16 March 1914, labour and ICA leaders spoke about the national question. Connolly and Markievicz shared a platform with P.T. Daly and William Partridge. Connolly proclaimed that labour would not accept the issue of partition and would fight a civil war that would surpass anything 'Ulster unionists' could do. Markievicz praised the workers for their efforts during the lockout, and highlighted some form of success for that labour dispute by claiming that it had laid 'the corner-stone' for a socialist Irish republic which would be owned by the workers and governed by the workers.[114] The presence of part of the Citizen Army's committee on the platform made it clear that it was to them whom Connolly was referring when he spoke of a civil war.

The following month, Connolly argued that there was either an inability or lack of desire on the part of the Irish Parliamentary Party to prevent the exclusion of a number of counties. The 'deal is done' he contended. The 'real crime' on the part of Redmond and Devlin was to open the question of Irish unity to 'bigoted and passion-blinded reactionaries'.[115] In another article in *Forward* in March, he stated that 'such a scheme should be resisted with armed force if necessary'.[116] With this in mind, he asked the working class to turn to the ICA's principles and concluded the article with an ominous rhetorical question that if Irish labour stood for the unity of Ireland, who would stop them?[117]

Clearly, within ICA leadership there was both a general opposition to partition and a belief that the British Parliament was impotent to stop such an amputation. Such opinions further developed the nationalisation and rigid militarisation of the army. However, this was not purely a result of the Amendment Bill on 9 March. Away from Westminster, other events transpired which helped foster such ideas. The Curragh mutiny, on 20 March 1914, had obvious implications regarding the importance of armed politics for the advanced nationalists of all shades. The issue of partition was brought to the forefront of Irish politics once fifty-seven out of the seventy officers stationed in the Curragh camp stated that if faced with the choice of initiating action against the Ulster Volunteers or dismissal, they would not engage against Carson's army. This was clear in April when Francis Sheehy-Skeffington spoke in the Antient Concert Building, Brunswick Street, Dublin on the issue, which he defined as 'the revolt of the army; the cry of who shall govern: the army or the people; and the Redmond surrender'.[118] Regarding the ICA specifically, Yeates wrote that:

the meeting to reconstitute the Citizen Army on more formal military lines [i.e. the adoption of its constitution and the implementation of an army council] may have been inspired by the announcement two days earlier by General Hubert Gough, officer commanding the 3rd Cavalry Brigade at the Curragh, and fifty-seven of its officers that they would resign rather than accept an order to march on Ulster and enforce home rule.[119]

Likewise, for the ITUC, the distinct possibility of partition was realised through the statement made from the camp in Kildare.[120] The officers' declaration in the Curragh resulted in the publication of a 'manifesto to the workers in Ireland from the Irish Trades Union Congress Parliamentary Committee' on 27 March 1914. According to the manifesto and the parliamentary committee which published it, the British Army stationed in the camp were a 'military junta evidently determined to thwart the will of the people.'[121] The declaration also had a nationalist ethos as the committee explicitly stated that it stood for the unity of Ireland and claimed 'Ulster in its entirety' before affirming its opposition to any attempt at division.[122]

Interestingly, the Curragh mutiny was viewed by the ITUC through the prism of a class conflict which further highlighted the perceived intrinsic connection between class and national issues. The position argued was that officers of the British Army would not fight against their own political convictions because it would have meant fighting against their privileged class. Likewise, then, the committee proposed that the non-commissioned officer in the army should not fight against his own class.[123] The manifesto contained a clear call to arms which was reminiscent of the rhetoric seen when the Citizen Army was being established, particularly Larkin's speech in Liberty Hall on 26 August 1913. The polemic argued 'if it is lawful for Carson to arm, it is lawful for us – the workers – to arm; if it is lawful for Carson to drill, it is lawful for us to drill; if it is right and legal for Carson to fight, then it is right and legal for us to fight for economic freedom.'[124] For the ITUC, the spectre of partition took on a sense of metaphorical corporeality after the event, and gave further credence to the anti-partitionist and anti-parliamentarian arguments outlined by Connolly and suggested by the Citizen Army's constitution.

The ITUC's manifesto was an implicit espousal of article 2 of that constitution. It was clear that both labour organisations were delving further into physical-force politics. Fox noted that the congress's discourse had all the hallmarks of Larkin who was at the time the chairman of the ITUC, as well as the vice chairman of the army and one of the key ideological drivers for said force.[125] Signed by the leaders of the national labour movement, the manifesto not only emphasised the right of workers to arm against the Ulster Volunteers but also gave 'powerful support' for the newly reinvigorated labour militia.[126] That the manifesto was written less than a week after the Citizen Army's committee and constitution were formed and accepted, that both documents were signed by Larkin, and that the *Irish Worker* published the two manuscripts side by side meant these documents were intrinsically connected to each other.[127]

It is true that there was a dichotomy within the ITUC's commentary on the Curragh incident and the army's anti-partitionist article 2. It can be suggested that the latter was implicit while the former was explicit. Certainly, while the issue of the division of the country was directly referenced by the ITUC, the congress did not mention the ICA in its manifesto. Rather, there existed a symmetry of ideas with regard to the ITUC's attitude to the Home Rule crisis, and the statement 'that the Citizen Army shall stand for the absolute unity of Irish nationhood, and shall support the rights and liberties of the democracies of all nations'.[128] Clearly, the phrase 'the absolute unity of Irish nationhood' was a product of the prevalent Ulster problem and the threat of partition, and it created a direct correlation with the manifesto issued by the ITUC.[129] O'Connor contended that by doing this, the constitution 'complemented' the anti-partitionist stance being taken by Connolly at the time.[130] An analysis of both the constitution and the ITUC's manifesto suggests that the ITUC were giving implied support for the development of the Citizen Army into an outwardly anti-Carsonist, anti-partitionist military force.

In April, the ICA continued to voice their opposition to the burgeoning threat of a divided Ireland, and did so in a more public fashion. This was exemplified by the national labour demonstration in Sackville Street where the first battalion of the Citizen Army paraded and unveiled the starry plough flag. The day was organised to protest against 'the suggested amputation of Ireland's right hand' and the ICA did not miss the opportunity to criticise Carson and the Ulster unionists.[131] In his speech, White argued it would be for the good of Ulster if they were to receive a blow from their enemies.[132] On 11 April, less than a week later, O'Casey further noted how the Ulster crisis helped transform the workers' army from primarily a 'defence corps' into an army concerned with Irish politics in general.[133] He wrote that the army could 'never allow political corrosion to suck from Ireland even a shred of one of Ulster's counties'.[134] This was a clear indictment of Redmond's handling of the crisis. Importantly, at this time Connolly continued to reiterate the goals of the militia. He asked the working class to turn to the principles of Árm Lucta Oibre na h-Éireann.[135]

It can be understood from his appeal to the Irish 'third estate' that this may also have been to help enable the body to increase its membership, particularly considering that this was a primary goal at the time. Since its embryonic stage, the Citizen Army had used the presence of the Ulster Volunteers and its sedition in Ulster as a justifier for their own existence. The seeming success of such militant unionist machinations and the intrinsically connected appearance of parliamentary impotency were clearly affecting both White and O'Casey when they penned the 'Labour Hercules' manifesto that was sent to various trades bodies in April 1914. While the piece was particularly hostile to the Irish Volunteers, it also stated that 'we have the Ulster Volunteers preparing for eventualities in the North'.[136] It must be recognised that the polemic was not overtly nationalistic nor did it contain anti-partitionist goals. Both R.M. Fox and Adrian Grant stated that the objective of this manifesto was to act as a propaganda tool to enable the development of the army.[137] However, the reference to the UVF, alongside the Irish Volunteers, reveals how the situation regarding Ulster in early 1914 further militarised the ICA.[138] Through this, it continued to enable the development of the force numerically, patially and as a more nationalist-conscious body.

5

'CLOSER COMMUNION IN THOUGHT, PRINCIPLE AND ACTION': RELATIONS WITH THE IRISH VOLUNTEERS

A t a time when the labour body was becoming more rebellious in nature, *Irish Freedom* was arguing for the same philosophy, despite contending that the Volunteer movement 'was defensive, not offensive'.[1] The paper ran articles entitled 'Prospects of Modern Revolution', 'Urban Revolution' and 'Street fighting'.[2] Furthermore, criticism of the DMP was also present in the paper's February 1914 edition which expressed antagonism towards the police and connected the police to the national question, contending the DMP was the arm of an invading power.[3]

The process of an increased prioritisation of republican goals for Árm Lucta Oibre na h-Éireann seemed to have had only a marginal effect on their relationship with the wider republican family. It is true that figures such as White, Markievicz and McGowan were in favour of co-operation with Óglaigh. However, this co-operation did not begin to transpire until June.[4] Not only was the restructuring of the ICA marked by an ethos of 'fierce independence' but after the strike and lockout its nadir was contrasted by the Irish Volunteers' ability to draw in men who had been associated with the labour movement.[5] Finally, O'Casey's grasping of the Citizen Army's pulpit created a period of outright hostility towards the Irish Volunteers which lasted until summer 1914.

The dispute between O'Casey and McGowan continued to fill the pages of Larkin's paper. Here it was made clear that there was distrust about the class dynamic of the Volunteers. O'Casey asked if the lot of the labourer would be better under the wealthy nationalist rather than under the imperialist; 'the stick which beats the worker' would only be transferred to the Irish Volunteers.[6] With the promise of Home Rule in the air, this period was defined by contested points of Irish nationalism and the battle for the shape of a modern, more independent nation. O'Casey's assertions rang loudly within such a context. For him the difference between the members of the two militias was the embodiment of the struggle for who would be heard in this new state. Naturally, he believed that 'not in the shouts of the deluded wage-slave Volunteer; but in the hungry-cry of the nation's poor is the voice of Ireland'.[7]

While this was obviously further aggravated after Redmond's seizure of command of the Irish Volunteers on 16 June 1914, it was the most pertinent essence of the dispute. McGowan believed that these fears were unfounded. He argued that O'Casey's contentions were fallacious and that it would be foolish for the nation's toilers to 'boycott the only movement which … has caused a flutter in the dovecotes of Downing Street and Dublin Castle'.[8] He believed that the nationalists within MacNeill's movement would not come to oppress the Irish labourer and that the interest of the country should 'overshadow' the immediate needs of the workers.[9] However, the following two months saw the friction between the two bodies begin to boil over.

In April, evidenced by clause 1 of its constitution and the adoption of the prefix 'Irish', the ICA asserted their symmetry with the general republican public. They were 'convinced' that the ideological descendants of Parnell, those that believed in the absolute unity of Ireland, would see the principles espoused by the March constitution and would 'range themselves beneath the banner that flies nearest the skies'.[10] This opening to the broader nationalist spectrum centred on the threat of partition. However, at this point, the army's competitive nature, which arose out of its rebuilding stage, rendered harmony with Bulmer Hobson and MacNeill's men difficult. O'Casey, in usual fashion, accused the paper *Irish Freedom* of engaging in empty rhetoric. *Irish Freedom* had published that the time for 'weak politics and weak men' had passed, i.e. parliamentary politics, and O'Casey responded by asking when would they take their own advice to heart.[11] Such a critique emphasised not a difference in ideology but a negative appraisal of the Volunteers' passivity, though O'Casey's general distaste for the body would surely have been a major instigating factor for this critique.

Later that month, the tension between the two militias became more vocalised and stern. This focused on the attempt of the ICA to use some of the Volunteers' halls for drilling. According to O' Casey, when the facilities at Croydon Park and Liberty Hall proved to be inadequate, a number of requests were sent to the nationalist bodies to use the Volunteers' rooms but all were ignored.[12] Indeed, at the beginning of March, even before the Citizen Army's re-organisation, O'Casey criticised the absence of replies from the Volunteers.[13] Finally, a letter written by O'Casey to the secretary of the house committee of the Gaelic League drew a reply with declined the appeal. After this, and much like the article on 11 March, he again used the podium of the *Irish Worker* to accuse the other nationalist militia of duplicity towards the labour movement. He quoted Secretary Irvine's reply, which stated 'I don't think the committee would lend it to any other organisation for drill.'[14]

For O'Casey, the lack of co-operation was a sign of hypocrisy as he believed the Volunteers were 'constantly prating' about how the needs of the worker would be best met by joining MacNeill's force.[15] Here he was probably referring to articles in *Irish Freedom* where appeals for membership were made to the working-class inhabitants of Dublin. At the start of the year, the paper argued that the Volunteers should seek to gain members from the 'widest possible base'.[16] Not only would the implicit lack of condemnation of the landowning and capitalist class have raised concerns from sections in the ICA but so too would Óglaigh's encroachment in the labourer society. O'Casey referred to this as the call to follow the path which the 'aristocracy subsidised'.[17] In March, a more aggressive plea for support from the left was seen in *Irish Freedom*. One article raised concerns that the national movement was becoming controlled by the elite and argued that the paper supported the working-class society.[18] It continued that 'many skilled workers' had already joined the ranks of the movement and the Volunteers stood for the defence of the rights and security of Irishmen of all classes. 'The value of the Volunteers,' it finished, 'should not escape us.'[19] Yet, while the first four months of 1914 saw relations between both militias restricted to various forms of propaganda pieces in their relative newspapers as well as criticism of the Volunteers by O'Casey, the following months saw deeper interactions with longer lasting effects.

On 16 May 1914, the *Irish Worker* reported that the ICA was organising a meeting in order to fill a vacancy that had arisen through Captain White's resignation from his position as chairman.[20] Larkin stated that White was compelled to resign because of a court martial which found that he was propagating the idea that labour's armed wing had not the ability to lift itself out of its nadir nor could it hope to supplant capitalism with a co-operative commonwealth. White, Larkin contended, was constantly arguing that the workers' salvation lay in the hands of 'the middle class and aristocrats'.[21]

While White's writings and beliefs may have led to this opinion being held in some quarters, the absence of any other sources relating to such a court martial indicate that this was just empty rhetoric from the labour leader. However, it does reveal the dynamic of distrust that centred on the more bourgeois nationalists. Fox contended that White's departure occurred because he was not happy with the limited range of activities that were possible under the auspices of the Citizen Army.[22] O'Connor argued that in fact it was the creation of an army council and his own egotism that led to White's exit, seeing him as 'a self-confessed "dictator"' who 'suspected that the real function of the army council was to clip his wings'.[23]

However, the parting between the ICA and its first leader had wider implications for its relationship with the Volunteers. While the early months of the year saw O'Casey develop a sustained attack on the other nationalist militia, White took a far more cordial approach to them. Indeed, White met the challenges of increased militarisation with an attempt to affiliate the ICA with the more successful Volunteer force.[24] While he would later write that it was impossible, he was trying to unite middle-class nationalism with working-class labour. At the time of the ICA's recruitment drives, he wrote to his mother that he was attempting to compel 'the National Volunteers to cease from their suspicious aloofness from anyone connected with labour and draw together the middle class and the labour national movements'.[25]

Too much significance should not be attached to White's proposal. Fox describes White's offer to place two units of the ICA under the control of the Volunteers as 'impulsive'. Certainly, given that the offer was made with the condition that the two units were to remain independent and affiliated rather than entirely co-opted evidenced that he continued to want a somewhat independent ICA. Either way, MacNeill responded that his militia could have no association with an organisation that had recently been in conflict with the police.[26] Evidently, at this point any sustained affinity was impossible on either side. However, it was true that White's eventual departure from the ICA removed their most supportive voice towards the Irish Volunteers.

After failing to gain access to Óglaigh na hÉireann's halls to practice manoeuvres, and the rejection of their chairman's scheme, the ICA issued a direct challenge to the Volunteers to a discussion between three members of the Volunteers' executive and three members of the ICA's executive. An analysis of O'Casey's account of this debate makes clearer the dynamics that were at play here. The playwright proposed that this challenge arose from the

Volunteers' attempt to encroach on ICA territory by establishing a base in Swords, and, more importantly, the suggestion that Redmond was about to seize command of Óglaigh's executive.[27] The ICA argued that the Volunteers were actually 'antagonistic' to the claims of the Irish worker and, therefore, sought to verify whether this was true or not.[28]

In June 1914, Irish Republican Brotherhood's members of the Irish Volunteers were attempting to block such a manoeuvre by Redmond; his eventual usurpation of the body in June that year gave O'Casey's argument credence.[29] The encroachment of the IPP into the Volunteers, as well as the split which arose out of that process, had significant consequences for the relationship of the two militias. Yet, of more relevance here was White's response to the conflict. The leadership of the ICA, be it O'Casey who penned the challenge or Larkin whom O'Casey accredited for the idea, erroneously attached their chairman's name to it. In a letter to the editor of the *Irish Times* White was quick to distance himself from the attack;

> I wish to state that I had nothing to do with it. In fact, I resigned from the chairmanship of the said council a week ago, doubtful of my power to prevent, and determined not to become involved in such a policy. In my opinion, the all-important point is the speedy formation and equipment of a Volunteer army implicitly or explicitly determined to achieve the independence and maintain the unity of Ireland, and I will not lift a finger to embarrass anybody likely to work for this end. For an 'army council' which has not yet created an appreciable 'army' to issue a challenge to the organisers of a strong and growing movement seems to me [a] little short of absurd. Nevertheless, I believe that for trade unionism to predominate over unionism is the line of least resistance to the unification of Ireland and I shall work along that line myself whenever and wherever I get the chance.[30]

Regarding White's departure, a number of things were revealed in this letter. There was clearly no sense of apostasy; rather, there was a continued avowal of the value of labour seen by the importance it was given in overcoming the sectarianism prevalent in Ulster. However, despite this favouring of syndicalism, there was certainly an element of resentment regarding the failure of the ICA to grow into a larger unit.[31] Indeed, his disillusionment with the Volunteers later that year over their own strength was suggestive of a level of egotism on White's part.[32] It must also be recognised that his antagonism with his fellow labour leaders appears to have begun earlier than the published challenge. In his memoir, White recalled a dispute with Larkin in December 1913, after Larkin had disparaged his father. When White referred to the 'defender of ladysmith', a name his father had earned fighting in the British Army, Larkin stated that this title was gained by defending the flag 'under which more disease and degradation had been experienced' than any other.[33] This caused acrimony between the two men.

White's memoir also hinted at another clash which arose out of an incident at Butt Bridge in Dublin in March. On 13 March 1914, the ICA was protesting, in what was known as a hunger-march, against 'the vindictive victimisation inflicted on the unemployed by the Dublin employers'.[34] According to Robbins these 'hunger-marchers' were met by Inspector Barrett and a body of the DMP.[35] Here a fight broke out between the two groups which led to the eventual charging of White for assault.[36] When White eventually settled the dispute the move seemed to cause consternation amongst his colleagues. White argued 'I was blamed by my own side for [a] weak good nature and the waste of the opportunity to score a decisive victory over the police. But then my own side were not shelling out some £10 a day for the case.'[37] Certainly, issues such as these had to play a part in his departure from the force. It appears likely that O'Casey's challenge to Óglaigh was the final straw for White. Either way, the circumstances surrounding the loss of the army's first leader were indicative of the frail and often hostile relationship that had existed between the two nationalist militias since their inception. However, at this point events on a national scale, such as the annual Wolfe Tone commemoration at Bodenstown on 26 June 1914, the Howth gunrunning on 26 July 1914 and the outbreak of World War I in July 1914 were beginning to have repercussions.

However, before these events are examined, commentary on O'Casey's resignation from the ICA in summer 1914 is needed. While the date of his departure has remained uncertain, it is definite that it occurred sometime between the Howth gunrunning and the outbreak of the hostilities in the continent. According to O'Casey, it occurred out of events which, if only tangentially, arose out of the union between the Volunteers and the IPP, which will be discussed later in the chapter. O'Casey's history of the Citizen Army described the organisation of a 'special meeting' to allow the council to decide whether, given this development they could allow members of the council to fraternise with the other nationalist militia.[38] In essence, this was a push to have Countess Markievicz, a member of Cumann na mBan, ousted from the force. According to Robbins, O'Casey's attempt to expel the female republican failed because of a slip of the tongue when he stated that he was afraid of no man, including Larkin. This led to a remonstration by Larkin and ensured the failure of the move.[39] Subsequently, it resulted not just in his resignation from the council but also in a complete severing of his connection with the ICA, and the eventual criticism of their ideals in his 1926 play, *The Plough and the Stars*.[40] Like White's exit, O'Casey's was indicative of a rivalry between the two armies. Interestingly, while the departure of the chairman removed the Volunteers' staunchest ally, O'Casey's exit took away their harshest critic. O'Casey believed that 'Pearse [was] worse than all' and therefore the playwright's presence within any future military unit would have been a major stumbling block for the union between the two bodies in Easter 1916.[41] However, Hanratty also argued that many members of the Citizen Army believed O'Casey resigned from the council because the situation was beginning to look dangerous and a rising was possible. He wanted an excuse to leave and one that would also have acted as 'a good face saver'.[42]

Despite such strong words, O'Casey also described the beginnings of a kindred relationship between the two bodies in June 1914. On 26 June 1914, the annual pilgrimage to Wolfe Tone's grave at Bodenstown took place under the management of the Wolfe Tone Memorial Committee. Given the continued references to the republican father figure and his clear influence on their ideology it is not surprising that the army council of the ICA would have wanted to play a role in the proceedings. It was here, according to O'Casey, that a 'fraternal association' and a hope for 'closer communion in thought, principle and action' began to develop.[43] Certainly, after this a series of national and international events, from the gunrunning at Howth to the outbreak of World War I and Redmond's polices over that issue conspired to bring the bodies closer together. The pilgrimage to Wolfe Tone's grave was seen by Seán Prendergast as something of 'first rate importance' and the value of it as the first occasion when both militias stood together in unity cannot be underestimated.[44] It is noteworthy that, at this point, one of the most important roles of the IRB was the organisation of this event and that it was the republican leader, Tom Clarke, who assuaged fears on behalf of the Wolfe Tone Memorial Committee about the attendance of the ICA.[45] Evidently then, this was the instance when the Irish Republican Brotherhood began to seek the involvement of the labour movement in the republican discourse.

While Bodenstown suggested a promise of union, June was also the time where the biggest threat to any form of fraternity arose. On 9 June 1914, an ultimatum by Redmond was published demanding that twenty-five people nominated by him were to be put on the existing committee of the Irish Volunteers.[46] On 16 June, the Irish Volunteers' provisional committee accepted this request. However, this approval was not voluntary. Redmond had threatened to establish a separate committee for the Volunteers, creating disruption and discordance within the organisation. Indeed, his proposal was met with an eight-man protest. Six of the eight men that signed the protest were members of the IRB.[47] However, despite this, his grasping of control seemed to confirm the Citizen Army's fears. On the effect of incorporation of Redmond's nominees, Piaras Béaslaí, who voted against the incorporation, wrote that 'the new departure was followed by a big increase in the paper strength of the Volunteers. Those interested in politics rather than military training flooded the drill halls and meeting places, apparently aiming at strengthening the party's control of the movement.'[48]

The change in Volunteer leadership was indicative of a movement towards the moderate Home Rule movement. As well as this, it increased the numerical strength of the Irish Volunteers. Both of these consequences fed into the competitive nature of Árm Lucta Oibre na h-Éireann. It can be argued that after being outmanoeuvred within the provisional committee, the rump of republicans and IRB men were pushed to a supportive position for the ICA in a way that had not previously happened. This explained Clarke's invitation to the ICA to attend the Bodenstown commemoration.[49] However, the labour men had not yet realised this. Instead, despite the comradeship which arose out of the planned Wolfe Tone anniversary, the division between both of the armies was widened by the inclusion of the nominees of the IPP on to the Volunteers' executive.[50] Naturally, given his involvement during the previous year, O'Casey met the capitulation to the IPP with harsh criticism. Reporting on the Bodenstown event, he referred to Redmond as a 'miniature Grattan', a man of 'property protecting parliament'.[51]

It should be recognised that in labour circles a genuine fear was held that the Irish Volunteers could have been used as yet another force to repress the Irish worker. Less than a month before the ultimatum, in April, Colonel Moore promised that the Volunteers could be used in the event of public disturbance to keep the peace, in essence to act as an auxiliary police force. The *Irish Worker's* response was filled with criticism. 'E.K.' evoked the industrial dispute of the previous year. He recalled Bloody Sunday when 'murderous ruffians ... butchered two of our fellow citizens and maimed hundreds of others'. He contended that in the absence of any repudiation, 'honest nationalist workers' would be bound to view the movement with nothing but suspicion.[52] Larkin added further criticism and described the soon to be IPP-led militia as 'a [Dublin] Castle-controlled organisation', adding that they would 'if given the opportunity, attack, baton, shoot and massacre the organised working class'.[53] After the Volunteers' capitulation to Redmond, whose party were at best apathetic to the struggles of the workers in 1913, it was natural that such labour fears would have been further aggravated.

The Howth gunrunning on 26 July 1914 and the death of three people in Bachelor's Walk later that day was a significant moment in Irish republican circles. The landing of arms and the shooting of civilians affected both the Irish Volunteers and the Irish Citizen Army and also revealed the complexity of their relationship with each other. For the Irish Volunteer Frank Henderson, the relationship between the two bodies 'was not very definite at the time'. He believed that by the time of the gunrunning there was both a degree of hostility and a degree of friendliness.[54] Co-operation rather than competitiveness defined their interaction throughout the day. Common ideals were of greater importance than on-going rivalry. Indeed, Charles Shelly, a member of the National Guard, suggested that the leading men of 'armed labour' must have known of the impending arrival on 26 July of the *Asgard*, with its cargo of 900 rifles and 26,000 rounds of ammunition destined for the Irish Volunteers. It was Shelly's opinion in 1953, that the ICA's exercise in Swords on the day of the landing was 'arranged purposely to keep us out of the way'.[55] Evidently, Na Fianna Éireann man James Carrigan, along with four others, used a trek-cart from Liberty Hall and joined the Volunteer procession at Beresford Place before travelling to Howth.[56] While Bulmer Hobson, years later, stated that the ICA knew 'nothing' about these activities, it does appear that there may have been some awareness and even minimal assistance from the labour movement.[57] Certainly, given Connolly's continued criticism of Hobson in 1915–16, Hobson may have been less inclined to credit the labour militia.

Another sign of support occurred at Clontarf near Croydon Park. Close to the Howth Road, the Volunteers encountered a barrier of police and military stationed around 150 yards away from them. In response, the Volunteers turned to the right and down a crossroad towards the Malahide Road. There they encountered members of the DMP, around seventy in total, and the Scottish Borderers, numbering around fifty, who attempted to seize a number of rifles from Óglaigh.[58] During the ensuing struggle Captain M.J. Judge, a member of the nationalist militia, was stabbed by a bayonet trust and about nineteen rifles were seized by the British forces.[59] The importance of the Citizen Army in the event arose from the fact that during the mêlée other Volunteers left some of their rifles behind which were retrieved by the labour force. These were left in a nearby ditch and taken by ICA.[60] Other Volunteers sought refuge from the attack in Croydon Park.[61]

Naturally, this event helped to reshape the manner in which both bodies interacted with each other. Some of the rifles made their way to both Croydon Park and Markievicz's residence and the next day Connolly's daughter, Nora, was put in charge of making sure the rifles obtained were returned to the Volunteers.[62] As a result of this some of the stockpile was gifted to the labour militia.[63] It is also possible that some members of the ICA may have attempted to come to the rescue of their brethren. It was reported that during the scuffle with the DMP and the Scottish Borderers that shots were fired by 'bystanders unknown' and not by the Volunteers; the shots caused injuries to two of the British Army's soldiers.[64] If the report was correct and it was not MacNeill's men who injured the British servicemen then the most likely people to have fired on the British army were members of the ICA. This would partially explain why they were given the Italian masseur rifles that had arrived at Howth and why the day signalled the beginning of the union of the two bodies.

However, the events on 26 July 1914 were not entirely cordial. An ICA man named Scully had brought a Volunteer leader, Colonel Moore, to Croydon Park in order to gather up the guns. According to Moore '... at this period the labour party was very hostile to the Volunteers ... I was putting my head into a hornet's nest.'[65] Initially Moore, when inquiring if there were Volunteer men or guns at Croydon Park, was told that there was none of either. In truth, Larkin and J. Mills were burying the rifles.[66] Scully was also court martialled by the ICA for his actions, in what may have been the first republican court martial of the era, and when he failed to attend the hearing he was expelled from the force.[67] However, despite this, when it did transpire that some of rifles were there, Moore later returned with Bulmer Hobson and described the labour men as 'civil' while the boy scouts belonging to the left-wing body helped to gather up the remaining munitions.[68]

Of even more importance to both the development of unity between the two bodies and to the movement of the ICA towards revolution was the

Bachelor's Walk shootings, 26 July 1914. As the British soldiers returned from Howth to the city they encountered a crowd at Bachelor's Walk, near the Halfpenny Bridge, who began to throw stones at the army men. One soldier was kicked to the ground and another was stunned by a flour-pot that had been thrown when a mob came down from Liffey Street threatening the army's flank. At this point combatants at the rear of the unit opened fire on the crowd. Once the firing had ceased three people had died and eighty-five had been injured. The three deceased were Mary Duffy, a 56-year-old widow; Patrick Quinn, a coal porter; and James Brennan, a messenger aged seventeen.[69] For the working class and the labour movement in Dublin, the incident was particularly poignant. The attack by the Scottish Borderers and the DMP evoked memories of the brutality they had faced when they suffered baton charges by the RIC and the DMP during the strike and lockout.[70]

The consequences of the shooting brought together the two republican armies in an official capacity. At the funeral for those who had died in Bachelor's Walk both the Volunteers and the ICA took their place in the guard of honour.[71] Indeed, this was the beginning of a pattern that would run over the next two years where both militias would share the podium at a series of national events, most particularly the funeral of O'Donovan Rossa in 1915. Greaves described this as a 'reconciliation of the two organisations'.[72] For O'Casey, 'the celebrated episode of the Howth gunrunning had engendered a fellow feeling between the rank and file of both movements, which was very near akin to comradeship'.[73] He pointed specifically to the existence of the military wings on both sides of the procession as evidence.

Given that the scene in Bachelor's Walk was reminiscent of Bloody Sunday, it produced a public reaction among both sections of the republican spectrum. It also added further credence to the widespread belief in the lack of impartiality within the British forces when dealing with nationalist militias in contrast to the Ulster Volunteers. Such a belief in the bias of the imperial apparatus ran through the early history of the ICA. Indeed, such duplicity in contrast to the Larne gunrunning can be identified by Bulmer Hobson's statement that 'I knew that the Liberal government in England, having already remained inactive on the occasion of the Carsonite gunrunning at Larne, would find it very embarrassing to take active measures against us.'[74] The impact of what was seen as yet another example of brutality and hypocrisy led to the furthering of the belief in the necessity of revolt.

After the shooting, William O'Brien published his view that such brutal force should have been met with the same by the labour movement.[75] The *Irish Worker* reported that O'Brien believed that the 'government authorities' would have always discriminated between the militant Ulster unionists and the nationalist militias whenever they thought repressive force was needed. O'Brien held 'the Liberal government' directly responsible for the atrocity and he exclaimed the belief that such actions needed to be met with force.[76] The ICA was the obvious manifestation for such an approach. Furthermore, according to Connolly's confidant in Belfast, Cathal O'Shannon, once Connolly heard of the events of the day he immediately concluded that it was time to seek out Irish independence and he asked to be put in contact with the IRB.[77] On the funeral of the Bachelor's Walk victims, Nora Connolly-O'Brien recounted:

> this was only five months after we had been beaten in the great strike; we wanted to show them how badly we really were ... I have never seen Dublin so deeply stirred as it was the day those funerals winded their way up Parnell Square to Glasnevin Cemetery. The youngsters and people from the teeming tenements lined the streets while thousands marched behind. There was not a soldier to be seen. The authorities had withdrawn them to their barracks. Surely now, I thought, the world will know that she holds us by force and that she would rather destroy and kill us rather than allow us to go free. But the world did not have time to show its care. We were on the edge of far greater carnage than anyone could have dreamed about.[78]

The carnage that Connolly's daughter was referring to was World War I. John Redmond's policy after the outbreak was one of the most significant factors that brought the fractious period in the two republican militias' relationship to a close. In the House of Commons, on 3 August, the IPP leader pledged Irish co-operation with the British Army's war effort and loyalty to the government in Westminster and argued that the coast of Ireland was to be defended by 'her armed sons'.[79] More importantly, on 20 September in Woodenbridge, Co. Wicklow, he argued that such a mere defensive orientation was not sufficient; contending that 'it would be a disgrace for ever to our country, and a reproach to her manhood, and a denial of the lessons of her history, if young Ireland confined their efforts to remaining at home to defend the shores of Ireland from an unlikely invasion'.[80]

This offer towards involvement in the British war effort not only created rancour amongst the more republican members of the Volunteers but also caused an irrevocable disunity which resulted in the official split in the movement four days later. Future Judicial Commissioner of the Dáil Courts Kevin O'Sheil was scathing of Redmond's policy. He described the Woodenbridge speech as one that was 'impregnated with imperialism' and a 'positive recruiting speech' which was a violent assault on deep-seated republican sensibilities.[81] According to Laurence Nugent, the following meetings of the Volunteers' executive were characterised by 'angry scenes' which led to the eventual fragmentation of the Volunteers into the IRB-controlled Irish Volunteers and the Irish Parliamentary Party-led National Volunteers.[82] Outside of those in Óglaigh, Redmond's speech would have been particularly abhorrent to ICA members who upon joining the force took an oath which stated that with the exception of assisting the revolutionary working class from another country, no soldier would fight outside the confines of his own border.[83]

On 24 September 1914, the members of the original provisional committee of the Irish Volunteers seized their old headquarters in Great Brunswick Street in Dublin.[84] A convention was signed which expelled Redmond's men from the army. Amongst the signatories were Eoin MacNeill, Bulmer Hobson, 'The' O'Rahilly, Pádraig Pearse, Thomas MacDonagh and Joseph Plunkett. Approximately 168,000 men enlisted in the National Volunteers while about 12,000 men stayed loyal to the original organisation. After the split, Bulmer Hobson became the general secretary of the Irish Volunteers while Thomas MacDonagh was made its director of training and Joseph Plunkett became its director of military operations. The IRB's takeover of the general council was then complete after Pádraig Pearse was made its director of military organisation. After this the IRB held the majority of the positions on the council.[85] Its ideology was thereafter exemplified by two main tactical stands. One argued that a revolution should only take place under one of three circumstances: firstly, the cessation of the war should be followed by a revolution in support of the claims of Irish nationhood; secondly, if there was a German landing in Ireland; and thirdly, if the Irish Volunteers were coerced into joining the war effort. The second tactical philosophy, best represented by IRB men like Clarke, argued that a revolution should occur if an opportune moment should arise.[86]

Given these principles, it is clear that the break from moderate nationalism and the presence of a more revolutionary ethic within the Irish

Volunteers removed a major cause of the hostility between the two extra-parliamentary nationalist forces. Certainly, for Larkin at least, his previous support for O'Casey's criticism had largely been based on a distrust of Redmondism.[87] The significance of this event was best described by the recollections of the labour army's last O/C:

> After the split in the National Volunteers in 1914, caused mainly by world war one, the army threw their whole weight in with the group of Volunteers who believed that their destiny was to fight to regain Ireland's freedom rather than the liberation of Belgium. Now that the leaders saw the possibility of striking a blow that would break the connection with England in their own lifetime, having in mind that 'England's difficulty was Ireland's opportunity' a new enthusiasm swept through all ranks, drills were intensified and route marches became the order of the day and night.[88]

The IRB men appeared to have been aware of this and seem to have immediately sought greater co-operation with martial labour. On the night of the Irish Volunteers' split, a document from its committee which detailed the events was given to William O'Brien and Peadar Macken and was subsequently delivered to Liberty Hall.[89]

With this in mind, it is significant that the plan for the first non-commemorative joint action between the two bodies was meant to have occurred just one day after the rupture and was described by Connolly as 'the first stirring blow' against Redmond's 'betrayal'.[90] On 25 September 1914, Prime Minister Asquith was due to speak at the Mansion House in Dublin, alongside Redmond and John Dillon, in an attempt to aid the recruitment of soldiers for the war on the continent. It was planned that approximately 100 soldiers comprised of IRB, Volunteers and ICA men would capture and hold the building the day before the rally was meant to take place.[91] The tactic had been used in Belfast when Churchill had planned to speak at a Home Rule meeting. There was an important difference between the manifestation of the plan in Belfast and its development as planned in Dublin; in Belfast the proposal had the support of the city officials while in Dublin the significant political powers of the city opposed any interference in a recruitment meeting.[92]

Led by the IRB and Clarke, a meeting at the offices of *Irish Freedom* in D'Olier Street was held where it was decided that a Sinn Féin man named Moran would cut the electricity to the building. Regarding the actual occupation, the plan was drawn up at a later meeting at Foresters Hall, 41 Parnell Square, attended by, amongst others, Richard Mulcahy and Harry Boland. The IRB were represented by MacDermott while Connolly was present on behalf of militant labour.[93] Twenty-five ICA members had gathered in Liberty Hall in anticipation, waiting for orders to march to 41 Parnell Square where the entire unit would then mobilise. The Women Workers' Union Clothing Co-operative, led by Delia Larkin, had prepared supplies of cheese sandwiches and refreshments. Larkin informed them that they were to head to St Stephen's Green were they would meet 'a man whom [they] know', who appears to have been Connolly, and a cohort of Volunteers. The combined body of Volunteers and Citizen Army men were then to occupy the Mansion House.[94]

Among Óglaigh, the faith in the success of the Mansion House occupation proposal was varied. Lynch claims that both he and Tom Ashe were against the scheme, believing that had the occupation gone ahead they would have been 'wiped out' during the project. Others such as Seán MacDermott were for it.[95] In the end, William O'Brien arrived at Liberty Hall to inform the labour men that the plan had been cancelled.[96] The decision was made on the basis of the asymmetric nature of size and strength between the British forces and the republicans. On the day of the prime minister's meeting, the Mansion House was well guarded by both the RIC and the National Volunteers, which signified the full extent of the break that occurred in the national movement. Only people with tickets were allowed to enter. The military and police presence around the area was also telling; soldiers were confined to their barracks in anticipation of any outburst of violence while armed police filled Grafton Street and other groupings of police were dispersed across the surrounding area in case of the need for back up.[97] The military strength for the ICA, at least, could not have been starker, as they had only ammunition for their Howth Mauser rifles; the Italian thumb-lock rifles they also marched with were used only for posturing.[98]

The failure of the protest to take place did not, however, lessen its significance. Letters from Connolly confirmed it as a precursor to the Easter Rising in that it was the first military movement of the joint forces. In September 1914, he wrote to O'Brien and contended that the 'Asquith meeting will be a military affair, and the city will be in the hands of the military to carry through'. He emphasised the importance of the encounter, writing that 'in a sense all our future is on the cast of that die'.[99] The role of the IRB as a mastermind in the planning was also present. Lynch asserted that the idea of occupying the Mansion House arose from the secret society as well as James Connolly. A few nights before the occupation was to take place a selected body of men were mobilised at 41 Parnell Square. It was at this meeting when they were equipped with rifles and ammunition.[100] While it would be over a year until Connolly, then as the Irish Citizen Army's commandant, would organise the rebellion within the IRB's military council, the political space which allowed such actions had begun to ferment in September 1914. The growing importance of Connolly was also evident. At a time when Larkin had already resigned from the ITGWU and was about to step down from the chair of the ICA's military council, Connolly was described as the 'leading spirit' of a group whose members included future proclamation signatories Tom Clarke and Seán MacDermott.[101]

The failure of the Mansion House occupation proposal led to Larkin's members launching a series of counter-demonstrations on the same day as Asquith's meeting, 25 September. A wagon described as 'an old brake drawn by two horses' was filled with ICA soldiers. Larkin was positioned in the front while behind the wagon marched the majority of the Irish Citizen Army.[102] The moving podium was drawn from Liberty Hall, across Thomas Street and on to St Catherine's Church, outside of which Robert Emmet had been executed. After a meeting was held there, the procession moved through St Stephen's Green and South King Street where another assembly was held at a site chosen for a Wolfe Tone memorial.[103] The locations chosen for these two protests were another clear reflection of the body's genuflection towards Irish republican history. The separatist element appeared in College Green. During this meeting Larkin roused the crowd, calling upon them to swear 'hatred of the empire' while, simultaneously, the Irish Volunteers confronted the DMP.[104]

Another confrontation occurred later that night. Once the ICA, supported by small numbers of armed Irish Volunteers, had travelled through Dawson Street and reached Grafton Street they realised they were outnumbered and surrounded by the RIC. To make matters worse a group of National Volunteers arrived, coming from the Mansion House direction. According to Robbins, it was Connolly who quelled the already flaring tensions.[105] Despite this atmosphere of hostility, no violence broke out and a festive spirit remained where songs such as *A Nation Once Again* were led by Seán Connolly. This was fortunate for the ICA, as according to Christopher Poole, while haversacks had been handed out no weapons were brought except for a minority who 'had small arms'.[106] According to Fox, this was a night where 'the Citizen Army had brought the rebel movement out on to the streets'.[107] While there was a hyperbolic sense to the statement, the night of 25 September was important in two ways; firstly, as a planned military action by a unified republican and socialist republican force; and secondly, as an indicator of Connolly's overtaking of Larkin as Irish labour's most influential figure.

Soon to take the leadership reins of the ICA, his prominence, particularly with regard to a republican Ireland, was reasserted in October. Echoing the pilgrimage to Bodenstown in June, the ICA and Óglaigh jointly celebrated the Parnell anniversary on 11 October 1914 while the National Volunteers waited an hour to parade around Glasnevin.[108] Here the two bodies held a joint meeting, chaired by Eoin MacNeill, outside the Municipal Art Gallery on Parnell Square. While this was a further sign of how the militant republicans were growing closer to the Citizen Army and further away from Redmond's cadre, there was an acrimonious incident between both militias that day. Believing he had been invited to speak, Larkin ascended the platform but was refused access by MacNeill. In response he held another meeting simultaneously at the other side of the square. It later transpired that it was Connolly who had been invited to speak.[109] Evidently, a degree of suspicion of the former ITGWU leader still remained, while the future 1916 martyr was seen as a comrade.

After Larkin's perceived snub at the Parnell anniversary in Glasnevin he gave an address speaking from an 'outside car'. His lecture was marked by a sustained critique of the various leaders of the Volunteers and a complaint about his treatment that day. However, when he delivered it he stood beside both Tom Clarke and Seán MacDermott. Undoubtedly, this support from such dominant figures in the militant nationalist movement would have helped ease the tension between both sides. Indeed, the support confirms the growing connection between the two armies.[110] Not only was this clear, but the influence of Clarke, as he had done in Bodenstown, in acting as a uniting force for the two militias was also visible. Certainly, despite the minor rancour between Óglaigh na hÉireann and Árm Lucta Oibre na h-Éireann during the Parnell anniversary, they both remained united when it appeared that a skirmish with the National Volunteers became a possibility. Outnumbering the combined forces by a total of four to one, Redmond's men marched down North Frederick Street and it appeared that they were going to march through the meeting.[111]

Upon orders, the Citizen Army blocked their path across the square using bayonets, while some of the leading Irish Volunteers attempted diplomacy, telling the Redmondites to go back home through Frederick Street and Dorset Street. In the end mediation prevailed and no serious hostilities occurred as the National Volunteers returned to the original path.[112] Aptly, Fox contended 'here – as in Easter Week – the Citizen Army and the militant section of the Irish Volunteers were comrades in arms. This showed the true alignment of the forces which any crises produced.'[113] It should be noted that at this point the ICA was still willing to promote itself as politically superior to the IRB's militia. In October, the *Irish Worker* gave 'credit [to] the Irish Citizen Army [as] it must stand that they were the only organised body to protest publicly at the "Wolfe Tone site" against "Redmond's recruiting policy".'[114] Despite this, at the start of the year their relationship with the Volunteers was marked by bitter criticism of class discrepancies and a competitive scramble for new members. However, on the eve of Connolly's taking over command of the ICA, the natural unity that arose from a commonality of aspirations between the two militias was surfacing more frequently.

6

'FOR A REPUBLICAN FREEDOM OF IRELAND': POLITICAL DEVELOPMENTS UNDER CONNOLLY

On 22 June 1914, in the Antient Concert Rooms in Brunswick Street, James Larkin resigned from the union of which he was the major totem pole.[1] While he still remained as the chairman of the ICA, by November of that year he had also quit that office and left Ireland for the United States of America.[2] The departure of the country's leading labour figure resulted in the ICA being led by its most rebellious, republican and revolutionary leader during its existence. While this alone had obvious implications for its move towards revolt in 1916, Larkin's exit and his time spent immediately upon arrival in the United States revealed more about the ideological positioning of the force and its leadership. His decision to seek a change of environment after the arduous union struggle of 1913 can be explained by his suffering of physical exhaustion and nervousness.[3] This led, upon his return to Ireland in 1923, to sustained criticism by his contemporaries. He argued that he travelled to the United States upon the desire of Pearse, Clarke and Connolly. However, this was met with criticism from William O'Brien and the widows Lillie Connolly and Kathleen Clarke, who entitled his narrative as the 'Revolutionary Mission Myth'. To disseminate these criticisms a pamphlet was also published which was entitled 'Some Pages From Union History: Why Larkin Went To America'.[4] Likewise, while Robbins recalled being 'under the powerful influence' of the labour titan, he wrote of losing his faith in him years later.[5] However, not everyone was a detractor; Christopher Poole, a leading figure in the ICA upon the outbreak of the Easter Rising, stated 'Larkin left this country for the Citizen Army. He was the best man for the purpose.'[6] Certainly, accounts of Larkin's speeches which were detailed in

American newspapers and British intelligence reports reveal a revolutionary rhetoric that not only echoed the policies settled upon by the IRB and others on the 9 September meeting but also suggested that insurgent leadership within the ICA was not restricted to Connolly. Certainly, Larkin's claim to have acted as a proto-envoy necessitates an analysis of not just his exit from the Citizen Army but his early time in the United States as well.

While White's departure from the militia centred on acrimony with the Irish Volunteers, Larkin's leaving did not revolve around such political dynamics. Allegedly, his move was to raise money for the ITGWU which was still frail a year after the great strike. Certainly, the union was bankrupt, in a state of heavy debt, and had suffered a significant drop in membership.[7] Indeed, in June 1914 Larkin spoke to Connolly about funds and described how he was in correspondence with the Workers' of the World American trade union leader William Haywood about arranging a tour. However, it appears this did not have Connolly's support. In a 15 June 1914 letter to O'Brien he wrote how he felt 'that [was] foolish, as Haywood's crowd have no money at all.'[8] It has also been suggested by Newsinger that Larkin left due to a consuming exhaustion.[9] Undoubtedly, the strain of the lockout had taken its toll on his health. He repeatedly thought of leaving and finally in October it was decided by both Larkin and his union that he would spend one year in the United States raising funds for the ITGWU.[10] Superintendent Lowe of the DMP read the situation as a more menacing undertaking and believed that there was reason to believe that his 'real object [was] to advance the German cause' in the war.[11] O'Connor contended that this was a narrow view and that Larkin's reason for moving was to make money from public speaking.[12] Whatever his reasons, he left Kingstown on 23 October for Liverpool. The following day he boarded the S.S. *St Louis* en route to New York.[13] Back in Ireland, Larkin had desired for P.T. Daly to take over the running of the ITGWU but after pressure from both William O'Brien and Thomas Foran, he acquiesced to letting Connolly take charge.[14]

After the culmination of the 1916 rebellion, and perhaps sensing the seeds of change in Irish nationalist circles, Larkin publicly stated that Connolly and he had drafted the 'declaration' that was signed by the 1916 leaders.[15] In 1924, John J. Lyng wrote to William O'Brien and described how Larkin framed his 'mission' to the United States as being to 'purchase arms in Hamburg for the Easter Rising'.[16] While such claims, amongst others, were denounced by many of his contemporaries in both Irish labour and republican circles, it does raise the question whether a leading light of the

ICA continuously spoke on the IRB's behalf about republican aspirations. This is particularly relevant given that during his last years in America Larkin was at a nominal level the 'commander in chief' of the Citizen Army. Indeed, given that while in the United States Larkin remained the 'titular general secretary of the ITGWU', and that his re-election as the Irish Citizen Army's president on 10 October 1914 was announced upon his departure to America, he can be understood as having remained a representative of martial labour.[17] Certainly, in their own notes in October 1914, the ICA outlined how they expected their 'commander' would return and how they wanted an army of 5,000 people in place for when that happened.[18]

Similar to Connolly's promotion of the ICA in Ireland, in the US Larkin advocated for Irish revolt and castigated the British war effort. Immediately upon his arrival, Irish-American republican John Devoy, leader of Clan na Gael, and Irish-American judge Daniel F. Cohalan, an Irish-American New York congressman, put him in contact with various German military attachés. While Larkin declined any salary from Clan na Gael, he spent his first months in the United States using their platform to disseminate socialist republican beliefs.[19] On 24 November, Larkin spoke at a meeting organised by Irish and German societies in the Philadelphia Academy of Music where Redmond was lambasted as 'England's recruiting sergeant'.[20] There he delivered a speech 'pregnant with revolutionary import' and a 'vision of the Republic of Ireland'. Not only did he denounce Britain and Redmond, and call for German aid to Ireland, but he also positioned himself within the burgeoning Irish revolutionary movement and stated that 'we have altogether about 5,000 rifles. We have few bayonets ... the men in our movement ... always answer the call of Cathlin-Ni-Houlihan.'[21] On 17 December 1914, he spoke to a mixed audience of Clan na Gael men and German-Americans at a meeting in Terrace Garden, New York organised by the New York Irish Volunteers.[22] Speaking on the same platform as John Devoy, he argued that in Ireland the time for compromise was no more and that it was time for action that was more radical than mere talk.[23]

Earlier that month, on 6 December, he spoke at another Clan na Gael meeting at the Brooklyn Academy of Music. According to a report sent from British Consul-General Courtenay Bennett to British Secretary of the State for Foreign Affairs Edward Grey, this was organised in order to collect money for the Irish nationalist movement and to enable greater fraternity between the Germans and the Irish. In that report Roger Casement was described as 'the official representative of Ireland to Germany', whose mission was likened to Benjamin Franklin's 1776 mission to France. Larkin spoke beside Kuno Meyer and G. Koeble, the President of the German-American National Alliance. At the meeting Larkin called upon all young Irishmen to return to Ireland in order to fight for its freedom and asked those who could not travel to donate money in order to provide arms and ammunition.[24] At the same meeting, John Devoy argued a similar philosophy to Connolly's argument about 'England's difficulty' when he stated that the war afforded Ireland 'the greatest opportunity' to achieve freedom.[25]

Gradually Larkin wandered away from Clan na Gael and dropped his 'German *Uhlan*'.[26] Evidently, the former ICA leader began his time in America arguing along similar lines to that by Connolly. Not only was his pro-German sentiment typical of martial labour in Dublin but so too was the sense of a coming revolution. Such views heard by those in attendance at his New York and Philadelphia meetings, reinforced the revolutionary drive that permeated republican circles in the United States and in Ireland. His departure from Ireland should not be seen as a disavowal of the ICA, as was the case with White's resignation. While Larkin's claim to have acted as sort of unofficial envoy for the revolutionary movement appears to have been spurious, he certainly did offer a voice of support across the Atlantic. Larkin's propagandising in the United States resulted in the arrival in Ireland, in time for the rebellion, of some munitions for the ICA. However, from this point until Easter Week, 1916, the ICA's political and military development was largely dependent on Connolly and the increasingly significant Michael Mallin.

In late October 1914, just before leaving Ireland, Larkin published a farewell letter and succinctly stated 'to my comrades in the Irish Citizen Army: in my absence Jim Connolly will take command'.[27] His final words set out the principles which would define the ethos of the army under his successor. He asked them to remember their constitution and the oath that Ireland was first and last and 'all the time'. Containing overtures of revolution and references to contemporary geopolitics it was better he decried, to die fighting in Ireland as a freeman than to die in foreign fields fighting for those who were Ireland's oppressors. He concluded that 'sobriety, unquestioned obedience for drill be your motto' and with that the force was left under the leadership of the man who would take them into outright revolt.[28] By November 1914, Connolly had become 'firmly entrenched' as the ICA's leader.[29] However, at an ideological level, the start of his reign did not act as a break from the force's politics of the previous year. Rather, Larkin's German fraternisation and rebellious speeches, the impact of the Home Rule crisis and the outbreak of World War I, as well as the growing comradeship with the Irish Volunteers indicate that Connolly's first year in charge is best defined as an escalation of the army's republican revolutionary drive. Indeed, prior to becoming its commandant, Connolly attended a meeting on 9 September 1914 in the Gaelic League's offices in Dublin which set out the provisions under which a rebellion, and the ICA's part in it, would take place. Most probably at the invitation of future proclamation signatory Eamonn Ceannt, he, along with William O'Brien, travelled to Seán T. O'Kelly's office in the Gaelic League's premises in 25 Parnell Square. Others in attendance included Pádraig Pearse, Joseph Plunkett, Thomas MacDonagh, Arthur Griffith and Major John MacBride. [30]

Beginning around 19:30 it was, for all intents and purposes, an IRB-led meeting and started with an opening statement by Clarke after which MacDermott spoke.[31] After protracted discussion it was decided a rising would occur under one of three contingencies: firstly, a German victory during the war; secondly, an attempt by Britain to enforce conscription in Ireland; and thirdly, if the war was about to cease without any of the other two circumstances coming to fruition (this was to better enable a claim for belligerent rights at a future peace conference).[32] Noteworthy, a further consequence of this meeting was the establishment of the Irish Neutrality League which Connolly headed, indicating that he was more than a passive participant.[33] It is also important that while William O'Brien was there to represent the general labour movement, Connolly was seen as being able to 'very definitely speak for the Citizen Army'.[34] While no official decision to rise had been made, the structure of the provisions meant that the ICA from that point onwards was set for some form of revolution.

On 28 October 1914, the first convention of the Irish Volunteers took place in the Abbey Theatre in Dublin and the interaction between the Volunteers and the ICA during the surrounding time period was markedly more cordial than in winter 1913. Not only was the conference advertised in the *Irish Worker* but at 18:30 on the night of the meeting a 'great demonstration and torchlight procession' began in Beresford Place where all national and labour bodies were present. MacNeill spoke at the event and the policies adopted at the convention were announced to the crowd at the labour centre while, keeping in tune with the heady republican atmosphere, the procession travelled around 'places sacred to the memories of the United Irishmen and other patriots'.[35] Furthermore, the Citizen Army, following orders from Connolly, also helped to guard the Abbey Theatre that night.[36] At the convention itself, it is also noteworthy that Seán Milroy of the ICA attended the meeting with a view to proposing an affiliation between both armies. This appears to have been made at Connolly's behest and the labour force would have, in turn, received two seats on the Volunteers' nine-person executive.[37] According to Greaves, this was rejected because the IRB felt it would make it more difficult for them to hold a majority position and to hide behind the moderates.[38] Here, a trend emerged where despite the eradication of the old hostility, the ICA, with Connolly at the helm, were more vocal and arguably impatient for revolution.

Certainly, at this point, their philosophies were aligned. When examined in the context of the ICA's principles, the Volunteers' policies adopted at the convention reveal that such symmetry existed. The first clause of the policy document stated that the Irish Volunteers sought 'to maintain the right and duty of the Irish nation hence forward to provide for its own defence by means of a permanent armed and trained volunteer force'. While this did not bear much relation to the ICA's March 1914 constitution, it echoed clause 2.a of the socialist militia's revised May version which detailed the desire to have a trained and armed body ready to defend the Irish people's right to the ownership of Ireland.[39] The second clause which the Volunteers adopted was 'to unite the people of Ireland on the basis of Irish nationality and a common interest to maintain the integrity of the nation and to resist with all our strength any measures tending to bring about or perpetuate disunion or the partition of our country'. This had obvious relevance to Connolly's anti-partitionist INL but also aligned with both the March and May ICA constitutions. Article 2 and 4 in the original document, and clause 2.b and 3 in the latter both spoke in anti-partitionist terms typical of the Irish republican tradition.[40]

The third feature of the Volunteers' policy document which was typical of the late 1914–15 period was that it sought to prevent the forcing of Irish men into military service. Neither of the ICA's 1914 constitutions dealt with this issue. However, the ICA's women's section's battle with economic conscription and, as shall be shown, the effect of economic conscription on the ICA in 1915 showed a parallel philosophy.[41] Other discrepancies existed between the various constitutions. Resulting from their socialism and, in turn, their internationalist class element, the ICA's constitutions sought the 'recognition of the rights and liberties of the world's democracies' which was missing from the Volunteer document of 28 October 1914.[42] Likewise,

Óglaigh's reference to abolishing Dublin Castle and the British military's system of governance was more overt than in the earlier proclamations.[43] It was not the case that this was the result of a more revolutionary ethic within the IRB-led Volunteer movement. Rather, it was due to the different worlds which existed between the March–May 1914 period and that of the post-Woodenbridge speech environment. Certainly, the Volunteers' refusal of affiliation suggested that concern over the appearance of moderation existed more so on the republican rather than the socialist republican side. This affected how the Citizen Army, led by the increasingly revolt-ready Connolly, dealt with their soon-to-be comrades in arms over the next year-and-a-half. It should also be stated that the presence of Connolly as the new leader of the labour militia was vital. For White, Connolly's influence had always been used 'to moderate the mutual hostility that smouldered, and occasionally flamed into passionate recriminations' between the ICA and the Irish Volunteers.[44]

While the edition of the *Irish Worker* which followed the Rotunda meeting in 1913 was highly critical of the event, the ICA's notes after the Volunteers' first convention not only congratulated the Volunteers on their success and the size of their turnout but also turned its gaze to America. The ICA argued that alongside the meeting in the Abbey, the Clan na Gael conference held in the United States brought 'a spirit of confidence that Irishmen here will not be false to the teachings of the brave men who laid down their lives for the land they loved'. The ICA also appealed to nationalists not to 'betray the cause for which so many great men offered up their lives'.[45]

Under Connolly, the force also published a new advertising handbill which read:

Reasons Why

You Should Join

THE IRISH CITIZEN ARMY

BECAUSE It pledges its members to work for, organise for, drill for and fight for an independent Ireland.

BECAUSE It places its reliance upon the only class that never betrayed Ireland – the Irish working class.

BECAUSE Having a definite aim to work for there is no fear of it being paralysed in the moment of action by divisions in its executive body.

BECAUSE It teaches that the sole right of ownership of Ireland is vested in the people of Ireland, and that that full right of ownership may, and ought to be, enforced by any and all means that God hath put within the power of man

BECAUSE It works in harmony with the labour and true national movements and thus embraces all that makes for social welfare and national dignity.[46]

Another incident in November 1914 not only highlighted the ICA's comradeship with the Irish Volunteers but highlighted the degree of political defiance then found within Connolly's army. On 12 November 1914, Captain Robert Monteith, one of the Irish Volunteers' military instructors, was dismissed from his Ordnance Department post and told by the British Army to leave the capital.[47] Twelve hours after he had been fired, he received his deportation notice requiring him to leave Dublin by 14 November and to stay away from proscribed areas. However, he refused to sign the document.[48] Monteith, who would later become embroiled in Casement's work in Germany, was of socialist inclination and had considered joining the pre-constitutional Citizen Army before a discussion with Tom Clarke led him to become a member of the Irish Volunteers.[49]

While Monteith never became a member of the socialist militia, they were quick to come to his defence. Monteith was the soldier who had given to the ICA four rounds of ammunition to arm their Howth Mausers during the Parnell anniversary commemoration on 11 October 1914.[50] This would not have been forgotten so shortly. In response to his deportation order Monteith, who had been a member of the British Army, sought out Connolly. Connolly not only advised him to contact the officers he operated under in the Volunteers but also issued a stop press edition of the *Irish Worker* and ordered a public protest in Beresford Place with a complete mobilisation of the ICA.[51] If the British government and army were to enforce their deportation order against Monteith they were to be 'resisted in arms'.[52]

On 15 November 1914, Liberty Hall held a protest meeting for Monteith during which the ICA was under the charge of Captain Poole who had been elected to the management committee of the force the previous week.[53] At the meeting Markievicz told those gathered that the women of Cumann na mBan were learning to shoot.[54] Here Connolly's oratory was noticeably filled with the rhetoric of the nationalist struggle; it was under his motion that the crowd swore not to stop fighting until Ireland was free from British rule. While DMP agents were at the meeting, they did not interfere with it because of the need to recruit men into the British Army. The echoes of the Bachelor's Walk shootings were still ringing out around Dublin and the British forces feared inflaming the already volatile public opinion.[55] Hostility though was bubbling below the surface as the DMP were met with 'a squad of Citizen Army [soldiers] facing them' in a 'turnabout with a vengeance'.[56]

Despite this atmosphere, or perhaps, being acutely aware of it, the Volunteers' executive decided that for tactical reasons that Monteith had to accept the order.[57] It was decided that he could be of better use to the body if he acted as an organiser based in the countryside.[58] While Connolly again appeared more willing to both challenge and subvert the government and the military than his larger nationalist brethren, Robbins argued that Connolly had his own tactical considerations when protesting the deportation order. It is true that no Citizen Army man was placed in the same position as Monteith. However, their army experience meant that others such as captains Richard McCormick, John J. O'Neill, Christopher Poole, as well as Poole's brother Vincent, who was not a captain, were at risk from the same threat. Even more importantly, the same could be said for the ICA's new chief of staff, Michael Mallin. Robbins suggested that Connolly envisaged a raft of deportations and sought to make known to the government his willingness to respond with, at the least, civic disobedience in the hope of preventing such happenings.[59] Certainly, British forces were serious about this practice and on 10 July 1915 Herbert W. Pinn, Dennis McCullough, Liam Mellows and Ernest Blyth were ordered to leave the country.[60] According to O'Shea, both the commandant and the chief of staff were 'very annoyed' that Monteith was allowed to depart.[61]

By 1915, it was clear that the Socialist Internationals had not only failed to prevent the outbreak of war on the European continent but also to issue a significant general strike in protest.[62] The absence of a 'mass-resistance' was met by Connolly with a renewed avowal for revolution.[63] Indeed, according to his Belfast confidant, Cathal O'Shannon, once Connolly heard of the outbreak of the wider conflict he unequivocally announced that a blow for Irish freedom must be taken.[64] Certainly, the impact and progress of the war on the revolutionary movement was so great that Metscher claimed it to have been 'the major factor that triggered off a rising'.[65] Connolly's criticism of the world war, for both national and socialist reasons, meant that in 1915 the political command and nature of the ICA was deeply shaped by the continuation of the European confrontation.

Through the Suspension of the Operation of the Government of Ireland Act on 18 September 1914, the conflagration in Europe brought an end to the parliamentary discourse surrounding the Home Rule question. However, for those intimately tied to martial labour, the two were intrinsically connected, which meant the war affected the socialist republican army's national policies. The Irish Neutrality League which was formed of Monday 12 October 1914 argued that the outbreak of the war would lead to a rigidity and a corporeality to the division of the country. Despite the passing of the bill, the league argued the question of partition would have not been settled until peace was reached on the continent, after which time it would be affected by an amending bill 'dictated by Sir Edward Carson'.[66] Bluntly, the INL stated 'this means the partition of Ireland'.[67] Interestingly, the INL also signalled a coming revolution and warned that by the culmination of the European conflict the British Army would possess nearly a million soldiers, be stronger than ever, and less dependent 'upon Irish goodwill', a clear swipe at Redmond.[68] While the INL was outwardly a non-partisan organisation, it was seen by O'Shannon as a 'recruiting ground' for republicans, as a cover 'for our other activities' and was linked to the Asquith protest meeting discussed earlier.[69] The republican nature of the INL could be gleaned from Seán T. O'Kelly's description of Connolly's opening speech as that of 'an Irish nationalist claiming the right of Ireland to full and complete independence'.[70] Given that Connolly was the president of its committee and that Francis Sheehy Skeffington and Markievicz were also officers it is unlikely that the INL did not have at least some symmetry of machinations with the ICA.[71]

Certainly, the ICA, nominally under their fictitious Belfast division, publically protested Irish involvement in World War I. A poster placed around the walls of the city read:

> You are asked to stop and consider what this war will mean to the working class of this city and country. War will mean more unemployment and less wages. Already the mills of Belfast are put on short time ... remember, all you workers, that this war is utterly unjustifiable and unnecessary ... we have no foreign enemy except the treacherous government of England – a government that even whilst it is calling on

us to die for it, refuses to give a straight answer to our own demand for home rule. We want Ireland not for peers or the nominees of peers, but Ireland for the Irish.[72]

Not only was the war connected to the Home Rule question but it was also linked to economics. Despite the industrial resources required by the British war effort, no substantial financial benefits were garnered by the common Irish worker. Only 2,169 people were employed in the munitions factories that were located on the island. While employers grew wealthier from the British military's need to harness industry, employees, however, did not experience such benefit. Rather, the labourer experienced a reduction in food and fuel supplies as well as a period of inflation and a reduction in spending power.[73] In contrast, as table 6.1 shows, financial benefit could have been gained through joining the British war effort. As the table illustrates, one factor that was a significant incentive for unemployed or unskilled workers was the presence of the British Army's separation allowances which were announced on 8 August 1914. Given that a labourer in Dublin would, in general, earn between sixteen shillings and eighteen shillings if he worked a forty-eight-hour week, it is clear that a combination of the separation allowance and the recruit's own army pay would have appeared attractive to

TABLE 6.1.

WEEKLY RATES OF SEPARATION ALLOWANCE, INCLUDING THE COMPULSORY ALLOTMENT OF PAY.

	Rank of soldier.				
	Private and corporal.	Serjeant.	Colour-serjeant.	Quarter-master-serjeant.	Warrant officer.
	s. d.	s. d.	s. d.	s. d.	s. d.
Wife	12 6	15 0	16 6	22 0	23 0
Wife and 1 child	15 0	18 0	19 6	25 0	26 0
Wife and 2 children	17 6	21 0	22 6	28 0	29 0
Wife and 3 children	20 0	24 0	25 6	31 0	32 0
Wife and 4 children	22 0	26 0	27 6	33 0	34 0
	And so on, with an addition of 2s. for each additional child.				
Deduction if in public quarters with fuel and light	6 0	6 0	7 6	13 0	14 0

Source: *Increased Rate of Separation Allowance for the Wives and Children of Soldiers*, [Cd. 7623], H.C 1914–16, xxxix, 513; Yeates, *City in Wartime*, p. 48.

someone typical of the ICA's membership. This is especially so considering the new recruit would also have received free board and lodging, further cutting down on household expenditure.[74]

It should be noted that Dublin, as a wartime city, experienced a rapid rise in the price of foodstuffs. Overnight the price of sugar rose from 2 1/2d a pound to as much as 6d, butter increased from 1s a pound to 1s 6d, flour from 10s a sack to 12s, and bacon from 1s 1d to 1s 4d.[75]

The financial benefits gained from joining the British Army meant that the war acted as a drain on the numbers of the Irish Citizen Army. While ICA men would not typically have supported the war effort, it is also true that those who were members of the force and those who were most likely to join the ICA were typically from the socio-economic background that needed to take the king's shilling. Furthermore, the widely held belief that the war would be over by Christmas made it easier for these men to join the British Army.[76] Evidently, many of the reservists for the British Army, such as Kearns, who had been used by the ICA as drill instructors had been called upon to serve. By winter 1914, the ICA was faced with the need to elect and promote new members; Jack Fitzpatrick was promoted from sergeant to captain of A Company while McGowan was moved to B Company.[77] It is noteworthy that at that time 2,400 out of the ITGWU's 11,000 members had also joined the British Army's war effort.[78]

Connolly believed that any ICA fight against the war and against capitalism needed to be based on the economic circumstances which resulted in the financial imperative to join professional armies. However, he also thought that transport unions would have to play a subsidiary role in the anti-imperial struggle. Thus, the ICA was to lead the way, and any inter-class allegiance would be achieved through relations between the ICA and the Irish Volunteers. The ITGWU could then, beckoned by the Volunteers and the Citizen Army, put a halt to the state's communication system.[79] With this in mind, members of the ICA began to battle the growing prevalence of economic conscription. While Ireland's conscription crises occurred between 1917 and 1918, the Irish working class suffered from economic conscription from the outbreak of the war onwards. Defined as the creation of a financial situation where young men, in this case particularly shop assistants, were placed in such dire straits that monetary rewards made joining the war effort a necessity.

Connolly argued that 'hunger-scription' was the 'recognition of the fact that the working class fight the battle of the rich, that the rich control the jobs or means of existence of the working class, and that therefore if the rich desire to dismiss men eligible for military service they can force these men to enlist.[80] Members of the women's section of the ICA, Nellie Gifford and Marie Perloz, were tasked with assessing the degree to which the Dublin workers were affected by economic conscription and to offer them 'some alternative'.[81] In order to do this, a room was set up on the top floor of No. 6 Harcourt Street, which was occupied by Sinn Féin.[82] The ICA, according to Larkin was used as a 'counter attraction to the recruiting officer and the call of militarism'.[83] It is also noteworthy that the 1913 strike and lockout was described by the *Workers' Republic* as an 'apprenticeship in brutality' and was seen as the first step of the practice of economic conscription. During the industrial struggle of 1913, the tools of using the 'means of production' and the 'weapon of starvation' to compel men to act against their own conscience were honed.[84]

As a force that bridged syndicalist and socialist theory, and by its nature and tradition sat in the ideological *milieu* of the international socialist movement, the ICA's political opposition to the situation on the continent must be framed in the wider spectrum of the pan-European left-wing response. While the so-called 'khaki fever' spread rapidly after the outbreak of war, the ICA stayed true to its syndicalist roots.[85] Its opposition adhered not only to the guidelines of the Internationals but it was also one of the few movements which refused to view class interests as subservient to the war effort.[86] Fearing the possibility of such a massive scale conflict, the International had made clear its opposition to such war at the Stuttgart conference in 1907. The congress of socialists resolved to use the force of the working class to prevent such mass confrontation; the resolution stated:

> If a war threatens to break out, the working class and their parliamentary representatives for the countries involved are duty bound, supported by the combined allied operation of the International [Socialist] Bureau, to do everything within their power to prevent the outbreak of war by whatever means they deem most effective; this will naturally vary according to the intensity of the class struggle and the aggravation of the general political situation.[87]

Here, it stipulated that in the event of the outbreak of Europeanwide war, it was the duty of the socialists and the working class of Europe to use all their strength and influence not only to bring a prompt end to the war but to manipulate the crisis in order to bring about the fall of the capitalist system.[88] The revolutionary aspect to such opposition was put forward by both Lenin and Rosa Luxemburg who were proponents of Engels's theory about how a pan-European war would foreshadow the collapse of the capitalist/imperial system. Thus, they both argued that in the event of an outbreak of war any revolt and social disturbance that socialists could cause should have as its aim not merely the cessation of war but also the overthrow of capitalist bourgeoisie rule.[89] Such sentiment was made more certain on 21 September 1915 when the Zimmerwald conference declared that its socialist members must fight for the 'oppressed nations' and the 'enslaved classes' through the proletarian struggle.[90]

Connolly expressed disdain at the failure of continental socialists to adhere to such principles. However, his polemics and his ideological positioning of the ICA reflected the principles of the various socialist congresses held over the previous half-century. His anti-militarism against the 'carnival of murder' centred on his belief that a victory for the British Army would eradicate any hope for the revolutionary movement and with it the hopes of the Irish working class.[91] Ireland, the country's leading socialist argued, would starve.[92] In more apocalyptic terms, Connolly saw the war as a sort of *Götterdammerung* for the European proletariat, writing that 'civilisation is being destroyed before our eyes … thousands of comrades with whose souls we have lived in fraternal communion are about to be done to death … are being driven to fratricidal slaughter in shambles where that hope [of a utopian society] will be buried under a sea of blood'. [93]

In the same article, an uprising of the working class was put forward by Connolly as the solution to the catastrophe. Certainly, given the war's numerical devouring of Dublin's labour, it is clear why such an opinion was held. Thus, in an article also written by Connolly, entitled 'For the Citizen Army', the ICA was presented as an antidote. Here he dissected how the labour soldiers stood against the involvement of Irishmen in the British war effort and how they 'leaped to arms' to fight the deportation order against Captain Robert Monteith.[94] The ICA's 'magnificently defiant demonstration' against the Mansion House meeting was seen by Connolly to have 'saved the situation for Dublin itself'.[95] Almost akin to days of the strike and lockout, the labour army was also seen as a potential force in the 'armed battling in the streets' to prevent both profiteering and the export of essential foodstuffs from Ireland.[96] Importantly, the ICA's notes in the *Irish Worker* concurred both with his analysis of the destructive power of the events in Europe and with the need for revolutionary zeal. The notes read 'one thing is certain – the sacrifice of human life goes merely on. The irresistible greed of the capitalist class [is] unsatisfied … if we cannot write Emmet's epitaph at least we can prepare the tablet'.[97]

Connolly believed that not only was the Citizen Army a protest body which would link with the union's ability to strike, a tool that the Second International envisaged using should global conflict occur, but that the ICA would also engage in a general workers' uprising. Indeed, this belief was the first step towards involvement in the 1916 rebellion. The sense that the Irish revolution could act as a catalyst for the overthrow of the world's monarchical and capitalist systems was made clear by Connolly almost from the outset of World War I. Ireland, he contended, 'may yet set the torch to a European conflagration that will not burn out until the last throne and the last capitalist debenture are shrivelled in the war pyre of the last warlord'.[98] These words were the expression of the hope and expectation that the struggle in Dublin and the ICA's role in it would be a prelude to an outbreak of European tumult and upheaval.[99] In this vein, the ICA adhered to the Second International's belief that 'if war nevertheless were to break out, it is their ["the working class"] duty to intervene ensuring a swift termination, and do everything within their power to utilise the economic and political crisis created by the war to rouse the masses, thereby hastening the downfall of capitalist rule'.[100] In October 1914, Connolly, with a particular eye to revolt against Britain, wrote that 'if it requires insurrection in Ireland and through all the British dominions to teach the English working class that they cannot hope to prosper permanently by arresting the industrial development of others than insurrection must come'.[101]

In March 1915, Connolly criticised the European socialist movement in the *International Socialist Review*, a magazine which had advertised his *Socialism Made Easy* pamphlet in August 1914.[102] In a piece entitled 'Revolutionary Unionism and War' he argued:

> The socialist forces in the various countries failed so signally to prevent, or even delay the outbreak [of war] … the signal of war ought also to have been the signal for rebellion … I believe that the socialist proletariat of Europe in all the belligerent countries ought to have refused to march against their brothers across the frontiers, and that such refusal would

have prevented the war and all its horrors, even though it might have led to civil war ... in none of these belligerent countries was there an organised revolutionary industrial organisation directing the socialist vote, nor a socialist political party directing a revolutionary industrial organisation.[103]

Noteworthy, he finished the article by writing that none of the socialist parties on the continent could call out the entirety of the transport services and thus prevent the war; that 'the failure of European socialism to avert war is primarily due to the divorce between the industrial and the political movements of labour'.[104] For Connolly, the labour political parties were to provide political leadership while syndicalists unions were to act as disrupting forces, and finally martial labour was to be in the frontline of the revolution.

Upon the outbreak of the war, Connolly spoke in Shakespearian terms, asking if all the mechanism of protest, resolutions, strikes, international working-class fraternity were all 'sound and fury signifying nothing'.[105] In a tone which resonated with a sense of the ICA in mind, he wrote of socialist and nationalist rebellion and argued that instead of dying in fields in places like Flanders and the Somme, men would have been better dying for their national freedom and the emancipation of their class (reminiscent of Larkin's last sentiment before his departure to the United States).[106] A 2006 analysis of the 'psychological characteristics ... based upon the verbal behaviour' of Pearse and Connolly found that during this period the labour leader was atypical of both Pearse and other political leaders in that he viewed the political world as being more conflictually defined than average. It also found that he had a lower level of confidence than average in his ability to control such matters.[107] This would explain why despite that the pattern of Connolly's verbal position between 1913–14 and 1915–16 was comparatively lower than Pearse's, the external conflict of the European war and the failure of international socialism to meet it were of greater concern to him. Connolly was, according to such comparative analysis, 'itching for a fight' to a greater extent than Pearse.[108]

The war also had further practical concerns. While the impact of economic conscription was a persistent concern since its outbreak, by 1915, ICA leadership also feared the implementation of governmental conscription and sought to counteract this. In December 1915, the effect of the interaction between the employer and the British Army could be seen. After an anti-recruitment rally during that month, Lord Lieut. John

Campbell Hamilton Gordon, First Marquess of Aberdeen and Temair called on the country's major employers to help 'facilitate enlistment' by dismissing men of military age.[109] On 2 December, Connolly wrote to Agnes Newman and described how 'the employers have already sent in their lists of "eligible" and "indispensable" men. It is on the lines I suggested it would be. All the true blues and sycophants are returned as indispensables.'[110] Previous to this, on Tuesday 20 July 1915, at a Dublin Corporation conference, Connolly sat behind Lord Mayor Alderman J.J. Farrell who spoke out against conscription. Farrell argued that Dublin's young men were being placed in the position of needing to join the war effort because of the 'effective means' of depriving them work elsewhere. Finally, the belief was offered by Farrell that the Irish Volunteers and the ICA were best equipped to successfully prevent conscription.[111]

Later that year, Connolly's confidant, William O'Brien, also publicly announced that the ICA was seen as a counterweight against conscription. On 25 October 1915, O'Brien, the acting secretary of the Dublin United Trades Council and Labour League (DUTCLL), wrote a rather moderate appeal to the city's working class. While the DUTCLL did not want to 'obstruct' those who held a genuine 'zeal for the British Empire' from taking the king's shilling, it asked the workers to join either the Citizen Army or the Irish Volunteers as this was seen to be 'the best means to avert conscription'.[112] Noteworthy here was the outlining that Óglaigh was another potential counterweight to conscription. This was a far cry from the days when labour arguments were explicitly made against the Volunteers. Nor, does it appear, that this was the first time that labour leaders were willing to call for the advancement of their brethren militia. A DMP 'Movement of Extremists' intelligence file for July 1915 detailed a speech given by P. Ryan to a crowd in Beresford Place where he dismissed his audience for not being interested in joining either militia.[113] Alongside this, that O'Brien positioned the extra-parliamentary forces in such a manner was also reminiscent of Connolly's tactics, just after he had taken charge of martial labour, during the Monteith incident. This, then, was an endorsement by general labour figures of Connolly, the commandant.

Connolly also wrote a scathing critique of the British military 'kite flying' exercise of introducing compulsory service into Ireland. Bluntly, he wrote on 24 October 1914 'we of the Irish Transport and General Workers' Union, we of the Citizen Army, have our answer ready. We will resist the Militia Ballot Act, or any form of conscription, and we begin now to prepare our resistance.'[114] Importantly, he indicated that this should have been a shared focus between the two ever more fraternal armed forces, and appealed to the Volunteers to take a similar stand. As will be discussed later in this chapter, the sincerity of his belief was garnered from the fact that this article announced his desire to turn the ICA into a revolutionary ready force. His contention not only that rifles would come but also that the Citizen Army would be filled not with 'parade ground soldiers' but men that were prepared to fight and die for Ireland, was prophetic for the lifespan of his military command of the body.[115] As the Monteith incident was about to prove, such a polemic was not mere empty rhetoric but a declaration of intention.

While republican leaders penned letters of distrust of ICA forerunners in 1914, 1915 was markedly different. Not only did the *Irish Worker* and, subsequently the *Workers' Republic,* devote sections to the Irish Volunteers but those on the other side of the republican spectrum were publicly approving of Connolly's thoughts and philosophies. In June 1915, the *Na Fianna Éireann* newspaper, *Fianna,* advertised Connolly's book *The Re-Conquest of Ireland.* According to the advertisment, all members of the boys' corps needed to have a copy of the text as in order to be a 'good soldier' they needed to know the extent and the results of the British Army's conquest of Ireland, past and present as well as to understand how such a conquest could be 'reversed'.[116] A collection of a series of articles written in 1912, Connolly's text was published in one volume in 1915 to encourage Irish people to re-claim their country.[117] The newspaper's reference to understanding how the British Army's conquest could be 'reversed' was particularly important. The term 'reverse' implied a greater socio-economic revolution as opposed to merely political change. This was in tandem with socialist thinking. Throughout 1915, political symbiosis between the ICA and the Irish Volunteers continued to develop. Referring back to the Bachelor's Walk shootings of the previous year, the second edition of the *Workers' Republic,* edited by Connolly, noted how workers could visit a memorial for the victims of the shooting at the headquarters of the Irish Volunteers at 2 Dawson Street, Dublin.[118] The paper continued to advertise the memorial throughout summer 1915. In July, it also published the new manifesto of Óglaigh.[119]

In 1955, Patrick Casey, the Newry Brigade Vice O/C, recollected that 'inspiration was sought from those Gaelic heroes of the past – Tone, Mitchel and O'Donovan Rossa. We were refreshed and exhilarated by our contact with those great leaders of the past.'[120] While Casey was a Volunteer, the same could be said for those who belonged to the socialist militia. Given this, it is not surprising that the two militias continued to meet at funerals and commemorations. In the aftermath of Larkin's departure there were fewer national platforms but both forces appeared side by side at the Manchester Martyrs' anniversary on 22 November 1914, the Wolfe Tone commemoration in Bodenstown on 26 June 1915, and the funeral of the old Fenian leader, Jeremiah O'Donovan Rossa on 1 August 1915.

On 22 November, the commemoration of the Manchester Martyrs' anniversary took place. The previous day, the ICA's notes contained a brief statement stating simply that they would take their place on the occasion which was to start in the early part of the day.[121] Around 2,000 people including approximately 1,000 men from Óglaigh, the ITGWU, the ICA, the AOH, the National Foresters and the Old Guard Union as well as six bands assembled at St Stephen's Green and marched via South Great Georges Street, Dame Street, and Sackville Street to Glasnevin Cemetery where the proceedings took place.[122] Interestingly, while the remembrance of the rebels in Manchester had always been important in labour circles since the emergence of Larkinism, Old Fenian and IRB leaders James Stephens and John O'Leary were also remembered as flowers were placed on their graves before the event was brought to a close.[123] Remarking on the day, the ICA's notes were self-congratulatory and commented on the smart dress of the force and the positive comments from the public that were heard as the procession passed along its journey.[124]

Typically one of the IRB's most important public roles, the annual pilgrimage to the site of Wolfe Tone's burial marked the second consecutive time the Volunteers and the Citizen Army stood in unison at the grave.[125] As had been the case in 1914, the ICA was keen to assert that their presence was equal to and no less important than that of the Volunteers; in 'equal proportions' both extra-parliamentary bodies were to keep the guard of honour at both the remembrance ceremony at the graveside and at the 'accompanying exercises'.[126] Of the approximately 1,500 travellers who arrived on trains which departed from Kingsbridge Station that morning about seventy were armed with rifles.[127] While Eammon Ceannt took charge of the general military arrangements, the Citizen Army were led by their new chief-of-staff, Michael Mallin. The ICA's notes recorded the event as an inspiration for all of those within the wider movement. The esteem for the old republican Tom Clarke, who had been instrumental in quashing tensions between the two militias in 1914, was seen as his appearance 'full of fight and faith' received particular attention. Finally, the ICA noted how they felt proud to be there to remember and honour the man who had expressed belief in the workers of Ireland.[128] It is also noteworthy that both forces travelled back together and after arriving at Kingsbridge Station they marched in accord until they reached Blackhall Street and were dismissed.[129]

Described as a 'venerable Fenian', O'Donovan Rossa died in the United States on 29 June 1915 and his body was brought back to Ireland for a funeral on 1 August which was effectively stage-managed by Tom Clarke.[130] Through Connolly, the labour army was represented on the O'Donovan Rossa Funeral Committee alongside others such as Clarke (President), Con Colbert, Edward Daly, Eamonn Ceannt, Pádraig Pearse, Joseph Plunkett and John McBride, all of whom would be executed for their part in organising the Easter Rising.[131] The importance of the burial and Rossa's revolutionary ideology could be seen in Connolly's argument that members of both the Citizen Army and the ITGWU were 'bound by honour' to attend.[132] The burial has been seen by Yeates as 'the first major manifestation' of a new 'unity of purpose' defined by Connolly's embracing of militant nationalism.[133] Although this embrace had a much longer gestation, the occasion did see the Irish Volunteers and the ICA display their unity of purpose and consciousness.

The funeral and Pearse's famed speech 'the fools, the fools, the fools, they have left us our Fenian dead, and while Ireland holds these graves, Ireland, unfree, shall never be at peace' has been understood by Matthews as the 'first signifier' of revolt.[134] Previous to this, such a sentiment surrounding the dead leader and the hope for the future had already been heard within the Citizen Army's circles. Meave Cavanagh, sister to the *Workers' Republic*'s cartoonist Ernest and ICA women's section member and 1916 dispatcher in her own right, had published a poem on 10 July 1915 which was dedicated to O'Donovan Rossa. With a motif similar to Pearse's declaration, the last lines of her poem read 'thousands who stand by his grave/ pledging their lives to fight on to the last/ give the lie back to the knaves who proclaim/ the faith he suffered for died in the past'.[135]

The republicans' attitude to the old leader and to the occasion itself was phrased more openly and more directly in the July *Rossa Souvenir*. There Connolly wrote a piece entitled 'Why the Citizen Army honours Rossa' which detailed how the event was not just a homage but was also focused on showing the ICA's devotion to the principles for which Rossa stood, namely that the freedom of the Irish people lay in the hands of the Irish people.[136] Robbins stated as much in his own memoir when he recalled the 'inspiring message' of the event as not being a lament over the graveside but a celebration of O'Donovan Rossa's labours for Ireland's cause.[137] For O'Brien, the funeral was a 'wonderful success like the McManus funeral of the Fenian days'.[138] The event was a platform for the advanced nationalist politics that the ICA was propagating. It should be noted that all the Dublin units of the pro-Redmond National Volunteers took part in the day.[139] However, similar to the ISRP and the 1798 centenary, the ICA questioned the right of moderate nationalists to honour Rossa as Connolly believed they had rejected Rossa's principles.[140] For Árm Lucta Oibre na h-Éireann's own part, its soldiers unashamedly stood with his ideals, pledged themselves for a republican freedom of Ireland, and reiterated their faith in not only 'the separate destiny of Ireland' but also in 'the ability of the Irish workers to strike for and achieve that destiny'.[141] According to the *Workers' Republic*, around 500 ICA men and women attended the funeral but this was probably exaggerated and it is likely that there were no more than a couple of hundred Citizen Army soldiers present.[142]

This movement towards a wider revolt-ready conglomeration of republican bodies did not indicate that the ICA's attention was exclusively placed on national ambitions. Rather, it seems the leader of both martial and trade union labour was attempting to bring these bodies closer together into a similar relationship to what existed during the army's pre-constitutional days. It is true that Connolly became 'increasingly preoccupied' with using the conflict in Europe as a launch pad for national insurgency.[143] Yet, Connolly envisaged the ITGWU as the medium for the wider struggle. Though in charge of the union, he did not share Larkin's illusions about it. Once taking charge of the ITGWU, Connolly ran it with more drive than Larkin had done. New branches in Tralee and Kilkenny were created and a national leadership was established.

Likewise, 1915 also saw the labour army return to its original purpose of a workers' defence corps. As his 'Revolutionary Unionism and War' article showed, Connolly's variety of ideological policies was connected into one wider homogenous revolutionary philosophy. Likewise, the political activity Connolly engaged in during his last years was spread across a number of organisations: The Socialist Party of Ireland (SPI), the Irish Trades Union Congress and Labour Party (ITUCLP), the Irish Transport and General Workers' Union (ITGWU) and the Irish Citizen Army (ICA). Interestingly, these organs represented the various political elements of Connolly's ethos

– propaganda, politics, trade unionism and militarism. Woggon argued that while these bodies were not officially connected: 'the SPI was not attached to the Labour Party, nor was the Citizen Army part of the ITGWU', there was a clear symbiosis of principles which suggested the means for complete revolution.[144] In July 1915, Connolly used the title 'Transport Union Citizen Army'. This was the first time since winter 1913 that this title was used and it use was an indication of his attempt to reinvigorate a more harmonious relationship with the trade union movement. This relationship was to act within the wider co-operative structures that he was attempting to build for the post-capitalist sovereign Ireland.[145] Likewise, for the O'Donovan Rossa funeral every member of the ICA was ordered to wear the red hand badge of the ITGWU, the first record of such an order since the days of the lockout.[146]

The year before the rebellion was one of the busiest years for both Connolly and Branch No. 1 of the ITGWU.[147] Upon taking over the union's duties, he found it was in dire straits both financially and organisationally. The main branch in Liberty Hall had not functioned properly for months.[148] Connolly did not abandon this responsibility in favour of his ICA duties. In June 1915, it was the tool of the strike rather than the gun which garnered the attention of the DMP as Connolly embarked on a series of steps in order to improve the ITGWU's standing.[149] These steps included reorganising branches in Aungier Street, Inchicore and Thomas Street; attempts to establish a new branch in Limerick, control of indiscipline in Sligo, to establish an accepted national standing committee, and to increase membership fees.[150] Renewed industrial agitation had an effect on the ICA, and its role as a workers' army. The Burns and Laird Lines strike in 1914–15 saw the use of the armed picket.[151] Despite the ICA's distaste over handing over weapons to the strikers, there was a quick response to Connolly's order for support. Between eight to ten men were ordered to march down to the quays with full ICA equipment and acted as an armed picket surrounding the shipping office.[152] This was successful, as after the ICA had been convinced to give their arms to the strikers the dispute lasted only a short duration and resulted in a 'considerable increase in wages'.[153]

In October 1915, the use of the armed picket seemed to be reaffirmed by the ICA when the army stated that while it was steadfast and always foremost regarding the national question it was 'never neglecting its own special function'. This claim would be tested immediately.[154] Within the year, the most significant trade union dispute centred on the City of Dublin

Steamship Company. The ITGWU's strike against that company lasted from October to December.[155] Previous to that, despite its membership largely being made up of ITGWU men, the ICA had ceased to be a 'trade union' army. Branch No.1's dealing with the Citizen Army in 1915 had typically focused on day-to-day issues such as rent for rooms in Liberty Hall, catering, and the opening of a tea and coffee bar to raise funds.[156] Likewise, while Robbins, a staunch union man, stated that no hostility existed between both labour organs, particularly because of the 'dual position' held by Connolly discussion at Branch No. 1 meetings was sometimes at least latently critical of the military wing.[157] In January 1915 the committee raised concerns over 'the question of shooting with ball cartridges in Croydon Park' which they viewed as dangerous, while in June criticism centred on the expense involved in the ICA's use of Croydon Park.[158] Yet, despite this, Connolly was able to use the ICA as an auxiliary force while simultaneously using the strike as a recruitment tool for the militia.

Throughout October, a number of disputes occurred in Dublin docks as shipping companies broke their agreements with dockers over rates of pay. Events were quickly transformed into a protracted conflict which often incited the Munitions Act. Through this, the leadership in Beresford Place and Croydon Park believed excessive policing by the DMP and RIC was occurring.[159] With this in mind, it is not surprising that a meeting of about 1,000 people was held on 14 November where the Dublin Trades Council not only gave full support to the dock workers but leaders William O'Brien, Thomas Foran, P.T. Daly and Connolly stood on the stage and attributed to the Citizen Army the improved union conditions then experienced.[160] The necessity for immediate action in the midst of a strike and the belief in its potential for success once again led Connolly to order the use of Árm Lucta Oibre na h-Éireann. However, as opposed to loaning rifles, the conflict was seen as a potential recruitment avenue as he believed those on strike could form their own ICA companies:

> large sections have been formed for drill, and every day the men are instructed in military exercises. We are thus rapidly becoming the best drilled body of men in Ireland. For a time, it was difficult to get our men trained, as dock work keeps men employed always in the evenings, but the employers are kindly helping us to get over that difficulty. Company after company locks out its men, and then we bring them up to Liberty Hall and take advantage of the opportunity

to drill and train them. When each dispute is settled that squad of men goes back to work, and some other squad gets locked out, and we get a chance to train them.[161]

The dispute was eventually solved in December 1916 through the arbitration of Thomas Foran and William O'Brien.[162] However, by October 1915, the military strength of the ICA was already evidenced as it 'alone' was preventing the British administration from doing in Dublin what they had done in Barry in Wales – sending soldiers in during a strike to do the work of the docker.[163]

7

'TO ENLIGHTEN AND INSTRUCT OUR MEMBERS': MILITARY DEVELOPMENTS UNDER CONNOLLY

Writing about his close friend, O'Brien contended that:

> it is well known that Connolly was responsible for the method of street fighting adopted in Dublin in Easter Week. He had lectured on the subject frequently in many parts of the country ... Talking on the same subject to the Citizen Army he explained carefully the kind of trenches that should be made, and how the defenders must protect themselves.[1]

From September 1914 onwards, after the IRB meeting in the Gaelic League's offices, Connolly's language became even more revolutionary and with that the ICA was set on a path of becoming militarily ready for any revolt that might occur.[2] One of the most important facets of this was the role of Chief of Staff Mallin. According to James O'Shea, once Mallin took the lead at Liberty Hall 'things started to hum'.[3] While he was given this title by Connolly, Mallin's association with the force began before the second change of leadership. Brian Hughes dated this as 'in the latter half of 1914, after the collapse of the lockout and before Larkin's departure in October'.[4] O'Shea recalled the Parnell anniversary where Larkin was denied a platform by the Irish Volunteers but spoke beside Clarke. O'Shea described Mallin as being the 'coolest man' at the event. Therefore, he was involved in the ICA from at least 11 October 1914.[5]

Mallin had previous British Army experience. In 1889, he joined the Twenty-First Royal Scots Fusiliers as a teenager where he served seven years in India.[6] He was given the rank of 'drummer' and the majority of his training focused on music. However, he did receive basic regular training and in 1894 he earned the grade of 'marksman'. Every year for the rest of his British military career he obtained either a first class or a second class in marksmanship.[7] While he never exceeded the rank of 'drummer' in the royal forces, it appears that his rise to the second highest ranked position in the ICA 'was due to his time spent on active service in India'.[8] Certainly, military experience was needed during a time when Connolly was attempting to turn the republican body into a military unit ready to strike for their ideals. Upon his promotion, both Mallin and Connolly set upon establishing military practices that had relevance to real life revolt.

Robbins recalled Connolly stating that 'if you [Thomas Foran] or anybody else expect that I'm going to waste my time talking "bosh" to the crowds in Beresford Place, for the sake of hearing shouts – then you'll be sadly disappointed'. Rather, Connolly preferred to 'give my message to four serious men at any crossroads in Ireland and know that they carry it back to the places they came from'.[9] This was indicative of a policy that was centred on the firmness of political will rather than any bombast or showmanship. Certainly, in the *Irish Worker* on 24 October 1914, the edition which announced that Connolly was taking over ICA leadership, the ICA's notes ordered all members to parade at 12:00 on 25 November at Croydon Park. There a stern approach to discipline was evidenced in that all rifles were to be 'thoroughly cleaned', that 'absentees would be noted', and that any companies or members who arrived late (a persistent problem up to that point) would be refused admission.[10] However, this did not mean that Connolly was not interested in increasing the numerical strength and the geographical remit of the ICA. Like his predecessors, White and Larkin, focus was placed on enlarging the army of the working class.

It has been contended that Connolly quickly asserted his authority within the force, diminishing the influence of Larkin.[11] Winter 1914 saw such reorganisation through the appointment of a new 'committee of management' on 9 November but also the continued development of new sections through the formation of a new company at Leixlip on 15 November.[12] At the formation of this company, the ICA was represented by its No. 1 branch, clad in uniform and accompanied by the Fintan Lalor Pipers' Band which had initially formed an armed guard in 1913. The speakers for the event were W.M. Partridge, T. Moss, J. Shelly and J. McGowan and they were introduced by J.J. Farrell.[13] Leixlip was mentioned in the royal commission's minutes of evidence on the rebellion as a location of 'considerable thefts of explosives and extensive manufacture of bombs' and was also a key ICA arms dump during the Anglo-Irish War of Independence.[14] It is also important to note that this was not the last base in the greater Dublin area formed under Connolly's leadership. In October 1915, the ICA's notes advertised that a new company was formed in the Church Road area under Lieut. Williams.[15] Likewise, a system similar to the structure employed by the Volunteers of organising boys through *Na Fianna Éireann* was also developed, again in November 1914, when the boys who showed an active interest in the events of Liberty Hall were organised into the 'Irish Citizen Army Boy Scout Corps'. This corps was led by Walter Carpenter.[16]

On 17 October 1914, shortly after the Redmond/Asquith recruitment rally in the Mansion House, the 'Cork notes' of the union's paper congratulated the 'Dublin men' who had 'forced the mollies to retire on Sunday at Parnell Square'. The notes then went on to emphasise the support of the socialist republican body and noted that 'the night of the Asquith meeting the only protests were made by Larkin and the Citizen Army'.[17] While this may have seemed innocuous given its ITGWU connections, it was the first evidence of Cork's growing inclinations for a labour militia which would see Connolly's force create its first battalion outside of the greater Dublin area. Two weeks later, the *Irish Worker* ran an advertisement which was clearly intended for the readership from the southern county. It read: 'rebel Cork your country needs you. Join the Irish Citizen Army Captain Mackey Section. Four Merchants Quay, Cork. Live and die in Ireland. Learn to shoot straight. The Captain Mackey rifle range is now open at the above address where men are trained for Ireland and Ireland only'.[18]

The *Irish Worker*'s 'Cork notes' gave more detail on the new development and stated that the Captain Mackey division had been inspired by Councillor Partridge. Politically, while the Cork ICA was enthused by the example set in Dublin of establishing a protecting force which ensured that 'no more tyranny' would be placed on the working class, it also appealed to those who believed in 'the old principle of an Irish republic' and was clear in its statement that it would work harmoniously with *Oglaigh* though not with 'Redmond's Union Jack scabs'.[19] A fortnight later such politics were reiterated when the 'Cork notes' stated that 'the principles of the Fenians are ours, brothers. Rally round the flags, boys.' At this point further developments had occurred as a committee had been formed, drilling had started and the shooting gallery had been deemed a success.[20] After a further two weeks a 'competent drilling instructor' had been appointed in Cork to lead the sessions which took place on Tuesday and Friday nights as well as Sunday at 13:00. Focus was also placed on training boys in the boys' section which was also considered to be going well.[21] However, this was the last record of the Cork unit in both the paper and its successor the *Workers' Republic*, so it seems that the Cork battalion was short-lived.

Of the five men that led the ICA during the ten-year revolutionary period, Connolly was arguably the most 'internationalist' thinker of all the five leaders of the ICA between the lockout and the Irish Civil War. Given this, it is not surprising that his vantage was not just focused on expansion in Cork but also outside of Ireland. As the Captain Mackey Section was being developed a more internationally-minded appeal was also published which stated that 'those willing to form companies of the army in … England, Scotland or America will by applying to Sec. No. 5 room, Liberty Hall, receive all particulars. God save the people!'[22] Given Connolly's connections and heritage, and that the Glasgow *Na Fianna Éireann* member Seamus Reader transported arms to Connolly, it is not surprising that it was in Glasgow that the call was answered.[23] Furthermore, the IRB had circles in Glasgow, Kiloyth, Paisley, Motherwell, Govan and Port Glasgow which would have enabled the formation of Citizen Army units.[24]

This transnational advertisment was published on 7 November 1914 and three weeks later the *Irish Worker*'s readers were told that the ICA's secretary had received correspondence from Greenock town in the greater Glasgow and Clyde Valley area the previous Monday, 16 November 1914. He had been asked to send membership cards as a 'number of young men' were keen on starting their own branch. 'This is only one of many branches,' readers were informed, 'that are about to be started across the water and all we can do just now is wish their organisation every success.'[25] A number of points can be extrapolated from this: firstly, given the development of 'armed nation' and citizen army theory within the British left at the time, it is important that this unit sought to align itself specifically with the Irish variety of the theory rather than establish its own workers' militia. There were already a number of Irish Volunteer sections in Britain which would eventually manifest in the Kimmage garrison. The Glasgow ICA was perhaps a product of Irish republican circles as much as the international socialist *milieu*. Secondly, it appears through the use of a passive voice and the giving of well wishes that there were no plans for a central authority and the Scottish ICA was to have been autonomous. Certainly, it appears that the Scottish ICA which was involved in gunrunning during the 1919–21 period had a central authority entirely separate from Dublin.

Under the leadership of Connolly and Mallin, the core principles of the ICA focused on 'a definite commitment to revolution and a willingness to take to the field in a short notice'.[26] While its political evolution over winter 1914–15 began to establish the former, to make certain of the latter, a renewed focus on drilling was needed. For ICA member Helena Molony, the tactics espoused by Connolly were 'unique' and contained elements of bluff and bluster. Fearing the attention of the Dublin police, she once questioned him why manoeuvres were publically posted on a blackboard outside Liberty Hall and was met with the response 'you know the story of wolf, wolf'. 'So naturally,' she recalled, 'I saw the wisdom of this.'[27] However, certainly more visceral elements were also introduced. Less than a week after the leadership change, 'a deputation from the Citizen Army waited on the committee [of Branch No. 1 of the ITGWU] and asked for permission to carry out a shooting competition on Sunday 29 November 1914'. Permission was granted.[28]

Thus, the first ICA notes after Connolly took charge advertised the holding of a musketry competition on 29 November. Here a gold cross gun badge was given to the best shot in the army while silver versions were also given to those who were the best shot in their respective companies.[29] More revolt-orientated exercises also began to be implemented. Training in street fighting began just days after Connolly's new role had been announced.[30] These classes examined 'essential points' such as the value of a good water supply, the importance of protection against fire, the need to break internal walls in a building so a whole street could be occupied through the interior, and the tactical fault in occupying a corner building without support from the flanks.[31] A year later, Kathleen Lynn, the ICA's medical officer, began training on topics such as 'hastily dressing of wounds in battle'.[32] During the inquest on the Easter rebellion, this practice was described by Mackenzie Chalmers, a retired British judge and civil servant, as 'obvious sedition' that was done 'for the purpose of carrying out those very objects into effect if they got a chance'.[33]

Likewise, Mallin introduced outdoor exercises which were noteworthy for two reasons. Firstly, these exercises were often done in co-operation with the Volunteers of Con Colbert's company furthering the comradeship with that militia, something that could not have happened a year previous. Secondly, these were mock offensive and defensive practices rather than the mere marching of earlier periods.[34] This was indicative of a change to more strategic and tactical drilling practices that will be discussed shortly. Equally, Connolly also asserted the value of outdoor exercises. Before he had taken command, discipline was seen to be one of the ICA's weakest points. Parades, commonly for recruitment drives, would often occur up to an hour later than they were meant to, prompting Connolly's quip 'I can always guarantee that the Irish Citizen Army will fight but I cannot guarantee that they will be in time for such a fight when it takes place.'[35] With that in mind, a system was put in place that if a mobilisation order was signed by Connolly then it meant that it was of the utmost importance and everything else must be dropped by the soldiers so that nothing would interfere with the order.[36] Prior to the Easter Rising, mobilisations to defend Liberty Hall from perceived attacks took place and were responded to rapidly, highlighting the importance of such a practice.

Naturally, this was a gradual process that required evolution. In Robbins' words it developed 'day by day'.[37] It began with the use of noticeboards in the Beresford Place centre. Notes were posted such as 'Dublin Castle to be attacked at midnight', 'Assemble at 11:30 p.m. to encircle the village of Chapelizod. Cavalry not to turn out' and 'Encirclement of Howth'.[38] This was then replaced with a more sectionalised system with 'section mobilisers' or mobilising officers (MO) who were responsible to contact a given number of men living near their home address. The city, for drilling purposes was then split into two sections north and south of the River Liffey, with an area mobiliser in charge of either section working underneath Thomas Kain, the chief mobilising officer (CMO) and the person in charge of keeping records of membership. Kain in turn took orders from Connolly and Mallin.[39] The rank of mobilising officer did not pertain to the wider structure of commandant, staff captain and captain. Rather, it was a separate delineation. The only MOs who were also officers of the whole army were Thomas Kain (Lieut. and CMO) and Thomas Donoghue (Lieut. and MO for the Dorset Street section). This structural development was reflected in the army's notes in the *Irish Worker*. In September 1914, individual battalions were given separate orders through the paper. In October, divisions were organised around Company A and B with a left and right half for each; while by November the paper only provided orders for Branch No. 1 of the army and others were told to drill as appointed by their officers.[40]

White had initially conceived a similar notion but based on a looser organisation of companies and battalions under which were smaller working

TABLE 7.1. ICA mobilisation system 1915–16

Section	Section name	Mobilisers		Members	
		Kain	O'Brien	Kain	O'Brien
1	High Street	George Oman, Martin Kelly, Edward Burke	George Oman, Martin Kelly, Edward Burke	36	30
2	Aungier Street	Not Stated	Not Stated	23	21
3	Inchicore and Crumlin	Peter Kinsella	Peter Kinsella	13	11
4	Capel Street	John Kelly	John Kelly	43	33
5	Gloucester Street	No information given at all but John Reilly is listed as a MO separately.	John Reilly	No information given.	34
6	North Strand	No information given at all but George Norgrove is listed as a MO separately.	George Norgrove, Thomas O'Donoghue	No information given	23
7	Baldoyle	Not stated	Not stated	14	15
8	Dorset Street	Thomas O'Donoghue, Owen Carton	Owen Carton	37	24
9	Church Street	Not stated	Not stated	16	16
10	North Wall	John Mahon	John Mahon	52	30
11	South Circular Road	James Kelly	James Kelly	14	14
12	Townsend Street	Terence McGuire	Terence McGuire	17	19

Source: Three Notebooks Containing Names of ICA members, 1915–1916, WOBP, MS 15,672, NLI; Matthews, *Irish Citizen Army*, p. 46.

units of eighteen men – sixteen regulars and two non-commissioned officers.[41] The sectional breakdown was recorded by Kain in his own notebook while the Bureau of Military History holds another copy sourced by William O'Brien. There are subtle differences between the two.

By January 1916 there were 339 members of the Irish Citizen Army.[42] According to O'Brien's record, 69 members are unaccounted for. As Kain left out the details for sections five and six, it is impossible to get a full count from his notebook, though he did detail every member in the other ten sections. If O'Brien's record is taken to have been correct regarding the Gloucester Street and North Strand sections and is then added to Kain's then there were seventeen members not recorded as belonging to any section.[43] General marches continued to occur and a 'Special Report on the Irish Citizen Army' was recorded by the Dublin Metropolitan Police on 22 September 1915. It stated that 150 members, forty-five of which were armed with rifles, marched from Croydon Park to Liberty Hall on 19 September.[44]

More important than the sectional changes was the development of more tactically orientated drill which focused both on the practical necessities of soldiers, as opposed to White's morale-centric conception, and the strategic points that a revolt in Dublin would centre on. Under Mallin and Connolly, the force improved so dramatically that it bore no 'semblance' to its previous military form and the ICA's men and women became 'thoroughly trained soldiers well drilled in the rifle'.[45] While the practice of perfecting training through mock attacks on various Dublin buildings and streets was incorporated into ICA training, drills also begin to focus on the potentially disruptive effect that ICA marches could have on military and civil defence authorities.[46] For O'Shea, the time was defined by drilling, and Captain Richard McCormick and Captain John O'Neill were also used by Mallin and Connolly to aid the practice.[47] Under White, this principle had never been done with any intention towards violent social and/or national revolution. Rather, it had been an attempt to inculcate a sense of discipline into the workers.[48] In 1915, focus was placed on methods that had practical value to strategies of revolt. From a tactical educational point of view, Mallin began giving instructions to the ICA in house fighting while this period also saw Connolly and Mallin write some of their articles which focused on insurrectionary warfare.[49]

The articles were a review of the military strategies deployed in various insurgent episodes such as Moscow in 1905, Tyrol in 1809, the Alamo in 1821 and Paris in 1830 and 1848. According to the two senior figures in the army at the time, these articles were intended 'to enlighten and instruct our members in the work they are banded together to perform'. Any discussion of the value of the political movement was absent as the arguments focused totally on the material benefits of the martial concepts undertaken. The hope was that they would provide the ICA members with a reference to 'perfect a Citizen Army able to perform whatever duty [which] may be thrust upon it', in other words revolution.[50] Beginning with the Moscow revolt, the seeds of Connolly's plans for the Easter Rising were visible. He erroneously argued, as the HMS *Helga* would show the following year, that 'a regular bombardment of the city would only have been possible if the loyalist population had withdrawn outside the insurgent lines'.[51] While the falsehood of this belief was to have consequences for the entire republican forces during Easter Week, 1916, the intention for his Citizen Army was clear. Certainly, he ended the piece on a positive message for them, namely that 'the professional soldier is in a city badly handicapped in a fight against really determined civilian revolutions'.[52] This would have been heart-warming for any foot soldiers of the urban force who were beginning to have their own mutinous machinations.

The series of articles concluded with a general assessment of street fighting which detailed advice on fortification and the construction of barricades.[53] Here Connolly was trying to impart knowledge to his soldiers on the value of terrain during asymmetrical warfare. In the street, the argument followed, troops became a good target for the enemy as they had to narrow their front and as the restrictions of space meant it was difficult to manoeuver in such surroundings.[54] Cities, he argued, as Paris in 1848 revealed, should be held through the erection of barricades at tactical points in streets while houses should be broken through so that passages could be made. These instructions were followed in Moore Street and the Royal College of Surgeons during the Easter Rising. The piece finished with a general analysis clearly aimed at his militia:

> The general principle to be deducted from a study of the example we have been dealing with is that the defence is of almost overwhelming importance in such warfare as a popular force like the Citizen Army might be called upon to participate in. Not a mere passive defence of a position valueless in itself, but the active defence of a position whose location threatens the supremacy or the existence of the enemy. The genius of the commander must find such a position, the skill of his subordinates must prepare and fortify it, the courage of all must defend

it. Out of this combination of genius, skill and courage alone can grow the flower of military success.[55]

The esteem of defence manifested itself in actual drilling sessions. Croydon Park was often used as a location for the force to practice defending their own strongholds, a clear imitation of what would be needed in any takeover of city buildings during a revolt within the capital. Robbins recalled that on one occasion, a volunteer while defending the house in the labour recreational centre was so eager that Connolly feared for the safety of the furniture they were carrying.[56] In truth, such practices had begun to be implemented in the latter months of Larkin's reign. On 12 September 1914, the *Irish Worker* advertised that on 27 September a Citizen Army tournament was to be held in Croydon Park which involved a 'night assault on a fortified position'.[57] Operating under a degree of drama, the manoeuvre was played out under the story that 'Black Luke', a famous cowboy, had arrived with his gang to raid the centre. A reward of £4,000 was offered for his capture 'and the Citizen Army [were] on his track'.[58] Similarly, in what was planned to be the body's last public display of the year, days before Larkin's departure for the United States, another training exercise told another story where an Irish emigrant caravan was attacked by Native Americans and the force, in the guise of the American army, was to come to the rescue.[59] Under Mallin, training was focused not on such fictitious stories but on the actual basis of strength of the force's opposition in Dublin. His own mobilisation notes showed an orientation that was focused on direct confrontation with Dublin's police and military units.[60]

The first noticeable facet about these instructions was that the divisions did not correspond to the sectional mobilising units as outlined by Kain and O'Brien.[61] Rather than an organisation based on convenience: training with those who lived closest to you, it was centred on an arrangement to cause maximum disruption to enemy forces. Placement of units revolved around major bases of the British military, such as Richmond Barracks and Royal Barracks.[62] Locations were then chosen on the basis of where was the best place to both gather information on the British forces and to impede such forces from gaining access to the strategic centres. In essence, the structure sought to create a cordon near areas such as Dublin Castle, occupied by the ICA during the Easter Rising, as well as Liberty Hall, the ICA's headquarters. The instructions also allowed for ICA members to respond to the movement of the British Army as the plan directed members of the militia to move to

TABLE 7.2. Michael Mallin's mobilisation notes, 1914–15

Inchicore section:	Section one: Back of James Street to observe and delay all movement from Richmond Military Barracks and Kilmainham Police Barracks.
	Section two: James Street fountain to observe all movements from Royal Military Barracks and support No. 1 section.
High Street section:	Section one: Thomas Street to support section in James Street taking up a position between Meath Street and Francis Street.
	Section two: To take up position at bottom of Bridge Street to observe and delay all members of troops from Royal Barracks along quays. If necessary fall back on section one in Thomas Street.
	Section three: Back of Church Palace to observe all movements of police coming from King Street; to hold on until sections from James Street and Thomas Street fall back.
Aungier Street section:	Section 1: Stephen Street to observe and delay movement of troops from Ship Street.
	Section 2: South Great George Street to support section in Stephen Street.
Unnamed section:	Section 1: Nassau Street.
	Section 2: Griffin Street.
	Section 3: College Street.
'Strong' sections:	Strong section at Liberty Hall to observe Store Street.
	Strong section at Abbey Street midway to O'Connell Street to observe Store Street.

Source: *Irish Citizen Army Notebook, 1914–15*, WOBP, MS 34,937, NLI.

bases to support their comrades in arms when support was needed. While the High Street section was positioned in opposition to the British forces across the Liffey, coming from the Royal Barracks and King Street, they were also ordered to assist the Inchicore section if needed.[63] It was also noteworthy that the majority of support orders were orientated towards units facing the barracks near Richmond and Kilmainham, indicative of a greater ICA concern with British units coming from that direction.

More offensive practices were also put in place, most importantly the mock attack on Dublin Castle. This had a specific importance as it was a centre of British intelligence in Ireland. The plans for this event appear to have been devised as a preparation for the Easter Rising. O'Shea recorded 'all this work had a bearing on what was very near and we believe it was a try out for the fight to come'.[64] Certainly, Lord Hardinge, the chairman of the royal commission which reported on the Easter rebellion, appeared to share this view and was probing in questions to Lieutenant-Colonel Nathan regarding the mock attack. He asked 'apparently they were having sham attacks on Dublin Castle ... was not it quite obvious that that meant they would seize the castle if they could?' He continued, 'did it not strike you at the time as rather extraordinary that these people should have been permitted to make a mimic attack on Dublin Castle and nothing done to prevent it? ... Did not it strike you as coming rather nearer home than the usual military parades?'[65]

On 23 October 1915, the ICA's notes in the back page of the *Workers' Republic* advertised a midnight mobilisation that was to take place that night. The information of the specific details was vague yet the nature of the activity was made clear by the statement that 'an attack and route march were part of the programme'.[66] Those who responded to the call carried out training for an attack on Dublin Castle which many of them would actually do less than a year later. Poetically, Robbins described the night as one characterised by a thick heavy fog. Under this cloud a complete mobilisation of all sections had been ordered and the secrecy of the manoeuvre was accomplished because individual company officers were given instructions which only pertained to their volunteers. These instructions outlined the route they were to take and the time they were to arrive at their final destination.[67] Naturally, the event garnered a degree of attention from the police.[68] In this instance, the ICA was able to make use of the insufficient numbers of DMP in attendance as the splitting of the labour army at Liberty Hall into different march routes caused consternation for the civil authorities.[69] Records show two discernible routes were taken by various ICA companies, though it is likely that there were others that were not recorded. One course was to march up Dame Street, then around the main gate of Dublin Castle before going up Castle Street and stopping at Ship Street.[70] Another march involved walking around the back of the stronghold through Bridge Street, Patrick Street, Wood Street and George's Street.[71]

As well as the practice assault on this centre of authority, the night also saw manoeuvres on different areas across the city. Seemingly practising principles of containment, attempts at 'holding' bridges were also made at Dolphins Barn Bridge and Binns Bridge.[72] In the *Workers' Republic* the week following the training exercise, an unnamed ICA soldier described how 'we had halted at Dolphins Barn Bridge at 00:00 sharp, and an official arrived from headquarters with orders that we were to hold the bridge until 01.30'. In a show of strength against the G-man present, fresh men continued to arrive periodically until the bridge was occupied by 'quite a respectable crowd and the inspector by the move of his lips seemed to be saying his prayers'.[73] Likewise, at the canal bridge in Drumcondra, a party of six was stationed with three either side of the bridge. This too drew attention from the DMP as the militia section were not there long when two men belonging to the police intelligence attached themselves to the group. These G-men seemed to have been more assertive than the officer at Dolphins Barn and performed an inquisition. Despite being given 'an earful', they left satisfied.[74]

The importance of drill was seen in the ICA's continued involvement and success in 'feist competitions'.[75] They took part in contests in Tullow, Co. Carlow; Father Matthew Park, Fairview, Dublin; and St Enda's School, Rathfarnham.[76] In July 1914, the Tullow feist was run by the Carlow AOH and was considered to be for the drilling championship of Ireland as squads from all over the country were expected to have entered.[77] Under Mallin and Christopher Poole, two ICA drilling squads totalling sixty armed members went through the required exercises under the watch of judges.[78] The chief judge was an ex-sergeant major of the British Army. The 'number one squad' of the ICA was awarded first place and won a flag and £5, while the latter squad tied for second.[79] According to Connolly, 'now that the army of the working class has held so magnificently its own, it calls for more recruits for the "great day"'.[80] One aspect of the drill training that was used for those events was a tactic that Mallin termed 'prepare for cavalry'. That was done when companies were marching in fours along a country road. Upon the order, the company would form an eight-man squad, four standing and four kneeling, with bayonets fixed. After this, the order would then come to 'rally' which involved surrounding Mallin in the hope of forming a ring of steel which it was believed would 'hold cavalry and beat an attack if there was no wavering'.[81]

During the White and Larkin eras the gradual build-up of an armament stockpile had been a focal point which was driven by the rivalry with the Irish Volunteers and the ICA's desire to be seen in equal measure as a proper militia. However, the quest for munitions was typically unsuccessful and the ICA often had to resign itself to drilling with empty guns. Robbins wrote of one occasion when the ICA was 'skirmishing' in Santry and Ballymun. While resting they met with the DMP agent Kirwan, known by them as 'Sheep's Eyes', who sought to obtain accurate information about the strength of their arms. According to Robbins, a number of the ICA men present decided to open their magazine clips and show Kirwan the contents. This was not for any jovial reasons nor was it done to bow down to authority. Rather, a more Machiavellian stratagem lay behind the men's reasoning; it was hoped that by some of the men revealing their bullets, Kirwan would assume that all of the Mauser rifles were armed, whereas in reality that was not the case.[82] Given that Connolly was growing the army into not just a republican extra-parliamentary force but one with increasingly outward revolutionary machinations, the ICA needed to increase their arsenal.

The ICA under Connolly's command showed a remarkable degree of ingenuity when gathering new armaments. The *ad hoc* nature of this build-up was expressed by Connolly when he stated that they were true internationalists because they used French bayonets on German rifles in the fight for Ireland.[83] Indeed, the logistics of this required some work as if left unaltered, the blade would lie across the rifle's barrel – about three-quarters of its length – which prevented the firing of the rifles. In order to overcome this, all bayonets were adjusted. To make these adjustments the spear was heated halfway up and then bent in order to make it clear of the mouth of the rifle.[84] Such ingenuity became increasingly important as the rebellion approached when more and more effort was placed on the construction of home-made weapons. However, for the time being attention was mainly placed on gathering weapons from outside sources. While some of the guns used at the time dated back to the ICA's involvement in the Howth gunrunning, others were acquired through one of Connolly's friends, a stonemason named Fred Bower who hid the guns between marble slabs. The presence of the British Army in the capital also enabled the Citizen Army to build up its stockpile. According to O'Shea, at this time the chief of staff was also working 'secretly, though with the knowledge and approval of Connolly' on the 'old Fenian idea of members of the army'.[85] So sympathetic British soldiers were used to obtain weapons. It should also be stated that while the ICA would commonly illegally purchase arms from willing soldiers, many times they simply resorted to theft.[86]

To cover the cost of these materials, an army equipment fund was established in 1915.[87] In his notebook for the force, Mallin wrote an extensive listing of the purchasing of the cache, general military equipment and recruitment drives. The costing, in pounds, shillings and pence, read:

TABLE 7.3. Michael Mallin's budget for ICA purchases, 1914–15

Item	£.S.D
Flags 1000	3 15 0
Flags 1400	1 10 0
Pins, Amulets and Markings	0 12 3
Bawl	0 00 2
Travelling by 4	0 02 0
Ammunition	0 05 0
Material for arm[s] and making same	0 12 3
Rifles	3 00 0
Revolver ammunition	0 03 6
[Further] revolver ammunition	0 02 0
Travelling Sutton (3)	0 05 0

Source: *Irish Citizen Army Notebook, 1914–15*, WOBP, MS 34,937, NLI.

Outside of flags, the biggest costs to Mallin were guns and ammunition. A number of factors existed which enabled the ICA to purchase arms through soldiers. Not only did the continuation of the war increase the potential stockpile but the employment of many of the ICA's members enabled a greater opportunity to garner such weapons. At a general level, the problems that the British Army faced with the 'loss' of arms reached such a height that by the end of 1914 they began to require their soldiers to leave their rifles at Kingstown upon arrival and to collect these arms when leaving by using a receipt.[88] Through their work in the docks, ICA members were in a good position to capitalise. According to Richard Corbally, he was 'always down around the boats fetching ammunition'.[89] Throughout the period from November 1914 to January 1916, a large amount of guns and ammunition travelled into Dublin's port, indicated by the seizure of weapons.

The close proximity between Mallin's house in Emmet Hall, at the Inchicore Branch of the ITGWU, and Richmond Barracks in Keogh Square created another avenue for the ICA to bolster their arsenal. Given that his house and the barracks were only separated by a high wall, Citizen Army men were quite easily able to obtain more guns from 'sympathetic Irishmen' who were members of the British Army. O'Shea described the proximity as follows:

> after entering the hall of [Mallin's house] and going about thirty feet there was a small room used for the committees. Immediately to the right was the entrance to a yard and opposite this door at the far side of the yard was the entrance to the kitchen of [the] Mallin family. When you turned out of the door to the right you took a left and faced the yard and at the end of what was one time a garden was the wall of the barracks.[90]

Robbins wrote of how in winter 1915, he was called to the Inchicore premises. Within less than a minute after arriving at Mallin's dwelling, he was sent home but with the added load of a Lee Enfield rifle.[91] He stated that other members were also ordered to make the same visit but eventually this source dried up.[92] According to Fox, James O'Shea was another involved in this work.[93] O'Shea recalled an incident when Connolly ordered him to 'pick up another man' and go to Ranelagh. After giving a password, the men were given a parcel each which contained high explosives which they then transported back to Liberty Hall. He learned that this was one of a series of similar missions and that 'a big lot' of explosives had been moved that night into the army's headquarters.[94] While not officially 'on the job', O'Shea recalled travelling to Portobello Barracks with Mallin on two occasions. There the ICA's senior officers would speak with 'men in mufti ... for a considerable time'. Indeed, given that Connolly and Mallin had two squads working for them in this vein it is clear that both these barracks were useful sites for gathering armaments.[95] It should be noted that in post-rebellion Ireland Richard Corbally travelled to Portobello Barracks where weapons were wilfully transferred by British soldiers.[96]

In one sense the increased martial atmosphere created by World War I helped enable the use of this strategy. However, it also created difficulties in that British regiments were quickly moved out of Dublin when required.[97] Thus, it was difficult for the ICA to consistently purchase guns from British soldiers. However, a number of other avenues for purchasing as well as importing were also pursued. Interestingly, three weeks after Larkin had announced Connolly as his successor, the new editor of the *Irish Worker* published an advertisement for John Lawlor and Son gun sellers which was strikingly printed directly under the ICA's notes. French Gas bayonets were

TABLE 7.4. Total of arms seized at Dublin Port, November 1914–January 1916

Date	Rifles and Guns	Revolvers	Rounds of Ammunition	Bayonets
November 1914	54	4	36,000	154
December 1914	51	0	0	85
January 1915	0	0	0	0
February 1915	1	1	7,600	0
March 1915	1	0	0	6
April 1915	0	0	1,577	0
May 1915	2	0	700	0
June 1915	101	0	550	0
July 1915	4	0	25	3
August 1915	8	0	50	0
September 1915	1	0	20	0
October 1915	1	0	100	0
November 1915	230	0	30,000	1
December 1915	50	1	160,326	0
January 1916	13	0	3,400	1

Source: Table Entitled 'Arms and Ammunition Seized at Port of Dublin by Police for Arms' Attached to Memorandum from DMP Chief Superintendent Owen Brien, 12 May 1916, Arms Importation and Distribution, CO 904/28, TNA.

advertised at 1s and 6d each while pikes were 7s and 6d. Cartridges could have been purchased at 13s and 6d per 1,000 while Lee Enfield rifles and Martini rifles were sold at 90s and 50s each respectively. Finally, waist belts were also on offer from a varying price of 1s to 2s and 6d each.[98] On 6 April 1915, the Lawlor and Son building at 2 Fownes Street, Dublin was searched by the DMP and six Harrington and Richardson five chamber revolvers and one seven chamber revolver were found.[99] Another raid occurred on the same property on 2 December 1915 which procured a much more significant stash: ninety-one .22 rifles; fifteen single shotguns; nine double-barrel shotguns; two Vetellic rifles; three muzzle loading rifles; two Mauser magazine rifles; one Mannlicher rifle; one Martini rifle; one carbine; one Steyn rifle; one express rifle; six Italian swords; three English swords; seventy-nine revolvers and pistols; 38,400 .22 cartridges; 24,000 B.B. cartridges; 1,550 Pin Fire cartridges; 150 Winchester rifle cartridges; 300 .442 rifle cartridges; 100 automatic pistol cartridges; forty .45 cartridges; as well as sixty packages and eleven boxes of various loose cartridges. Alongside these, 'a large quantity' of holsters, pouches and khaki slings were also seized.[100]

Contact was also made with sources outside of Ireland. Naturally, given the growing socialist and feminist movements in the Clydeside region and the attempted formation of an ICA unit in Greenock, as well as the Irish Volunteers' use of that region, contact was made with Scottish radicals. William Omen, the 16-year-old member of the ICA's boys' corps was involved in the attainment of gelignite which had come from Scotland.[101] In 1914, the Glasgow *Na Fianna Éireann* man Seamus Reader was brought into the IRB. For the previous two years Countess Markievicz had been his guide for his various journeys around Dublin. Likewise, Cathal O'Shannon also travelled to the Clyde region to enable the development of such connections. These contacts also enabled the transfer of arms.[102] During Reader's trips to Dublin he would typically bring over five boxes of munitions containing detonators and revolver ammunition. Certainly, some of this material would have gone directly to the IRB, especially as he dealt with Clarke. However, he also dealt with what he termed as the 'Surrey House cliche [*sic*]', i.e. Connolly and Markievicz. Indeed, he spent time with ICA members McGowan, de Coeur and Molony taking down British Army recruitment posters that were posted in Dublin. Furthermore, it appears that Connolly had been quite open with him about the plans for the 1916 rebellion. Reader recalled 'most of the talking I had with Connolly was in Surrey House in the morning or at night. He more or less told me about the [Easter] Rising. In November and December, I knew definitely from the Countess and Connolly that there was going to be a rising or a fight.'[103] Reader was also aware that prior to the rebellion Markievicz had issued orders to Frank Murray to transport explosives from Glasgow to Dublin. Murray's activity continued after the rebellion with his expenses paid for by Árm Lucta Oibre na h-Éireann.[104]

Likewise, America was successfully used as another avenue. This was a logical source to tap given its long tradition of supporting Irish republicanism which had been built up through Clan na Gael. Furthermore, Larkin was active in the United States agitating for greater support in the approaching national struggle. The DMP reported that again through Scotland, via Glasgow in this instance, Clan na Gael was shipping arms wrapped up in woollen goods.[105] In Liverpool, Italian thumb-lock rifles were packed between shavings and marble slabs before being imported into Ireland and put in the care of McGowan, who alongside James O'Neill was the most senior of the men involved in munitions work at that time.[106] The result of this was that in the second week of April 1916, the police noted that the Citizen Army had not only a 'slight increase' in rifles but also twenty American shotguns.[107] William Omen recalled being called into Liberty Hall one night to be told that such a cargo had been 'landed' and safely brought into the labour base.[108] At an event in Chicago, shortly after the Easter Rising, Larkin dramatically spoke to the American audience in attendance. After he stacked three rifles on the stage and held one aloft he said 'perhaps you don't know who brought these kinds of rifles into Ireland. Of course you don't, because the press has never told you. Well it was Angela Spring-Rice, sister of Ambassador Spring-Rice. It was she who smuggled them in to us.'[109] The staff-captain of the ICA during the Easter Rising, Christopher Poole, recorded the importance of his former leader in this regard. According to him, Larkin 'sent arms from America, shotguns etc.'.[110]

Arms acquisitions were also attempted in less cordial terms. While dockside robbery of tools and scrap metal was important to the creation of home-made munitions in 1916, at this stage focus was also placed on raids on British drill halls and arms dumps. Efforts were made to abscond with arms from these places on at least two occasions. In the St Margaret's area of Dublin, Tom Daly, known as 'blackguard', Corbally and other ICA members spotted a building which they viewed as strange-looking: it was surrounded by two iron gates and had a very low-lying roof which seemed 'grass-grown'. After hearing from a so-called 'herder' that it was full of RIC explosives the unit made pretence to clear the territory but waited until the opportunity arose where they could confirm this information.[111] When further investigation revealed this to be correct, Connolly was informed and ordered what ended up as two failed raid attempts, one on the following night and the other a 'short time after'. The first was botched because the units involved did not realise that the building was reinforced with a concrete roof underlined with steel. Despite a couple of hours work, they could not gain access.[112] Approximately two weeks later, orders were issued for a more extensive attempt. With smoking and talking prohibited so as not to alert onlookers, O'Shea alongside Martin Kelly and Michael Donnelly formed one unit that attempted to cut the gate down while another part of the squad acted as watchmen. However, after the alarm was sounded and the ICA men were fired upon, the attempt was called off and never repeated.[113]

The importance of Connolly's leadership was best described by the last leader of the body before the struggle was given up in 1923. According to Hanratty:

> It was left to James Connolly, who possessed to a marked degree the qualities of realism and idealism, to mould this force into the historic army it later became. It required a man with those qualities to overcome the many obstacles the young army was faced with in the succeeding months. Not only had he to overcome the obstacles of the absence of drill halls and instructors but he had also to face a shortage of ammunition, arms and equipment.[114]

8

'UNDER ARMS IN LIBERTY HALL': FINAL PREPARATIONS FOR THE EASTER RISING

The 1915 period saw the ICA intensify its training and create greater harmony with the Irish Volunteers. This pattern continued during the first months of 1916 until the Easter Rising. While greater fraternity existed between the Citizen Army and the wider republican family under Connolly, than the previous two ICA leaders, variance in revolutionary drive, or at least a perceived difference on Connolly's part, meant there was still an absence of trust within the various army lobbies in 1915.[1] Immediately upon the turn of the year, a formal union between the ICA and the IRB was created during Connolly's mysterious disappearance from Dublin, 19–21 January 1916. His disappearance is examined within this chapter. This resulted in a formalising of plans for the rebellion. Likewise, the need for a stockpile of weapons became increasingly important, and bomb making was a defining feature of the January–April 1916 period. Liberty Hall was transformed into far more than a labour base.[2] This brought the ICA into a quasi active service where defence of the headquarters was a full-time occupation for many of the ICA's service men. The chapter also examines how such outwardly radical and militant activities had implications for the ICA's relationship with the ITGWU.

Towards the end of 1915, Connolly was contemplating the idea that the ICA might have to act not only as a 'vanguard', in Matthews's terms, for a coming revolution but may also have been faced with the challenge of being the only militia involved in an Irish rebellion.[3] It was true that Connolly had continued to meet rebellion leaders such as Tom Clarke and Con Colbert during the year.[4] Evidently, he was not content with the pace of the movement towards revolution as a complete mobilisation of the ICA was ordered in the first months of 1916. All members present were asked three questions in order to assess if they were prepared for the coming conflict; 'are you prepared to take part in the fight for Ireland's freedom?' 'Are you prepared to fight alongside the Irish Volunteers?' 'Are you prepared to fight without the aid of the Irish Volunteers or any other allies?'[5] If the answer to all questions was 'yes' then each ICA member was given a secret army registration number. That this number was subsequently imprinted on a block to be carried on the neck of the individual soldier in order to enable him or her to be identified 'in the event of complete annihilation' made clear the gravity of the situation.[6] Not only was it clear that the ICA was now set on a path to rebellion but as the third question shows, they would be willing to go it alone if needed.

Throughout 1915, Connolly had criticised the Volunteers for what he believed was their rigidity in not moving plans along since the 9 September 1914 meeting. According to Undersecretary Nathan's statement given to the commission examining the rebellion, from the latter part of 1915 onwards, the leaders of the Citizen Army were seen as 'urging violent action on those of the Irish Volunteers'.[7] A month after the IRB meeting in the Gaelic League's offices on 9 September, Connolly stated that the Volunteers needed to recognise that their fight was a 'struggle to the death' and that there was 'but one effective weapon – the daring appeal of the revolution'.[8] O'Brien recorded that during the O'Donovan Rossa funeral when Pearse was speaking in revolutionary tones, Connolly stated 'you people are great admirers of dead Fenians. What you don't admire are the men who are alive and prepared to do the things they did and tried to do, which causes you to admire the Fenians.'[9] Robbins also recalled being at a meeting in November 1915 which had been organised to 'commemorate one of our martyred patriots'. There, Pearse stressed that past insurrections in Ireland had always occurred too late. To this Connolly replied 'will this one also be too late'.[10] Given this, it seems that T.A. Jackson was accurate when he claimed that a meeting between the IRB and Connolly occurred in January 1916 because the old secret society was afraid that Connolly was excessively and overtly seditious and would draw the British forces upon them.[11]

By January 1916, the IRB's own military plans were progressing well except that it was becoming apparent that Connolly might bypass them.[12] It was in this context that on Wednesday 19 January James Connolly disappeared from Dublin's labour circles and did not return until Saturday 22 January. He spent these days engaged with the other putative leaders of the rebellion, Pearse, MacDermott and Plunkett, where plans and dates were discussed, shared and set. Before the end of the weekend he had become a member of the IRB's military council.[13] According to O'Brien, the idea that this event began with a kidnapping of Connolly appears to have originated during the internment of the participants of the Easter Rising in the Frongoch camp between April and December 1916. A number of ICA prisoners had argued that Connolly was more responsible for the revolution than any of the other leaders. Some of the Volunteers disagreed and one of them stated that the Volunteers' leadership knew how to handle him as they had taken him prisoner in January 1916 until he agreed to fall in line with them.[14]

William O'Brien's notes recalled a conversation he had with Harry Walpole on 9 June 1947. Not only was Walpole a member of *Na Fianna Éireann* and lived with Markievicz in Surrey House, Leinster Road Dublin, but also, alongside Eddy Murray, John Shallow and Louis Marie, he acted as a bodyguard to Connolly. The terms used in this record did suggest some sort of captivity. O'Brien recorded that Walpole 'was satisfied that Connolly was held by the IRB and that while in custody [he] had come to an agreement with that body'.[15] Similar terminology was used by Capt. Richard McCormick who alongside Mallin and Seán Connolly met Connolly upon his reappearance. Here the expression used was 'released' by the IRB which suggested that Connolly was unwillingly held.[16]

However, Morrissey's work recently implied that there was no kidnapping but that Connolly, after encountering some Irish Volunteers, went immediately but also voluntarily to meet with Pearse on 19 January 1916 and that he then stayed 'of his own free will'.[17] Certainly, four reasons have been put forward by Lorcan Collins which challenge the idea of the kidnapping: firstly, logic dictates that if Connolly had been held against his will some type of repercussions would have occurred, they did not; secondly, it is fair to assume that once Connolly was informed of the IRB's plans that he would have wanted to spend hours studying and arguing about the details; thirdly, it is also possible that Connolly did, indeed, go for a long walk to 'digest' the revelation (his own explanation for his disappearance); fourthly, it is likely that Connolly was sworn to secrecy and would not have been able to give an explanation no matter what it was.[18]

Another indication of Connolly's acquiescence to a meeting is that in the middle of the three-day period a letter addressed to Larkin and signed by 'Wardell' arrived at Liberty Hall. The letter mentioned 'missing the tram' and that they would 'meet tomorrow at two'. This was taken to be a coded letter from Connolly ordering that the ICA should not be mobilised as he would soon return.[19] If he had been captured it is unlikely that this type of communication would have been possible. Furthermore, on 5 March 1950, O'Brien had a conversation with Denis McCullough regarding the incident and noted that McCullough was positive that Connolly had not been kidnapped by the IRB's military council. McCullough was present at a meeting of that council on 23 January 1916 in the town hall in Clontarf and was told by MacDermott that it was felt that the ICA's commandant, chief of staff and Markievicz were 'liable to start the fight at any moment' and that once fighting started nothing could be done to stop the Volunteers joining the effort.[20] O'Brien, a close confidant of Connolly, also stated that based on his 'intimate knowledge' of Connolly if he had been kidnapped he would have resented it to such a degree that he would have refused to discuss plans with his captors.[21]

BMH witness statements reveal that IRB men Frank and Ned Daly and Eamon Dore, had been charged by the IRB's military council with the task of making contact with Connolly and bringing him to the meeting on 19 January 1916. Dore recalled that the IRB's decision was taken because the labour leader 'had been causing trouble, affecting [sic] a contempt of the IRB and the Volunteers, or disbelieving the earnestness of the intentions in these organisations'.[22] Fox contended that 'the incessant demand for revolt' not only was the cause of ire for the Volunteers but, for those who agreed with the socialist thinker, it was a catalyst for a fear of an attack or suppression by the police.[23] While he did not indicate when the order was given, Dore had been ordered by Seán MacDermott to meet Ned Daly at Seamus O'Connor's office in Dame Street where Frank Daly was also present. They waited there for about half an hour before Ned 'decided to go out to find out how things stood'. After twenty minutes he returned and told his two colleagues that everything was arranged and they could leave.[24] His recollections continued:

> From what I learned at the time and immediately afterwards about this matter, I gathered that it was Seán MacDermott who took action on behalf of the supreme council and probably in consultation with them, to have a showdown with Connolly. Connolly was to be invited or persuaded to accompany him to a house in the vicinity of Castleknock … It was intended that if Connolly refused to go voluntarily he was to be arrested and [be] brought there under guard, and it was for this reason that Ned and Frank Daly and I stood by in O'Connor's office.

Apparently Connolly did agree to go with MacDermott and so our services were not required in the matter. [25]

Despite the recollections and rhetoric of some former ICA members, it does appear that Connolly was not forcibly detained.

In truth, the greatest significance of the event lay not in whether Connolly had been kidnapped or went willingly but in the consequences of his disappearance: the settlement on plans for Easter Week, 1916, and the near mobilisation of the ICA which cemented their path towards revolution.[26] Upon arriving at the IRB's meeting on 19 January, Connolly met Pearse, MacDermott, Plunkett and possibly MacDonagh and Clarke for deliberations. Geraldine Plunkett, sister of Joseph, recalled how these meetings would go on all day and her brother would not return home until late at night as they had found it difficult to get Connolly to discuss anything. Eventually agreement was reached. Geraldine also recorded how she was told that Connolly later said 'I have been beaten at my own game', by which she took to mean both the military plan and that the council was as anxious as him 'to put the future of Ireland on a basis of abstract justice'.[27] When Connolly later met McCormick, Mallin and Seán Connolly, he shared with them the plans that had been settled upon between 19 and 21 January.[28]

Robbins contended that the following week's edition of the *Workers' Republic* revealed that a significant change in Connolly's outlook had occurred.[29] Collins argued that the language in this edition was 'more subdued' and that it was filled with a sense of prophecy.[30] The piece argued that the time for more didactic rhetoric regarding the issue of independence had passed. Rather, a 'seed' had been planted and the time for it to ripen had been reached. Connolly wrote 'for the moment and hour of that ripening, that fruitful blessed day of the days ... [the republican forces were] ready ... will it find you ready too?'[31] It is clear that it was written in the context of the IRB and Connolly's agreement for revolution. It should be noted that for Mallin these plans were not entirely convincing. When he was shown the plans for the rebellion his response was to ask where the 'B' plan was as he felt that the plans did not leave enough room for contingencies and that they were bound to break down.[32] Despite concerns such as these, the newly created formal alliance between the IRB and the ICA was mutually beneficial. While Connolly acquiesced to hold off on a rising for a relatively short extension, he secured far greater support for the ICA than if they had revolted on their own. The plans also increased the likelihood of a rebellion being more than a symbolic gesture. The agreement reached in late January also eradicated the threat of a sudden socialist republican movement destroying the IRB's own machinations.[33] Importantly, the IRB had no significant apparatus available for military instruction and, as the Irish Volunteers had done in 1915, would have been glad to make use of Connolly's teachings.[34]

McCormick also recorded two notable features of the settlement for the plan of joint action. Firstly, he stated that Connolly had argued for the use of the bank building facing Trinity College as the general headquarters for the insurrection because it was facing the college. McCormick remembered Connolly as saying that '[the headquarters] might as well be in a cellar as [the] GPO'. However, Pearse was against this idea as it was an old parliament building and the General Post Office was settled on. Secondly, McCormick contended that '[Connolly] had made the IRB agree to a labour programme.'[35] Certainly, elements of the proclamation echoed the ICA's constitution. The proclamation's declaration of 'the right of the people of Ireland to the ownership of Ireland and to the unfettered control of Irish destinies to be sovereign and indefeasible' contained the exact philosophy of clause 1 in the ICA's March 1914 constitution.

Principles regarding suffrage, children and equal opportunities to all citizens were typical of the ideas espoused by leaders like Connolly and Markievicz. In essence, the wording and the egalitarian essence of the document was largely a product of Connolly's socialist thinking.[36] According to Mulholland, it was Connolly above anyone else 'who provided that unifying ideological frame for feminism and nationalism'.[37] While the collapsing of the respective ICA and Irish Volunteer titles did not occur until later in the year, Connolly's inclusion into the IRB's military council marked the point when their paths formally converged. Indeed, shortly afterwards, James O'Shea was told by his chief of staff that he was to join the IRB, while less than a month later Frank Robbins joined the secret society.[38]

While it has been argued that Connolly was not kidnapped, his disappearance was a cause for consternation within Árm Lucta Oibre na h-Éireann.[39] Mallin was instructed by his leader that if at any point he should go missing for some days then the chief of staff was to lead the labour militia 'out' and they were to take Dublin Castle.[40] Indeed, the day before Connolly's return, 21 January 1916, Markievicz informed O'Brien that there was a pact within ICA leadership not to tolerate the arrest of any leader. If it was to happen, they were to start their own insurrection.[41] Certainly, upon Connolly's disappearance Mallin came close to calling a mobilisation of the

ICA and the reason it did not occur was due to both the letter addressed to Larkin as well as a conversation he had with O'Brien and Markievicz. He, along with O'Brien, had arrived at Liberty Hall not long before 'Wardell's' note arrived. When O'Brien, Markievicz and Mallin discussed the note they decided not to take any action until 14:00 on Friday when they would go to the post office in Lucan to see if they could ascertain any more information.[42] When the time came, Kathleen Lynn drove Markievicz and Mallin's wife, a Lucan native, and William O'Brien, but the trip did not clarify anything.[43]

Sometime between Friday 21 January and Saturday evening 22 January, Mallin eventually sat down with members of the IRB's military council. An IRB deputation visited Mallin in order to ask him to 'hold his hand'.[44] During the meeting, Mallin informed the delegation that should Connolly not be found by a certain date then the Citizen Army was to take to the streets of Dublin. He also stated that if he too was captured the force would rise none the less. According to Robbins, who talked with Mallin about the event, when the military council's delegation asked what the ICA could do with such paltry numbers, Mallin replied 'we can fight and die, and it will be our glory and your shame if such does take place'.[45] In the end Connolly returned to Surrey House on Saturday evening.

It appears that Mallin's role in this event should not be exaggerated. According to IRB man Diarmuid Lynch, Connolly's release was due to him having acquiesced to the council. Lynch asked why would they have released Connolly as they would have been able to handle his chief subordinate.[46] Connolly appears to have met with the IRB willingly. Therefore, it is probable that his return was the result of the settlement of a strategy rather than his release being secured by other ICA figures. Certainly, the leader's vanishing did reveal a preparedness for revolt amongst the ICA's other commanders. Furthermore, while the ICA had been preparing for some form of uprising since late 1914, Connolly's deliberations with the IRB cemented a path for a joint revolution which, while a possibility, was by no means destined since 9 September 1914. After this the ICA became absorbed into the preparations and the execution of the IRB's Easter rebellion.[47]

As Casement's diplomacy with Germany showed, despite the progress with plans for rebellion, arms remained a problem for the revolutionaries. By the beginning of 1916, there was an even greater drive to increase and improve the stockpile of weapons. Throughout late 1915 and early 1916, the aim was not just the procurement of guns but the making of bombs and other armaments. For instance, James O'Neill focused on this work in

1916.[48] Within the wider republican family, bomb-making factories were established by Scottish and English Volunteers in Kimmage as well as by other Irish Volunteers at Pearse's St Edna's school in Rathfarnham. The socialist republican militia was no different.[49] During the months prior to the rebellion, the ICA's headquarters in Beresford Place became more than just a trade union centre which housed a labour army but was for all intents and purposes a bomb factory.[50] According to Matthew Connolly, an 'armoury had been established on the first floor which was a busy place where grenades were made, cartridges "altered" and bayonets heated and reshaped'.[51] This practice was so important that in January while inquiring about a new 'Glasgow Fianna IRB bomb', Mallin tried to arrange a meeting for O'Neill and McGowan with the O/C of the Scottish Brigade, Seamus Reader.[52]

During this period, a number of the unemployed members of the ICA, alongside 'a selected number of members who frequented Liberty Hall in the evening', manufactured grenades and bullets which were converted from regular shotgun ammunition. The shotgun cartridges were melted down in order to create a space where four bullets could be placed into the original cartridge. Each casting was recompressed in order to enhance the effect. These were then tested, which revealed that they were most potent at a distance of no less than '180 yards'.[53] Likewise, shrapnel and explosive material was made out of materials such as 'baggin' cans, tin boxes for snuff, tobacco tins and various other metal objects.[54] To make these, a hole was put into the lid of the can which enabled a fuse to be put through and come out on the top. A further total of four holes were bored into the side of the cans while one more was made on either end of it which were then fastened with a bicycle adjuster normally used for altering a back wheel. The ends of these also protruded through the lid which was then fastened down tightly which completed the bomb.[55]

A number of other men, often leading officers in the ICA were also involved in this type of work. To ensure the success of such a practice, work had to be done on gathering explosives and scrap metal. James O'Shea contended that because he worked in a foundry and knew many 'republican sympathisers' he was able to get 'a lot of jobs done' in this regard.[56] Likewise, James O'Neill was a building contractor and when asked by the Advisory Committee of the Army Pensions Board in 1935 about what he was doing prior to the Easter Rising he replied 'preparing munitions'.[57] John White, who was an ICA member from 1913 to 1917, also was 'actively engaged in Liberty Hall assisting in the manufacture of munitions' during the month prior to Easter Week.[58] In 1915–16, Seamus McGowan was also involved in arms development.[59] O'Neill wrote that he 'was sent to assist me on many occasions when experimenting with guns and bombs. That was in 1915 and later still when I gave my whole time to the manufacturing of munitions.'[60] Fox suggested that George Norgrove and Elliot Elmes, amongst others, were deployed to assist McGowan and that their work led to the testing of weapons at St Enda's school in Rathfarnham as well as in the farm of Frank Lawless at Saucerstown, both in County Dublin.[61]

In order to ensure the success of the armaments work, explosives and scrap metal had to be gathered. Many of the ICA's soldiers worked in the city's dockyard or other manufacturing intensive locations which meant they could go about this work unnoticed by the police. Robbins stated that 'very often it was found that two or perhaps three Citizen Army men would have their eyes on the one sledgehammer'; items like this were used in the Royal College of Surgeons during Easter Week. From his own position working for the Dublin Dockyard Company, Robbins took some of the 7-lbs sledgehammers while other equipment that went missing included pieces of lathes, files and borings which were used in the preparation of the homemade propellants.[62] Furthermore, as Robbins worked for the Inchicore foundry, he was able to gather metal from there, as well as make contact with others who could provide the same assistance. Steel bars were made which were planned to be used as tools to force open doors. These bars were each about 18 inches long and designed to have a curve and lever at one end. Given his connections, O'Shea was 'a key man' in this project.[63] He detailed how the practice of establishing such crowbar-like equipment began. Through Mallin, Connolly had asked him if it was possible to get these types of bars and ordered him to start developing the most suitable type. Eventually he brought back to Connolly two samples, both of which were steel: one with a chisel and the chosen one which had a chisel point and a bend at each end. He described the process of how each of these was made: 'when the furnace was going about a half hour I used to retire up on stage with the steel bars cut to about eighteen inches put them in and with a big hammer I would put rough points on them, also bend. After that I got a friend at the benches to temper and put a final edge on them.'[64]

Similarly, O'Neill's work was of assistance to the ICA's attempt to create more weaponry. He was also suitably placed as his employment, from 1914 onwards, as a building contractor allowed him to have a permit for keeping and using explosives for work.[65] In 1915, he began work for a Captain Jones of the Lancer Regiment, building a house in Montpelier Hill.[66] According to Fox, Jones put him to work cutting nicks in lead pipes as part of an experiment for a new British Army bomb to be used in France. In his claim to the Army Pensions Board O'Neill gave more detail and outlined how Jones was making hand grenades.[67] His letter described how this evolved into the ICA's first explosive-making practice:

> I first learned how to make a bomb. This information I transferred to Jim Connolly, who was a close personal friend of mine and about August 1915 I demonstrated to him the manufacture and use of bombs. This took place at Croydon Park ... and was witnessed by Thomas Foran and J. Smith ... after the demonstration Connolly remarked to me that I had the honour of making and throwing the first grenade on behalf of the republic and added that before it is all over the people you are making them for will be throwing them at each other.[68]

O'Neill was then given instructions to make as many hand grenades as possible and to give them to Connolly. According to Christopher Crothers, McGowan and he began to make the grenades.[69] By the time Connolly vanished in January 1916, O'Neill had amassed and delivered 'quite a large amount' of explosives.[70] During Connolly's disappearance, Mallin ordered that all arms and explosives were to be collected and examined. After Connolly's reappearance on 22 January these grenades were left in a stockpile in Lucan.[71]

After this event, an old back room was used in Liberty Hall where McGowan and O'Neill had set up some old machines and manufactured 'all sorts of war equipment'.[72] Outside of the grenades, one of the projects was the creation of a machine gun. Robbins contended that this idea originated from 'a man named Hughes', probably Patrick Hughes, who was reputed to have been a veteran of a South American revolution.[73] Like the other munitions, the materials for this project came from a variety of engineering shops as well as the docklands 'without the knowledge of the owners' and it was hoped that the gun would have been made to use the makeshift shotgun cartridges that were also being developed.[74] McGowan claimed to have made four or five of these machines. However, this was dismissed by O'Neil who stated 'I wish he did'.[75] It appears that there were a number of failed attempts at making the weapon and that once it was eventually completed it was tested and found to be defective to a small degree. This was near to the date of the rebellion and given the conditions, Connolly felt that more time was needed to fix the flaw than could be afforded and thus he deemed that the work on the machinegun should be abandoned.[76] The development of a stockpile was not without casualties. A gun was fired accidently on 31 January 1916 wounding Hanratty. He was in hospital until 3 August 1916 and missed the Rising.[77]

This munitions and armament work caused consternation for the British authorities and both James O'Shea and James O'Neill received the attention of the DMP. The stockpile that O'Neill had left in Lucan was subsequently discovered in January by a gamekeeper and was reported to the police. The DMP believed that the material was there in preparation for an attack on Redmond and Asquith's train. An investigation into the incident found that O'Neill was buying explosives 'quite heavily'. This caused O'Neill to hide out away from his home.[78] Likewise, before 19 January, O'Shea was caught attempting to steal copper for his work creating crowbars. On 26 December 1915, he was arrested by G-men and once his affiliations were discovered he was questioned on the intentions of the ICA, where their rifles came from, and if Mallin's aims were true or if he was a British spy.[79] O'Shea eventually faced trial but was released sometime between late January and mid-March 1916.[80]

Such developments turned Liberty Hall into far more than a trade union centre. From early 1916 onwards, it began to resemble more of an army base than anything else. It operated as a barracks for the ICA, the location of printing for the proclamation of the soon to be declared republic, and a storehouse for weapons belonging to the entire republican forces. Collins contended that there were in essence two sides to the building. The ITGWU base upstairs where union activities and dues were organised and downstairs where the planning of the revolution occurred.[81] Indeed, the ITGWU's minutes for the period reveal that no matters regarding the ICA were discussed by Branch No. 1 between 29 September 1915 and 12 April 1916.[82] This indicated how separate these activities were. Frederick Norgrove, who was on 'armoury work' at this time, recalled how during these months the ICA were getting everything ready for the rebellion in Liberty Hall. Up until the day before the insurrection it was increasingly becoming a base of operations where the necessary tools for revolt were being gathered. During a royal commission's hearing on the matter, the Right Hon. Lord Wimborne, P.C. described a letter he wrote to Chief Secretary Augustine Birrell on 23 April 1916. According to him, it read:

Nathan will not have time to write by this post, so I send this in haste to let you know that this morning two men held up the caretaker of the magazine of the quarry works at Tulla, 10 miles south-west of Dublin, and abstracted 200 lbs. of gelignite which they conveyed to Liberty Hall. The object of this theft is not known, but it may be connected with a threat to Mr. Watson that one of his ships (City of Dublin Steam Packet Company) would be blown up on the 24th instant. It may be also that it was stolen for a still more sinister purpose.[83]

On the same day as this arrival, Connolly spoke to the Citizen Army in order to impress upon them the significant degree to which they had become a proper army and the level to which the centre of Larkinism had become an army base. After a republican flag was raised on the roof of Liberty Hall and bugles were sounded in traditional military fashion, he told the soldiers around him that this was their barracks and that they were not to leave until called upon to defend the flag that had been hoisted.[84] In truth, for many Beresford Place had become a near permanent base since the middle of March when there was a succession of mobilisations of the labour army to protect the labour centre from raids by British forces.[85] There was a squad of Irish Citizen Army soldiers based there from March onwards. O'Shea recollected that this was around 18 or 19 March 1916.[86] Seditious activities by the Citizen Army and more so by the Volunteers had increased pressure on the British authorities to respond more forcefully. March 1916 saw a series of raids and the seizures of politically radical newspapers such as the *Gael*. This in turn necessitated the guarding of the labour building.

On 8 August 1914, four days after Britain had entered World War I, the Westminster Parliament passed a Defence of the Realm Act (DORA) which granted 'His Majesty in Council' powers to ensure the safety of 'any means of communication' as well as to prevent any communication with Axis forces.[87] In August of that year, an amendment was made which stipulated that this also extended to the power 'to prevent the spread of reports likely to cause disaffection or alarm'.[88] With the publication of DORA, warnings were given by the British Army on 2 December 1914 to the printers of *The Irish Volunteer*, *Irish Freedom*, *Sinn Féin*, *The Leader* and the *Irish Worker* amongst others, regarding the seditious nature of the publications. Two days later the *Irish Worker*'s next edition was published and it was felt by the authorities that it 'still contained matters contravening the regulations'. All copies of the paper were seized and the removable parts of the printer as well as the type were confiscated.[89] By March 1916, such raids were not unknown to the Citizen Army. However, given that the ICA's base had become an arsenal, the stakes were much higher and a police search was not something which could have been afforded. In Rose Hackett's words 'as there was a lot of ammunition and stuff being made at Liberty Hall, it would have been serious, at that stage, if it were to be seized'.[90]

Throughout summer 1915, DMP reports stated that apart from a few paragraphs, the *Workers' Republic* did not contain anything warranting serious attention.[91] It was not until 5 November 1915 that DMP reports viewed the paper, along with *Nationality*, as one which contained 'notes of an anti-British character'.[92] However, Liberty Hall sold other subversive newspapers and was still at risk from unwanted official attention in March 1916. Following the government's decision to suppress the nationalist paper the *Gael*, of which some 1,000 copies were seized from Joe Stanley's printing works on Liffey Street, another attempt to access the material at Eden Quay was made by the DMP on 26 March. This led to another, and final, mobilisation of the ICA.[93] After the raids on Stanley's, the *Gael's* type frames were brought to Liberty Hall.[94] ICA soldiers such as Robbins and Martin Kelly were armed as they attempted to get the frames.[95] After the DMP finished in Stanley's, they turned their attention to the shop in Eden Quay run by Jane Shanahan and Helena Molony.[96] This shop not only sold copies of seditious newspapers such as *Spark* and the *Nation*, but it was also the location of where the 'the work of the women's section of the Irish Citizen Army started in earnest'. For instance, items such as the grey-backed shirts which were worn in the '[General] Post Office garrison' were made there at the time.[97] Perhaps most importantly, the shop led directly into the printing room in Liberty Hall.[98] Michael Molloy, who worked on the printing of the 1916 proclamation, stated that the 'main purpose' of the police raid on 26 March was to locate the position of the printing press used by Connolly.[99] According to Joseph Brady, the attempt was understood by 'those in the hall' as a tool to garner 'a general survey' given the degree to which the mood of revolution was palpable.[100]

Hackett's and Brady's versions of the raid on 26 March differ in one respect; she contended that she was alone in the shop when the DMP raid occurred, while he wrote of seeing three women behind the counter. However, both recalled the police had no warrant for their actions and that Connolly, when he arrived from upstairs, saw the DMP's agents holding papers and told them 'drop them, I will drop you'.[101] Both also spoke of a sense of anxiety felt while waiting for the police to return. Hackett said that nothing was found when the DMP reappeared, but this did not diminish the significance of the mobilisation. Brady contended that within an hour a large contingent of ICA men had gathered around to defend the building while through the rest of the day Hackett could see them 'in their working clothes, coming from all directions of the city to [Liberty] Hall'.[102] According to the following week's *Workers' Republic*, when the DMP did eventually return 'the defenders had been augmented, and the Countess among others was lovingly toying with a large automatic, while a number of rifles were pepping round the corner'.[103]

In a manner, the 26 March mobilisation was the successful acid test of Kain's mobilisation system.[104] Certainly, the CMO was sought out by Connolly as the order travelled to a variety of places across the city. O'Shea had arrived at Liberty Hall not long after the first attempted DMP raid and passed Connolly, who was carrying a loaded .45 calibre gun, at the stairs. He was told to go to room number seven where he found Markievicz who was also armed and Nora Connolly 'writing in a hurry' and 'working hell for leather signing the papers'. He was then ordered to make his way out of the building, past the G-men who had camped outside and deliver the notes at once to Kain at Arran Quay.[105] Brady also recorded that the Countess had told him 'Christy, when you get to Emmet Hall and see Commandant Mallin, tell him to see Tom Keane [*sic*] and he is to get the guns.'[106]

Kain stated to the Advisory Committee of the Army Pensions Board that the order quickly travelled across the city. He detailed that he 'was responsible for all the mobilisation. Connolly asked me to devise a scheme of mobilisation, to get the addresses from the men, and also to be able to mobilise them from their work.' He continued that 'as a result of that, the time the military authorities raided Liberty Hall, I was able to mobilise the men in a very short time'.[107] That day Robbins had been in conversation with Elliot Elmes at the dockyard when they were stopped and were given an order signed by Lieut. Kelly which told them to get their section organised immediately, fully armed, and to proceed to their headquarters by the Liffey.[108] O'Shea described the mobilisation as a 'great success' where jobs were stopped and men ran out of 'foundries, fitting shops, forges and building jobs' while carters left their horses in the street while they got their rifles.[109] Many went so far as to bring their horses with them to the quay.[110] In the same vein as the O'Donovan Rossa funeral, Maeve Cavanagh wrote a poem honouring the incident. Entitled 'The Call to Arms', the last stanza read 'They kept their vigil, brave and true/ No foe their fort assailed/ The British Bull-dog, loath to woo/ New dangers, backed and quailed,/ And slunk to kennel, baffled, sore,/ Too scared to bark or bite,/ To weave his dastard plots once more/ 'Gainst me he dare not fight.'[111] A week before the publication of this poem, the ICA's notes argued that the British government had made a 'coup' in an attempt to discourage the 'national forces' by attempting to supress all of their papers; the article read that 'endeth the first chapter' and asked 'who will write the next?'[112]

The majority of those who arrived at Liberty Hall on 26 March ended up spending the night at the base and slept in various rooms on bare boards in the building without any covering.[113] From this time onwards, a permanent guard operated in the building which worked in shifts.[114] While some kept their arms at home for fear of another raid, 'two big halls' were used in the building for their stockpile.[115] William Oman, who during this time had spent four weeks between the Meath Hospital and Stillorgen Convalescent Home for appendicitis, returned to what he described as an 'armed camp'. From then until Easter Monday, Oman formed part of a permanent guard on the building.[116] Oman was not atypical of the force. Elliot Elmes had been mobilised from the month previous to the rebellion where he was in the ICA headquarters 'nearly all the time'.[117] Likewise, Christopher Crothers left his home about two weeks before Easter Week and was based there permanently.[118] The chief mobilising officer, while not there all day and night, was based there during the daytime and in the week before the rebellion he gave up his job entirely and 'lived in Liberty Hall'.[119] The guard system operated in a manner where those who were unemployed were expected to remain there all the time while those who worked were 'allowed' to do so and expected to do about three or four nights of armed guard duty a week.[120] This process of being 'under arms' in the base acted as an important deterrent against the authorities. Right up until Easter Sunday, 1916, Nathan and Lord Lieutenant Wimborne had deliberated over the possibility of another search of Liberty Hall. This was abandoned after it was decided that such an attempt would have needed artillery.[121] Had Liberty Hall not been under guard, it is unlikely that such measures would have been necessary.

Such activity was typical of a garrison preparing for insurgency and was aptly described by Matthew Connolly:

a constant armed guard was being kept, day and night, on the premises, particularly on the machine room ... during these weeks immediately preceding the [Easter] Rising, armed men could be seen, on guard at the entrance, on the stairs and landing or in the corridors, some in dark green uniform, some in their ordinary clothes … they were all fully armed, and the building resembled a military barracks in everything but in name.[122]

Simultaneous to munitions creation, ammunition was collected from around different Dublin centres on a handcart which was then brought back to Liberty Hall for storage.[123] Sometime between early and mid-April, Robbins was part of an armed group sent by Connolly to Seán MacDermott's house on the North Circular Road near Russell Street. They were ordered to resist any inquiries or interference from the DMP and when they reached the rebel leader's dwelling they were met with a number of cases filled with shotguns. These were loaded up onto the handcart and brought back to the base.[124] In mid-April, 3,000 rounds of shotgun cartridges were brought from the Larkfield garrison in Kimmage to Liberty Hall where men were 'put to work on them' for four days. This involved taking out the shot with which they were filled, melting it down with extra lead and then moulding it into 'buck shot slugs and refilling the cartridge as the slugs cooled.'[125] In the immediate period before Easter Week, the women's section of the ICA was busy preparing supplies. Hackett, amongst others, was 'terribly busy' making knapsacks as well as first-aid packs.[126] Similarly, Mary Allen recalled being in Liberty Hall 'doing first aid all the time'.[127] While this type of training began in 1915, the ICA's notes in January and February 1916 continued to assert the importance of the work. A guide specifically prepared for the ICA entitled 'Irish Freedom: First Aid Outfit' was published which detailed twelve types of injury and what to do if these occurred.[128] A week later another article appeared which was labelled 'First Aid on the Battlefield'.[129] Food supplies also had to be prepared and the women's section of the force was also involved in this. On Easter Sunday, food was being prepared upstairs, large joints were cooked and 'the co-operative girls' were cutting bread, butter and cooked meat.[130]

The final significance of the ICA headquarters as a garrison in April 1916 was that it was used to print the Proclamation of the Irish Republic. On Good Friday, William O'Brien, Joseph Brady and Michael Molloy were called to Connolly's office and told that there was work.[131] On 21 April 1916, Thomas MacDonagh had told the military council about MacNeill's countermanding order. Likewise, they had become aware of Casement's arrest in Kerry as well as that the *Aud* had sunk. Despite the knowledge of the countermanding order and the other problems, on Good Friday the three men were brought upstairs in Liberty Hall and introduced to MacDonagh who handed them out the document to be transferred to type. As was usual in the building, Citizen Army men were guarding the room while the document was being printed.[132] It does seem that ICA members were also on a special post in order to protect the room. No one was allowed to contact the printers. Even Markievicz had to wait upon the re-arrival of Connolly. In order to do this, soldiers stood guard at three areas: the fanlight over the entrance at the co-operative stores, the door leading into the machine room at the concert hall, and at the rear entrance.[133] Some 2,500 copies were eventually printed, parcelled up and delivered to Helena Molony.[134]

Clearly, the ICA had turned Liberty Hall into a military base in the immediate period before the rebellion, but, this had implications for their relationship with their old parent body, the ITGWU. Connolly had hoped that the trade union front and the revolutionary underground could have acted together in order to encourage every shade of nationalist sentiment. Certainly the conditions of some working-class families were improved by the separation allowances which were received by the spouses of British Army servicemen. This in turn made a 'spontaneous rising' less likely. It was, then, even more important for the ICA to appeal to the wider labour movement. Greaves considered a lecture held on St Patricks Day on the theme of Robert Emmet to be part of this strategy.[135] However, the ICA did not take part in this commemoration. Speaking at the event Connolly objected to the presence of the more moderate and less rebellious Eoin MacNeill and Bulmer Hobson.[136] The evolution of the labour militia as well as its nationalist Volunteer sibling, and the ICA's position between revolutionary radicalism, trade unionism and nationalist agitation was encapsulated in that moment. By March 1916, radicalism had developed to the point where Connolly was willing to deal with, and join with, the IRB's military council, yet the ICA refused to associate with the less seditious leaders of the Óglaigh. This was contrasted by the ITGWU standing on the same platform as the less militant republicans.

On 8 April 1916, the *Workers' Republic* announced the decision to hoist a green flag over Liberty Hall.[137] The paper was clear that this was an ICA decision and not one made by the ITGWU. It was decided by the ICA council 'as a symbol of [their] faith in freedom', to show a 'fortress' held by Irish arms as an emblem of 'national redemption' and a re-born Ireland.[138] This decision raised 'murmurs of dissent' from members of the ITGWU.[139] While the base had been turned into an arsenal, the public nature of the potential display and the response from British authorities that it might bring may have been the cause for such dissent. The 12 April minutes of Branch No. 1 of the ITGWU included a proposal from William Fairtlough, and seconded by William O'Toole, to open a discussion to the general members on the matter of the raising of the flag.[140] Upon the suggestion of Thomas Foran, five people agreed to hold a special meeting the next day to allow Connolly to 'discuss the question' and to see if the matter could be resolved. At this meeting, Fairtlough along with S. Kelsh, F. Fitzgerald, A. Leahy and J. Farrell continued to argue that a public plebiscite was needed. Connolly replied that he had taken up a position from which he was not going to retreat and would resign, ostensibly to stop rumours of disunity. This action led to a private discussion between Farrell and Connolly, after which the motion was withdrawn and it was agreed to raise the flag.[141]

For Robbins, perhaps tainted by his union involvement, the flag issue was not evidence of any 'open hostility' between the two shades of labour, which any 'reasoning and sensible people' would see.[142] While it was serious enough to almost bring about a change in trade union leadership, there was truth to his claim that it was the most acrimonious incident that had occurred between the two bodies during the previous three years. However, what it did reveal was that Connolly, who struggled to achieve a majority in favour of his proposal, would not have been able to bring the union into the same political space as the ICA. There was no possibility that the union would take any official part in the revolution.[143] While internal labour relations had not irrevocably split, the army and the ITGWU were certainly now on different paths. There is no record of what was said between the president/ commandant and Farrell but any contention that Farrell changed his mind after being informed that the rebellion was near, seems unlikely. Hanratty stated that the militia had agreed to leave the Beresford Place building upon the establishment of an Irish republic and it is likely that this was the reason that allowed the flag to be hoisted.[144] That event marked the weakest connection between the two bodies since the Transport Union Citizen Army was created. However, considering that the ICA was about to be subsumed into a wider republican army, it was natural that they had planned to move away from the trade union base to a building befitting a state army.

By midnight on 22 April 1916, Eoin MacNeill's countermanding order was beginning to travel to the various counties and thus rescinded all manoeuvres for the following day, 'owing to the very critical situation'. This was a cleverly written message and the deeper meaning of terms such as the 'critical situation' and 'other movements' would not have been lost on the most informed republican figures who would understand he was granting no sanction for a rising. The ordinary Volunteers were also likely to simply follow the instructions as given by their chief of staff.[145] Importantly though, as this was not an IRB document, it had no official implications for the ICA. Indeed, in Liberty Hall many members of the Citizen Army were inclined to take the demobilisation 'lightly'.[146] Yet, as the ICA's plans had become entirely intertwined with the plans of the IRB and the Irish Volunteers, the decision was made to simply bring the labour soldiers on a route march. This also had the benefit of avoiding intense police attention at Liberty Hall.[147]

At about 16:00 they received their order and set out across Butt Bridge, along College Green, down to Dublin Castle, and back to Liberty Hall which was 'more like a military barracks than a trade union'.[148] Not only did this reveal the degree of the intertwining of the republican militias but also the willingness and desire for revolution on the part of the ICA. Easter Sunday, for the workers' army, was marked by an atmosphere of despair and anger. In Norgrove's words 'we were all tensed up and nothing happened and on our arrival back in the hall the men were told they were to be confined to their barracks'.[149] McGowan recalled that the emotional turmoil was so much for Seán Connolly that with tears streaming down his face, he threw off his gear and said to James Connolly 'here is my equipment, do what you like with it'. Apparently, others had the same response.[150] Robbins recalled the general mood and wrote 'some cursed. Some prayed that things would be righted. Others went gloomily, while others forced a smile, saying better luck next time'.[151]

Despite this, throughout 23 April, preparations for the following day were constant. At 10:00 a meeting of the IRB's military council was held in room number seven of Liberty Hall and did not dissolve until 16:00, suggesting that it was immediately after its culmination that the ICA route march was undertaken.[152] McGowan also took the 'entire IRB council' on an inspection of the munitions and stores held in Beresford Place. Given the timeframe it is probably true that this occurred before the meeting took place.[153] Connolly also made a number of promotions in order for them to have the authority needed in battle. Thomas Kain remembered how, on Good Friday, a number of people were commissioned 'who practically held no rank previous to that'.[154] On Easter Sunday, O'Neill and McGowan became quartermaster and assistant quartermaster respectively.[155] O'Shea also recalled how officer commissions were handed out the previous day and Christopher Poole produced a complete list of these which identified General James Connolly, Commandant Michael Mallin, Staff Captain Christopher Poole, Captain Seán Connolly, Captain Richard McCormick, Captain John O'Neill, Lieut. Michael Kelly, Lieut. Thomas Kain, Lieut. Robert de Coeur, Lieut. Thomas Donoghue, Lieut. P. Jackson, Lieut. Countess Markievicz.[156] As will be detailed further in the succeeding chapters, the rebellion marked a merging of both republican militias. This then raises the questions of why the promotions were made so shortly before the ICA was to cease as an independent force. It is likely that it was largely due to the work they would have to do during the rebellion. According to Christopher Crothers, 'prior to the [Easter] Rising they were given the rank of staff captain for the purpose of being able to take control of any number of men that would be given to them when the fight actually broke out'.[157] It might have also been that in case of Connolly's own death and if a socialist republic was not established, this would have ensured continuity if they split with the Volunteer movement. Connolly was reported to have said to his force 'in the event of victory, hold on to your rifles, as those with whom we are fighting may stop before our goal is reached. We are out for economic as well as political liberty'.[158]

Yet, despite such rhetoric the grander unifying cause was not lost. Connolly continued to be at pains to stress that Liberty Hall was now an army garrison and before the soldiers spent their final peace time night he pointed to the building and told them 'this is your barracks'.[159] For Connolly, as well as those marching and encamped in Beresford Place, they felt that they were no longer merely members of a socialist workers' army but that they were the nation's combatants. Oman contended that they 'were to consider themselves soldiers' while Rose Hackett wrote that 'every man and woman, and every boy and girl, that had marched on this day were now soldiers of Ireland'.[160] Here, on the final day before the rebellion, their political allegiances were made clear. John O'Keffe recollected that some days before the insurrection, his leader stated that 'being the lesser party we join in this fight with our comrades of the Irish Volunteers. But hold your arms. If we succeed, those who are our comrades today we may be compelled to fight tomorrow'.[161] However, too much should not be made of this seeming prophecy of civil war. The men and women of the Citizen Army were also told by their commandant that there was no longer an ICA nor an Irish Volunteers but an army of the Irish Republic.[162] In his pension claim, George

Oman phrased it eloquently when he stated 'the Citizen Army ceased to exist on Monday of Easter Week'.[163] Likewise, for James O'Neill 'when the joint forces were brought together on Easter Sunday there was no distinction between the Volunteers and the Citizen Army'.[164] As succeeding chapters highlight, divisions between the republican militias were perceived to have been eradicated and they were to play out the struggle for independence as part of a wider republican force. Only if their comrades failed to adhere to a total holistic revolution would the ICA break away. The complexity of the ICA's relationship with the Irish Volunteers was best expressed by John Hanratty in 1955.

> During the [Easter] Rising the Irish Citizen Army had to shelve its identity, for as their leader James Connolly told them on the eve of the [Easter] Rising: 'You are going out to fight not as the Irish Citizen Army, not as Irish Volunteers but as soldiers of the Irish Republic.' But while they may have shelved their identity, they never really lost it, as witness the despatch notifying the unconditional surrender of the GPO garrison and its environ with James Connolly's specific agreement for similar action by the Citizen Army in the Stephen's Green command. The document was signed by P.H. Pearse as well.[165]

9

'BAPTISM OF FIRE': STEPHEN'S GREEN AND THE ROYAL COLLEGE OF SURGEONS

At Liberty Hall on Monday, 24 April 1916, James Connolly, Pádraig Pearse as well as a contingent of Irish Volunteers and ICA soldiers marched along Eden Quay and down Sackville Street. Seamus Robinson and five others, equipped with a rifle, two shotguns, two 'small arms' and a supply of homemade explosives, succeeded in capturing a building in Bachelor's Walk. The others proceeded to the General Post Office where the proclamation was read out by Pearse and the rebellion was instigated.[1] Previous to this, the Citizen Army's soldiers had gathered and were counted by Connolly and Mallin before a list of names was read out as Mallin gave a speech that was 'to the point with no word wasted'.[2] About a week before this the officers had been informed of their positions but it was at this point when each man knew his squad as well as his posting. This was at around 05:00 on Monday 24 April, and once finished, final preparations were made. Rifles were cleaned and oiled while the equipment was given a last examination. James O'Shea saw:

> women working … with a bread cutting machine … they were cutting bread and meat as rations. Also, there was another squad working on bandages and iodine. Each man had issued to him two days' rations and a first aid outfit. There was a crowd of men with Seamus McGowan at bombs, filling and packing them. There was the last-minute rush going on.[3]

At 11:30 William Oman sounded the fall-in both inside and outside Liberty Hall. As he assembled and fell into marching order he watched as the Volunteers from the Kimmage Garrison marched in front of Liberty Hall.

This symbolised the unity of the two militias whose relationship was once defined by antagonism. Oman was standing beside Captain Seán Connolly and overheard James Connolly, now the commandant general of the Dublin Division, tell him 'good luck Seán. We won't meet again.' Commandant General Connolly also told Seán Connolly the length of time he had at his disposal to get to Dublin Castle.[4] With that the City Hall garrison led by Captain Connolly left the building to reach their base. Michael Mallin and Richard McCormick were also charged with leading the largest ICA garrison to their base in St Stephen's Green.[5]

Not only was the St Stephen's Green section the largest group of ICA soldiers but it also was the location of fighting for both its second-in-command, Mallin, and its most famed female volunteer, Lieut. Markievicz. Furthermore, action in the GPO was a combined effort with republican forces while the City Hall occupation was a much smaller affair. The Green covered about a total of twenty-two acres of uncovered land and was about a quarter of a mile long.[6] Importantly, unlike the General Post Office with obvious telecommunication implications and City Hall as the seat of local government in the city, this open area was not only of insignificant military value but also as a wide space it was a tactical nightmare for the insurgents engaging in asymmetrical warfare.[7] O'Brien has argued that the area was to have been used as a 'transport depot' which was capable of acting as a link for the bases of the joint forces throughout the city.[8] While Fox noted that as a central location with a running supply of fresh water (something which Connolly had stressed the need for) it was not only a 'space for transport' but also 'a base for activities throughout the city'.[9] Certainly, the Green was a transport centre for those approaching the city from the south-east of Dublin.[10] Captain Richard McCormick had been told by Connolly that '500 men [were] to occupy [the] Green [as] it was to be a base for [the] wounded on account of [the] water supply. Also men could be transferred to any point on the Green to repel the advance of British troops.'[11]

Nonetheless, the St Stephen's Green section was different from the other bases occupied during the week. The others were far more strategically located or symbolically important. Certainly, Mallin's mobilisation plans, which detailed a Citizen Army cordon around key areas, included Dublin Castle and City Hall, as well as Sackville Street and Liberty Hall, indicated no movement in the Green.[12] Furthermore, Connolly was of the opinion that the Green was a more dangerous location than the ICA's other main garrison, City Hall.[13]

Before any of the soldiers arrived at St Stephen's Green, positions had to be taken where a small body of men could delay the British Army coming from Portobello Barracks. Led by Captain Richard McCormick and Christopher Poole, this type of obstructing tactics was typical of Mallin's instructions and was one of the more successful features of the Green garrison. According to Robbins, McCormick took command of the job which was 'to engage and delay the advance of the British troops approaching from Portobello and Wellington Barracks long enough to allow the main section of our forces to dig themselves into their allotted defence positions in St Stephen's Green'.[14] McCormick claimed to have been in charge of 'four outposts' near the Green. However, statements made by Poole and Christopher Crothers argued that it was Poole who was the senior officer in this project.[15] Both captains, however, were in agreement that the orders for the Green mission were to 'check the enemy's advance' and to 'hold the enemy in check until the positions were taken up'.[16] For this to be completed, Sergeant Joseph Doyle commanded a section of sixteen men at Davy's public house which faced Portobello Bridge in order 'to dominate the bridge' and, once the British Army were in range, to delay them as long as possible. Lieut. Michael Kelly took charge of another section of sixteen which took position at the railway bridge over the Grand Canal in an attempt to support Doyle's men and to cover them during their retreat.[17] John O'Neill was to support Kelly's men by occupying the railway bridge over Harcourt Road while the temporary headquarters was to be in the railway station on that road.[18] Certainly, that location was one of the better placed in order to halt the British soldiers crossing from Portobello.[19]

This practice of delay and support was typical of the guidelines set out by Mallin in his Citizen Army notebook.[20] After cutting tramway wires at the railway bridge, Doyle's men were successful in occupying the public house and at circa 13:30 they were faced with British soldiers coming from the barracks. They fired upon these men causing their withdrawal. A similar incident also occurred before 16:00 when they were ordered by McCormick to fall back onto the railway station having archived the goal of obstructing British troop movements. At the same time Kelly's force also received this message and returned to the temporary headquarters in the railway station.[21] According to Robbins, 'the British had in fact attempted to advance from the barracks in Rathmines by way of Portobello Bridge, but after a brief encounter with our men in Davy's they beat a hasty retreat'.[22]

Certainly, the tactics used near Portobello Bridge were successful, but the Citizen Army's manoeuvres in St Stephen's Green were generally one of the less effective aspects of the rebels' plans. It has been contended by Hughes that the most salient feature about Mallin's rebellion experience was that it was different from his didactic articles which appeared in the *Workers' Republic* from spring 1915 onwards.[23] One of the strongest messages that Mallin had tried to inculcate was the importance of terrain and the use of geography as an advantage. He had written of the effectiveness of street fighting in that the larger body of men could be hemmed in which granted an advantage to the smaller unit. Yet, during the Easter Rising his men camped in one of the least built-up spaces in the city.[24] According to McCormick, it was 17:00 when they eventually departed through the 'line left [of the] rail and through Stephen's across from [the] train coming in'. After this, they 'fell back on Harcourt Street as ordered then [the] whole party returned on[*sic*] [the] Green'.[25]

According to the royal commission which reported on the rebellion in Ireland, the revolutionary soldiers began arriving at St Stephen's Green in 'two and threes' and by 11:50 they had been reported to the police for locking civilians out.[26] This included a gardener who was ordered to hand over his keys as well as a Roman Catholic priest who was shortly let back in to hear confessions before leaving again.[27] Immediately afterwards, the republican forces began to fortify their position: the houses around the square were examined by Mallin and others. The most suitable places for occupation were then selected to house the ICA's best shooters. Barricades were built up using all the available vehicles.[28] In his *The Insurrection in Dublin*, James Stephens described one of these barricades: 'in the centre of this side of the park a rough barricade of carts and motor cars had been sketched. It was still full of gaps. Behind it was a halted tram, and along the vistas of the Green one saw other trams derelict, untenanted.'[29] One of the most visual and important tactics initiated at this point which did adhere to Mallin's principles, was the digging of trenches. The process was described by James O'Shea: 'we marked out a trench or gun pit in front of the railings and looking towards Dawson Street. We dug for a couple of hours and made a nice job of it, putting some bushes around it as camouflage. We made a shelf for bombs and the shotguns of two lads.'[30] F.X. Martin has understood the construction of these trenches as 'the high point of futility'.[31] Hughes contended that the use of these channels may have derived from Mallin's experience in India and a wider awareness of its use on the continent during World War I.[32]

Undoubtedly the trenches were completed to ensure adequate protective fortifications and create a siege-like situation in which the Green could be held. The major problem for the ICA garrison was the lack of men, which made it impossible to occupy the nearby Shelbourne Hotel and led to a 'hold' type tactic.[33] However, there were a number of problems with the trenches. Firstly, some of the trenches were not built to be fit for purpose. O'Donoghue noted one that was only 12" by 12". 'Such parameters renders it worthless in contrast to the type of trenches Mallin had described in 1915.' The trenches in India established a 'state of defence by digging deep and very wide trenches … too wide for the troops to jump across'.[34] Secondly, as the trenches in St Stephen's Green were being dug it was noticed that the soil had begun to roll down the grass outside the bushes. This indicated to those watching that not only was this practice being used but also identified their location which rendered this type of camouflage useless.[35] The openness of the Green terrain was also a weakness as the British Army gained good vantage from the overlooking buildings and exposed the republican army to fire.

While the use of trenches in the Green was not successful, the erection of barricades outside of the Green did prove to be a success. Seamus Kavanagh detailed how he 'went round to the different gate entrances into the Green, and got the men to erect barricades inside and dig trenches with the small number of trench tools' which we had'.[36] In the same way as Mallin's notes on trench construction, this tactic had been learned by the ICA from Connolly's lectures on street fighting.[37] All of Monday 24 April was spent using 'carts, cars, furniture and other large items' in order to create these blockades.[38] O'Donoghue 'stopped many cars of all descriptions and put them in the barricade'.[39] It is true that not all of these blockades were sufficient as cars returning from the Fairyhouse races were able to pass at Harcourt Street despite the heavy fire.[40]

It is arguable that if the orders for the Green were simply to take and hold the park, digging the trenches, however ineffective they were, was about the only thing that could be done to secure some safety.[41] It is true that they provided valuable cover for Johnnie McDonnell and ICA man Thomas O'Donoghue. During a barrage on Tuesday morning, both men used a rifle trench in the centre of the pathway in the Green for refuge.[42] However, its limitations were revealed as it was after this salvo that Mallin told O'Shea that it had become necessary to evacuate to the Royal College of Surgeons in Ireland (RCSI).[43] In truth, the park was never suitable for any sustained occupation.[44] By Monday evening, the inadequacy of military supplies in the Green had already become apparent. A group which consisted of Robbins, Fred Ryan, John Joe Hendrick, David O'Leary, Markievicz, Mary Hyland

and Lily Kempson were sent to take over and hold the RCSI building. According to Robbins, this had a two-fold purpose. Firstly, in order to search for rifles and ammunition in the Officers' Training Corps attached to the RCSI and then to return to the Green. Secondly, Robbins and three men were to continue to occupy the medical institute.[45] However, it was not until Thursday that they found a stockpile of eighty-nine rifles and 24,000 rounds of ammunition.[46] Instead of leaving only four volunteers there, conditions in the Green were worsening to the extent that on Monday night there were about sixty republican soldiers stationed in the Royal College of Surgeons.[47]

Furthermore, an attack on Tuesday morning forced the entire republican body to fall back into the RCSI. O'Shea recalled the assault that happened during daybreak on Easter Tuesday when the British forces mounted machine guns at the Shelbourne Hotel and the United Services Club. These guns were used to 'rake the Green up and down. All the bushes and grass along the railings got it.' O'Shea had to lie still for close to half an hour until the machine guns stopped firing. However, after that snipers began to shoot at any known trenches. He described how he 'got hell for about an hour or more' and that this volley resulted in the death of one republican.[48] Estimates of the deaths caused by this volley have varied. Foy and Barton cited the belief of the British officer who commanded the hotel that the casualties numbered eleven while they also referenced Fox's contention that there were only a few fatalities.[49] Stephens wrote that 'inside the Green's railings four bodies could be seen lying on the ground. They were dead Volunteers.'[50] Another facet of this attack which caused consternation for the ICA's soldiers was that the shooting also peppered the Red Cross centre in the park established on Easter Monday. For Robbins 'the British [Army] flagrantly abused the sanctuary of our Red Cross shelter ... near the south-west corner of the Green and which had a large Red Cross flag flying from it'. He believed 'there was no legitimate reason or excuse for their action'.[51] Certainly, it was not long after this that the order was given by Mallin to evacuate for the Royal College of Surgeons.[52] Robbins stated that 'it was quite evident that our comrades within Stephen's Green could not continue to remain there because of the open space which did not afford sufficient cover. Consequently, Mallin took the earliest opportunity of issuing an order to relieve to the RCSI.'[53]

As well as those who moved to the RCSI, all those belonging to the ICA's boys' corps were ordered to go home entirely, further reducing the numbers in the garrison. Crothers stated 'at about 13:00 on Tuesday

Madame Markievicz came to me and told me she wanted all the boys. I went around and the only boys I came upon were Paddy Butler and Mick Dwyer and I brought them over and Madame instructed us to leave the post and go home as it was too dangerous, we were so young.'[54] It was noon when Peter Bermingham went to the York Street gate to join his comrades in the RCSI building while Crothers left between 13:00 and 15:00.[55] After they and all the others had gone Mallin, Michael Kelly and O'Shea were the last to leave the Green.[56] It was just before 15:00 when a British Military Operations Circular stated that the park had been freed of all rebels. By the following day the imperial authorities had seized control and occupied St Stephen's Green.[57]

Crossing over from the Green to the RCSI was no easy task. Wisely, O'Donoghue had advised the soldiers that while they were to take the shortest route, 'under no circumstances' were two men to go through the same bush or rush in the same manner or same direction so to prevent the machinegun from pre-selecting its target.[58] In an Old IRA Literary Society lecture, Robbins stated that 'it was during the retirement from the Green that we sustained our first losses, a small number of our men being killed and wounded'.[59] O'Shea remembered thinking that they were fighting against good marksmen as he concentrated his fire upon the windows of the Shelbourne Hotel. He was proved right as it was during the exit from the Green when Michael Doherty was sprayed with rounds from a machine gun. O'Shea remarked 'I actually saw the bullets strike him. The side of his face seemed to be gone.'[60]

As well as the onslaught from the British soldiers, the republican soldiers faced attacks from civilians. Indeed, McCormick told Hanratty that the crowd were 'hostile' upon the evacuation and that he was jostled on York Street.[61] At another point Robbins looked down York Street towards Aungier Street and saw McCormick, Kelly and Michael Donnelly facing difficulty. They had left No. 113 St Stephen's Green and had attempted to access the RCSI via a rear laneway but were 'beset' by a number of non-combatants. Robbins recollected that 'one man had a hatchet, others had different weapons, including iron bars. Blood was oozing from Captain McCormick's forehead. All this took place outside the line of fire from the British. There were about ten or twelve civilians involved in this incident.'[62] While not all of Dublin's inhabitants were unsympathetic to the republicans, this type of aggression was not surprising given the prevalence of 'separation women' who would have been dependant on separation allowance and whose husbands were reliant on British Army pay. The feelings of the city's civilians were put aptly by Stephens;

> Was the city for or against the Volunteers? Was it for the Volunteers, and yet against the [Easter] Rising? It is considered now (writing a day or two afterwards) that Dublin was entirely against the Volunteers, but on the day of which I write no such certainty could be put forward. There was a singular reticence on the subject. Men met and talked volubly, but they said nothing that indicated a personal desire or belief ... no expression of opinion for or against was anywhere formulated.[63]

Once the first arrivals reached the RCSI, they did not face difficulty taking control and securing it. Upon arrival at the front door, it was quickly realised that it was nearly vacant and while it took a 'length' of time to open the front door, after this was done they quickly gained control of it. This indicated that despite a day of action in the neighbouring park, the British forces did not think of defending the RCSI. This is surprising given the Officer Training Corps stockpile that was housed there.[64] Once entrance had been gained, Mallin was informed of the arrival of the other republican soldiers. The caretaker was also questioned. He and his family were eventually locked up after an orange sash was found in his room. This sash would have indicated unionist principles which went against the republican ideals that the ICA were then fighting for. The front door was then locked and barricaded with 'anything moveable'. The back door at the corner of York Street was seen as a safe door to have unlocked and one soldier was posted there with the order to let in those who were thought to have been friends of the republicans.[65] However, one of the unintended consequences of locking the front door was that it made it more difficult for people such as O'Shea and Mallin to find safety. Once they had exited the Green via York Street and 'broke cover' all 'hell was let loose'. After they found the front door closed they were attacked by 'one of the soldiers' women'. While O'Shea fixed his bayonet at her, Mallin took all precautions to avoid civilian casualties and they were able to rush to the back door and were let in after hammering at it with the butts of their rifles.[66] Once inside, Robbins barricaded the door and Mallin rhetorically asked him 'wasn't that a narrow shave?'[67] Mallin had come so close to the firing line that a bullet had pierced his hat.[68]

Simultaneously, in order to secure the College of Surgeons, watchmen were positioned on its roof and the use of passwords was adopted in order to grant access to the various entranceways.[69] This was the type of work that had been honed during the use of Liberty Hall as a garrison from March 1916 onwards. After entering the building on Monday and locking the caretaker away, the rest of the day was spent 'on the roof with bombs and other war material'.[70] When Mallin arrived, he appeared to have ordered this type of work to continue due to a report that the college was going to be attacked, though O'Shea felt that they 'had plenty of bombs and shotguns in case it did come off'.[71] With republican riflemen on top of the RCSI and opposed by British machine gun fire from the roofs of the Shelbourne Hotel, the Alexandra Club and the United Services Club 'a triangular duel opened' across the skies of the wider Green area.[72] Scottish republican and suffragette Margaret Skinnider described how she was 'on the roof, sniping from the roof with the [I]CA men'.[73] However, before Tuesday was brought to a close, the ICA's soldiers were instructed by Mallin to leave the roof and they were taken to the RCSI's lecture hall and given tea and cocoa.[74]

As well as providing greater cover, the RCSI building offered far more hospitable shelter for the soldiers. The floors were filled with mattresses and pillows. A fire was lit in one of the classroom fireplaces at the back of the building and was used to make porridge.[75] O'Shea also recalled enjoying tea and cocoa once the new base had been secured on Tuesday.[76] The ground floor was turned into a dining room and sleeping quarters while Mallin used the floor above it as an office. A sick-bay and a mortuary were also established in a lecture room and an examination room, respectively.[77] However, a rigidly disciplined manner was taken to its upkeep. For Oman, this was far more so than in the Jacob's factory garrison where he had previously been engaged. The barrack-like atmosphere in the RCSI was evidenced in that they had 'to make down our beds and, in the morning reveille … we had to make our beds up etc'.[78] This approach was important as the location acted not only as a safe house but also a place for armament creation. While the munitions belonging to the Officer Training Corps had been found in the RCSI on Thursday, jars of chlorine were found on Monday and were brought to a window where they were to be thrown at any passing armoured cars.[79] Likewise, old Bourneville cocoa and Bluads Health salts cans were used to hold gunpowder so as to make a somewhat less advanced version of the bombs that had been developed in Beresford Place.[80]

In the RCSI, the Citizen Army was able to draw on the house-fighting lectures that Connolly had given in 1915. According to Brennan-Whitmore, for Connolly, barricades were of less importance than to seize city blocks, 'fortify them and then punch holes leading from one set of premises to another within the block, so as to facilitate the massing of men at one threatened point'.[81] The RCSI provided far more suitable grounds for this type of work than St Stephen's Green could. When the College of Surgeons was captured, the republican soldiers began to break through the walls into the neighbouring houses northwards towards Grafton Street and southwards towards Cuffe Street.[82] From Tuesday onwards the chief of staff attempted to take a more offensive approach through the establishment of new outposts in the nearby houses.[83] One plan was developed which involved O'Shea, McCormick, O'Neill, Mick Kelly, M. Donnelly and M. Tuite. They were directed by Mallin to travel past the Turkish Baths near York and Cuffe Street. They were to then travel towards Grafton Street and rush to Sibley's bookshop in the hopes of wiping out a machine gun nest that had been set up in the United Services Club.

Initially, the plan was to do this along the streets. However, after firing broke out Mallin ordered that they were to 'break through from house to house'.[84] This followed the principles that Connolly argued for the previous year.[85] With Markievicz acting as a guide, a long plank was stretched across one of the windows of the RCSI to the roof of the Turkish Baths beside it. Once the ICA's soldiers had crawled over this they began to break through the walls of the houses.[86] The method was to use a seven-pound sledgehammer to break a hole in the wall big enough to allow one person to 'crawl through'. The 'lower portion' of the house was then barricaded with any furniture available.[87] O'Shea recalled 'we started to work with a will and sometime between 00:00 and 01:00 we stopped for rest and sleep. We had then got as far as May's music shop'.[88]

After the occupation of May's shop, the group was able to gain entrance to Alexandra Ladies' Club. This was demanding work as the wall was made of brick and concrete. Eventually they got through and McCormick, Robbins, O'Neill, O'Shea, Kelly and Michael Donnelly jumped the four to five feet drop to the club's floor.[89] Here the danger of not following the training they had received the previous year became apparent. In his lecture to the Old IRA Literary Society, Robbins described how 'the telephone bell rang, and against all advice given by Connolly in his lectures to the ICA, Capt. John O'Neill lifted the telephone and spoke over the wire. Immediately a fusillade of gunfire raked the building.' Robbins contended that the men were lucky as the majority of them had returned to the house which they had previously taken over and those who remained dropped to the floor in order to avoid the onslaught. 'Had it been otherwise,' he continued, 'this little plan would have borne fruit for the British forces.'[90] O'Shea recollected similarly. Once the phone was answered McCormick grabbed it and smashed it. However, it was too late as a burst of machine gun fire opened which destroyed the windows and walls instantaneously. 'We all had to lie flat for nearly an hour,' O'Shea remembered. He had been told by McCormick that a telltale sign was that all the shops and houses from South King Street to Cuffe Street had already been damaged by this type of fire.[91]

A number of other plans like this continued to be made by Mallin. An ICA unit under Lieut. Kelly, and supported by a section under Kavanagh, was also charged with the burning of buildings on the north side of the Green in order to 'quieten the enemy forces'. However, through a 'misunderstanding by the latter this movement was a failure'.[92] Likewise, on the west side in South York Street, a small party of republican soldiers were captained by Lieutenant Robert de Coeur.[93] Here a different defensive tactic was used. Instead of the barricading system deployed by O'Shea, Kelly and the others, the lower floors of the house were left untouched in the hope that they would appear as if they had not been used by the rebels. Rather, the stairway was carefully sawn through to allow men to pass but with enough of the stairs left to bear its own weight in order to allow for the creation of a secret passageway.[94] O'Donoghue was also ordered by Mallin to lead a group to go to the back of the Russell Hotel beside St Stephen's Green and attack the building as information had been received that it was manned by British troops. He was ordered not to attempt to take the building or to attack it but only to pressure it. The instructions also stipulated that if it was impossible to do that or if they were attacked before their position was 'consolidated', they were to set fire to the two houses near the hotel and return to the RCSI.

Amongst a group of twenty soldiers involved in this attack was the labour leader William Partridge along with Freddie Ryan, Martin Foy, George Campbell, Michael Carlton and Robert O'Shea.[95] Margaret Skinnider was also in charge of a group of five men.[96] Their work involved house occupation as they were to reach Russell Hotel by occupying two houses on Harcourt Street and 'getting in through the shops'.[97] Surprisingly, there was no British sentry posted at the Cuffe Street corner and they reached Harcourt Street without receiving trouble from the British Army. At Cuffe Street, Partridge and another man were charged with the task of using the butt-end of their rifles in order to break the glass on the doors of a photographic supplies shop. However, in the commotion of breaking into the shop it appears that

To the People of Ireland!

"Our Freedom must be had at all hazards."—Wolfe Tone.

The time has come to practice the advice of Fintan Lalor, namely: to train our hands and our sons' hands, for the day will come when we and they will have to use them.

The workers must be disciplined and alert if they are to enjoy the just proceeds of their labour. It has been well said:

"The Price of Liberty is Eternal Vigilance."

The methods of discipline and alertness and the means of power to train our hands, are provided by

THE IRISH CITIZEN ARMY.

This organisation embraces the full principles of Republican Democracy; its aim is to sink the difference of Birth, Privilege and Creed under the common name of the Irish People. It stands for a Union of Progressive Nationalism with the Democratic forces of Ireland, and its policy is to achieve that, for which

Theobald Wolfe Tone died, and John Mitchel suffered—

AN INDEPENDENT IRELAND.

Irishmen! Join the Citizen Army NOW and help us to build up an Irish Co-operative Commonwealth.

All inquiries to be addressed to:

HON. SEC., LIBERTY HALL, DUBLIN.

Muscail do Mhisneach, a Bhanba!

CITY PRINTING WORKS, 13 Stafford Street, Dublin.

'To the people of Ireland' by the Irish Citizen Army (ICA) (MS15,000/8/14. All images courtesy of the National Library of Ireland).

Liberty Hall Headquarters of the ICA, Dublin (NPA DOCG53).

Group of Irish Volunteers and ICA soldiers inside the General Post Office, Dublin, during the Easter Rising (NPA GPO2).

The ICA lined up under the banner 'We serve neither King nor Kaiser' outside Liberty Hall, Dublin, 1914, with a crowd observing (KE199).

Half-length portrait of Countess Markievicz with gun, facing sideways, undated (NPA MGU).

Constance Markievicz and Michael Mallin under arrest, 1916 (NPA DOCA1).

Scene in the General Post Office, just before its evacuation during Easter Week 1916 (NPA POLI11).

Sean Ó Congaile: Sean Connolly,
undated (NPA PERS5).

Michael Mallin, Commandant of
the Irish Republican Army. Executed
8 May 1916 (NPA POLF195).

James Connolly, *c.*1916 (NPA POLI10).

Press photo of Jim Larkin outside the Imperial Hotel, Dublin, 31 August 1913
(NPA POLF100).

REASONS WHY

YOU SHOULD JOIN

The Irish Citizen Army.

BECAUSE It pledges its members to work for, organise for, drill for and fight for **an Independent Ireland.**

BECAUSE It places its reliance upon the only class that never betrayed Ireland—the Irish Working Class.

BECAUSE Having a definite aim to work for there is no fear of it being paralysed in the moment of action by divisions in its Executive Body.

BECAUSE It teaches that "the sole right of ownership of Ireland is vested in the people of Ireland, and that that full right of ownership may, and ought to be, enforced by any and all means that God hath put within the power of man."

BECAUSE It works in harmony with the Labour and true National Movements and thus embraces all that makes for Social Welfare and National Dignity.

Companies Wanted in Every District.

RECRUITS WANTED EVERY HOUR.

Apply for further information, Secretary, Citizen Army, Liberty Hall, Dublin.

Irish Paper.]   *City Printing Works, 13 Stafford Street, Dublin.*

Handbill: 'Reasons why you should join the Irish Citizen Army' (MS15,673/8/2).

Partridge's rifle fired an unintended shot which set off an exchange between the two armies. The mission was abandoned because of this. All moveable items were placed in the centre of the shop. Turpentine was then poured over them and set alight, and the unit made a hasty return to their base. During the mêlée, Skinnider suffered three wounds and Frederick Ryan was killed. She recalled 'Partridge and another man helped to carry me back to the College of Surgeons that night.' On Sunday 30 April, she was taken to St Vincent's Hospital where she spent seven weeks recovering.[98]

Despite the attacks on the hotels, events were conspiring against the rebel forces. Not only had the *Helga* gunboat destroyed Liberty Hall on Wednesday but by Thursday British forces had managed to create an effective cordon between the north and south of Dublin city.[99] Given that the main purpose of the occupation of St Stephen's Green was the creation of a transport hub for the entire republican army, the ICA garrison in the RCSI now served little value. Furthermore, on Thursday, Christina Caffrey, who had been a courier of information from the RCSI and the GPO, was arrested and taken into Trinity College by two officers.[100] This meant that any form of effective communication with the headquarters in the GPO had been cut off and the ICA in the College of Surgeons was placed in the position where they had to wait as passive actors in the rebellion.[101]

Robbins's sense of isolation could be seen from his description of Thursday as 'a day of rest' when the republican soldiers had 'plenty of time on our hands'. Similarly, he contended that 'nothing of an extraordinary nature happened' on Friday. O'Shea recalled that 'there was very little of importance' between the events at the Alexandra Ladies' Club and Saturday.[102] The ICA men and women speculated about 'a great fight at Mount Street', of Larkin's return to Ireland, and of German assistance landing with Casement. Robbins recalled 'we had very little real knowledge of what was happening in the city'.[103] This was best encapsulated on Thursday night when Markievicz and O'Donoghue went onto the roof of the RCSI to attempt to ascertain the location of nearby fires. O'Donoghue remembered 'the flames were so intense that we decided the fires were somewhere about [the] College Green area, but we could not understand this as we did not know of any of our forces being in position there'.[104]

At 09:00 on Sunday 30 April, the remaining officers in the RCSI were called upstairs where Mallin, holding a typewritten document, was located. In what was described as a 'very painful duty' he attempted to read out Connolly's official instruction of surrender before passing it to his men.[105] After this, an order was sent to all of the surrounding houses for the soldiers to return to the RCSI where they were also informed of the surrender.[106] Naturally, it was not received well. O'Shea, when he heard of the news, pleaded with his leader to 'take to the hills' and had a long argument with him that only ended when O'Shea was told that they had begun the fight as soldiers following orders and they would end it following the commands of their commandant.[107] The first thing that Robbins noticed was the 'awful gloom' and how he was being told that 'something awful was about to happen'.[108] Others reacted in a similar manner. Some entered a stage of denial and disputed if it was in fact Connolly's signature. De Coeur and O'Donoghue considered a mutiny and the possibility of arresting Mallin. This idea was disregarded after Mallin told them much the same as he had O'Shea: 'we came out as an army and we are now going to surrender as an army'. Upon acceptance, O'Donoghue went to the room where they had imprisoned Laurence Kettle, the perceived strike-breaker whom some labour men had heckled at the Irish Volunteers's formation at the Rotunda in 1913. O'Donghue went there so that he could cry away from his comrades. He was not alone and saw 'men in all postures overcome by grief and some [who] appeared to be in agony'.[109]

The republican soldiers were then assembled in the lecture hall where the surrender took place.[110] The news was read out by Mallin who also 'spoke a few sad words' and was followed by speeches from Markievicz and Partridge. The option was also given to those who wished to attempt to escape to do so before the arrival of the British Army. Not only were they not to be thought less of if they did but some were given instructions to leave. After this the final act of defeat lay at the feet of Mallin as he lowered the tricolour and massed a white flag.[111] With this, British officer Major de Courcy Wheeler, who apparently was surprised by the sparse numbers of republican soldiers in the RCSI, entered and gave his commands to the prisoners. They were told that they were to get blankets as such items might be needed and they were then formed in twos and marched out of the building.[112] They were marched down the Green, through Grafton Street and College Street, and into the lower castle yard. After being stationed there for a couple of hours they were then brought past City Hall through Lord Edward Street and Thomas Street, and passed St Catherine's Church, where they had previously rallied. Finally, they arrived at Richmond Barracks where they awaited their internment.[113]

In truth, the attempt to hold St Stephen's Green was one the least successful of the republican operations during Easter Week. While it did have value as a transport hub and a place for the injured, its sprawling open ground made it unsuitable for the type of insurgency engaged in. The occupation of the RCSI provided far safer grounds. Not only were more offensive practices employed from there from Wednesday onwards but it also allowed men from Jacob's factory to 'get backwards and forwards'.[114] Certainly, while communication with the GPO was lost on Thursday, they were able to hold the RCSI until the capitulation on Sunday 30 April when the message of surrender reached Mallin.[115] However, its isolation as a post meant once communication with the GPO was lost the soldiers in the Green garrison were reduced to inactivity. The republican force also suffered seven deaths in the wider St Stephen's Green area.[116] Robbins pointed specifically to the deaths of ICA men James Fox, Philip Clarke, George Geoghegan, Frederick Ryan, as well as the execution of Mallin on 8 May.[117] Yet, despite the surrender, the Green's garrison remained resolute. Many had broken down when they heard the news of the surrender. However, once Mallin appeared again, they became determined to face their respective fates. Emily Norgrove argued 'in this way [they] preceded under military escorts to Dublin Castle, and from there to Richmond Barracks, from which place that evening we were deported to England'.[118] It was this steadfastness that would serve them during their internment and during the re-organisation period of 1917–19 before the outbreak of the Anglo-Irish War of Independence.

10

'THAT SMALL GARRISON CARRIED OUT THEIR ORDERS': DUBLIN CASTLE AND ITS ENVIRONS

If one of the most striking features of the St Stephen's Green garrison was that it began in conditions unusual to the ICA, the same could not be said of the republican unit that attempted to seize control of City Hall and its wider area. Not only had they carried out a mock attack on Dublin Castle in winter 1915 but they had also planned to attack the castle if they were the sole insurgents in the rebellion. However, the official plan for Easter Week never included an occupation of Dublin Castle.[1] The joint republican forces did not consider that the capture of the building would be too difficult, a contention supported by Head Constable Folan who believed 'the Volunteers could have easily taken the castle, there was not a gun in it, and any ammunition to be found was blank. Indeed, MacNeill's countermanding of the parade order had lulled the Dublin Castle authorities with a sense of security'.[2] However, the republican leadership believed that the castle was too spread out and that any occupation would have required 'hundreds of men'.[3] The castle made strategic sense for the republicans to attack even if it was not going to be occupied. Not only was it a central fortification for the British administrative authority but was also seen around the world as a symbol of their control in Ireland. Burning the citadel had been considered by the rebel leaders but was dismissed as it contained a Red Cross hospital and should any of the patients have died during an attack it would have severely damaged the Irish cause.[4] Wisely, it was decided by the leaders that the best approach was to isolate it from the other bases.

In order to achieve that goal, William Oman noted that the 'intention was to control the whole square' around it.[5] While City Hall on Cork Hill was the designated headquarters for this battalion, Emily Norgrove detailed the other outposts. As well as City Hall, these included Henry and James's Tailors shop on Dame Street, the lower castle entrance on Cork Hill, the churchyard on Nicholas Street, Synod Hall at Christchurch Place and the *Daily Mail*'s office on Dame Street.[6] Oman gave an account which differed slightly from Norgrove's version. According to Oman, the Engineering Post beside City Hall as well as the Rates Department, which Robbins contended would have 'dominated the castle', were also to be taken. A group from Jacob's factory was to command two houses in Stephen Street which overlooked the barrack square in Ship Street, opposite Leitrim House. Oman also stated that Martin Kelly was to take charge of the group in the *Daily Mail*'s office, Elmes was to take charge in Henry and James's shop while George Oman was to lead a party of five, including William (contradicting Hanratty's membership listing), up Castle Street to enter a house beside the steps of Ship Street. They were to enter an overhead viaduct which overlooked the upper and lower gates of the barracks in the hope of covering the entrance gates.[7]

The IRB's military council also hoped either to capture the telephone exchange or to destroy all the wires connected to it as well as the wires which passed from the castle through the manhole in Dame Street by the lower castle yard.[8] This was part of a larger citywide plan where Andy Fitzpatrick and Arthur King were to cut wires in Talbot Street while Tom O'Donoghue and others were to do the same at Church Street Bridge. Sam King and George King were also involved in this type of work in Palace Street and Lombard Street, respectively. However, the Volunteers detailed to work with Martin King at the telephone exchange did not turn up and the task was not completed at all.[9]

As the Dublin Castle map shows, this plan was sufficient to create a complete cordon around the castle. If that map is compared to the ICA Drill map it is clear how close this plan was to the drill system conceived by Mallin in 1915.[10] As Seamus Pounch recollected 'the Citizen Army had this project in their hands'.[11] However, when the attack on the castle occurred on 24 April things quickly went against the plan. Oman recalled seeing sections break off to take up their positions at Henry and James's and the *Daily Mail*'s office while the main body of men turned towards the main gate of Dublin Castle. Here uncertainty began to creep into his mind as his group was meant to be five minutes ahead of the main group of men. For him, this caused 'a quandary [about] what to do'.[12] It must be noted that it was the rigidly timed nature of the plans that caused consternation for Mallin when he was shown them.[13]

More drastically, a decision by Seán Connolly, the commander for the entire attack, led to a complete deviation of the republicans' plan. When he saw Constable O'Brien attempt to lock Dublin Castle's main gate, Connolly ordered him to step aside. When O'Brien refused to do so, Connolly fired, causing the first casualty of the rebellion in Dublin.[14]

Connolly's brother George described the event: 'the policeman on the gate made an effort to stop us going in. My brother Seán drew an automatic and told the policeman to stand back. The policeman made an effort as well as I can remember to draw his baton or something I do not know. My brother shot him.'[15] The head constable of the RIC, Peter Folan remembered that 'after the shots, commotion started immediately. The Volunteers – 15 or 20 of them –made to go in through the gate into the yard, which they did.' Molony remembered Connolly shouting '"get in, get in"– as if they already did not know they were to go in.'[16] Oman too appeared to be surprised by the action and he was told to 'run' by his senior officer. He and his party left for their intended positions.[17] This indicates two points: firstly, that after firing, it was Captain Connolly's decision to enter the castle, and secondly, the decision was taken on his own counsel.

A number of potential reasons for Connolly's actions have been put forward by Michael Foy and Brian Barton. Firstly, he may have seen O'Brien's movements as threatening and acted upon that. Secondly, he had wanted the Citizen Army to begin the Easter Rising with a 'dramatic act just like the Volunteer and Fianna attack on the Magazine Court'. Finally, and more strategically, he had conceptualised a situation whereby if the British soldiers attempted to recapture the building, they would have been outflanked by the republican forces in the surrounding buildings.[18] Kain told Fox that James Connolly's last words to him on 23 April were that the ICA was to have the 'post of honour'. While others were to take up their defensive positions, the City Hall garrison was to attack and to 'open fire on the stroke of the Angelus bell'.[19]

It was noon when the Citizen Army's unit approached Dublin Castle. It is possible that this glorification of the offensive may have been the cause of Connolly's attack on O'Brien. Kain's pension claim appeared to suggest a further cause. According to him, he was due to occupy City Hall but when they got near the gates it became apparent to Captain Connolly that 'the fellow who was to take the castle did not turn up'. Lieut. Kain was then told by Connolly to take the guard room but not to go 'an inch further', in essence to attempt a raid rather than a full occupation. Once the republicans got to the gate, Kain remembered, the instructions were given to everyone 'to try to knock out the sentry'.[20] From this it can be gathered that the breach into Dublin Castle may have been intended as a temporary measure to secure further munitions and/or possibly with the goal of destabilising a sentry in the hope of making the occupation of the surroundings areas easier. It is also possible that it was a combination of some if not all of the above reasons.

Whatever the reasons for Connolly's decision, with his orders for Kain in place, he began to focus on the occupation of City Hall. The ease of this project was described by Molony who stated 'we went into the City Hall and at once manned it'.[21] This ease of entry was because it was a bank holiday and there was no one in the place. Connolly, who worked as a clerk in the building, may have had a key and certainly Molony had no recollection of any doors or windows being broken open, so, once they had climbed over the railings of the building they got access without much delay.[22] Certainly, the municipal building was completely taken over by 13:00.[23] With the seizure successfully completed, work began bunkering down in order to make the place a suitable garrison. An appropriate place for a hospital was sought and once the kitchen was found so too was a 'large dish of fruit – oranges and apples' – which were to be kept for any wounded combatants. While the occupants attempted to '[sit] pretty' an exchange of gunfire between the roof of Dublin Castle and the roof of City Hall had begun, which was 'very heavy for the first hour'.[24] Both Shanahan and Molony went to the top of the hall's roof and witnessed both the death of a young British soldier in Ship Street as well as the first death of the rebels.

Two hours after Connolly fired the shot that killed O'Brien, he became the first casualty of the republican forces. The ICA's chief medical officer, Kathleen Lynn, who had reached City Hall not long after the constable's death, recalled the incident. Once she had got past the gates she met the garrison chief and was told that it would be wise if a number of people went up to the roof. There she saw Connolly walking towards other republican soldiers on the roof and standing upright, despite having being told of the value of crouching and taking cover. He then dropped to the ground, 'mortally wounded' from the bullet of a sniper. The wound had caused him to bleed heavily from the stomach and her belief was that first aid would not have done anything to save him.[25] With Connolly's death, Kain, who was on his way to take the castle's guardroom, become the chief officer in Dublin Castle while a man named O'Reilly took charge in City Hall.[26]

Once the news of Connolly's death reached the GPO, it was decided that reinforcements were needed in City Hall. George Norgrove stated that 'I went into the GPO first by the Henry Street entrance. I led the men in, and afterwards when Connolly was shot I brought reinforcements to the City Hall.'[27] He was initially meant to be stationed in St Stephen's Green where, according to the original plan, he was to take a body of men to occupy the Shelbourne Hotel, but at the last minute the plan was changed and he was detailed with the occupying company to the General Post Office.[28] Thus after Connolly's death, Norgrove was repositioned a second time as he brought Michael Lambert, John Poole, John Nolan, Denis Farrell, Louis Byrne, Michael Sexton and Tom Walsh to the municipal building.[29] According to Hanratty, the last piece of advice given to Norgrove from James Connolly was that the rear of City Hall was secure and that an attack would come from the front. This was because of the belief that the force on Bishop Street 'would spread out and occupy Stephen Street, principally Booths, and dominate Ship Street and the castle yard'.[30] For Robbins 'this meant that even the important job in the GPO which had involved Norgrove's transfer from the St Stephen's Green garrison had, in turn, to be neglected to buttress the rapidly deteriorating situation around the castle'.[31] Perhaps most importantly, on the day of the declaration of their republic, Connolly's death drained the Irish soldiers of all morale. Molony described that after this 'the men in the main positions fired desultory shots all day. They fired at anything they saw'.[32]

In the castle, after O'Brien's death, the two sentries who were stationed beside him fled into the guardroom to the right-hand side of the castle's gate.[33] Citizen Army volunteers Thomas Kain, Philip O'Leary, Thomas Daly, George Connolly and Christy Brady, along with James Seery were successful in their attempt to take this room while it was Kain's job to lead this section.[34] At this time, one of the homemade bombs that the ICA had devised in late 1915 and early 1916 failed to explode when it was thrown through the window of the guardroom. After the failed explosion, the republican soldiers rushed the room and the sentinels were ordered to put their hands up before they were disarmed.[35] Naturally, this granted the men the ability to increase their arsenal by taking some of the guards' Lee Enfield rifles. However, while Kain pointed this out to some of the men, the guns were not collected because the republican soldiers felt 'in case of a rush … they might forget the way the bolts were drawn'.[36] The republicans remained armed with guns including their Holt Mausers.[37]

In the guardroom, five of the men took positions at the different windows and 'loopholes', while one watched over the four prisoners. However, while this lasted a few hours, they were under 'heavy machine gun fire' for nearly the entire time and did not have any food. Thus, at some point during the night Kain decided it was necessary to evacuate the castle.[38] With the conditions for the rebels worsening rapidly, this was a 'very nasty job' as the men did not know where either their colleagues or enemies were positioned. They left through an old cellar window and withdrew to Lahiff's plumbing shop in Castle Street (though the original plan as ordered by Kain to George Connolly was to go to Christchurch Place).[39] In order to take cover they bored their way into the cellar and stayed at Lahiff's until Wednesday night. Once they sensed 'the British were hot foot after us' and heard 'them tramping about upstairs' the conclusion was made that the house was being billeted. With this knowledge, they began 'trying to bore through the walls without making too much noise'. However, the group were discovered on Wednesday night when the floorboards were taken up. Once they were captured they were brought to the barracks in Ship Street where they were kept until Sunday 30 April, after which they were marched to Kilmainham Gaol.[40]

Back at City Hall, the situation was continuing to deteriorate. A combined group of 180 men from the Third Royal Irish and the Tenth Royal Dublin Fusiliers had reached the castle.[41] By 'dusk' another group of British soldiers had arrived and had done so without any difficulty from the republican forces.[42] If during the previous morning the castle was largely unoccupied and poorly defended, this was no longer the case. The British Army soldiers at the castle were able to focus on attacking City Hall. Shanahan remembered that it was at 18:00 when 'the big attack opened on us and the troops came up and the attack lasted about two hours. They broke into the building and took us prisoners.'[43] Difficulty arose for the republicans in City Hall when the British Army succeeded in bringing a machine gun into use on Castle Street. Both City Hall and the *Daily Mail*'s office came under an enormous onslaught.[44] It is worth noting again Connolly's last piece of advice to Norgrove that the rear of City Hall was secure and that an attack would come from the front.[45] This had important implications as the republicans had placed their support to the front of the building. As a result, they were poorly positioned when attacked by the British Army from the back of the building.[46] While the rebels stationed on the roof replied with a salvo of their own, the discrepancy in force meant that their efforts were in vain.

Secretary of the Post Office A.H. Norway was in Dublin Castle when this attack began and he was struck by the sound of rifles and the 'shattering bursts of bombs'.[47] Likewise, John O'Leary also remembered the ringing and echoing of the bullets fired as well as how these periods were preceded by 'ominous silence'.[48] In City Hall firing was coming from every angle and continued until darkness. Furthermore, the force of the volley had meant that there was no electric light and 'no way of escape'.[49] The only point of illumination had been beams from the moon, and with the cloak of darkness as their aid, the imperial forces were able to rush the building at the point of bayonets and capture the rebels. Certainly Lynn recalled being ordered to put her hands up by 'a voice in the dark'.[50] Like Kain and his troops at Lahiff's, the prisoners were also taken to Ship Street.[51]

Events did not go much better within the surrounding buildings. Throughout the entirety of Monday, the *Daily Mail*'s office and Henry and James's shop came under fire from Ship Street Barracks. Those stationed at the tailor's shop were 'forced to evacuate' on Monday night and reached the GPO on Tuesday.[52] In Ship Street, the rebels took a position which commanded the gates of the barracks. However, there the period was marked by general inactivity. Initially there had been 'no stir' for 'quite a while'. Later the republicans fired at British troops who had come out on the roadway inside the inner gates but those soldiers took immediate cover and once again there was 'quite a lull'.[53] At around 14:00, William Oman attempted to move a few yards in order to better ascertain the situation in the castle but was immediately shot at by a sniper. He was hidden by an arch but would have been exposed to fire from both Ship Street and all of the castle's buildings. In essence, he was completely impeded from making any progress.[54] After another two hours the battalion heard the sound of cheering. This was caused by a group of British soldiers coming in open formation down past Christchurch onto Little Ship Street in order to support the castle. They spotted the rebels and once one of the rebels' homemade bombs, like Kain's, failed to go off, a barrage of bullets was levelled at the small rebel base. It was feared that a cordon would be made and the men surrounded, and it was decided that the best course of action was to evacuate, with each man responsible for his own safety. After evacuating, Oman went to Jacob's on Tuesday and after that to the aid of the men in the RCSI.[55]

The action in the area surrounding Dublin Castle led to the death of four ICA men: Capt. Seán Connolly, Jack Reilly, George Geoghegan and Lewis Byrne. Two others were also wounded: Tommy Coyle and Jack Findlay.

However, for Emily Norgrove, who was active in the garrison, it was also a source of honour. She wrote:

> I think we may say with pride that that small garrison carried out their orders ... They could have retired before the breach was made but their orders were to hold on at all costs and so they stood their ground. Well might that affair express surprise for that small garrison had held the post for ten long hours, under continuous fire, from trained troops – operating from their own base, Ship Street Barracks.[56]

This was a confrontation that the ICA had planned and trained for meticulously. While the killing of O'Brien and the subsequent movement into the castle grounds appears not to have been authorised by James Connolly and the other rebel leaders, it is not likely that these actions severely affected the encounter in any negative manner. In truth, the ICA's belief that the castle was a location that would have been impossible to hold for a significant length of time was accurate. While it was startling that the garrison was held for less than one day, this was largely a result of the difference in firepower between the British and Irish forces rather than any tactical or strategic mistake on the part of the revolutionaries. The Citizen Army failed to occupy the centre of British authority in Ireland, yet their intention had been to isolate the castle from the other republican operational bases of the Easter Rising and their actions drew British resources away from centres such as the GPO, the new republican military headquarters.[57]

11

'LEFT WHEEL, CHARGE': THE GENERAL POST OFFICE

While units were busy going to St Stephen's Green and City Hall, the commandant of the ICA, in his new role as the Dublin Division's commandant general, led the largest republican garrison to their headquarters in Sackville Street. Connolly was accompanied by Commandant General Pearse as well as Plunkett. Proclamation signatories Clarke and MacDermott had travelled ahead of them in a car.[1] About forty of the unit to be stationed in the actual GPO rather than the wider area encompassing Sackville Street, Cabra Bridge and Fairview, were ICA soldiers. This comprised just over one-quarter of the body.[2] The GPO unit also saw seven members of the ICA's boy scouts active. Walter Carpenter was in charge of these. According to Lieut Robert de Coeur, Carpenter held the rank of 'captain of the boys'.[3] As well as Carpenter, these were Louis Byrne, Roderick Connolly, Patrick O'Neill, Joseph Keeley, Frederick Norgrove and Lawrence Corbally.[4] Winifred Carney, Connolly's secretary, travelled along with them and was the only woman in this march.

Henderson recalled that it was at 11:50 when the order 'column, attention. Quick march' was shouted by Connolly.[5] The republican unit travelled through Abbey Street, and as news of the occupations of places such as Boland's Mills and the Four Courts had not yet become widespread, they were met with unconcerned bystanders who saw it as just another march by the Citizen Army and the Irish Volunteers.[6] Having passed through Abbey Street, the unit turned right and faced what was soon to become the centre point of the newly declared Irish Republic, the GPO. The building itself was one of the more impressive ones that was taken during the week. It stood at over 200 feet wide and 150 long and was three stories high. A product of late-eighteenth- and early-nineteenth-century design, it was marked by a large sorting office surrounded by small personal offices which ran along to and looked out upon Henry Street; a glass partition separated this from a public office in the front of the building, and in the levels above a staff restaurant and a telegraphic office were housed.[7]

It was 12:05 when the battalion faced this large edifice and began the process of occupation. Outside the William Martin Murphy owned Imperial Hotel, the order was given 'left wheel, charge'. With this, twelve men entered the GPO via the Henry Street entrance and immediately went to take control of the upper floors while another group took control of the roof. All 'vantage points' were taken and defensive measures were put into use: all glass partitions were smashed and large books as well as any other suitable equipment available were placed at windows to enhance the security of the building.[8] Men were also told to go to the cellar and fill mailbags full of coal so that they could also be used as barricades at the windows. Meanwhile, a unit moved to the back of the municipal building towards 'The' O'Rahilly's car as well as towards a horse-drawn cart which had been filled with supplies and ammunition. This ammunition was then taken to the main office and sorted.[9] Michael Staines, who had arrived in O'Rahilly's car, described the equipment as 'Mauser, American, Howth rifles and .308 rifles ammunition, .25, .32, .38 and .45'.[10] As Liberty Hall was not to be abandoned until 16:00, when O'Neill and McGowan brought the final supplies to the GPO, this was an important step to immediately secure the base. Staines also led a group of six to the top floor where some staff and soldiers remained. Here they were met by a group of six Connaught Rangers who demanded them to halt but after Staines shot one of them and inflicted a 'scalp wound' they surrendered as it became clear that the Rangers had no ammunition.[11]

With the GPO secured, the outward signs of the republic needed to be shown. It was 12:30 when the republican tricolour flag was raised at the Henry Street corner and a green banner inscribed 'Irish Republic' was erected overlooking Princess Street.[12] Staines hoisted the flags and Pearse and Connolly were on Sackville Street preparing for Pearse to read out the proclamation of the Irish Republic. At this point, Michael Cremen left the GPO to go to Sherrard Street to collect equipment and overheard Connolly say to the newly installed president 'thank God Pearse, we (or I) have lived to see this day'.[13] Then the proclamation, which bore elements of ICA ideology, was read out.

Back in Liberty Hall, the key ICA munitions workers, O'Neill and McGowan were engaged in preparing supplies that would be needed in the

General Post Office. On Easter Sunday, the ICA's commandant had told O'Neill that as Liberty Hall was the 'then GHQ', both men were to remain there continuously until they received further orders. This was repeated during the departure on the following day when '[Connolly] instructed [O'Neill] to remain and defend Liberty Hall until [O'Neill] got word to go to the GPO and [Connolly's] instructions were that McGowan would remain with [O'Neill]'. While they waited, around forty-five Volunteers and ICA men who were late mobilising arrived.[14] They had been ordered by Connolly not to take any offensive action against the British forces unless they were attacked by them. This precautionary measure was implemented in order to stop a British convoy that passed along the quays from engaging in an onslaught. At the same time, they began creating an avenue to exit the labour base and worked through the back of the houses which faced Eden Quay. This opened an avenue through Marlborough Street.[15] Eventually they received a dispatch from Connolly that they were to go to the new headquarters in the General Post Office, but there is some dispute over when this occurred. Ruairi Henderson asserted it was at 15:30, while O'Neill contended he did not receive the order until around 17:30.[16] According to Frank Thornton, they were 'in occupation of Liberty Hall until about 17:00 when we left with all stores, etc. for the GPO'.[17] Around fifteen lorries, cabs and other motorised modes of transport were used in the move. All stores and munitions were brought with them and when they arrived in the GPO they were given over to a unit on the ground floor of the building.[18]

From Tuesday onwards, O'Neill led a party of men making bombs at the back of the sorting office. According to Michael Staines, O'Neill's Citizen Army experience of the previous months showed its importance in the wider struggle.[19] About twenty men were engaged in this work and McGowan operated as his assistant at all times. O'Neill described how 'we still had to manufacture bombs but we also had to defend our own windows and to look after the engineering section as the man who was O/C engineers "Slattery" was wounded'.[20] In O'Neill's own pension claim, he stated that because of Patrick Slattery's injury, when he arrived both Pearse and Connolly told him that he was to be appointed as 'head engineer to the forces'. He also claimed that he acted as the quartermaster (QM) to the general headquarters (GHQ).[21] Oscar Traynor dismissed this and stated that the 'engineer-in-chief' was a man named Captain Breen, a staff battalion officer of the Second Battalion, while Brian O'Higgins acted as the quartermaster.[22]

It is possible that O'Neill was referring to Liberty Hall as the GHQ when he discussed being a QM and Traynor contended he was speaking about the Citizen Army in that case.[23] While neither Breen nor O'Higgins recorded a pension claim or a witness statement, Seamus Ua Caomhanaigh recalled that he thought it was O'Higgins who was responsible for the manufacture, distribution and use of the homemade bombs.[24] Ua Caomhanaigh was stationed on the GPO's roof where some of these explosives were used and may have conflated the two roles of creation and supply. Certainly, Staines, who also claimed to be the general quartermaster of the Dublin Brigade in 1916, was not any less credible.[25] Traynor did state that had the rebellion been 'general', Staines would have acted as 'QMG [quartermaster general] in the headquarters command' while 'Brian O'Higgins acted in that capacity' in reality.[26] This would suggest Staines was the more informed source. Diarmuid Lynch also referred to O'Neill as being not only 'one of Connolly's right hand men' but also having had aides in the armoury based in the GPO's sorting room.[27] Certainly, under either scenario, it is likely that given their experience both McGowan and O'Neill played key roles in the creation of munitions at the sorting office in the GPO.

This was not the only location on Monday where the ICA played vital roles. For the first two days of the rebellion, the GPO unit largely focused on occupying and buttressing strategic locations and the Citizen Army provided significant numbers of men at these minor posts.[28] Edward Doyle and Andrew Conroy were two ICA men who formed a six-man unit, under Seamus Robinson, which occupied Hopkins and Hopkins in Sackville Street at 12:30 on Monday (Robinson also stated that an ICA man named 'Andy Fitzpatrick' was also active there but he is not mentioned in the ICA's membership listings. It is possible that this was either Edward or Matthew Fitzpatrick).[29] This jewellery shop was a 'small but crucially important' garrison as it was located opposite Kelly's gunpowder store, occupied by Peadar Bracken and located between Bachelor's Walk and Lower Sackville Street. These two bases formed a front which looked across College Green and Trinity College where it was likely that any British Army counter-attack was to come from.[30] The entire garrison in the two shops, let alone Robinson's 'half-company', was formed in an 'ad hoc' fashion so it is unlikely that there was a tactical reason for the involvement of the Citizen Army men there. Rather, this was a by-product of the coalescing of the Irish Volunteers and the ICA.

Gaining entrance to the jeweller's shop proved far more difficult than entry to the RCSI or City Hall. This was because the entrance to the building was secured by 'roller shutters' which were locked in place by bolts.[31] These did not give way after Robinson hit them with an axe. Thus, after a short consultation, it was decided that not only would it be easier to secure entry via another means but by leaving the shutters untouched the building's exterior would remain protected.[32] Seamus Lundy and Cormac Turner then initiated the takeover of a quayside house through the first floor. They were able to bore through the wall and enter the upper portion of the shop. This was the floor which they had intended to occupy.[33] Fortification and a search of the premises were than instigated. The location was found to be deserted and all the furniture that could be found was used to create a barricade.

Much like the base in the RCSI, it was also hoped to tunnel through the walls of other adjoining buildings to both enhance the blockade and enable communication with 'the wireless section at the corner of Abbey Street'.[34] Unfortunately for the republicans it was then discovered that not only had they no food but that the roof of Hopkins and Hopkins was completely unsuitable as a firing point as it provided no cover.[35] The republican soldiers were stationed at the windows of the base when they received word from the GPO and asked for reinforcements which led to the arrival of Conroy and supposedly Fitzpatrick. Doyle arrived later and brought the only service rifle that was present at the base. Conroy had been equipped only with 'small arms' while Lundy, Turner and Robinson all had shotguns. However, a 'fair supply' of homemade explosives was also present. With the six men and their weapons in situ the shop was secured and the rest of Monday was eventless.[36]

Further afield at around 16:00 a ten-man strong detachment of the ICA was sent to occupy the chemical works near Annesly Bridge in Fairview. Led by Thomas Craven, who had come over from Liverpool, they were dispatched to take hold of a position in the Dublin and Wicklow Company's fertiliser factory at the Drumcondra side of the bridge.[37] Previous to this, Gilbey's Wine Branch Depot had been occupied by two units under Captain Tom Weafer, who actively engaged in fire with the British forces in their attempt to travel from Farther Matthew Park to the GPO.[38] The ICA men were then sent by Connolly as a reinforcement party.

Both the factory and the offices of the company at the North Strand corner were seized by the republicans and barricades were erected which granted command of the bridge area. It is noteworthy that on the night of the ICA's mock attack on Dublin Castle, 23 October 1915, the ICA had trained to hold the bridges there.[39] Republican casualties were suffered during the North Strand occupation on Easter Monday, 1916. A letter written by First

Company First Battalion member John Saunders in March 1938 stated that an ICA member was injured on Monday evening when he accidently shot himself. He remembered that thirty or forty men had marched down Talbot Street from the GPO en route to Fairview which suggested that it occurred on that mission. The republican soldiers had been ordered to break in doors and after about five or ten minutes of beating these doors with rifle butts, one of the guns went off shooting its possessor.[40] According to Christopher Crothers, the action there had a significance for Vincent Poole, whose brother Christopher led the occupation of the Harcourt Street intersection along with McCormick. In 1914, Vincent was expelled from the Citizen Army for drunkenness and insubordination. He joined the struggle against the British military with the republican men on their way to Fairview and this, Crothers contended, was how Poole re-established himself in the ICA.[41]

On the second day of the rebellion, British Army snipers and machine gunners who were positioned at Trinity College and Westmoreland Street began to litter Sackville Street with fire.[42] In response, Connolly decided to increase the perimeter between the GPO and the non-republican controlled area. At 07:30 he ordered the erection of barbed wire across the ends of Sackville Street, both to keep civilians away from the danger zone in the centre of the city's main street and to prevent the looting that had occurred on Monday. A sufficient quantity of barbed wire was not available and it was decided to secure the overhead tram wires by blowing up their iron base. The subsequent explosion failed to collapse these poles but did take down the wires.[43] Connolly also set about enhancing the defensive parameter on the Liffey side. This involved the occupation of the Imperial Hotel across from the GPO. A garrison of twenty men occupied the hotel.[44] Seven ICA men were involved in that unit. These were George Oman (who just prior to this mission was promoted to the rank of lieutenant),[45] Patrick Tuohy, Michael Finnigan (who had been active in Fleet Street the previous night),[46] Patrick Devereux, Charles Smith (who on Monday was involved in occupations at the telephone exchange in Temple Bar and at Fleet Street),[47] John Redmond and Andrew Redmond (this is according to Hanratty's membership files but Redmond's pension reads that he was stationed in the Metropole Hotel). They were aided by other men from the Second Battalion, Dublin Brigade of the Irish Volunteers.[48]

Frank Thornton was instructed to lead the party and he took over the Imperial Hotel at around noon. He then began to bore holes through the walls which connected the hotel to the buildings on either flank.[49] Immediately the republican soldiers 'started getting ready the place which involved sandbagging windows and laying in water, according to the instructions we received. Every landing and every room – every receptacle that would hold water was carried up from the tanks.'[50] After this task was completed, the tricolour was flown from the roof. However, it was on Wednesday when the temporary victory of the ICA over Dublin's capitalist class was signalled as the starry plough was also massed.[51] Thornton recalled:

> During the insurrection I received a request from my commander in chief, James Connolly, to erect 'the plough and the stars' on the Imperial Hotel alongside the tricolour already flying there. I immediately agreed, and only succeeded after great difficulty as it had to be erected under fire, but up it went – 'the plough and the stars' – and there it stayed.[52]

The hotel was owned by William Martin Murphy, with whom the ITGWU had battled so feverishly three years previously. Flying the flag of the ICA therefore was not only an act of defiance against the British military but also against the employer class of nationalists like Murphy and Kettle, thus signalling that the new republic sought to defend the working and employee class.[53] It was both a gesture of revenge and a reaffirmation of the egalitarian principles of the proclamation and the ICA's constitutions of 1914. According to Devereux, the remainder of the work in the Imperial Hotel centred on guarding both the roof and the lower parts of the building.[54]

By this time Doyle, Conroy and their comrades in Hopkins had drilled as far as the Dublin Bread Company (DBC) near Abbey Street, where, since the previous day a number of Volunteers had been stationed in order to use it as a sniper post, 'to protect our wireless station' and 'to observe Lower Abbey Street and Lower O'Connell Street'.[55] Despite that the soldiers stationed in the DBC had also begun to bore through to Hopkins, but the walls between the two bases were too sturdy for a passageway to be made.[56] This was because many of the walls in the area were made of solid concrete and the republicans' tools had little impact.[57] In order to circumvent this problem a platform at the back of the building on the first floor was established which enabled communication between the two bases.[58] At the same time, supplies needed to be replenished and it was felt that extra manpower was also necessary. Both Turner and Robinson recalled going to the GPO about this problem. They stated that they met with Connolly and George Plunkett, respectively. Turner stated that his conversation with Connolly resulted in the arrival of

Conroy at Hopkins and Hopkins. However, Conroy had arrived there the previous day so it is likely that Turner was confused over the dates and only Robinson travelled to the GPO on Tuesday.[59] According to Robinson, Plunkett told him that the GPO unit had no men to spare.[60] While firing could be heard throughout the rest of the day, these were the most eventful incidents for the Hopkins-based men until Wednesday.

For those stationed along the Liffey and across Sackville Street, Wednesday was a turning point when the might of the British artillery began to be used, and by Thursday, used to stunning success. On Tuesday, four eighteen-pounder field guns had travelled from Athlone and arrived at Trinity College. Due to the force of the recoil of their fire, it was necessary to fix the trail of the gun in the ground. This caused the British Army problems mounting them because of the paved nature of the streets and it was necessary to 'dig up the cobble stones before the guns could be used'.[61] However, by Wednesday morning two of the guns had been erected in Tara Street. Worse for the republicans, the HMS *Helga*, a gunboat which had been on active anti-submarine patrol duty in the Atlantic had also arrived in the city from Kingstown.[62] Robinson stated that his 'first recollection of Wednesday was hearing the sound of artillery fire and with the aid of a homemade periscope we saw a boat in the river just beyond the railway building shelling Liberty Hall'.[63]

The British Army soldiers stationed on the *Helga* believed Liberty Hall was the headquarters of the insurgent movement and it was the first building to be shelled. This began ineffectually as the *Helga*'s first shot struck the lower portion of the steel framework of the bridge that ran across to the station at Tara Street.[64] After that the gunboat moved further up the river to get a less obscured angle and was aided by the eighteen-pounder Howitzers in Tara Street. The combined fire-power quickly destroyed Liberty Hall.[65] Described in Sinn Féin's rebellion handbook as a 'thorn in the side of the Dublin police and the Irish government' as well as 'the centre of the social anarchy in Ireland, the brain of every riot and disturbance', there was certainly a symbolic importance to the destruction of the Beresford Place building.[66] In Brennan-Whitmore's words, it was 'destroyed simply because it was the home of the Transport Union and the Citizen Army'.[67] Given that Liberty Hall had been evacuated on Monday, its shelling provided little tactical advantage to the British Army. After this, the gunboat attempted to fire on the GPO but a direct shot was not possible because of the *Helga*'s position. In total the *Helga* fired only about forty rounds during the Easter Rising.[68]

Also on Wednesday, the ICA and Volunteer men stationed at Hopkins and Hopkins began to experience heavy fire, this time directed from the fire station on Tara Street. However, this shelling did little damage.[69] While the republicans had to 'keep our heads down', the fusillade did no more than chip 'the brickwork around the windows'.[70] The Howitzers located in Trinity College gradually began to have a greater effect. They peppered Sackville Street and made it nearly impossible for those in the GPO and the Imperial and Metropole hotels to go to the open ground.[71] Liam Tannam, who had previously fired at the *Helga* from the roof of the Dublin Bread Company, was in the middle of Sackville Street when a machine gunner started to trail him with the 'bullets ... striking the roadway at my feet'.[72]

A British Army 'nine-pounder' had also been established at the junction between D'Olier Street and College Street and begun to attack Kelly's gunpowder store with devastating success. By 14:30 on Wednesday, the upper portion of the shop had been ripped apart and the republican soldiers stationed there were ordered to evacuate and join those at the Metropole Hotel.[73] By the end of the night, the chimney stack on that hotel had been struck and collapsed. This resulted in a stream of molten lead flowing into the building's interior as the shell had been filled with molten wax which subsequently melted and coursed into the building.[74] At about 17:30, the area around Hopkins jewellery shop, where the Citizen Army comprised fifty per cent of the garrison, was also on fire. An order had been received, through a Volunteer lieutenant stationed in the Dublin Bread Company that the place was to be evacuated. This was queried by Robinson as the building itself was in a relatively stable condition. However, the command was obeyed. They left via the Hibernian bank in Abbey Street, travelled through that street and into North Earl Street before they individually rushed past the far side of Nelson's Pillar.[75] But when they arrived at the GPO and after a conversation with Connolly, it became apparent that it was only the DBC's tower which was ordered to be abandoned.[76]

By Thursday, conditions for the republicans continued to worsen. The GPO was coming under increasing danger of catching fire and it was becoming progressively difficult to hold onto the minor bases. In the same vein as much of the other smaller barracks across the city, the Imperial Hotel suffered from a shortage of supplies. At this stage they had run out of foodstuffs and Noel Lemass as well as two others had to cross to the GPO, under British fire, in order to refill their stocks. They were given bread and then rushed back to the hotel unharmed.[77] Making matters worse was that on Wednesday afternoon the large water tank on the top of the hotel's roof was hit by enemy fire which created four bullet holes through which water began to leak, reducing the republicans' water supply.[78]

Liam Tannam described the effect both the incendiary shells and the fires had on the Sackville Street garrisons:

> the water, of course was quite useless and these incendiaries melted the lead I understand, and so the building was set on fire. It burned from top downwards, floor after floor … finally, pieces of burning timber began to fall from the ceiling over us … there was a grave danger that the ceiling would now collapse bringing a burning mass down on top of us.[79]

The Imperial Hotel was also on fire. The fire had started in the basement on Thursday night after a shell had landed there and exploded. All the men were put to work tackling it but with no water to put it out the fire kept spreading. Soon the hotel was 'filled with smoke … [and] the men were being suffocated with [it]'.[80] The fire in the hotel was burning so severely that Thornton was forced to lead his men in an evacuation during the small hours of the night and they retired into the Earl Street district where they stayed until the surrender. [81]

According to Smith, the Imperial Hotel was abandoned between 04:00 and 05:00 on Friday morning.[82] This evacuation was done by smashing the building's wall until they got to an area where they could cross Earl Street, Cathedral Street, Marlboro Street and Thomas's Lane. At the lane, they stayed at the back of a chapel until they were taken prisoner later that day.[83] Daly described that this work was done with 'practically no tools … we used pokers, and anything, but lucky enough I had three of these long chisels we had for the purpose … we worked right through the day and night, and the result was that we were able to get right up to Earl Street'.[84] Importantly, the order that Connolly had given Thornton was to hold onto the building until they were 'blown down by shell fire or burned down' and concluded that 'the British must not occupy these buildings'.[85] The evacuation, therefore, was not a failure for the ICA and the Volunteer men stationed there. However, the retreat from the hotel did not happen without casualties. During the process of breaking through walls, Smith received an injury to his knee which subsequently 'necessitated the amputation of my leg'.[86]

Sometime between Wednesday and Thursday an attempt was made to re-occupy Hopkins and Hopkins jewellery shop after the erroneous interpretation of Connolly's order. This effort was carried out under the command of ICA man Andrew Conroy rather than Robinson. Conroy stated 'I was sent back in charge, including Senator Robinson; he came back under me, because Connolly knew me personally and the rest were nearly strangers to him.'[87] Robinson confirmed this, writing in 1935 that 'a few hours after we reached the GPO James Connolly told Conroy (whom he knew personally) to take charge of about thirteen men and re-occupy the Hopkins and Hopkins – Abbey Street section'.[88] The change in command may have been a result of the incorrect decision to leave the garrison in the first place or it may have been because the Citizen Army soldiers originally had arrived at the jewellery shop after the other three Volunteers and Hopkins, therefore, was already under someone else's command.

The Hopkins garrison attempted to return along the same route that they had come from. When they reached Marlborough Street, machine gun fire opened on them which not only wounded Frank Scullin but impeded the path of the majority of the unit and in the end only Conroy, Robinson and one other made it to the jewellers.[89] Conditions there were worse than when they had left it as it had received a barrage of bullets from both machine guns and rifles. The three men could not reply to that type of firepower with the arms that were at their disposal. By Friday, they were left with no option but to evacuate and it was during the subsequent return to the GPO that Conroy was wounded by a bullet to the hip. Robinson saw him 'leap into the air. He had obviously been hit but he continued to run and reached the shelter of the houses at Manfield's Corner where I lost sight of him.'[90]

Thursday also saw James Connolly's severe wounding. With the encroachment of British forces, a barricade had needed to be established on Prince's Street and Connolly had been out examining this work when he was hit in the left arm. It seemed to be a flesh wound and was dressed by Doctor James Ryan before the commandant went back to his tasks – this time establishing an outpost on Liffey Street. However, there a sniper was able to inflict a much more severe wound to Connolly's left leg, which shattered two inches of his shin bone.[91] Aluminium rods were secured to either side of his leg in order to immobilise it and were kept together in plaster of Paris, with a 'window being left for dressing the wound'.[92] A bed was also acquired and he was placed on it but he refused to stay in the casualty ward and was taken to the main hall of the GPO.[93] On Thursday, in a piece intended for the republican soldiers entitled the *Hour of Victory*, he stated that he would be able to continue as a military leader. He wrote '[I have] got my bed moved in to the firing lines, and, with the assistance of your officers, will be just as useful to you as ever'.[94] However, the nature of his injuries rendered him incapable of the same level of command that he had exercised during the previous four days. Making matters more difficult was that Pearse had suffered from sleep deprivation. Consequently, two of the leading strategists for the revolt were incapacitated by midday Thursday.[95]

Even without Connolly's injury, the GPO was in an increasing fragile position. Throughout Thursday and Friday it had been assaulted by British Howitzers, machine gunners and snipers. By about 15:00 on Friday, the British Army had perfected their range, after a direct hit on the portico of the building, and began another heavy bombardment which created severe fires across the General Post Office.[96] By the evening 'the whole place went on fire' which was 'if possible, even more destructive than the one of the previous night'.[97] While Tom Clarke stated he would never leave the place alive, a danger existed that the roof would collapse on those inside. Evacuation had become inevitable and 'The' O'Rahilly had begun efforts to create a mode of retreat via Moore Street.[98] In 16 Moore Street the final headquarters of the republicans was established. There a conference between the leaders began and future action was decided. The plan devised by the new commandant, 18-year-old Seán McLoughlin, to connect with the Four Courts was dismissed by the majority of those camped in the house out of fear that it would result in too much loss of life. While Clarke wanted to keep fighting, it was decided that surrender was necessary. Elizabeth O'Farrell went out into the street with a white flag. The rebellion and the ICA's 'baptism of fire' had ended.

12

'SWEPT UP': EXECUTIONS AND INTERNMENT

With the Easter Rising over, the vengeance of the British political authorities came and the trials of the republican leaders began, *in camera*, on 2 May 1916. Deputy Judge Advocate General Alfred Bucknill believed that the legal preview for the court martial was by no means definite. While the authority emanated from the military emergency measures, specifically the Defence of the Realm Act (DORA), this did not take into consideration the case of armed insurrection and the charge of 'aiding the enemy' was added in the cases against the republicans. Justification for this was based on Pearse's last letter to his mother where he wrote of German assistance.[1] By operating in this way under DORA, the British administrative authorities were given far greater judicial control than normal, as legally any court martial which operated under martial law was subject to the regular courts once the period of emergency had ceased.[2] Rather, the leaders of the rebellion were all tried under a Field General Court Martial (FGCM), as an Ordinary General Court Martial (OGCM) was deemed impractical.[3]

This Field General Court Martial mode of trial meant that the republican soldiers were heard by three judges who did not have to be legally qualified. However, any death sentence had to be agreed by all three as well as confirmed by General Maxwell, the commander in chief in Ireland.[4] This was typically a blunt instrument and was conceived with the idea of ensuring discipline in the front line during war rather than for processing treasonous citizens. Furthermore, legally speaking, such a system was to be conducted in public, though as these court martials were typically held at the 'front' this was often impossible. Yet, this still ran counter to the secretive *in camera* principle which the Easter prosecutions operated under. Finally, no judge advocate presided over these hearings, as was the case under an Ordinary

General Court Martial.[5] Yet despite such inconsistencies, the trials began on 2 May when Pearse, MacDonagh and Clarke faced their hearings before being shot the following day.[6]

In total, only five ICA members were court martialled: James Connolly, Michael Mallin, Vincent Poole, William Partridge and Countess Markievicz.[7] Connolly and Mallin were both sentenced for execution while Markievicz was condemned to death but this was commuted to life in prison. Likewise, Vincent Poole also received a death sentence but it was commuted to five years. Partridge, the only one who was not originally to be executed, was sentenced to fifteen years' penal servitude remitted to five years.[8] After the trials of Connolly and MacDermott, Maxwell sent a letter to Prime Minister Asquith which detailed the three conditions under which the fifteen death sentences had been given: firstly, 'those who signed [the] proclamation of [the] provisional government and were also leaders in [the] actual rebellion in Dublin'; secondly, 'those who were in command of rebels actually shooting down troops, police and others'; and thirdly, 'those whose offence was murder'.[9] Connolly obviously fitted into the first division and Mallin into the second. The perception of Markievicz as a leader of the St Stephen's Green garrison probably placed her in the second as well. There is not sufficient evidence to state under which condition Poole was sentenced to death. However, it is plausible that he was placed in the third category.

On 2 May, a confidential note written by Brig-Genl Joseph Byrne detailed the manner in which the executions of Pearse, MacDonagh and Clarke were to take place. Once the 'Sinn Féin prisoners' had received their death sentences they were to be separated, 'so far as circumstance permit' and then asked if they wished to see any family or friends. A number of motor cars were stationed at Richmond Barracks to enable the transportation of these relatives who were to be taken back home before 03.30 on the day of the shooting.[10] After the visitors had departed, the execution process began. The rifles belonging to the rifle party were loaded by other men behind their backs. One rifle was left with a blank cartridge and the eleven others were filled with ball cartridges. Four firing parties were to fire in turn, with no man knowing which rifle contained the blank. Once the prisoner was shot a medical officer certified his death and his body was 'immediately removed' to an ambulance with a label pinned to his breast which identified him. The instructions then stated that once the ambulance was full, it was taken to Arbour Hill, via the garrison's chapel, and once each body was in position 'a priest [was to] attend for the funeral service'.[11]

On 5 May, Mallin, as prisoner number 78, faced court martial.[12] According to the general commanding the forces in Ireland, L.B. Friend, the offences were neither of a 'minor character' or 'practicable' to be tried by an Ordinary General Court Martial, so he convened a Field General Court Martial under Col. E.W.S.K. Maconchy, L.E. Col. A.M. Bent C.M.G. and Major. T.W. Woodward.[13] Mallin was charged, and pleaded not guilty to two offences. The first offence charged against him was that he 'did an act to take part in an armed rebellion and in the engaging of war against his Majesty the King, such an act being of such a nature as to be calculated to be prejudicial to the Defence of the Realm and being done with the intention and the purpose of assisting the enemy'. Alongside Markievicz, Connolly and Seán MacDermott, as well as other republican soldiers, Mallin faced another offence which stated he 'did attempt to cause disaffection among the civilian population of His Majesty' but he was cleared of that.[14] This second charge was of much lesser significance than the former and was not punishable by death. In practice the court considered the question of 'assisting the enemy' first and once the prisoner was convicted of this allegation, the latter was typically dropped as procedure. In that sense not guilty for the latter did not equate to innocent.[15]

It appears Mallin was not a well-known figure within British military or police circles. Within some of the DMP's files he was mistakenly referred to as 'James Mallin' and 'Michael Mullen'.[16] During the trial Mallin attempted to conceal his leadership using the British Army rank he obtained while stationed in India. He attempted to portray himself as a band instructor who had thought he was going out on general manoeuvres but got unwittingly caught up in the events on Easter Monday.[17] However, it appears that his role in the 'Instructional Warfare' articles gave away his true significance. The first witness, a DMP constable, John O'Connell stated that the *Workers' Republic* referred to him as 'Chief of Staff of the ICA'. Another witness, Constable C. Butler, also contended that he knew the rebel for the previous six to eight months and had seen him dressed in uniform with a revolver at the head of the Citizen Army alongside James Connolly. A third witness, Captain H.E. Wheeler, who was on duty outside the RCSI on 30 April, also remembered Mallin saying that he was the commandant of the garrison.[18] Furthermore, a document had been found on one of the prisoners which was signed by Connolly and mentioned his second in command as one of the various leaders, alongside MacDonagh, Kent, de Valera and Daly.[19] This meant it was nearly impossible for Mallin to escape the initial more significant charge and he was sentenced to death and subsequently executed sometime between 03:45 and 04:50 on 8 May; the same day as Seán Heuston, Con Colbert and Éamonn Ceannt.[20]

Two days before his execution, Countess Markievicz became the first and only woman to face trial and she was sentenced to death for her part in the rebellion. She faced the same two charges as the man she served under in St Stephen's Green. She pleaded guilty to the latter but not guilty to the more serious former.[21] Despite this, when questioned by the deputy judge advocate she responded that 'we dreamed of an Irish republic and thought we had a fighting chance'.[22] The wording of the charge 'did take part in an armed rebellion ... with the intention and the purpose of assisting the enemy' was important as it meant that this was not a disowning of her part in the rebellion but a recognition of the belief that the Easter Rising was done with the sole purpose of Irish independence and not with the goal of assisting the German war effort. She was found guilty of the first charge. However, the court recommended a degree of mercy due to her gender and she was commuted to penal servitude for life.[23] She seemed to have been acutely aware of the value of her gender in receiving the lesser sentence; Lieut. William Wylie recorded in his memoir that she made this argument and stated 'I'm only a woman. You cannot shoot a woman; you must not shoot a woman.'[24] Given the public outcry after the executions and the increased support for republicanism that followed, the execution of a woman was something that the British forces could not afford to do, politically speaking. Due to the commuting of the sentence, she was able to become the leading female figure of the Irish revolution and remained a central leader within the Citizen Army.

Connolly was given the prisoner identification number 90 and, due to his injuries, was taken to the Red Cross Hospital, Dublin Castle where his possessions amounted to 'a £1 note; a 10 pound treasury note; a watch; and a wallet'.[25] Here two doctors passed him fit to stand trial and on 9 May he was charged with the same charges that Mallin had faced previously. Like his most immediate understudy, he also pleaded not guilty to both. As opposed to trying to hide his leading role he appeared to make a political showcase of his hearing, in a similar manner to that of Robert Emmet. This was evidenced by his request to have a copy of his last statement given to his wife as well as by his effort to hand a second copy to his daughter, Nora. Enright described the statement as 'emotionally charged' and written at a point when 'Europe was locked in a war sustained by nationalist feeling.'[26] It sought to highlight the hypocrisy of the British Empire in its justification for its war effort. In the statement, Connolly contended that 'we succeeded in proving that Irishmen are ready to die endeavouring to win for Ireland their national rights which the British government have been asking them to die to win for Belgium'. Finally, at a time when the international community appeared to be at war for small nations, he stated 'we went out to try and break the connection between this country and the British Empire and to establish the Irish republic. We believe that the call we thus issued to the people of Ireland was a nobler call ... believing that the British government has no right in Ireland.'[27]

With the failure of the rebellion to achieve political independence, those who took an active part in Easter Week, 1916, were faced with the retribution of the British political and military authorities through imprisonment. While Maxwell oversaw the execution of fifteen of the rebel leaders, around 1,800 of the ordinary soldiers who went 'out' were simultaneously being interviewed and assessed before being deported and sent to various internment camps across Britain, most famously Frongoch in north Wales.[28] The *Sinn Féin Rebellion Handbook* detailed eighty-one ICA soldiers who were transported from Kilmainham Gaol and Ballsbridge by boat to British prisons between 30 April and 15 June 1916. Knutsford Prison received twenty-five prisoners, Stafford Prison received thirty-four prisoners, nine were sent to Wakefield Prison, Wandsworth Prison housed another eleven ICA men and two ICA men were sent to Lewis Prison.[29] Forty-nine of the ICA left on 30 April and this group included James O'Shea, Frank Robbins and Richard Corbally. Another five, Matthew Burke, John Byrne, Michael Delaney, George Fullerton and Patrick Murphy departed for Knutsford on 2 May. On 6 May, nine people arrived at Wakefield prison. Matthew Connolly, Jas Hyland and Seamus McGowan left for Stafford on 8 May as nine others, including Thomas Kain, travelled to Wandsworth. Two each were moved to Lewis, Wandsworth and Knutsford on 19 May, 1 June and 15 June respectively.[30]

Robbins described the boat trip and his arrival at Holyhead:

During the trip some men became ill, and having no room and being unable to move, had vomited on their nearest colleagues or on themselves. This will give an idea of how closely packed we were. There were, of course, no lavatories. The stench in the hold was overwhelming ... it must have taken about eight to twelve hours from the time we embarked until our arrival at Holyhead. While lined up at

Holyhead railway station we were the object of a great deal of curiosity. Most of the people assembled there indicated ... we were traitors and murderers. Some of the other epithets directed at us were even less complimentary.[31]

James O'Connor, an Irish Volunteer who was transported to Wakefield, had a similar experience. At the North Wall, he and his compatriots were placed in the cattle stalls of a cattle boat on its way to Holyhead and were given no food except for dog biscuits. Like Robbins, once they reached the British port they 'got a bad reception' which remained as they travelled through England.[32] Charles Brown of the Macroom Company of the Volunteers concurred with this assessment. He remembered when about 1,100 internees were marched in a cattle ship, handcuffed in pairs and placed in the space normally meant for such animals where 'things became very unpleasant' once sea sickness set in.[33] Seán O'Duffy also contended that these boats were so overcrowded that they were 'deplorable' and that having once arrived they were shown hostility by the British public who referred to the prisoners as 'dirty dogs'.[34]

Before leaving the various prisons and scrubs all of the men were handed a notice which informed them that under regulation 14B of DORA they were to be interned on the grounds of being 'a member of an organisation called the Irish Volunteers or of an organisation called the Citizen Army which have promoted armed insurrection against his majesty ...'[35] However, removal to the more permanent bases was a protracted affair. O'Connor was in Wakefield for a fortnight before being moved to Frongoch.[36] Meanwhile, many of the men in Knutsford were moved to the Welsh base during the middle of June while about 150, including William O'Brien, were transported there on 24 June.[37] In Stafford, the news of the impending movement reached Frank Henderson in early July.[38]

Once an old Welsh whiskey distillery, the camp was initially used to hold German Prisoners of War (POWs) but during summer–winter 1916 it was the home to the remaining men of the rebellion and those who would go on to attempt to break the British imperial yoke during the Anglo-Irish War of Independence. It was constructed in two separate parts: the south camp which lay in the depression of the valley and housed the buildings of the distillery, and the north camp on higher ground adjacent to the railway station through which the prisoners arrived.[39] It was in the north camp that the ICA served their internment alongside IRB men and Irish Volunteers as one united body of soldiers of the Irish Republic.

London-Irish Volunteer and member of the Kimmage Garrison, Joseph Good stated that during the entire period in the Welsh camp, the members of Larkin and Connolly's army 'sank their identity as a separate military body and had no special billets, officers or leaders. They accepted leadership from the Volunteers.'[40] Certainly, while it appears that it was during this time that competitiveness led to the claims of Connolly's kidnapping, as noted in Chapter 5, in general the Irish Volunteers and Irish Citizen Army remained united.[41] Referring to those 'out' during the Easter Rising, Matthew Connolly stated 'we were now merged with the Irish Volunteers, under the titles of the Irish Republican Army'.[42] Likewise, Andrew Conroy recollected the mobilisation of 'the officers of the IRA including the late Thomas Clarke, Joseph Plunkett and others for the meeting which was held in Liberty Hall on Easter Sunday'.[43] While these were retrospective accounts, contemporary accounts of the internment period showed that despite the failure to achieve independence, both the sense of formal unity as well as the belief in the existence of an Irish republic remained in late 1916.

In Frongoch on 26 August, James O'Neill referred to himself as both the quartermaster of the Citizen Army and belonging to the IRA when writing about the continuation of the struggle: 'they sent us to this cold English prison and our spirits they tried hard to break but dear lad we're more willing than ever to lay down our lives for thy sake'.[44] On 22 December 1916, Richard McCormick, detained in Reading Gaol, stated that he held allegiance to Ireland only and none to any king. Here he was even more certain of the formation of the IRA and the collapse of the ICA into a joint republican force as he wrote 'Cpt. Irish Repb Army, Late Irish Citizen Army'.[45] Likewise, on the same date and also in Reading, McGowan used the term 'late Citizen Army' and the initials 'IRA'. He continued in the prophetic tone of O'Neill by arguing 'our leaders are gone but we hang on just for another day and then we strike just for our rights and blow their [sic] to clay'.[46] In republican terminology the use of the term 'IRA' was an identifier for the 'IRB' at war.[47] It was a clear signal for the continuation of the republican armed campaign despite the failure of the rebellion at Easter. As a correlation to this, the term 'IRA' signified the continued existence of the joint forces during the internment period. Two important facets should be noted here. Firstly, O'Neill, McCormick and McGowan were all ICA officers in 1916 and, therefore, represented more than the ordinary soldiers' opinion as they were some of the most senior voices with the ICA at that point. Secondly, they all held commissioned ranks within the ICA after their release which indicated that their referrals were not part of a disavowal of the labour movement or were anyway atypical of those who took part in the Anglo-Irish War of Independence under the auspices of the labour militia.

Good's statement was then partly true. All divisions between the two republican militias had been eradicated and the remaining ICA leadership appeared to have followed Connolly's belief in a uniform republican body. However, it was not accurate that they accepted leadership from 'the Volunteers' *per se*. Allegiance was given to the wider newly formed army derived from the IRB rather than the militia formed at the Rotunda in November 1913. Certainly, the concept of the existence of the IRA was not restricted to those who had operated within the command of the old workers' defence corps. Others figures referred to the new republican army in such terms; including: Joseph Reader Robinson (Glasgow regiment IRA, 22 December 1916, Reading), Seajan Ó'Callaig (Captain Staff of Commander in Chief IRA, 22 December 1916, Reading), Tomás MacCurtain (Brigade Commander IRA, Christmas 1916, Reading) and Tomás Ó Grabám (Captain IRA Dublin Division, Reading).[48]

Importantly, in Frongoch it was decided by the POWs that they, with the approval of the British authorities, were to accept responsibility for the control of the internment base.[49] This meant that rather than being housed as a group of former active service men, those interned acted as a proper army unit which created a continuation from the Easter Rising. The British officers in the camp were seen as 'ordinary guards' who were past the point where they were able to fight at the front lines, and were described by Tomás MacCurtain as not capable of doing anything. Given this, an understanding gradually developed that the internees were to take care of the day-to-day running of base.[50] It is true that such a mutual understanding was not acceptable to all of the republicans. The argument followed that any tasks done by the IRA men relieved a British soldier of responsibility and was thus an aid to the enemy.[51] In Robbins's words 'many of us felt that this co-operation should not be given to the British military'.[52] However, the argument which won out was that such self-organisation was something that the force could do itself, that it would show discipline, and would help prevent the idea amongst the British soldiers that the republicans could not control their own military.[53]

In order to conduct such control, an IRA army council had to be established. According to Brennan-Whitmore, 'the control of the camp was entirely in the senior officers of the Irish Republican Army'.[54] Led by

Commandant J.J. O'Connell, the council comprised thirteen figures but importantly no one from the Citizen Army sat on it. Labour typically centred on fatigue work within the cookhouse, dining hall, latrines and yard offices. Drilling was also done after permission had been granted by the British military authorities.[55] These marches took place three times a week. At 11:00, the men were formed up with the company commanders lined in a single file quarter-column and the regulars lined in the same fashion to the right of their respective commanders. Lasting an hour, these marches were conducted outside of the camp and granted an opportunity, Robbins believed, to admire the Welsh countryside and as well to enjoy a short period of mental relaxation.[56]

While the work of the republican council in Frongoch was not typically subversive, the sense of renewed insurgency was never lost and this operational control helped create 'the organisation nucleus of the new revolution'.[57] The ICA's belief in this can be seen in O'Neill's, McGowan's and McCormick's sentiments. One prisoner of war, Liam O'Maguire, wrote of the hope for the future when writing 'the patriots of 1916, they failed say you, yes, but with their failure achieved success'. 'Success in establishing still higher, stronger and nobler;' he continued, 'the splendid ideal; in the hearts and minds of Irishmen and Irishwomen of an Ireland free and independent'.[58] While another, Seán MacGarigal, argued for 'the cause over all ... learn to labour and to wait'.[59] With this in mind, Frongoch became a revolutionary university which, in MP Tim Healy's words, was 'to the Irish what Sandhurst was to the British soldier'.[60]

Brennan-Whitmore recalled that the cream of the revolutionary movement had been 'swept up' by the British authorities and brought to a 'huge training camp' were they had 'carte blanche' to develop their military practices through training and lectures. He contended that the time spent in internment gave the republican soldiers an incalculable military advantage. In Frongoch communication networks and operational structures were put in place while old ICA and Óglaigh na hÉireann men were able to discuss, refine and understand each other's ideological position.[61] It, in effect, acted as an incubator for a renewed and a larger revolution, both politically and militarily.

13

'WE WERE PREPARING':
REORGANISING THE ARMY

The fall of Herbert Asquith as British Prime Minister over the struggles of the war effort in Europe took place on 6 December 1916 and he was replaced by David Lloyd George who decided that it was time to end the internment of the rebels who had been sentenced for their part in the Easter Rising. A general amnesty was declared in December and the majority of prisoners were released on Friday 22 December 1916.[1] Throughout early 1917, political focus across the wider republican community was on rejuvenating Sinn Féin in an attempt to cut the link between the British administration and the Irish community. In the military space, cautious attempts at reorganisation and public defiance began to be made.[2] These steps were also taken by the Irish Citizen Army. According to McGowan, they 'were preparing for conscription, procuring arms and distributing them.'[3] Even before the amnesty, and possibly under the guise of the Connolly and Mallin Social and Athletic Club, which was established in the aftermath of the rebellion, labour men who had evaded arrest had decided to 'keep going until the men came out of jail'. This even led to the find of forty-five rifles, largely old Mausers, in a hall in Lower Pembroke Street.[4] More formal structures were re-established in 1917. According to Hanratty, James O'Neill was made commandant of the newly revived organisation early in the year.[5] Given the affiliations during the internment period, it is interesting that in such a quick space of time an attempt to reassert the Citizen Army's independence was made.

It can be argued once the official unity of republicans occurred on Easter Sunday and Easter Monday there ceased to be a need for a reformed independent Citizen Army; that the body stepped away from its initial primary function as a workers' defensive wing when it separated from its parent union in March 1914 to assume the role of a revolutionary instigator. But that too had ceased to be pertinent in post-rebellion Ireland.[6] As indicated by their future co-operation with the IRA, it is unlikely that this quasi-split between the Volunteers and the ICA resulted from significant ideological divergence. Rather, it may have resulted from the Volunteers re-establishing itself across the country and it was logical for the ICA to do the same.[7] Similarly, as no formal united structures had ever existed outside of Connolly's co-option onto the IRB's military council, it may have been the case that this was the simplest form of reviving the republican struggle. Evidently, it was felt that before creating a scheme of operation within the wider republican forces, it was necessary to reform the labour army to agree upon the way in which this was to be done. 'The first job,' O'Neill stated, 'was to reorganise the army and the second [was] to see how we could work best in conjunction with the HQ of the Volunteers.'[8] An attempt to formalise such structures was made in 1917.

In the aftermath of the release of the internees in December 1916, the majority of the ICA felt that the militia should remain an autonomous organisation, separated from the Volunteers. The ICA's own constitution, in particular the labour clauses, was to be retained. Particularly relevant was that all Citizen Army members should be, where possible, members of a trade union, and should be ready to work for the unity of Ireland and 'the recognition of the rights and liberties of the world's democracies'. A conference was held where the ICA was represented by O'Neill and McCormick while Brugha and Collins represented the Volunteers. At this meeting it was decided that both organs would keep their respective constitutions and their status of independence but would not engage in any armed operations without informing the other army first.[9] It seems for the labour men their sense of identity, most profoundly manifested through their constitution, was not something which they could give up.[10] This was a logical position to take given the ICA's internationalist outlook as well as the persistent belief amongst its members that the militia needed to present itself as a proper army. However, others saw the labour army's desire for autonomy in more self-aggrandising terms. Oscar Traynor, a lieutenant during the rebellion, stated 'the position I find was immediately after the reorganisation in 1916, the Citizen Army was very difficult to co-operate with, whether they had superiority complex or not ... I rather imagine they felt they were the initiators of the whole thing.'[11] O'Neill gave an account which painted a more cordial picture and stated:

After 1916, I met Cathal Brugha. We discussed the thing, as how it reconciled to the Volunteers, or vice versa. We found it was not possible. We were not prepared to fuse. Then it was decided the two people should exist as independent units, and work in close co-operation with each other. We wanted particularly to cover this point. There might be cases where the Citizen Army might take action other than what would be approved by the Volunteers, and it was from that point of view we had to keep in touch with each other.[12]

The problems with creating a unified body appear to have been a case of practicality rather than any ideological divergence. Traynor may have been correct in pointing towards an egocentric element. Indeed, the ICA's belief in Connolly as the instigator of the rebellion led to the belief amongst ICA soldiers that the labour militia was the forerunner of the revolution, as evidenced in the emergence of the kidnapping myth. The force, during the Anglo-Irish War of Independence, was described by Hanley as an army with an 'obsession' regarding its autonomy and status. Evidence for this can be seen in that McGowan was 'disciplined' by the ICA's army council in 1920 for allowing his title to be used at a Larkin support meeting. Further evidence was that when former member Seán McLaughlin criticised the army in a report for the Third International, which focused on working-class organisations in Ireland, the ICA issued a warrant for his arrest.[13] Given the countrywide nature of Óglaigh and the capital-centred nature of the labour force, it is possible that issues such as seniority and spheres of influence may have been impediments to the ICA remaining as a part of the IRA. Certainly, no form of hostility hindered co-operation either throughout that period or during the Anglo-Irish War of Independence. While the ICA 'functioned definitely as an independent army', this was always 'in conjunction with the IRA'.[14] The ICA's general pension file suggested that during the 1917–18 period the Volunteers and the Citizen Army leadership met three to four times a year.[15]

With the death of Connolly and Mallin, Christopher Poole had been left as the most senior officer in the ICA and contended that he had taken charge of the force until O'Neill's appointment, which was made 'some time before Count Plunkett's election'.[16] According to John Hanratty, Poole could have been looked on as an O/C for the short period between the release of prisoners and the succession of O'Neill. However, Hanratty also contended that that was a period of disorganisation and there were no official ranks used in practice at that point. Hanratty stated there was no rivalry or jostling for the head position. Rather, the eventual selection of O'Neill was due to the belief amongst the other remaining officers that he was the best suited for the role.[17] This was an opinion shared by Poole. He confirmed that he 'withdrew in favour of James O'Neill'. However, he inaccurately stated that the commandant held no rank before 1916.[18] While O'Neill eventually resigned in 1922, in the aftermath of O'Neill's promotion to commandant, Poole remained on as staff captain. This position was also held by Richard McCormick and Michael Kelly. McGowan officially became the ICA's director of munitions, Kathleen Lynn became its surgeon general and Hanratty was awarded the position of quartermaster.[19] Further restructuring occurred in 1918 when an operational division was drawn across the city with the creation of the North Side ICA and the South Side ICA commanded by staff captains Martin Kelly and Richard McCormick, respectively.[20] Also by 1918, the ICA's council was also firmly re-established. In an 18 July 1935 statement to the Advisory Committee of the Army Pensions Board, James O'Neill outlined its construct and remit. It consisted of the commandant, the quartermaster as the 'next senior rank' (Hanratty was appointed to this position in 1918) and the four staff captains. O'Neill stated that the council 'met at least once a week and sometimes more frequently; they decided the general policy of the Army and the general activities all along'. When asked did the council decide on whether operations would be carried out or not, he confirmed 'yes, they did'.[21]

In Poole's words, the activity during this period was simply 'organising'.[22] McGowan stated that at this time he was 'tremendously busy and active in re-organising and rebuilding the ICA organisation and munitions departments'.[23] Hanratty also provided a listing of their general activities: commemorations, such as the first anniversary of the Easter Rising, funerals, such as that of Thomas Ashe on 26 September 1917 or W. Partridge in November 1917, public events like the reception for Countess Markievicz in November 1918, and military operations like the defence against the raid on Liberty Hall on 13 November 1918 and the Dublin dockland raid on a American supply boat also in 1918.[24] In order to turn the republican movement into a sustained widespread and successful campaign, such political measures were needed and were typical of the wider movement's efforts to legitimise both the republic proclaimed the year before and the violence that was soon to follow.[25] The armament work was in the tradition of the activities of 1915–16 but was also drastically needed during the rebuilding phase of 1917–19. Work in drilling also recommenced and was conducted two nights a week in a small committee room at the back of Liberty Hall, which had been restored in the aftermath of the Rising. Focus was placed on musketry instruction and rifles practice and, according to O'Neill, was taught by 'expert trainors [sic] ... who were musketry instructors ... [and] had all their scientific method of training'. Field practice was also carried out during the weekend.[26]

By May 1917, republicanism was in the air once again and it travelled around the streets of Dublin. ICA women's section members Helena Molony, Winifred Carney, 'Jinny' Shanahan and Madeline ffrench-Mullin all decided that it was important to commemorate the first anniversary of the strike for independence and the death of the labour leader, Connolly.[27] In Liberty Hall, women were assigned the task of making tricolour flags while a man named West printed out copies of the proclamation written on the original typewriter which Hanratty, O'Neill, McGowan and McCormick had excavated from the rubble of the original Liberty Hall. The regular soldiers of the ICA were used to post these across the city.[28] In 1936, Jane Shanahan recalled 'the anniversary of Easter Week we got a second issue of the proclamation printed ... and we got the flags on each position that was held by the military forces during Easter Week'.[29] Molony also remembered that both she and Shanahan barricaded themselves into Liberty Hall using coal from a coal room and went to the roof to hang a commemorative banner and wait for the arrival of the police. While the DMP did eventually enter the building, having had to shovel out the coal and take down the republican message, Molony recalled 'the scroll remained on Liberty Hall for several hours. It attracted great attention, and crowds gathered – the same as happened in O'Connell Street when the flag was flown.'[30]

That day, 12 May 1917, showed that Liberty Hall stood defiant against British imperialism in the same manner as it had done when the 'we serve neither King nor Kaiser' flag had been massed on its façade. However, aspects of the event revealed how the more heated post-rebellion atmosphere began to break the relationship between the ITGWU and the ICA. Despite the hoisting of a flag that said James Connolly had been murdered on 12 May 1916, the union appeared to be unwilling to publicly support outward separatist machinations. During the rebellion, the ITGWU had lost £1000s belonging to their members while, after the Rising, their headquarters lay literally in ruins.[31] The rebellion and the subsequent imposition of martial law as well as the arrest and deportation of many trade union members had left trade unionism in Ireland in a critical position. While the destruction of the capital city during the week had created a 'dislocation of industry', it was also argued in the ITUC's 1916 annual report that the employers and press could point to the collapse of the republican effort as the 'end of militant trade unionism'.[32] The congress, at its annual meeting in Sligo in August 1916, was unwilling to take a firm stance on the Easter Rising's rights or wrongs.

> as a trade union movement we are of varied minds on matters of history and political development, and, consequently, this is not a place to enter into a discussion as to the right or the wrong, the wisdom or the folly of the revolt, but this we may say, that those amongst the rebels who have been associated with us in the past, who have led and inspired some of us with their love of their country and their class were led to act as they did with no selfish thought but purely with a passion for freedom and a hatred of oppression.[33]

Given this equivocal response, it was not surprising that by 1917 ICA members felt that the union 'did not want the Citizen Army men [in Beresford Place] at all. They were only tolerated, they were there on sufferance.'[34] Hanratty, O'Neill and Poole had all been deployed by the ICA to help Count Plunkett in his election campaign for the Roscommon by-election in February 1917.[35] On 4 February 1917, the day his election victory was announced, Árm Lucta Oibre na h-Éireann men had hoisted a tricolour on the Beresford Place building in celebration but this was quickly ordered to be taken down.[36] By August of that year, the ITGWU, facing financial difficulties, sought to distance itself from the history of the armed labour wing in its attempt to claim for damages to Liberty Hall. The ICA were simply 'tenants of Irish Transport Union' rather than having a shared leadership. The union was also keen to assert that 5,000 of its men, 2,000 of which were fatalities, had been engaged in British Army's effort in the 'European war'.[37] Molony believed that the ICA was only tolerated in their old base because of the memory of Connolly and the ITGWU did not have the 'courage' to tell the army to leave.[38] Certainly, the ambivalent 'facing both ways' position taken in Sligo in summer 1916, meant the ITUC and the ITGWU had severed any political symbiosis with the army of the workers.[39]

The divergence between the ICA and the wider labour movement's leadership in their willingness to take part in the republican campaign was expressed by Hanratty. In 1922, he stated that the union had been 'taken over' by men who did not share the interest of the army. This takeover, he argued, was despite twice being approached by the ICA with the aspiration of renewing co-operation and assistance.[40] Certainly, 1917–19 saw a sustained divergence in political ethos which led to the splitting of the connection between the Citizen Army and ITGWU. Undoubtedly, the union began to take a more moderate stance on political issues in comparison to the army. Robbins returned to Dublin in early 1918, after having worked in America, and found 'the close co-operation which had previously existed officially between the Irish Transport Union and the Irish Citizen Army seemed to have gone completely'.[41]

By 1918, the Irish political scene was even further radicalised as the continuation of the conflict in Europe once again raised the spectre of conscription. This threat sparked 'mass popular protest' in Dublin in opposition to the potential implementation of conscription.[42] In the Ulster counties opposition to conscription was not restricted to nationalists, as working-class loyalists were also active in attempts at impeding the measure.[43] Certainly, opposition to that type of government policy also acted as a republican rallying call. In the southern counties, nationalists did not hesitate to meet the challenge and neither did the ICA. Throughout the 1914–15 period, armed labour had consistently offered itself as a solution to both British Army recruitment and what it saw as 'economic conscription'. In early 1918, when the issue of parliamentary enforced conscription was threatened, they did not change their course.

While he did not provide detail on the actual work undertaken, ICA man Andrew Conroy, who was made lieutenant in 1918, was tasked with impeding conscription. He stated that he was one of the men detailed, given passwords and instructions by the ICA to proceed to various locations where they were to operate should there have been an attempt to enact conscription in the country.[44] It is likely that the ICA's leadership expected their men to act as a line of resistance at individual places in a similar manner to their plan to mobilise during the Monteith deportation incident. Evidently the women's section was involved in fundraising to help provide assistance for the undertaking. According to Shanahan, during the period 'that must have been the time of conscription. You might remember a period where you were not supposed to gather outside churches and make collections, sometime in 1917, there was some decision arrived at that we would meet outside churches and hold demonstrations.'[45]

After the rebellion, Bryan Mahon, Britain's general officer commanding (GOC) in Ireland, issued an order that required Óglaigh, the Sinn Féin

League and the Citizen Army to surrender all of their remaining arms. While an untitled RIC report stated that this was only 'partially complied with', a total of 4,075 arms were confiscated.[46] For a force that had historically struggled to gather an adequate stockpile of weapons, this may have rendered the ICA's work of 1915–16 null and void. According to Robbins, when the initial reorganisation of the force occurred 'we held a number of meetings at the Eden Quay end of Liberty Hall, and one of the first things we decided to concentrate on was the procuring of arms'. However, he also contended that 'there was neither money nor contacts nor any form of organisation'.[47] The ICA returned to the methods of arms acquisition that had been used from late 1914 up to the Easter Rising: importation and purchases from sympathetic British soldiers. It was under these conditions that Commandant O'Neill, McCormick and McGowan began rebuilding the arms and ammunition stocks of the ICA. McGowan wrote that from April 1917 to March 1918 he was continually involved in the 'purchase, and actual thefts of rifles from British soldiers' which was done with the 'collaboration' of the Volunteer J.J. O'Connell.[48]

While the Dublin Port authorities did not view 'the Sinn Féin Volunteers'' attempts at importation of arms as a success, the docks and the quays were valuable grounds for the ICA.[49] McGowan worked with a man named Hughes in creating contacts with sailors on boats in order to increase their stockpile.[50] Likewise, under the Irish National Aid Association and Volunteers' Dependents Fund (INAAVDF), Molony established a shirtmaking factory along the quays which had a two-fold purpose: its profits were used to pay wages to the female members of the ICA, and its location was ideal 'as a post for people calling on the quays'. The place was permanently open and sailors would often arrive in to inform the women what type of valuable 'goods' were coming through the port. In this way, she contended, the base acted as 'a type of intelligence depot for getting [the arms] in'.[51]

This depot appears to have been quite successful in receiving arms from Glasgow and Liverpool, two traditional port cities friendly to the Irish republican cause. According to Molony, two Glasgow men were involved in this type of work, one named Moran and another named Whyte but known as 'Blanco'.[52] She did not know the exact amount of arms and ammunition which were smuggled in because at that time she felt it was not customary to ask for precise details. However, she contended that 'a lot of arms' and 'a considerable amount' of bombs were brought over.[53] Dennis Farrell was one of several people termed as 'boat workers' who were working on troop ships at the North Wall who took in revolvers and ammunition and brought them to McGowan in Beresford Place.[54] On two occasions Reader travelled to Dublin with his brothers Friel and Carmichael, to give a combined total of 100 detonators to the ICA.[55]

In a similar manner to the use of Richmond Barracks prior to the rebellion, Portobello Barracks provided a useful location where the ICA was given guns. Commandant O'Neill and Captain McCormick seemed to have initiated this work. McCormick used to travel around various public houses and 'get talking to' various people who could have been of help and he paid them 30 shillings for each rifle. Through this *modus operandi* he was able to receive three rifles from Portobello on 25 September 1917.[56] This work was not a one-time occurrence as it continued throughout the pre-war period and provided a relatively significant number of arms. On another occasion in 1917 both Corbally and O'Shea, along with about seven others, travelled across Leinster Road to Portobello Barracks where they were handed about twelve rifles which were then placed on Corbally's cart before being left in an arms dump in Gardiner Street.[57] The method of the work occurred in this fashion:

> The position was that there were two soldiers in the barracks who got the stuff ready and had it fairly handy. Very few of our fellows actually handled the stuff. Most of the work was done by scouts on bicycles. The man who actually brought the stuff was a man named Corbally, who brought in a horse and car and took it away from Mount Street. Myself [Christopher Crothers] and two others shifted it afterwards to Leixlip. O'Shea was in on the removal of [the] stuff after the first dump. There was a grave risk attached to that whole job.[58]

John Craven was also used as a transporter while James Keogh was often handed the guns once these jobs were complete.[59] Certainly, Portobello was particularly valuable as Corbally received twenty-seven rifles from there. However, it was not the only target. McCormick and James Keogh were involved in the procurement of guns from Islandbridge Barracks in 1918.[60] Similarly, around four or five times a week, though sometimes he would not have a job for a week or a month, Corbally would go around to various barracks in the hope of purchasing munitions. He would pay £1 for one rifle and 30 shillings or £2 for a couple of rifles.[61] Keogh recalled that Corbally was 'kept very busy' in this assignment while McCormick received a total of twenty-six guns.[62] Some of these rifles and certainly the four which were obtained from Islandbridge were brought out to Lucan where it was hoped to raise a column there, though such plans never came to fruition.[63]

One soldier who was particularly useful to the ICA in their attempts to gather arms after the rebellion, was Edward Handley, whom James O'Shea came in contact with sometime in 1917. After becoming friendly, O'Shea told him the ICA was out to 'rob, murder, or buy guns'.[64] Handley served in the Fourth Battalion, Dublin Fusiliers, enlisting out of economic necessity, and had been in Dublin on sick leave in 1916 after having been wounded on duty in France. On account of this injury, as well as having failed to return to the army, by 1917 his rank was reduced from sergeant to private and he was sent to Portobello to work as a storeman; thus, he was in a perfect position to aid the needs of the ICA.[65] Previously, Handley had worked in White's public house at 79 The Coombe, which was owned by the Volunteer Andy Redmond where he got to know a number of men in the area who later became members of the Citizen Army. Given this, it was natural that James Keogh, Matt Burke and O'Shea questioned him over the possibility of getting arms.[66]

Handley informed Keogh that he would be able to pursue the task if he was able to get a suitable turnscrew which would allow him to take apart the guns. Keogh worked at the railway station in Inchicore and was able to make such a screw which was used to strip rifles. After this was done, a meeting took place at the back of the sports field in Mount Thomond Avenue near Harold's Cross were O'Shea and Craven took the rifles.[67] Once four to five of the guns were gathered they were then brought to The Coombe where they were left in the house of a Mrs Pidgeon who had first met O'Shea at the time of the Howth gunrunning. She stored the guns in an old chimney which was camouflaged so well that they remained hidden despite a number of raids.[68]

The work was dangerous as the British Army knew that the guns had been taken. However, they never suspected Handley but believed that they were being taken by traders visiting the barracks.[69] The Citizen Army men were almost caught on two occasions. In one incident, Craven, O'Shea and Kelly had left The Coombe at about nine o'clock with ten rifles concealed in sacks as well as 'No.9 bombs' and some automatics. They were transporting them across the city in Craven's van when they got caught in a hold-up at College Green, and only avoided a search when Craven told a soldier that he was running late to get a train. On another occasion, they were stopped outside of the capital when they were carrying 'a big cargo of stuff'. While the policeman only wanted to know if they had seen the sergeant down the road, they were prepared to pull guns on him.[70]

Not all of the Citizen Army's attempts at acquisitions were done with the aid of sympathetic British Army servicemen. In his outline history of the 1917–23 period, Hanratty wrote 'USA Supply Boat 1918'.[71] He was referring to the USS *Defiance* which was a US Navy transport vessel that had docked in Dublin on its way back from Dunkirk for Hampton Roads with the purpose of shipping huts and stores belonging to the United States Expeditionary Force. When the dockers in Dublin realised that the ship held cases of revolvers, ammunition and rifles, they quickly informed the ICA. Seamus McGowan was smuggled in on the pretence of being a docker.[72] James O'Dwyer was one ICA volunteer who worked in the docks at the time and he appears to have been one of the first to spot the potential for a raid.[73] While an armed US marine was stationed on each gangway of the vessel and other US guards were placed in positions in the deck and hold, the ICA worked in conjunction with the Third Battalion of the IRA and was able to offload many of the munitions that were on the vessel.[74]

Other ICA men involved in this expedition were: Christopher Poole, whom Fox contended was in charge of the project though Poole did not claim this, Peter Coates, George Connolly, Laurence Corbally, whose role was to transfer them to Liberty Hall, and Richard Corbally, who confirmed that the materials taken were ordinary service rifles. Richard Corbally said that 'a good bit' of rifles and revolvers went through his hands. James O'Shea carried seven guns out of the USS *Defiance* strapped to his body.[75] While the cases had to be broken open in the hold by dockers without being observed by guards, the republican soldiers worked in groups and were sent to the quays for eight hours a day where they were handed the munitions from those who received the necessary permits. At the same time, tin lavatories that were found on the quays were used as transfer stations.[76] According to Connolly, 'the way it was we passed it from one to another. We did not go down and get a load of stuff and walk up to the hall. We waylaid one another at street corners.'[77]

The raid on the USS *Defiance* proved to be arguably the most successful in the force's ten-year history. Fox estimated that fifty-four .45 revolvers, 2,000 rounds of revolver ammunition, 5,000 rounds of Springfield ammunition and various amounts of Verey lights and pistols were smuggled off the ship while a member of the *Defiance*'s crew was also paid off to lower a further twenty-four .45 automatics over the side of the ship, in a canvas bucket, to a boat waiting below.[78] Alongside this, the Springfield rifles had to be left on the ship as they were too cumbersome to carry. McGowan estimated that nearly one hundred .45 revolvers were taken from the ship as it lay in the South Wall.[79] Hanratty contended that fifty-six Smith & Wessons, twenty-five automatics, 4,000 rounds of .45 cartridges and 6,000 rounds of Springfield ammunition were secured. He also stated that they 'failed to get the rifles'.[80] The smuggling had to be stopped after the captain of the ship discovered that a number of the ship's crates were now empty. He had also been informed by one of his crew who, in turn, had been asked by one of the Volunteers if he had any guns for sale.[81] However, before this the ICA and the Volunteers had clearly secured a windfall and they were eventually moved from Liberty Hall to the dump in Leixlip.[82]

Shortly before this raid, the unit was engaged in active service in the defence of Liberty Hall. Despite the sense of impartiality that ITGWU had tried to cultivate post-rebellion, they still bore the suspicions of the DMP who believed that on occasion the ITGWU's influence was expressed in a 'distinctly political type'.[83] Such distrust manifested in a raid on Liberty Hall on 24 December 1917. DMP agents were looking for bombs and other explosives and given that there was no opposition to their arrival it can be deduced that the ICA was not involved.[84] However, a year later the ICA returned to its March–April 1916 purpose of defending the base. Armistice Day 1918 saw an outbreak of celebrations amongst unionists and nationalists alike. However, in the midst of such a festive atmosphere, Liberty Hall, the Mansion House and the Sinn Féin offices were attacked by a group of British soldiers. According to Mary Allen, some ICA members were in Liberty Hall that night.[85] They quickly rushed to its defence as they went to the roof and began to throw stones over the heads of the mob. The British soldiers were kept at bay but did manage to break windows and caused £200 worth of damage before they were taken away by the military police.[86] While this was nothing more than a small fracas, it had a symbolic importance. On the day when peace across Europe was announced, the latent antagonism between some republicans and some British soldiers emerged. Within the coming months, the beginning of a full-scale war was to occur and the ICA was faced with the task of aiding the IRA.

14

'We stand solid for an Irish Workers' Republic': The War of Independence

On 21 January 1919, the First Dáil, though illegal according to the Westminster Parliament, was convened for the first time. At the time, Countess Markievicz, who in O'Neill's opinion was the second in command of the ICA, had run in the 1918 elections which granted the Irish Parliament its democratic mandate.[1] During her political career as a *Teachta Dála* (Member of Parliament), letters from her which varied from ICA obituaries, to letters to American Clan na Gael leader Joe McGarrity, to criticism of the police, were signed with the title 'ICA'.[2] In this manner, she represented a political wing of the labour military body. However, as the assassination on 21 January 1919 of two policemen at Soloheadbeg, County Tipperary, signalled, this was a period defined by a prolonged military campaign as well as political agitation. Through the actions of the South Tipperary IRA Brigade, the Irish Citizen Army was faced with renewing their attack on the British Empire.

In some quarters, the ICA has been seen as being politically lethargic during the Anglo-Irish War of Independence. According to an Army Pensions Board report, 'generally speaking, the Citizen Army did not take a fully organised part in the Black and Tan fight. Individual members of that organisation did undoubtedly operate with members of the IRA.'[3] Traynor, when asked about the ICA not wanting to fight, said they were disorganised. Likewise, the 1919–20 minute book of the ICA has been interpreted as highlighting an interest in day-to-day issues and formality during the period rather than the wider political struggle.[4] Hanley wrote of the Citizen Army during the Anglo-Irish War of Independence and subsequent Irish Civil War, that 'the organisation was never clear on its political and military purposes and was hidebound both by a petty application of formal discipline and by the tendency of its members to use it as a social club'.[5] Certainly, for Robbins, the lack of a definitive Connolly-ite policy was the fault of its new leader. He believed O'Neill's actions were best defined by procrastination and that without the guidance of the likes of Mallin and Connolly, the ICA 'in no way resembled or held the outlook which was dominant up to 1916'.[6] However, one issue that questions this was that each year between 1917 and 1920 O'Neill was re-appointed as the commandant of the force by its regular soldiers.[7]

Certainly, for his own part, O'Neill argued that 'the Tan War was not a stand up fight, it was guerrilla. In proportion to their numbers they gave just as good service as the Volunteers.'[8] It must be recognised that there were other factors which hamstrung the small army. Hanley recognised that the ICA, at this point, lacked any definitive and homogenous ideological drive and contained members who, at various levels, supported republicanism, Larkinism, 'mainstream labour' and communism.[9] Furthermore, in contrast to the Easter Rising which focused on the capital city, the Anglo-Irish War of Independence was typically at its most intense in the Munster region while in Dublin full-scale urban IRA ambushes were noticeably 'remarkable for their rarity'.[10] Considering this, it was impossible for the labour army to engage in operations in a comparable sense to the countrywide Irish Republican Army. Despite such limitations, attempts were made to assist the wider movement. For instance, in 1921, the ICA's army council decided to transfer twelve of their rifles to Tipperary IRA units.[11] In 1935 Hanratty contended that during the War of Independence 'almost all the rifles in our possession went to the Volunteers for use down the country'.[12] According to their director of munitions, the council met, deliberated, and decided to send the material to the Munster ASU. It appears this was a definitive policy rather than the actions of any individual as stated by the Army Pensions Board.[13] Evidently, efforts to create a co-operative relationship with the wider Irish Republican Army defined the ICA during the 1919–21 conflict.

However, criticism can be directed at O'Neill and the ICA's leadership for its inactivity in various industrial and agrarian working-class struggles from 1917 onwards. Hanley was correct in his statement that 'the army council's minutes for 1919–20 mention no incidence of armed backing being given to labour, aside from the stewarding of the Connolly commemoration in June 1919'. He continued that 'despite the prestige and status gained by its involvement in the 1916 rising the ICA played no real role in working class struggles during the 1919–21 period … but given the explosion of working-class militancy throughout the period, its inactivity in that field was its major weakness'.[14]

Despite the deterioration of the ICA's association with the ITGWU, its relationship with the IRA during this period was more cordial. Sustained formal union with Óglaigh proved impossible in 1917, but this was not the case by the outbreak of the Anglo-Irish War of Independence. Statements by both O'Neill and the typically critical Traynor, indicate that the commandant was meeting IRA leader Michael Collins nearly once a week and this enabled greater co-operation between the bodies.[15] Murray contended that he regularly saw Collins and O'Neill in Kirwans public house in Parnell Street.[16] O'Neill described the relationship in general terms and stated 'we let them start anything they wished, as long as they fought in the one common cause'. He continued 'our instruction in these cases to such people who wanted to organise sections in the country was for them to act in close co-operation with the Volunteers'.[17] Certainly, Robbins attended a meeting with Seamus Robinson, Archie Heron and Frank McCade with the object of cementing this harmony.[18] Likewise, McGowan often acted as both a guide and a point of contact for various IRA men. According to Edmond O'Brien, from Limerick, both he and James Scalon were guided by him at meetings at the army offices of Phil Shenahan as well as at interviews with figures such as Michael Collins, Seán Tracy and Dan Breen at Flemings Hotel in Gardiner Place, Dublin. In this manner McGowan 'was indispensable in getting [IRA] comrades and [O'Brien] in touch with each other day and night and his services were often in demand'.[19]

A system of reassignment was also put in place where those who wished to were able to permanently move into the Irish Republican Army.[20] This was not a simple disavowal of militant Larkinism as the soldiers could not simply leave the ICA and go to any 'Volunteer' unit that they wished but typically had to apply for a transfer which implied an acceptance on the part of both forces.[21] In O'Neill's words 'a man got a definite transfer from us to the Volunteers or from the Volunteers to us. There was very close co-operation'.[22] Indeed, the ICA used to recruit and then transfer these men over to the IRA.[23] Traynor contended that those who transferred did so because they wished to escape the 'inactivity where they were'.[24] However, reasons for such movement were not restricted to frustration with martial labour policy but were often a result of personal situations. George Oman 'did not get transferred [he] left the Citizen Army, [he] gave up the Citizen Army'. However, his brother William joined B Company First Battalion IRA simply because George had joined previously. Internal ICA politics was the cause of the departure of James O'Shea in May 1922. He was one of the ICA's most active members and he became an intelligence officer in A Company of the Third Battalion IRA.[25] Economic reasons were another cause. For

TABLE 14.1. ICA men who transferred to the IRA post-rebellion

Name	Date
Peter Bermingham	1916
Patrick Bradley	10 January 1917
Peter Carpenter	March/April 1920
Walter Carpenter	1922
Patrick Carroll	1921 (truce)
Owen Carton	1917
George Connolly	1921
Patrick Dury	1917
James Gough	1917
Francis Kelly	February 1917
Hugh Kelly	Summer 1920
James Kelly	1918
Joseph Kelly	1918
Edward Kelly	December 1918
Shawn Nolan	1918
Thomas O'Donoghue	1920
William Oman	September 1919
George Oman	1918
James O'Shea	1922
Vincent Poole	1920
Andrew Redmond	1918
John Redmond	1919
Thomas Shiel	1918
Michael Wade	1921 (truce)
Joseph Whelan	1917

Source: See individual claims within the Military Service Pension Collection.

instance, Martin Shannon left the ICA on 6 February 1919 because he had been let go from his position in Jacob's biscuit factory and moved to Scotland for employment.[26] Similarly, Thomas Shiel moved to Wicklow and joined the IRA's Second Battalion of the Carlow Brigade which operated there.[27] Furthermore, others such as Andrew Redmond, William Scott and Peter Bermingham left the ICA before the outbreak of the Anglo-Irish War of Independence and this could not be seen as a result of a failure of ICA activity.[28]

A similar operation occurred with some movement in the opposite direction and people such as Joseph Doolan transferred to the ICA.[29] The November to December 1920 period also saw the development of a new company composed of the South County Dublin ICA and A Company, Fourth Battalion Irish Volunteers.[30] The unit operated under the leadership of the Citizen Army rather than a co-operative effort as the IRA's men were 'transferred' into ICA.[31] Denis Dunne was one of the last people to move between the bodies and he transferred from the anti-treaty IRA to that battalion in 1922, shortly before the bombing of the Four Courts.[32] Seán O'Neill was referred to as the leader of the unit but it was Pádraig Ó Broin who acted as its organiser and representative on the Citizen Army's leadership council. He 'had authority from the ICA headquarters to organise the section and to carry on his activity in co-operation with the local Volunteer unit'.[33] During his time in Óglaigh, Ó Broin had served as a squad leader, section commander, quartermaster and company adjutant, and had also been a member of the 'Teeling Centre' of the IRB prior to the Easter Rising. Thus, he was in an excellent position to act as an organiser.[34] He had also been a short-lived member of the Citizen Army during its pre-constitutional days before leaving in December 1913.[35] Such familiarity may also have aided his promotion.

The consultation arrangement between the Volunteers and the Citizen Army did not always run successfully. Failures in communication occurred on one occasion during a Citizen Army planned raid on Kingsbridge Station where it was hoped to abscond with two waggons of military stores which were held there. However, it was discovered that the Dublin Brigade of the Volunteers had raided the station first. Collins explained the incident by informing the Citizen Army that he had not been told of the Dublin Brigade's plans. After this incident an arrangement was made where the Dublin Brigade and the Citizen Army would be in direct contact. Such an arrangement held steadfast during both the Anglo-Irish War of Independence and the Irish

Civil War.[36] Another area where Oscar Traynor argued co-operative efforts were impossible was the organisation of Q Company in 1919.

Q Company was formed in early 1919 by the Dublin Division IRA when the IRA's headquarters realised that seamen and dockers who had experienced hardship during the lockout had been supplying groups such as the Hibernian Rifles militia and it was 'realised that if these men were properly organised they could obtain as much arms and munitions as the funds at their disposal could purchase'.[37] Q Company comprised both sailors and dockers who in Traynor's words were 'the type of men who might be members of the Citizen Army, but they were not'.[38] It is accurate that the general pension file for Q Company only mentioned the ICA concerning general quay work which predated its formation, and that no individual ICA member who submitted a pension file claimed involvement in Q Company. Given this, it seems Traynor's contention was correct.[39]

It is possible that the absence of ICA involvement in Q Company resulted from its confidence in its own systems as it is unlikely that the ICA did not have the necessary mechanisms in place to help in the smuggling in of arms through the quays. Christina Caffrey was carrying armaments over from Glasgow every three months until the truce. She had been sent over in 1917 by Molony and ffrench-Mullen, suggesting that this was part of the work undertaken by the ICA's shirt-making factory front organisation along the quays. Initially, it was hoped that she would get a job in a munitions factory but it was felt by Liam Gribbons that it would be 'less suspicious' to get work making garments. Contact was then made with Joe Robinson and Seamus Reader and through Frank Murray, Charlie Diamond and a man named O'Callaghan, explosives began to be carried over to Liberty Hall from early 1917 onwards.[40] Roderick Connolly, James's son, was also the captain of A Company of the Glasgow IRA in 1918, which contained ICA and IRA men. Diamond stated that through Connolly's direction a 'valuable' collection and transportation of munitions to Ireland occurred.[41] Certainly, the Scottish republican, James Corbett stated that Murray organised a contingent of seamen on the Glasgow to Dublin line and 'was thus enabled to deal expeditiously with large consignments of material', which was similar to Q Company's work.[42] Likewise, the buyer for the Light Machine Gunner Staff, James FitzGerald, stated that Murray was 'supplying me [FitzGerald] with gelignite and detonators for GHQ at a time when they were urgently needed, and was largely due the credit for a good amount of munitions we got from the ICA'.[43]

For her own part, Caffrey remembered 'on one occasion I brought revolvers. I had nine but I had to bring three at a time. I was about six months bringing these over, then I had boxes of detonators which I had to bring over.'[44] Murray stated he was detailed to purchase material from Scotland between 1917 and 1921, and was 'backwards and forwards' throughout the period. In this way a regular supply, an average of once a week, of gelignite and explosives were gained.[45] Murray termed himself the 'ICA representative for Scotland' while the Old IRA Scottish Division viewed him as the 'purchasing officer' for the ICA, which they saw as a 'full-time occupation'.[46] According to Seán MacMahon, Murray was responsible for 'procuring large quantities' of munitions which were 'invaluable in carrying on the war during years 1919–21'. Corbett estimated that he handed over one ton of gelignite and many thousands of detonators to Murray.[47] Notably though, Murray was not held in high esteem amongst some leading IRA men on both sides of the channel. Joseph Vize, a key IRA organiser in Glasgow, felt that he was 'anything but safe' and in September 1919 Vize expressed to Collins that he was not surprised to see that Murray had been arrested.[48] Murray's arrest was a result of being found with a ticket to a parcel store in a Glasgow cloakroom and, for Collins, this confirmed his lack of suitability.[49] Diamond also came under criticism from Michael O'Callaghan who contended that in 1918 he gave Diamond £40 worth of explosives for free and they were then sold to O'Neill for £50.[50]

Further avenues of obtaining weaponry also existed. By July 1919, the British Home Office felt that the independent Scottish Citizen Army had developed a 'scheme for collecting cartridges of pit explosives' of 'considerable quantitates' which they transported via Hamilton and Bothwell.[51] By the turn of the year, the transfer of weapons from Glasgow to Ireland was operating at a steady pace.[52] It would have been unlikely that some of this material did not make it to their socialist cousins in Ireland. Certainly, it was not uncommon for the same source to be used by the two Irish organisations. Murray worked for the ICA before he also worked for Óglaigh na hÉireann. Importantly, he noted miners were another source where he garnered explosives.[53] Vize pointed to another man named Nolan who also worked for the two Irish groups. Corbett transported arms for the ICA before focusing entirely on the IRA, after a falling out with the other two suppliers. Furthermore, during the Anglo-Irish War of Independence, the Irish Citizen Army travelled to Glasgow alongside brigades from Cork, Sligo, Mayo and Tipperary to the purchasing committee which operated there under Vize.[54] In 1919, Robert de Coeur was also involved in the procurement of explosives from cross-channel sources and he sent people across the channel once it was felt safe.[55] As noted, McGowan also worked with a man named Hughes to use sailors and others on boats in the Dublin docks to secure weapons, another system akin to Q Company, though it is probable that he was the receiving end of Murray's line.[56]

Hanratty argued that at its height the Citizen Army possessed 'about ninety-six rifles, 3,000 rounds .303, five owt. explosives, gelignite, dynamite and samsonite, fifty-six Smith & Wessons, twenty-four .45 automatics, fourteen German Mauser automatics' as well as 6,000 rounds of Springfield ammunition, 4,000 rounds of .45 ammunition, 3,000 detonators and a stockpile of hand grenades'.[57] Evidently, they remained active and successful in gunrunning to such an extent that the IRA, not just in Tipperary but also in Dublin, requested the use of these munitions. The Fourth Battalion was given arms by the South County ICA unit on three occasions.[58] Traynor recalled that 'he [O'Neill] seem[ed] to have an unlimited supply of war material'.[59] Regarding his own purchase from Árm Lucta Oibre na h-Éireann, completed in early 1921, Traynor remembered:

> immediately after I took command of the Dublin Brigade, I found we were very short of explosives, viz., rifles, ammunition, and so on, and in the course of endeavouring to find ways and minds to add to our store, it was suggested to me we could get such store as we required from the Citizen Army. I was sort of surprised I had not thought of that myself. I immediately got someone to get information if it would be saleable. We got in touch, and he was prepared to give us a supply of gelignite. We purchased a large quantity of gelignite, some rifles, and rifle ammunition ...[60]

In 1921, Seán MacMahon (IRA Quartermaster General) and James Fitzgerald (IRA Purchaser) paid £70 for munitions from the ICA. Ten Lee Enfield rifles, three Ross rifles, thirteen Lee Enfield rifles in bad condition, two Howth rifles, one shotgun, twenty-four bayonets, fifty shotgun cartridges, 2,093 rounds of .303 ammunition, 130 rounds of Howth ammunition, one .22 rifle in bad condition and one .38 rifle in bad condition were taken from the Leixlip dump on 23 February 1921.[61]

Likewise, McGowan was involved in the creation of bombs and landmines for Óglaigh na hÉireann men such as Gerry Golden. McGowan contended that his work of 'acquiring arms continued throughout the period 1 April 1919 to 31 March 1920'.[62] Golden confirmed that such work was completed, though he specifically mentioned the 1918–19 period.[63] The importance of this type of work was seen in that on two occasions Collins wrote to the IRA in Glasgow and expressed the need for explosives.[64] By 1921, the South County ICA unit, after it had incorporated the Fourth Battalion Volunteers, was also involved in the 'casting of slugs and [the] refilling of shotgun cartridges'.[65] This was done around twenty times and about half a dozen ICA men were involved in this work where they would spend a whole day in the home of Pádraig Ó Broin working on the task.[66] The group was also involved in arms gathering and in November 1920 they absconded with Black and Tan rifles from the Rathgar area of Dublin while further 'arms and equipment' were also gathered in Stillorgan, Donnybrook, Bray, Terenure, Harold's Cross, Kimmage, Mercer Street and Dominick Street. In January 1921, a landmine was received from the Gormanstown Aerodrome and more guns were taken from Harold's Cross shortly before the outbreak of the Irish Civil War in June 1922.[67] House searches were also undertaken and a Winchester rifle was taken from one house in Highfield Road in Rathgar.[68]

By 1919, Edward Handley had been transferred to Wellington Barracks and with his aid McCormick led a raid on the barracks.[69] Handley remained the ICA's greatest source for weapons during the 1919–21 period. With the aid of a sympathetic 'policeman', Handley was able to make use of the practice that soldiers would leave their rifles outside of huts when going to lectures on wet days. After he had taken these, he would wait until the same policeman was on duty and then pass them out at a back gate near Harold's Cross Bridge. That soldiers had to pay for the 'lost' equipment also seemed to have worked to his advantage as such compensation 'seemed to satisfy the authorities'. It was true that some searches began to take place periodically but he was also warned of these in advance by the same policeman.[70]

By 1920, a hut at the North Wall was established by the British Army where men on leave had their rifles taken from them. This not only acted as a drop-off point for arms that were to be transferred to Ship Street Barracks but also attracted a number of men who wished to sell their rifles. This provided a fertile base for Handley and he was even able to appropriate five or six rifles which belonged to the Black and Tans, whom he said 'were very often drunk ... [and] were not particular about keeping the numbers of their rifles ... [which] made the tracing of any lost rifle very difficult'.[71] Another base was established at Kingstown for men on leave via Holyhead where the record-keeping was more diligent. Here the sergeant major kept a book where the names and numbers of the men and their rifles were logged. However, a flaw existed whereby the weapons that were faulty were sent to Islandbridge Barracks to be fixed and were not itemised. Handley's job was to oil and clean the rifles, and bring those with defects to the other centre. He would carry four of them, two slung on each shoulder. After he arrived at Westland Row two of these were handed over to the ICA's soldiers and when he arrived back at Kingstown the missing rifles were crossed off as being re-issued.[72] According to Handley, he was able to transfer over a hundred rifles and revolvers to the ICA, though this was probably an exaggerated estimate. It is also noteworthy that Handley was never held up by the IRA and he believed that they were aware of his work.[73]

The use of ICA homes as safe houses was also a defining characteristic of the war years. The acquisitions of arms, often done with the help of J.J. O'Connell, necessitated the creation of dumps to house these munitions. While Leixlip was a key centre during the immediate post-rebellion period, other locations were now sought. O'Neill and Ó Broin's unit held a dump at Piperstown, Tallaght and at the back of a church by Mount Argus.[74] Sometime between 1920 and 1921, a dump was also established in Marino, to where Frank Robbins brought twenty-five rifles. The rifles had originally been stored in a dump in The Coombe while Robbins also brought a collection of material previously held in Bridgefoot Street to the dump in Marino.[75] Molony was also often active in this regard and though she never had more than five of six rifles in her possession she 'constantly had [arms] either to pass them on or keep them in safety'. Through her, they were kept in Leeson Street which was raided during the war and a stash was found.[76] Republican soldiers were also often housed in such places when they were 'on the run'. Soloheadbeg men such as Dan Breen, Seán Hogan and Seán Tracey along with Seamus Robinson, Ned Ryan and Jimmy Scanlon were safeguarded in 140 Drumcondra Road, the home of McGowan.[77] Kathleen Barrett who, despite holding no rank, considered herself an ICA member, both carried rifles to her home and gave William Carn a key to this house as well as giving him permission 'to send or bring when she was away from home any IRA men who needed a place to stay in'.[78] O'Shea used 29 The Coombe, the house beside his home, as an arms dump, stuffing them up the chimney before calling Edward Burke when they were ready to be moved again.[79] Patrick Kiernan also stored rifles for the South County Dublin unit.[80] A 'dreadful amount of gelignite and detonators' was also kept in Christina

Caffrey's home. The place was often raided but nothing was ever found as the material was given to James O'Neill and Robert de Coeur.[81]

Even though Hanratty refuted the claim that the ICA was involved in an 'economic fight', he also described the Citizen Army's activity during the 1920–1 period in similar terms. He stated 'they had various activities. They enforced the boycott. They burned sacks belonging to Paul and Vincent and Shackelton's Mills at Lucan. They boycotted tobacco and they dumped some in the Liffey.'[82] Here he was referring to the Belfast boycott, the sanction undertaken by the Dáil in January 1921 to shun goods coming from the Belfast area due to the discrimination and attacks suffered by the nationalists and Catholics under the newly consolidated Northern Irish government. Under Seán O'Neill and Pádraig Ó Broin, the South County unit served notices about the embargo in winter 1920–1.[83] However, as the typical work of the more urban North County Dublin unit was that of a labourer, this ICA unit was in a better position to know which of the Dublin firms were working with Northern Irish companies and acted on that.[84] O'Neill stated this when he contended that 'due to the positioning of our men we were again able to destroy a great-deal [sic] of the Belfast boycott material. Notable among this was the dumping of tobacco in the river at [the] Custom House and [the] burning of materials at Shackelton's, Lucan'.[85]

Mentioned by O'Neill and Hanratty, the action in Lucan was clearly held in high regard amongst the ICA's army council. James O'Shea, Caffrey, Sloan, Michael Donnelly and both King brothers intercepted a van at Amiens Street and forced the driver to go through the poorest parts of the city where the goods were unloaded and left for the inhabitants.[86] The job of the interception was taken off an IRA ASU in Dublin and was also seen to be of importance in the wider struggle as Lucan was 'occupied' by the Black and Tans at this point.[87] In his outline history, Hanratty also mentioned the burning of military waggons at Spencer Dock in 1919 as well as action against the Dock Milling Company and the throwing of tobacco into the Liffey in 1920.[88] Three lorries carrying six tons of the smoking product were commandeered before they were brought to the river and dumped over Butt Bridge. Likewise, during the burning of the Custom House, Shackelton's again received ICA attention.

While the ICA was directly engaged in skirmishes with their enemy, in truth these were never of any real significance. There were about 130 total ambushes on Crown forces in the capital during the 1919–21 period yet ICA-organised incidents only took place a handful of times.[89] O'Neill contended they were on armed patrols on 'a very few occasions' and he justified this by stating 'it was a question of overlapping [with the IRA] again, a question of which job it would be advisable for us to do'.[90] Patrolling was more typical of urban IRA activities rather than direct ambushes in rural areas. While similar to an ambush, this involved no specific targets but the creation of opportunistic moments by the covering of known enemy movements by a group of up to thirty or forty republicans.[91] Ó Broin stated that in January 1921 the South County ICA unit begun 'intensive' activity in such work in an attempt to obstruct the British Army.[92] He also noted that they 'fired a few shots at Tallaght' and that they were out in Tallaght and Dundrum on about half a dozen occasions.[93] He contended that apart from these occasional scraps there was no 'big fight' with the Black and Tans.[94] Another attack was planned but never went ahead. Described by O'Neill as 'one of our best arranged military jobs at the time', one incident which had been planned was an attack at Sidney Lodge which was frequented by a group of Black and Tans. Information was gathered and given to the local IRA unit, and Collins approved the ICA to take action but this was called off at the last minute.[95] A plan was also constructed for the ICA to break out the IRB man Frank Teeling from Mountjoy Prison but he was moved to Kilmainham before this could occur.[96] Given Ó Broin's connection with him, the plan was not surprising.

They were, however, involved in two incidents at Eden Quay and Burgh Quay where they fired at passing lorries.[97] Laurence Corbally was also involved in a shooting at Ryan's public house on Gloucester Street. Here four British soldiers had entered the pub and were made to hold up their hands. After a row broke out, firing started and Corbally, who was passing, shot at them.[98] Other engagements occurred at Bachelor's Walk, one near the quays at the Custom House, one at Sandymount and an attack at London Bridge Road during which the vice commandant of the Auxiliaries was shot.[99] While no official part was taken in the burning of the Custom House, an ICA ASU was stationed nearby which took part in the incident once they became aware of the events. They had been stationed at Liberty Hall but were able to fire at the enemy. Later that night they also re-entered the building and recovered the guns that had been left behind by the IRA.[100] After the Black and Tan sacking of Balbriggan on 20 September 1920, during which twenty houses on Clonard Street were destroyed, McGowan was ordered 'to stand' for an attempted reprisal at the barracks in Gormanston.[101] While this was not an ICA planned operation it was a typical example of leading Citizen Army figures having active interaction with Óglaigh.

Engagement with the British Army also occurred during a commemoration of James Connolly's birthday on 5 June 1919. William Oman described the Mansion House gathering for this as proscribed but it was not. However, British authorities had told both the ITGWU and the Lord Mayor of Dublin that it would not be welcomed.[102] Along with a significant crowd, a large contingent of DMP agents gathered to block access to the route along Dawson Street. A group of ICA men comprising Thomas Kain, Laurence Corbally, James O'Shea, William Oman and Philip O'Leary were present, and there was an altercation between the two forces.[103] During that fight O'Shea pulled out a gun and in the midst of his attempted arrest the ICA's men felt that they 'had to participate, to overcome the police, and give him a chance to get away'. Both Oman and Kain confirmed that they had fired shots. No members of the ICA were injured but four of the authorities and a civilian named Margaret Hayes were wounded.[104] These skirmishes signalled the breakdown of the British administration's hold on peaceably maintained authority. However, none of these incidents were significant to the wider republican struggle.

Of more significance were the instances of civil resistance that were instigated by rank-and-file members of the Irish trade union movement. Two key cases of industrial action taken against the British Army and police were the general strike called by the Limerick Trades Council on 14 April 1919, also known as the Limerick soviet, and the embargo of British military personnel and supplies which was undertaken by Irish railway workers from May 1920 to December 1920. While these protests were more effective than the ICA's direct confrontation with the British Army, they also characterised Ireland's part in the Anglo-Irish War of Independence as 'a spontaneous movement of the mass of the people' rather than 'the work of a handful of fanatical terrorists'.[105]

In the first weeks of April 1919 Limerick city was experiencing a period of heightened tension over the death of the trade unionist and republican Robert Byrne. On 21 January 1919, Byrne faced a British Army court martial for possession of a revolver and ammunition. He was sentenced to twelve months imprisonment and he did not receive political status. By March, Byrne had gone on hunger strike and on 12 March he was transferred to the Limerick Workhouse Hospital.[106] On 6 April 1919, a local IRA unit attempted to rescue Byrne but in the ensuing struggle both he and an RIC constable, Martin O'Brien, were fatally wounded.[107] In response, the city and part of the county was declared a 'Special Military Area' by General C.J.

Griffin on 11 April. Troops were deployed onto the bridges over the Shannon and all citizens required a pass from Griffin if they wanted to travel across these. In order to receive a pass, a letter had to be forwarded to an RIC sergeant. The costs of the extra policing led to an increase in rates.[108] On 12 April, workers in the Condensed Milk Company's Lansdowne factory went on strike in protest at these permits. The following day a meeting was held by the Limerick Trades Council at the Mechanics Institute, Hartstonge Street where the council called a general strike beginning on 14 April.[109]

Around 14,000 workers went on strike. Fifty RIC men were sent to Limerick by Deputy Inspector-General W.M. Davies for support and permission was also granted to General Griffin to seek further military support.[110] The supply of vital resources such as water, gas and electricity were taken control of by the strike committee.[111] The committee also printed a currency and its own newspaper, the *Workers' Bulletin*. However, despite the inroads quickly made by the soviet, the protest never gained the support of the national executive of the Irish Labour Party and Trades Union Congress (having changed its name from Irish Trades Union Congress and Labour Party in 1918). William O'Brien believed that the executive of the ILPTUC 'gave Limerick all the assistance in their power. Anything that was not done was due to lack of machinery rather than lack of desire or earnestness on the part of the executive.'[112] But the reality was different. Labour leaders feared the consequences that would have resulted from a national strike against the British military. Such an action would have made the labour movement the forerunner in the republican struggle and would likely have led to violent confrontation with the British authorities. This was not a risk the labour leadership was willing to take.[113]

Thus, while labour leaders such as the ILPTUC's treasurer, Thomas Johnson, were sent down to Limerick from Dublin between 16 April and 22 April, the congress's national executive sought to avoid any confrontation with the British military or the RIC. The executive proposed a policy of an organised evacuation of the city.[114] The strike committee rejected this proposal and without national support they were forced to call off the strike on 27 April.

According to Thomas MacPartlain, the soviet 'was a win ... because since then the military tyranny had not placed a ban upon any industrial centre.'[115] Similarly, Secretary of the Limerick Trades Council James O'Connor contended the workers of Limerick 'made the greatest fight ever made by any united body of workers in a big city. They showed the world that the workers were able to run the city in spite of the presence of any foreign government.'[116] However, it was a movement instigated by the rank-and-file workers of Limerick rather than the national labour movement. Lysaght contended that the soviet 'was handicapped by labour's national leadership'.[117]

The rail embargo of British military goods and soldiers was another example of civil protest caused by the 'spontaneous action' of Irish workers.[118] According to Townshend, the railway strike against the British military was 'notable amongst other industrial actions of the war period in its duration and its clear nationalist political orientations'.[119] The report of the 1920 annual conference of the ILPTUC stated that in 'the present strike against the carrying of munitions of war, the workers used their "industrial franchise" for political and social purposes'.[120] The strike began independently of labour leadership and was a result of British labour's 'hands off Russia' campaign which saw British workers refuse to load munitions onto cargo that was destined for Poland in order to fight the soviet regime.[121] According to the 1920 annual report of the ILPTUC, 'immediately following the refusal of the London dockers to ship munitions of war to Poland [in mid-May 1920], a steamer arrived in Dublin containing a cargo of military equipment ... the Dublin dock workers refused to discharge this cargo'.[122]

Other dock and rail workers quickly joined the embargo. On 27 May 1920, workers in the railway station in Harcourt Street, Dublin refused to load rifles which were bound for the RIC in County Wexford. In Queenstown, Cork, the *Czaritsa*, a British Army transport vessel, twice failed to land its cargo of machine guns.[123] These incidents seriously impaired the British government's ability to sustain any peaceably maintained authority in Ireland. The actions caused not only practical difficulties for the British Army but also took place at a time when Sinn Féin was raising questions about who was actually governing Ireland. Alongside tactics such as the Dáil courts and the 'police' activity of both the IRA and the ICA, the general strike questioned whether the British government had already lost its ability to govern the country.[124] On 25 September 1920, Chief Secretary for Ireland Hamar Greenwood told the British Cabinet that the strike had put the government 'in a humiliating and discreditable position'.[125]

However, by winter 1920, the British government and the Irish rail workers had entered a stalemate. The strike denied the British military the ability to transport soldiers and supplies but it also threatened to 'paralyse the entire Irish economy'.[126] Between July and October, passenger services had ceased to exist in large swathes of Ireland.[127] By November 1920, over 1,000 Irish workers had been dismissed from their jobs. On 17 November, the *Irish Times* published Johnson's view that an 'economic war with England would throw back the social life of Ireland for perhaps a hundred years'. It was becoming evident that Irish labour's resources were running thin and that the strike could not be sustained for much longer. On 21 December 1920, the Irish railway workers voted unanimously to end their strike.[128] In the ILPTUC's 1921 annual report, its national executive told the railway and dock workers that '[their] protest for six months has been unique in the annals of the labour movement'.[129] While the strike was called off in December 1920, it was viewed as a moral victory for the Irish workers. Again in their 1921 annual report, the ILPTUC's national executive advised the same workers who had carried out the strike the year previous to 'offer to carry everything the British authorities are willing to risk on the trains'.[130] According to Costello, this was 'a policy that both suited the reality of the situation and brought continued disruption to the British military effort in Ireland'. The word 'risk' was clear in its implication that labour had begun to support the republican movement.[131]

In contrast, none of the ICA's skirmishes were significant to the wider republican struggle. Of more impact was that the Anglo-Irish War of Independence saw ICA–IRA relations develop in an amicable way. Not only was a transfer system of soldiers put in place but the ICA provided munitions to the IRA both in Dublin and in the more intensive Tipperary region, and they also provided safe houses to figures such as Dan Breen. Alongside these actions, intelligence provision, as opposed to physical confrontation, was a key component of the ICA's role in the conflict. No distinct unit existed and the policy, according to O'Neill, was that 'each man did his part as best he could'.[132] Traynor contended that 'they took information from any and every source'.[133] Despite this *ad hoc* nature, valuable information was gathered by the ICA and divulged to their IRA comrades.

While the Countess, with her position as a TD, was an obvious conduit between the two sides, in reality the 'chief lines' of intelligence came through Christopher Crothers and Robert de Coeur.[134] Crothers, in particular, was seen by O'Neill as having had a 'peculiar connection' with people involved in the British secret service and 'seemed to be able to find out these things', and he accredited him with providing 'valuable information which was responsible for the destroying of British intelligence staff in Dublin'.[135] Crothers identified Thomas Millea and Kate Murphy as two agents who aided him. Millea lived in a house in Mount Street while Murphy worked for a Mrs Sankey whose house was a 'call office' for the British intelligence staff stationed in the city. In his pension Crothers asserted that a British agent named Bennet lived with Millea in Mount Street while in his witness statement he contended that Bennet stayed with Murphy in Fitzwilliam Street.[136] Nonetheless, Crothers transferred information regarding the location of guns and police agents to Paddy Kennedy and was eventually introduced to Michael Collins. The information he received from Millea and Murphy led to arms raids at 3 Percy Place and at Great Brunswick Street.[137] Crothers defined the process: 'I used to visit the house in Fitzwilliam Street once or twice a day. Any documents I could get I took and handed them over. When they left that house they scattered and it was then that the group of people were of assistance to me.'[138] O'Neill also accredited him with discovering the 'Ross handbills' and discovering the centre where they were produced.[139] These handbills were 6" by 4", sought to teach the best method for Irishmen to inform on the IRA, and asked for letters to be addressed to D.W. Ross. Crothers remembered:

> Miss Murphy came to me with three of four of these posters and informed me that the men staying at the house had hundreds of these posters and that they were out all night posting them up ... I went with her to No. 15 Upper Fitzwilliam Street and on top of a wardrobe in the front drawing room there were actually thousands of bill heads ... I took a number of the bill heads that evening to Captain de Coeur and when he saw them he immediately took me to the house of the O/C Intelligence, Dublin Brigade ... as a result of this I was asked to try if possible to get the name of every man who was in the house and if possible to report more regularly on what was occurring there.[140]

For his own part, de Coeur was not as involved in this work as Crothers but he did pass knowledge on to Barney McMahon which led to the burning of military stores at the Midland Railway.[141] De Coeur's position as the secretary of the ICA's army council meant that he transferred to McMahon the data that Crothers discovered. One particular example saw Murphy transfer information emanating from Pembroke Street to Crothers, which eventually found its way to McMahon and aided in the assassinations of fourteen British informants, intelligence officers, MI5 agents and Auxiliaries on Bloody Sunday, 1920.[142] In a manner that was characteristic of the ICA's involvement in the Anglo-Irish War of Independence, no action was taken on the Pembroke Street information until it was discussed with the IRA, lest it interfere with the wider conflict. In this case, Dick McKee informed O'Neill that any individual Citizen Army action was not to go ahead as 'it might spoil things for a bigger job'.[143]

Naturally, the ICA remained active during the Anglo-Irish War of Independence and this was a cause of fear for the ITGWU who, as far back as 1917, dreaded that labour militancy would not only lead to the closure of Liberty Hall but to the union being declared illegal.[144] After the outbreak of the conflict in 1919, the atmosphere, in O'Neill's words, 'became very hot [as] the labour people became nervous'.[145] The ITGWU's fear of British Army raids was so significant that by February 1919 McGowan was asked that the ICA's officers would be 'careful' when giving out instructions so as to avoid enhancing such fears. However, the escalation of hostilities meant this proved to be impossible and by April the military wing was asked by the trade union to cease drilling or to leave Liberty Hall. Their response was to 'carry on drilling quietly'.[146] A succession of raids throughout the year meant that this was not considered sufficient.

Considered one of the republican headquarters and levelled in Easter 1916, Liberty Hall remained a fixation in the suspicious minds of the British military authorities in post-rebellion Ireland. In August 1919 alone, the Beresford Place building was raided on three separate occasions, once on 2 August and twice on 22 August. These raids resulted in the arrests of figures such as Peter Ennis and Christopher Quigley.[147] A further search on 24 November led to the seizure of seditious literature, bombs, a revolver, ammunition and rifle training rests.[148] This was part of a 'crescendo of repression' which indicated the view of Dublin Castle that the ITGWU was one 'of the revolutionary agencies it was their business to put down'.[149] Alongside this, the union's paper the *Voice of Labour* was suppressed on 20 September 1919, after which the ITGWU had to give a guarantee that no future copies were to be printed until permission was granted by the 'competent military authority'.[150]

Given this background, the ICA was asked to leave Liberty Hall in November 1919. This was not without precedent. At a 20 May meeting of Branch No. 1 of the ITGWU in 1917, Thomas Foran read out a letter served by the police and issued by a magistrate which authorised the closure of Liberty Hall unless steps were taken. While these steps were not recorded in the minutes, it was clear that this was to do with the Connolly and Mallin

Social and Athletic Club, a group organised after Easter 1916 to keep active those ICA figures not interned. The committee, while not prepared to sign any document, did agree to a 'verbal undertaking' to these steps.[151] As result of this the club was eventually asked to leave the building altogether on 30 May 1917.[152] The ITGWU's push against the Citizen Army was therefore not atypical. The period also marked the longest duration where the ICA was not mentioned in the union's minutes.[153]

This did not mean that the Citizen Army was completely ostracised from general labour as they moved to the Trades Council Hall in Chapel Street.[154] They eventually moved to 35 Parnell Square where, in Robbins's opinion, they 'safeguarded it ... because it was threatened be [sic] people who suddenly woke to life'.[155] Also in November 1919, Liberty Hall held a meeting where Cathal O'Shannon stood beside labour leaders such as Markievicz, Eamon MacAlpine and Thomas Johnson and 'dwelt upon the extreme necessity of military as well as political action'. Notably this attitude was recorded in the *Watchword of Labour* which, like the *Workers' Republic* and the *Irish Worker* before it, published a section devoted to the ITGWU.[156] The Socialist Party of Ireland (SPI), which held meetings in Liberty Hall, seemed to take a particular interest in the ICA, perhaps because the stated aim of the SPI was to 'destroy the monarch of this and every other country'. Thus, it was closely aligned with the revolutionary goals of O'Neill's men.[157]

At the International Socialist Conference in Stockholm in 1917, the SPI claimed to speak on behalf of the ICA as well as the ITUCLP. They appealed to the 'proletariat of all countries' and to the conference itself to support the claims of the Irish people and the Irish nation, especially regarding the claim for admission to a peace congress after the culmination of World War I.[158] In September 1921, Roderick Connolly argued for the potential of the Communist Party of Ireland (a breakaway group of the SPI formed in late 1921) to '[have] a nucleus in the ICA, the IRA and any other organisation that contains members possible to exploit for revolutionary socialism', though this came to nothing.[159]

15

'IRISH WORKERS' REPUBLIC, WITHOUT FEAR AND WITHOUT COMPROMISE': SPLIT AND CIVIL WAR

The truce period in 1921 also saw the Citizen Army begin to reapply to the ITGWU to hold meetings at Beresford Place. ITGWU officials responded that

> if it was only a room they wanted for two or three nights in the week for members of the band only, the committee would see about granting the application on certain conditions which would have to be agreed to on both sides. On the other hand, if it was a club room they wanted for their sole use, they could not have it as there was not sufficient rooms in the hall at present for the different sections of the union.[1]

No further discussion was held until January 1922 when Robbins successfully applied for use of 'the big room' for the militia itself on 5 January. The ICA's piper's band was granted a large room for practice on 26 January.[2] The difficulty in reaching this point was made clear by O'Neill in his statement about the raids and their effect on the ICA in Liberty Hall: 'on some occasions it was raided, during the Tan War. On one occasion they got some rifles, and on another, they tore up the floor, etc. We had great difficulty in trying to get back. We had to take it forcibly, really.'[3] Simultaneous to these discussions, the ITGWU was attempting to create a new nationwide Irish Workers' Army, which they hoped would incorporate the Irish Citizen Army and would take a neutral stance on the Anglo-Irish Treaty. According to a membership form for the Irish Workers' Army, it sought 'to defend the country against foreign aggression, to defend the workers against attack during labour disputes, to assist and maintain the rights of the workers and to support the movement towards the establishment of a workers' republic'.[4] The committee was to be comprised of five members of the Irish Citizen Army and five representatives of the trade union movement while every member had to be, 'wherever possible', a member of a trade union recognised by the Irish Labour Party and Trade Union Congress.[5]

On 18 January, a letter was sent to labour officials in Birr, Dundalk, Mullingar, Newcastle West, Tipperary, Clonmel and Ballina in order to assess the potential for this 'in view of the change which has now taken [place] in the political life of the country'.[6] It was hoped that some of the working-class members of the IRA in these areas could have been persuaded to join this new force.[7] By this point the ICA was drilling out of the brick works in Dolphin's Barn and was approached by O'Brien regarding affiliation with the Irish Workers' Army. Initially, the ICA was cautiously open to such action on the condition that they were to keep their separate identity as a distinct regiment.[8] Michael Donnelly and John Byrne both spoke of the growing demand for such an organ within the trade union movement and in March O'Brien stated the response from the various branches was 'very encouraging'.[9] While the Irish Workers' Army was a short-lived entity, within the context of the burgeoning movement towards civil war, its creation led to a split in the ICA. By March 1922, James O'Neill was court martialled, sat a tribunal, and was removed from the ICA's army council as a result of accepting payment for arms from the South Tipperary IRA Brigade without the permission of the ICA's council.[10] With his departure, James Larkin, though in America, was made the spiritual leader of the body as its commander in chief while John Hanratty was made its operational controller as O/C.[11] On 21 June 1935 Hanratty stated that he was appointed Commandant of the Citizen Army in May 1922; the titles O/C and Commandant may have been used interchangeably in 1922. It does seem that the memorandum only used Larkin's name for posterity.[12]

Hanratty only tentatively agreed with the aspiration for a wider labour army as he feared a loss of ICA control but also hoped that it would lead to greater funds.[13] The former fear, however, was realised when an 'Anti-Militarist Meeting' was organised by the ILPTUC on 17 March 1922. Michael Kelly, who sat on the subcommittee of the developing Irish Workers' Army, arranged for a Citizen Army guard to be present. However, the ICA's army council felt that the meeting was explicitly pro-treaty, and Kelly's claim to have acted under the 'higher authority' of the Irish Workers' Army's executive also caused acrimony. In response, the ICA's leading figures in the nascent Irish Workers' Army: Kelly, Donnell, Byrne and O'Shea were removed from the Citizen Army, and the ICA declared itself against the Anglo-Irish Treaty.[14] At this point many in organised labour, including Frank Robbins, were struggling to maintain impartiality between the two nationalist sides.[15] A split had taken place.

On 14 April 1922 – the same day that Rory O'Connor instigated the anti-treaty occupation of the Four Courts – a meeting took place between former ICA men Kelly, Robbins, Byrne, Donnelly, O'Shea and ITGWU men O'Brien, Thomas Johnson, Cathal O'Shannon, Dan Morrissey of Tipperary, Gilbert Lynch of Dundalk, a man named Butler from Waterford, as well as a delegate from Tyrrellspass and two men from Limerick.[16] It was at this meeting where the men who had belonged to the Citizen Army were officially appointed to the Irish Workers' Army's executive committee. The agenda for the meeting is in Table 15.1.

On 1 June 1922, Hanratty, Major Richard McCormick, Capt Robert de Coeur, QM Alfred Norgrove and Adjt Joseph Sheehy wrote a memorandum on behalf of the anti-treaty ICA.[17] They accused the ITGWU and the recently constituted Irish Workers' Army as 'dragoon[ing]' the Irish working class into 'association with the murderers of Connolly'. Hanratty *et al* stated

TABLE 15.1.   Agenda for ITGWU and ICA meeting regarding the formation of the Irish Workers' Army

---

(1) Statement on general position and necessity of army

(2) Reports on work already done in country

(3) Organisation:

    a. Method of forming units

    b. Connection between local units and centre

(4) Convention

    a. Basis of representation

    b. Date

(5) Finance

(6) General points raised but deferred from previous sections.

Source: Agenda for a 14 April 1922 Meeting Regarding an Irish Workers' Army, undated, Irish Citizen Army Documents, WOBP, MS 15,673 (1), NLI.

they refused 'to become the willing organisers of British imperialism'. They followed Larkin's belief that the treaty would lose Ireland its soul, stood for 'an Irish workers' republic, without fear and without compromise', and positioned themselves 'against the treaty with the British Empire ... [and] against any compromise with the Irish capitalist class'.[18] In response, on 13 June 1922, a circular was written by the Irish Workers' Army's executive committee which by June had begun using the title Irish Citizen Army. They criticised the 1917–22 ICA leadership as having failed to carry out the goals of the ICA as well as having declined to work 'in harmony' with organised labour. The ICA was also accused of having refused to protect the workers and having done nothing to 'organise the country'. In contrast, the ITGWU was seen as having done everything possible to aid labour's military wing since its inception. The circular also claimed that the ICA was not removed from Liberty Hall in 1919 but that it chose to leave 'owing to the frequent raids by Black and Tans'.[19] The committee was explicit in the statement that they did 'not stand for empire' but for 'the protection of the workers, for the aspirations of the Irish working class for the workers' republic ... [and] for unity'.[20] The reference to aspirations in contrast to the immediacy of the anti-treatyites' letter was indicative of the general divide caused by the Anglo-Irish Treaty signed on 6 December 1921. The letter signed by the anti-treaty ICA on 1 June 1922 evidenced an allegiance to the Irish Republic affirmed in both 1916 and 1918 while the Irish Workers' Army's circular written on 13 June supported the stepping stone theory as argued by Michael Collins. It should be noted that O'Shea eventually took part in the Irish Civil War as an 'Irregular', suggesting that allegiance to the pro-union Irish Workers' Army did not require agreement with the deal bargained by Collins, Griffith *et al.* in December 1921 in London. Larkinite and union sympathies also played a part in the dynamic.

During the truce period, there was little activity that the ICA was able to involve itself in. The North County Dublin unit established a training camp near the IRA camp in Sutton.[21] Likewise, camps were established in Kilbarrack and Tallaght where twenty of the South County unit's men were trained.[22] However, the occupation of the Four Courts on 14 April 1922 meant they were soon forced into action. While the ICA remained a staunchly republican and anti-treaty unit, the controversy over the attempted Irish Workers' Army indicated division over the issue, and some older members took an active part in the Irish Free State's force. Luke Bradley joined the First Eastern Division and was wounded in 1923.[23] George Campbell was a private in the Motor Service Transport Unit; John Conroy enlisted in A Company of the Dublin City Guard on 2 March 1922; and William Egan held the rank of corporal in Second Section, B Company, First Battalion, Dublin City Guard.[24] Other former Citizen Army men who took part on this side in the Irish Civil War included: Francis Fitzpatrick, Martin Foy, John Joseph Hendrick, Peter Jackson, Thomas Michael Jennings, Patrick Joseph Drury, Edward Tuke, Michael Dwyer and James Donnelly.[25]

The ICA began to receive communication from the 'Irregular' IRA almost immediately after the labour split. On 15 May, the general headquarters in the Four Courts issued a letter to Hanratty which stated 'I would be anxious to attend a meeting of either the officers or a parade of the men of the ICA as soon as possible.'[26] Communications continued to a point where it was soon understood that should the 'Irregular' force be attacked, the ICA would engage in supporting them.[27] On the evening of 27 June 1922, the Dublin City Guard, which was part of the Free State army, established positions in Chancery Place, Bridewell Street and the Four Courts Hotel. This created a cordon around the republican-controlled Four Courts. At 03:30 an ultimatum was issued by the Dublin City Guard to those inside the Four Courts to evacuate or face an assault. At 04:15 the building began to be shelled.[28]

A meeting was held in the home of Robert de Coeur where it was agreed to mobilise the ICA. It was also agreed that those belonging to the Citizen Army, while keeping their own separate identity, would take orders from the Dublin IRA's O/C Oscar Traynor.[29] Hanratty stated that 125 ICA soldiers took an active part in the Irish Civil War.[30] However, as the Four Courts building was locked down, activity was largely centred in the surrounding area such as Barry's Hotel, which was established as a brigade headquarters, and the Hammam Hotel which had been occupied by Traynor on 29 June.[31] Figures such as McCormick also took part in the fighting at Roy McMahon's and Griffith's boot shop in Capel Street.[32] Garry Houlihan also put McGowan in charge of the barricading force at Findlaters as a supporting mechanism for the defence of the Hammam.[33] While sandbagging proved to be successful initially, Collins's army was able to use heavy artillery, which resulted in a gradual anti-treatyite retreat from the city's bases. ICA figures such as James Maguire were captured on 3 July.[34] On 5 July, the headquarters at the Hammam raised a white flag which ended the first battle of the Irish Civil War.[35]

Ó Broin's unit was active in ambushes on Free State troops in June 1922. At 09:00 on Wednesday 28 June, a unit in Terenure began standing for an attack. A dispatch was sent to the O/C in the Rathfarnham barracks and at 01:00 on the following Friday the Citizen Army men carried out an attack which secured two rifles. Interestingly, despite this, Ó Broin told his commandant that 'arms [are] wanted badly' and asked 'send us six rifles or shotguns'.[36] The men were also active in Glenasmole in 1923.[37] On 26 July Hanratty received another letter from Traynor which expressed the hope to instigate a better operational structure and 'to get a section of [Hanratty's] command working on both north and south of the city'. In the north side, contact was to be made with Commandant Sweeney at 16 Cadogan Road while Mr Cohen at 14 Wexford Street was to be the contact on the south side.[38] Through this nexus, two things were hoped to be achieved: firstly, the widest possible net over the city would be placed and secondly, any potential overlapping of the two republican bodies would be avoided.

This led to the ICA being co-opted to an assignment with the Fifth Battalion (Engineers), termed by the ICA as the 'Night of the Bridges', on 5 August 1922. The plan was to separate Dublin city from the wider area by both destroying the communications network and collapsing the city's bridges. The Free State Army's capture of Liam Clarke, who was in possession of the plans, meant that it was destined for failure. Free State army patrols were sent to all likely bridges and 104 anti-treaty soldiers were arrested. Ernie O'Malley was told these arrests crushed the Dublin Brigade and led to the arrests of its most active members.[39] The activity on 5 August resulted in the arrest of fourteen men belonging to Árm Lucta Oibre na h-Éireann, including Edward Burke, Patrick Buttner, Patrick Joseph O'Neill and, most importantly, John Hanratty.[40] McGowan had been arrested previous to the engagement, on 4 July.[41] Likewise, Robert de Coeur had also been captured in July and was interned until December 1923. Ó Broin was arrested on 20 August 1922.[42]

Citizen Army man James Keogh's recollection on 20 June 1935 was similar to what O'Malley was told. Keogh stated that the ICA was 'practically wiped out' after the 'Night of the Bridges'.[43] Patrick Carroll expressed a similar sentiment, stating 'all our lads were arrested'.[44] As well as Hanratty, de Coeur and McGowan, since 1916 the force had lost the services of leaders such as James Connolly, Michael Mallin, James O'Neill, Thomas Kain (who had no activity after the truce) and James O'Shea. Richard McCormick had taken part in the 'Night of the Bridges' affair but had evaded arrest and continued to transport munitions to Tipperary after this. However, in truth, the loss of such operational command was too significant for the ICA as he was the only remaining officer left after the 'round up'.[45] Given this, the force failed to continue to perform an active part in the war outside of the internment camps. Activity from this point onwards was summed up by the position of Alfred Norgrove who stated 'the arms were left with me after the "Night of the Bridges." The O/C was arrested that night and I became QM after that. A lot of the stuff was left in my house all the time and was there until it was got.' He was later arrested once the dump was found.[46] Hanratty referred to three activities in 1923: 'column at Leixlip, fight in Glenasmole Lodge, and intelligence work'.[47] However, in truth, the ICA's ability to contribute significantly to the conflict had been eradicated after the arrests on 5 August 1922.

16

'THE PLACE IT CARVED OUT':
LEGACIES

The Irish Citizen Army was always a much smaller army than the Irish Volunteers and, subsequently, the Irish Republican Army, so the force received less attention in both the academic or public space. However, the ICA did leave behind a lasting legacy. This manifested itself in three spaces: the armed movement, the political and the public. While the ICA failed to provide significant activity within either the republican or labour movement after the 'Night of the Bridges', the 1920s saw intermittent attempts at creating new left-wing armed organisations. In 1929, Roddy Connolly suggested to the James Connolly Workers' Club that a new 'Workers' Defence Corps' needed to be created.[1] However, it was not until 1934, after the formation of the Republican Congress, that the ICA was revived. According to one of the congress's joint secretaries, Patrick Byrne, an attempt was made at creating a new military wing by 'resurrecting' the ICA and some Citizen Army veterans were 'dug up' to give the wing 'legitimacy and colour'.[2] However, Hanley was probably correct in his assertion that the former ICA soldiers saw the potential in the congress as much as they were manipulated by it.[3] A 3 January 1935 ICA memorandum described the need for a battle on three fronts in the fight against capitalism: 'industrial unity, a socialist party, and the Citizen Army'.[4] McGowan was the most famous of the ICA's veterans who were involved in this venture but others such as John Purcell, Joe Doyle, Liam Kelly and Seamus O'Brien also met with the Republican Congress's leadership.[5] However, a split in the Republican Congress occurred in 1935 as Roddy Connolly and Michael Price called for the congress to become a socialist political party, while Peadar O'Donnell and George Gilmore argued the need for an appeal to a wider base. The ICA also split but the majority of the men and women stayed loyal to Price who became their chief.[6] The

Price-led ICA had 309 members based across the country. It remained a proponent of armed-force politics but argued this should only occur in the final stage of the overthrow of capitalism, after widespread support for a popular revolution had been gained.[7] However, Matthews was correct in her assertion that by 1936 'their role was now reduced merely to pageantry' as their activity was confined to appearing at Fianna Fáil and Labour Party organised commemorative events.[8]

Militants paid homage to the ICA throughout the Northern Irish troubles from 1968 to 1998. In 1981, the British Maoist organisation Big Flame stated that an armed group known as the Revolutionary Citizen's Army had recently been organised and followed the 'political line' of the socialist organisation People's Democracy.[9] Given the socialist leanings of People's Democracy as well as the use of the name Citizen's Army it is apparent that this militia was drawing upon the heritage of Árm Lucta Oibre na h-Éireann. However, the absence of sources pertaining to the Revolutionary Citizen's Army suggests that the organisation was ephemeral. Two longer lasting paramilitaries which drew upon the revolutionary legacy of the ICA were the Official Irish Republican Army (OIRA) and the Irish National Liberation Army (INLA).

In December 1969 the OIRA split from what became the Provisional Irish Republican Army (PIRA), largely over the issues of abstention from Dáil Eireann. The paramilitary wing assumed a more Marxist outlook than the PIRA and, in January 1970, it argued it was no longer an 'elitist force, divorced from the struggles of the people'.[10] It is also noteworthy that its Derry newspaper was titled *The Starry Plough*. Clearly, OIRA leadership in Derry was trying to claim a heritage to the socialist force that went 'out' in Easter 1916. The INLA also claimed to be part of this tradition by adopting the starry plough after its formation in 1974. Regarding the wider issue of Northern Irish murals, Judy Vannais noted that after the 1994 IRA ceasefire the starry plough was one part of the 'traditional vocabulary of Irish nationalism' which began to disappear from the 'lexicon' expressed by these murals. Images such as the flag, the Easter lily and the phoenix were replaced by symbols which articulated the new republican demands of the new political process, such as the withdrawal of the British Army, the disbandment of the Royal Ulster Constabulary and the release of political prisoners.[11] However, an Institute of Irish Studies survey on the display of public emblems in Northern Ireland found that in the months of September and October, from 2006 to 2009, the starry plough was the most likely republican or unionist paramilitary flag to be on display in Northern Ireland.[12] Evidently, the most distinct symbol of the ICA as well as its legacy of an armed campaign for a socialist republic of Ireland was relatively in vogue within some republican communities over ten years after the Good Friday Agreement.

In Britain, a number of left-wing political parties and civic action groups have been inspired by Connolly and the ICA. One of the most influential and long lasting of these is the Connolly Association (CA). The CA was established in 1938 in England as the Connolly Club but changed its name to the Connolly Association after the end of World War II. In 1955, it drew up its constitution which was adopted at its conference in Birmingham that year. The constitution stated that its aims and objects were 'to organise Irish men and women resident in Britain for the defence of their interest in [the] united struggle with the British working class movement'. In particular, the association sought 'to win support for the struggle of the Irish people for a united independent republic, and to fight for the removal of all obstacles placed in their way by British imperialism' and 'to stand for [the] equitable treatment for all Irish people living in Britain'.[13] In 1963, the Connolly Association argued that its 'fundamental' concept was that the interest of the 'Irish in Britain as Irishmen [were] in no way contrary to their interests as workers'. This, the CA argued, 'follows directly from Connolly's teaching that the struggle for Irish independence and the struggle for socialism and the betterment of the workers in Ireland [were] not contradictory but complementary'.[14] The CA remains active with the same aims and objectives.[15]

The Irish Workers Group (IWG) was a Trotskyist group formed in London in 1966. As the golden jubilee of the Easter Rising approached the IWG published a pamphlet entitled *The Irish Revolt 1916 and After* which used the example of the ICA to justify their criticism of the Connolly Association and C. Desmond Greaves who was the editor of the association's paper, the *Irish Democrat*. According to the IWG, 'as the history of the Citizen Army shows Connolly maintained at all times the independence and separate ideology of the working class, never hesitating to criticise the weakness of those people who were for the time being his allies'.[16] The IWG argued that 'Greaves and his like imply' that because an economic and political Irish revolution first requires a 'bourgeois democratic revolution' it was wrong to put forward any ideology which might have criticised the beliefs of middle-class revolutionaries.[17] However, for the IWG, Connolly's statement supposedly made on Easter Sunday, 1916, that the ICA should hold on to their rifles was evidence that a socialist armed campaign required a wider rank-and-file Marxist revolutionary movement rather than an association with a 'small clique' of militant nationalists.[18] In essence, the IWG used the history of the ICA as a justification for its own exclusively socialist revolutionary strategy.

A number of political parties have claimed inheritance of ICA principles by carrying versions of its flag, the starry plough. By the centenary of the Rising, dissident groups such as Real Sinn Féin and Éirígí marched under the flag while the more mainstream Sinn Féin continues to use the starry plough as a banner. Interestingly, the Labour Party, under the proposal of their leader Dick Spring, stopped displaying the flag in 1991. According to an unnamed party spokesman, the *Irish Times* reported, the decision was made because the party wished 'to be seen as a political organisation that people associate with 1990, rather than with 1915'.[19]

By May 2016, in a post-Good Friday Ireland filled with an atmosphere of commemoration the Labour Party was keener to assert its lineage to James Connolly, the ICA and those from the labour movement involved in the Irish struggle during the second decade of the twentieth century. On 15 May 2016, the Labour Party's then leader and Dáil Éireann Tánaiste, Joan Burton, spoke at the James Connolly commemoration at Arbour Hill, Dublin. Burton initially stated that it was a privilege on a personal level to speak at the event as she was the granddaughter of ICA member James Burton. According to her, 'Connolly's legacy' was 'an independent, democratic, and by international standards, prosperous if far from prefect state'.[20] Burton then connected Connolly's principles with the Labour Party's policies on social equality. He was 'a staunch and committed feminist', she believed, and his 'core vision was one of equality' which was 'a vision the Labour Party has sought to fulfil from its foundation'.[21] Interestingly, she inferred a privileging of Connolly over the other proclamation signatories, to whose legacy the Labour Party has less of a claim. She quoted historian J.J. Lee's contention that Connolly was in a 'class of his own' and she contended that Connolly was the 'most remarkable thinker' in twentieth-century Irish history.[22]

Sinn Féin is another political party which identified itself as left-wing in the years approaching the centenary of the Easter Rising. On 6 February 2015, the party launched their national programme to commemorate the rebellion's centenary. At this event, the speech of Sinn Féin's then president Gerry Adams provided interesting contrasts from Joan Burton's talk. Reflecting on Sinn Féin's identity, Adams drew upon the anti-imperial and anti-partitionist elements of the 1916 revolutionaries in a manner which

Burton did not. Adams argued that the 1916 proclamation and the Easter Rising was a 'declaration heard around the world – that we were no longer colonised citizens'.[23] He also contended that partition meant the continued relevance of the question of Irish self-determination. He argued that the proclamation was 'a freedom charter for this whole island and all the people who live here … the struggle is not over … our island was partitioned … [which has] distorted life on this island ever since [its implementation]'.[24] Adams, like Burton, also drew upon the socially progressive elements of Connolly and the other revolutionaries' thought when he stated the rebellion's proclamation 'guarantees religious and civil liberty and is avowedly anti-sectarian. It promotes equal rights and equal opportunities for all citizens. It addresses Irishmen and Irishwomen.'[25]

On 11 May 2016, Paul Murphy, the Anti-Austerity Alliance's (AAA) TD for Dublin South-West, spoke at Pery's Hotel, Limerick on the subject of 'James Connolly: His Life and Ideas'. Murphy presented a holistic view of Connolly's legacy, refusing to confine it to merely the national struggle. Rather, Murphy suggested Connolly's 'core central ideas' were that he was an internationalist, that he 'identified an agency for change which was the working class', and that he was a revolutionary in the 'struggle for … fundamental change in how our society operates'.[26] Cian Prendiville, an Anti-Austerity Alliance spokesperson and councillor for Limerick City and County, argued that AAA was part of the tradition of these ideas. He contended 'AAA is inspired by Connolly's internationalism and vision of socialism.' He also claimed that 'Connolly also argued that [the] working class cannot simply struggle on the industrial field, and not leave the political field to the bosses's parties. In that same vein the AAA was formed to take the struggle against austerity onto the political field.'[27]

It is noteworthy that Murphy established his view of Connolly and by extension the ICA's legacy in opposition to mainstream political parties such as Fine Gael, Fianna Fáil and Sinn Féin. He stated that Connolly is celebrated by 'the establishment in order to neuter and dull the revolutionary content which is what Connolly stood for' in order to create a 'myth of origin' which conceals that the roots of the state lie in the counter revolution of the 1920s.[28] This Murphy believed was a 'one dimensional view of Connolly as a martyr of 1916'.[29] In perhaps a false juxtaposition, Murphy argued Connolly was 'an internationalist rather than a nationalist'. Implicit in this was that the 1916 Easter Rising was not the highpoint of Connolly and his Citizen Army's legacy but was an aberration. For Murphy, perhaps challenging parties who attempt to represent both the nationalist and the socialist traditions, 'we should not accept anybody who says that Connolly was a nationalist. He was an anti-imperialist, yes. But he was not a nationalist.' Likewise, the Easter Rising, he believed, should be seen as a rebellion which was 'premature' and did not present 'a sufficiently independent clear socialist message'.[30]

Evidently, a variety of political parties have taken different aspects of Connolly and the ICA's ideology in order to publicise their own policies. However, the legacy of the Citizen Army is also felt by the public. The East Wall for All website was established in May 2012.[31] The site was created to display 'all things to do with the East Wall [area] of Dublin' and has allowed descendants of ICA soldiers to outline their family's contribution to Irish history and to present memorabilia relevant to Ireland's revolutionary situation from 1913 to 1923. Articles on topics such as '"The Fighting Old Guard": The O'Doherty family in the North Dock' and '"He Was Buried From Stephen's Green" The Life and Death of James Corcoran – North Dock Resident, Trade Unionist and Citizen Army Volunteer' as well as items such as a photograph of Connolly which he gave to Christina Caffrey in March 1916 have been published on the website.[32]

Outside of this local project, aspects of the Irish Citizen Army's ideology remain pertinent to the Irish nation as a whole. President of Ireland Michael D. Higgins wrote 'one of the most remarkable legacies of the ICA for us today is, I believe, the place it carved out for women'.[33] While complete gender equality did not exist within the force, the militia was undoubtedly progressive in its attitude towards its female members. A forward-thinking approach to the issue of gender equality remains important today. It is also true that the activity of the ICA's female soldiers in 1916 allows for a significant inclusion of the female voice in the history of the Irish independence movement. It is noticeable that in a 16 March 2016 *New York Times* article entitled 'Eight Women of the Easter Rising' four of the women discussed were members of the ICA: Kathleen Lynn, Countess Markievicz, Margaret Skinnider and Rose Hackett.[34] Certainly, the opening of Hackett Bridge in Dublin in 2014 highlighted the degree to which these women's personal histories resonate in contemporary Irish society. Aspects of the ICA's constitution also remain relevant to modern Ireland. Clause 3 of the Citizen Army's revised constitution stated its 'recognition of the rights and liberties of world democracies'.[35] In a time of significant upheaval in geopolitics as well as the uncertainty surrounding the European Union, this clause remains as relevant in 2016 as it did in 1916. Finally, it is significant that 'the first and last principle of the Citizen Army [was] the avowal that the ownership of Ireland, moral and material is vested in the people of Ireland'.[36] President Higgins was correct in his assertion that 'the ambition of those who formed or joined the ICA was not confined to replacing an alien landlord class with a native one ... their objective was to transform Ireland's social, economic and cultural, as well as political, hierarchies'.[37] The aspiration for true holistic equality in all sectors of society is one a modern democracy must keep at its foundation.

APPENDIX 1

ICA CONSTITUTION, 22 MARCH 1914

That the first and last principle of the Citizen Army is the avowal that the ownership of Ireland, moral and material is vested of right in the people of Ireland.

That the Citizen Army shall stand for the absolute unity of Irish nationhood, and shall support the rights and liberties of the democracies of all nations.

That the Citizen Army shall be open to all who accept the principle of equal rights and opportunities for the people of Ireland.

That one of its objects shall be to sink all differences of birth, property, and creed under the common noun of the Irish people.

Before being enrolled every applicant must, if eligible, be a member of his trade union, such union to be recognised by the Irish Trades Union Congress

Source: *Irish Worker*, 28 March 1914.

APPENDIX 2

REVISED ICA CONSTITUTION

1. That the first and last principle of the Citizen Army is the avowal that the ownership of Ireland, moral and material is vested of right in the people of Ireland
2. That its principal objects shall be:
   (a) To arm and train all Irishmen capable of bearing arms to enforce and defend its first principle.
   (b) To sink all differences of birth, privilege and creed under the common name of the Irish people.
3. That the Citizen Army shall stand for the absolute unity of Irish nationhood, and the recognition of the rights and liberties of world democracies.
4. That the Citizen Army shall be open to all who are prepared to accept the principles of equal rights and opportunities for the people of Ireland, and to work in harmony with organised labour towards that end.
5. Every enrolled member must be, wherever possible, a member of a trade union recognised by the Irish Trades Union Congress.

TO THE PEOPLE OF IRELAND
This is the time for action. All political organisations are preparing for the future. Shall labour remain apathetic? Remember, workers, that

THE PRICE OF LIBERTY IS ETERNAL VIGILANCE
Put the advice of labour in practice by joining now

THE IRISH CITIZEN ARMY,
Which stands for the cause of labour and erects its constitution on
the principles of

WOLFE TONE AND JOHN MITCHEL
Enlist at once and help us to create

THE IRISH CO-OPERATIVE COMMONWEALTH
GOD SAVE THE PEOPLE
All particulars from

THE HONORARY SECRETARY,
Irish Citizen Army,
Liberty Hall,
Dublin

Sources: *Irish Worker*, 9 May 1914; *Irish Worker*, 22 Aug. 1914; Irish Citizen Army Constitution, undated, in James O'Neill, MSP, 34REF8368.

APPENDIX 3

OUTLINE HISTORY OF 1917–23 PERIOD BY O/C JOHN HANRATTY

1 April 1917–31 March 1918	
Demonstration Easter Monday	1917
Mass at Tallaght	1917
M. MacDonagh Funeral	July 1917
Portobello Barracks	23 September 1917
T. Ashe Funeral	26 September 1917
Portobello Barracks	3 October 1917
W. Partridge Funeral	November 1917
1 April 1918–31 March 1919	
USA Supply Boat	1918
Countess Reception Westland Row	June 1918
Canal Boat Lucan	1918
Countess Reception Dun Laoghaire	November 1918
Defence of Liberty Hall	13 November 1918
General Elections	1918
Coleman's Funeral	1918
De Valera's Reception Merrion Gate	6 March 1919
1 April 1919–31 March 1920	
Dawson Street Scrap	12 May 1919
Norton's Funeral at Swords	July 1919
Burning Military Waggons Spencer Dock	1919

1 April 1920–31 March 1921	
Burning of Belfast Materials Paul and Vincents	
Tobacco thrown into Liffey	
Shackleton Mill Lucan	
Amiens Street Station	
Dock Milling Company	
Demonstration re: Hunger Strike	
1 April 1921–11 July 1921	
Sydney Parade	
12 July 1921–30 June 1922	
Tadgh Barry's Funeral	November 1921
Civil War	28 June 1922
1 July 1922–31 March 1923	
O'Connell Street area	1 July 1922
Bridges	5 August 1922
1 April 1923–30 September 1923	
Column at Leixlip	
Fight in Glenasmole Lodge	
Intelligence Work	

Source: Outline History of the 1917–23 Period by O/C John Hanratty, undated, 1913–23 Documents I, Hanratty Papers, Kilmainham Gaol.

APPENDIX 4

SOUTH COUNTY DUBLIN ICA MEMORANDUM OF ACTIVE AND GENERAL SERVICE, 1920–3

November 1920
Black and Tan rifles collected in Rathgar Area. General drills (indoor and outdoor). Rifle and revolver practice. Watching suspected persons and houses. Outpost duty. Patrol duty (armed and unarmed). Collecting arms and equipment. Helping deserters from the British army. Serving notice re: Belfast boycott goods on firms.
Detective duty: Watching movements of British military and police. Guarding houses where meetings of the republican forces were being held in the following areas: Terenure, Rathgar, Harold's Cross and city of Dublin etc. Carrying and removing arms backwards and forwards.
Arms and equipment were collected in the following areas: Stillorgan, Donnybrook, Bray, Rathgar, Terenure, Harold's Cross, Kimmage, Dublin city (notably Mercer Street and Dominick Street).
Red Cross lectures carried on at Moira Cottage, Rathgar Avenue under the instruction of M.O.J. Doolan and J. Kearney.
January 1921
General arrests of IRA in south County Dublin. Intensive ICA and Irish Volunteer activity started to obstruct enemy forces. Sections ICA on night duty at regular times in Malahide, Sutton, Tallaght and other areas.
January–July 1921
First-aid equipment commandeered from Grafton Street for use of unit. Landmine got out of Gormanstown Aerodrome. Ambush planned by Comdt. Seán O'Neill in Tallaght area. Harbouring men and women on the run.

Police Duty: (armed and unarmed) Second Lieutenant P. Kearney in charge of police section. Houses in south County Dublin guarded by ICA men when asked for protection. Property recovered by ICA men and handed back to owners.

Circulating section: *An tÓglách* newspapers circulated. ICA members of printing trade assisted.

Munitions: The casting of slugs and refilling shotgun cartridges, carried out by members of ICA, assisted in collecting war material, etc.

General obstruction of enemy forces and those connected with them.

July 1921–1922 Truce

General field and company drills at Tallaght and north County Dublin.

1 July 1922 – Outbreak of Civil War (28 June)

Rifles got at a house in Harold's Cross. Mobilised for hit-up of Free State troops to: blockade roads; take empty house for Red Cross at Kimmage; get cross cuts, saws and axes for tree felling; for armed patrol duty; detective duty, general routine duty; for mountain column at Tallaght area; to get food at Rathfarnham and Tallaght. In conflict with Free State troops at Glenasmole, July 1922.

20 August 1922

Comdt. Seán O'Neill and Capt. Padg Ó Broin arrested at Moira Cottage, Rathgar Avenue.

August 1922–September 1923

Mobilised for duty in city of Dublin at Aungier Street, north city. (Duty at Rathfarnham Barracks, Ballyboden Post Office, etc.)

Outposts and armed patrol duty, 1922–3

Mobilised to work on tunnel going into Mountjoy Prison. Job put off owing to men being arrested in house adjoining. Arrangements were made to have carpenters and carters supplied by ICA men. Red Cross commandeered at Clonskeagh. Helped to commandeer rifles from Wynnfield Post Office, Rathmines. Harbouring and assisting men and women of the republican forces. Collecting food, clothes, etc. for families of prisoners of war.

Source: Memorandum by Pádraig Ó Broin on the Subject of the South County Dublin ICA Unit's Active and General Service Between 1921–23, 1 June 1935, 1913–23 Documents I, Hanratty Papers, Kilmainham Gaol.

APPENDIX 5

DEPORTATION OF ICA MEMBERS, 1916, TO BRITISH PRISONS

To Knutsford on 30 April

1. Bradley, Patrick
2. Campbell, George
3. Carpenter, Peter
4. Charleton, Michael
5. Courtney, Daniel
6. Donnelly, Michael
7. Dunn, Andrew
8. Foy, Martin
9. Gleeson, William
10. Kelly, M.
11. Kelly, William
12. McCormick, Richard
13. Nelson, Thomas
14. O'Donoghue, Thomas
15. O'Shea, James
16. Robbins, Frank
17. Shannon, Martin
18. Tuke, Edward

To Stafford on 30 April

1. Bryan, Thomas
2. Burke, Edward
3. Chaney, William
4. Coates, Peter
5. Craven, Bernard
6. Carroll, Michael
7. Carton, Owen
8. Cullen, Patrick

9. Conroy, John
10. Corbally, Richard
11. Doyle, Joseph
12. Dwyer, James
13. Gleason, Thomas
14. Henry, Fred
15. Jackson, Peter
16. Joyce, Edward
17. Kelly, James
18. Keogh, James
19. King, George
20. King, Martin
21. Little, Jas.
22. MacDonagh, Joseph
23. Mahon, John
24. Maire, Louis
25. Nolan, Michael
26. O'Connor, John
27. O'Reilly, Joseph
28. Poole, Christopher
29. Poole, Patrick
30. Seery, J.
31. Tuohy, Patrick

To Knutsford, 2 May

1. Burke, Matthew
2. Byrne, John (Joseph)
3. Delaney, Michael
4. Fullerton, George
5. Murphy, Patrick

To Wakefield arrived on 6 May

From Ballsbridge

1. Mannering, Edward
2. Scully, Thomas
3. Tully, George
4. Williams, Patrick

From Kilmainham

1. Byrne, Joseph
2. Lambart, Thomas

3. McMahon, Dan
4. Nolan, John
5. O'Reilly, John

To Stafford, 8 May

1. Connolly, Matthew
2. Hyland, Jas
3. McGowan, Seamus

To Wandsworth, 8 May

1. Brady, Christopher
2. Dwyer, James
3. Kain, Thomas
4. McManus, M.
5. Nelson, Thomas
6. Norgrove, Alfred G.
7. O'Leary, Phillip
8. Poole, John
9. Sexton, Michael

To Lewis, 19 May

1. Daly, Thomas
2. Wade, Michael

To Wandsworth, 1 June

1. O'Neill, John
2. O'Neill, John

To Knutsford, 15 June

1. Halpin, William
2. Kelly, John

Source: Sinn Féin, *Sinn Féin Rebellion Handbook Easter 1916*, pp. 69–87.

APPENDIX 6

IRISH TRANSPORT UNION AND GENERAL WORKERS' UNION BRANCH

No. 1 Minutes Relating to the Irish Citizen Army

22 April 1914: An application from the Secretary of the Citizen Army asking for permission to hold an *aricheort* at Croydon Park was next considered. It was agreed to grant permission to hold same on the third Sunday of May.

30 June 1914: A deputation from the [Fintan Lalor's] band appeared before the committee in reference to the uniform, and suggested the same colours of uniform as the Citizen Army, with the addition of gold facing stand up collar and glazed piqued cap with lanyard and tassel.

8 July 1914: An application was also read from the Secretary of the Citizen Army Women's Ambulance Corps for use of grounds to hold an open air concert. This application was also referred to Gen Sec. [for] consideration.

20 August 1914: A deputation from the Citizen Army applied to the committee for the use of Croydon Park grounds on Sunday 27th Sept to hold a display to raise funds to pay off some debts. It was unanimously agreed to grant same.

27 October 1914: A deputation from the Citizen Army waited on the Committee and asked for permission to carry out a shooting competition on Sunday 29th Nov 1914. Permission granted. They also applied for permission to create a miniature rifle range in Liberty Hall. Permission to create same granted. They also applied for the permission to run a concert for the benefit

of the boys and girls who had helped in the recent displays. The committee informed them that in this case they would have to apply to the Women Workers for use of [the] large front room. The dispatcher then withdrew.

22 November 1914: A letter was read from the Citizen Army Secretary re: money due by army for uniforms etc. Secretary to furnish same.

29 November 1914: A deputation from the Citizen Army waited on the Committee re: shooting range in Croydon Park. It was agreed to consider the case later on.

6 December 1914: Correspondence from Citizen Army re: rifle range adopted with the recommendation that no preference be given to numbers of No. 1 Branch – no more than any other branch of the army.

13 January 1915: The question of rent for the room used by the Citizen Army was next discussed at some length. Some members expressing the opinion that as nearly all the Citizen Army were members of the union it would be rather exacting to press them for rent under present circumstances. No further action was taken in the case.

27 January 1915: The question of shooting with ball cartridges at the butt in Croydon Park was next discussed at some length. The committee were firmly of the opinion that the practice was dangerous. When B. Conway moved and J. Cunningham seconded that the shooting practice be suspended until further notice and that a printed notice to that effect be posted up. Agreed.

10 March 1915: A letter was read from the Secretary of the Citizen Army Council asking for permission to open a tea and coffee bar in connection with the council. The Secretary was instructed to reply the same asking the council to send a deputation to [the] next meeting of the committee to have a conference on the matter.

24 March 1915: A deputation from the Citizen Army Council waited on the committee regarding the opening of a tea and coffee bar in connection with the army. After due consideration of the matter permission was granted, for opening of same.

26 May 1915: A request from Citizen Army Council for use of Croydon Park on alternate Sundays in July and August was next discussed. P. Ford moved & P. Doyle seconded that the case be left open to a special meeting for consideration.

2 June 1915: The chairman called the attention of the meeting to the request of the Citizen Army for the use of Croydon Park for every alternate Sunday in July and August. He considered that was too big a request as it appeared to him they wanted the union to foot the bill for rent and give them the use of the place for the best months of the summer. Mr Connolly explained the Citizen Army did not want anything unreasonable but it was necessary to state something definite in their application and it rested with the committee to say what dates they could grant the use of [the] park to [the] Citizen Army for one Sunday in July and one in August for the present.

21 July 1915: IC Army to be granted either says they choose a special badge to be got for O'Donovan Rossa funeral.

4 August 1915: Catering for Citizen Army sports to be given under their own control.

29 September 1915: Deputation re: raffle … Citizen Army Room re: Committee […]. Adopted to give 2: 2: 0 approved.

12 April 1916: Wm Fairtlough raised the question of the action that was supposed to going to take place on next Sunday vis the raising of a flag over Liberty Hall. And he now moved that a general meeting of the members [be called] before the flag is raised in order that the general body may have an opportunity to decide whether this flag is to be hoisted or not. This was seconded by Wm O'Toole. Thom[as] Foran moved as an amendment that the matter be adjourned until nine o'clock tomorrow night and asked J[a]m[es] Connolly to be present and discuss the whole question. M. McCarthy sec[onded]. 5 for.

13 April 1916: Wm Fairtlough, S. Kelsh, F. Fitzgerald, A. Leahy and J. Farrell having spoken against the wisdom of the transaction and expressed the opinion that the general body should be consulted about the matter. Mr. J Nolan expressed the opinion that the flag should be hoisted. Mr Connolly

explained his position in the matter and stated that he would not appeal to the general body against the decision of the council as he had worked harmoniously with them since he took up the position he occupied and he would hand in his resignation rather than fall out with the committee or give it to anyone to say that there was disunity in the ranks. Personally he had taken up a position from which he was not going to retreat, nor did he expect any Irishman would do so.

30 December 1916: The Chairman raised the question of [the] deported men away. It was decided to take off 8 months that were away. Agreed.

21 January 1917: The General President in opening the proceedings paid a tribute to the memory of the late Jas Connolly who had conducted the business of the union for Mr. Larkin during his absence aboard up to the date of the insurrection [in] Easter Week when he placed himself at the head of the Irish Citizen Army and took the field with his men to fight for the freedom of Ireland and the liberty of the working men and women of Ireland. He (the President) could not express in words the sorrow he felt for the loss the workers of Dublin and not alone Dublin but all Ireland had sustained by the death of their esteemed colleague Mr. Connolly who had been shot by order of a District Court Martial. In closing he said he would ask Mr. W O'Brien, Secretary of [the] Dublin Trades Council to say a few words to the meeting before proceeding to business proper.

21 January 1917: Mr O'Brien then addressed the meeting at some length and paid a glowing tribute of respect to the memory of the late Mr Connolly and to his unselfish labour and sacrifices on behalf of the workers of the world at large. He also referred to other members and officials of the union who had been imprisoned, deported or who had fallen in the fight for Irish freedom on Easter Week. At the conclusion of his remarks, all members present showed the marked respect in which they held their departed comrades by standing up and uncovering their hands.

29 April 1917: The question of commemorating the memory of the late James Connolly General in Command of the Dublin District IRA was again under discussion and it was finally decided to drape the hall and close same on the date of the anniversary of his murder by the British government.

13 May 1917: Mr Dillon raised the question of a member of the Citizen Army attempting to assault the caretaker of the hall and asked that the man who was guilty of this action be brought before the committee on next Sunday to answer for his conduct.

23 September 1917: An application was made by Commandant O'Neill of the ICA for the use of the old band room for practice as they were about starting a Piper's Band. Jas Dillon moved that the matter be deferred for more definite information as to the control, hours of attendance, etc. This was agreed.

3 February 1918: P. Nolan raised the question of drilling being carried out in the hall and stated how he had been approached by a number of members of the union [in] relations to having same stopped before the authorities take steps to have the hall closed. Nolan said he would not have raised the point only he was, along with the Gen. President, when the arrangement was made with the Lord Mayor regarding the prohibition of drilling or other illegal acts in the hall and had pledged his word along with the President that nothing of the kind would be allowed in the hall. After some discussion it was decided to have a conference with the ICA Council with a view to having some definite understanding on the matter.

17 February 1918: R. de Coeur, J. Hanratty, M. Donnelly comprised a deputation appointed by the Council of the CA to wait on the Committee of the Transport Union to try to ascertain the relations existing between the two bodies. It was decided to appoint a deputation to meet AC [Army Council] on Monday night. The following were selected on the deputation: Mr Foran, President, Jas Gannon and O'Neill Sec.

3 March 1918: A deputation from the CA waited on the committee to ask permission to carry on Swedish drill. Permission granted.

5 December 1918: Jas Doyle and M. Donnelly applied on behalf of ICA for the use of the concert hall on a Monday night previous to Christmas for the purpose of holding a concert to raise funds for the ICA. The committee stated they had no objection to the application and told the deputation to get in touch with the concert committee and arrange what night would be

available and suitable for them to have their concert. The deputation thanked the committee and withdrew.

13 March 1919: The chairman read a letter from the ICA re the home coming of Countess Markievicz and the reception in connection with same. The question of bringing out the large banner was discussed at some length and owing to the lateness of the hour of arrival it was decided not to bring it out and it was decided to arrange with Mr Foran to send a deputation meet Madame.

6 October 1921: J. Byrne and M. Donnelly attended the meeting as a deputation from the Council of the ICA applying for the use of a room in the hall for the Pipers Band to practice in. The committee having heard the application and explained to the men who formed the deputation that if it was only a room they wanted for two or three nights in the week for members of the band only, the committee would see about granting the application on certain conditions which would have to be agreed to on both sides. On the other hand, if it was a club room they wanted for their sole use, they could not have it as there was not sufficient rooms in the hall at present for the different sections of the union. If these conditions were satisfactory when they had consulted their council they could come back and let the committee know and then have a proper agreement entered into.

5 January 1922: F. Robbins applied for the use of the big front room for Sunday evening at the HOC for a meeting of the ICA for an hour or so. Mr Pepper moved and Mr Ryan seconded that the room be granted on this occasion. Agreed.

26 January 1922: ICA Pipers Band was granted use of large room for practice on the motion of M. Donnelly. Seconded by M Pepper.

Sources: Minutes of Committee Meetings of the ITGWU February 1914–February 1916, Together with Minutes of the Strike Committee October 1913, MS 7298, NLI; Minutes of Committee Meetings of the ITGWU June 1915–April 1916, MS 7303, NLI; Minutes of Committee Meetings of the ITGWU June 1916–June 1919, MS 7299-300, NLI; Minutes of Committee Meetings of the ITGWU September 1920–May 1925, MS 7304-7308, NLI.

ENDNOTES

Chapter 1

1   *Daily Herald*, 24 Jan. 1914; *Daily Herald*, 26 Jan. 1914; South County Dublin Unit ICA to John Hanratty, 31 June 1922, 1913–23 Documents I, Hanratty papers, Kilmainham Gaol; James O'Neill, 29 March 1935, in Irish Citizen Army, Military Service Pension Collection (MSPC), RO 10A. While *hÉireann* is the correct spelling, ICA sources used *h-Éireann* and this is used in the thesis when referring to Árm Lucta Oibre na h-Éireann.

2   Ann Matthews, 'Vanguard of the Revolution? The Irish Citizen Army, 1916' in Ruán O'Donnell (ed.), *The Easter Rising Among the Nations* (Dublin, 2008), pp. 24–36.

3   Charles Townshend, 'Historiography: Telling the Irish Revolution' in Joost Augusteijn (ed.), *The Irish Revolution, 1913–23* (London, 2002), pp. 1–16; Peter Hart, 'Definition: Defining the Irish Revolution' in Augusteijn (ed.), *The Irish Revolution*, pp. 17–33.

4   R.F. Foster, *Vivid Faces: the Revolutionary Generation in Ireland 1890–1923* (Milton Keynes, 2015), p. xvii.

5   James D. Fearon and David D. Laitin, 'Ethnicity, Insurgency, and Civil War' in *The American Political Science Review*, 1 (2003), pp. 75–6; James Ron, 'Paradigm in Distress? Primary Commodities and Civil War' in *The Journal of Conflict Resolution*, 4 (2005), p. 448.

6   Foster, *Vivid Faces*, p. xvi.

7   Ibid. p. 3.

8   International Socialist Congress, *Full Report of the Proceedings of the International Workers Congress London July and August 1896* (London, 1896), p. 4.

9   J.D. Clarkson, *Labour and Nationalism in Ireland* (New York, 1925), p. 288.

10 Bernard Campbell Ransom, 'James Connolly and the Scottish Left' (unpublished PhD, University of Edinburgh, 1975), p. 291.

11 D.R. O'Connor Lysaght, 'The Irish Citizen Army 1913–16: White, Larkin, and Connolly' in *History Ireland*, 2 (2006), pp. 16–17; Jean Jaurés, *Democracy and Military Service* (Kent, 1916).

12 International Socialist Congress, *International Workers Congress London*, p. 73.

13 Ibid. p. 4.

14 International Working Men's Association, *Resolutions of the Congress 1866 and the Congress of Brussels, 1868* (London, 1868).

15   *Advocate of Peace*, Jan. 1869.

16   Harry Quelch, *Social Democracy and the Armed Nation* (Clerkenwell Green, 1900), p. 6.

17   James Joll, *The Second International* (Boston, 1974), p. 111.

18   International Workingman's Association, *Documents of the First International* (London, 1964), p. 144.

19   International Socialist Congress, *International Workers Congress London*, p. 4.

20   Granville Fortescue, *Fore-Armed: How to Build a Citizen Army* (Philadelphia, 1916), p. 167.

21   *Fortnightly Review*, Sept. 1915.

22   Máirtín Seán Ó Catháin, *Irish Republicanism in Scotland 1858–1916: Fenians in Exile* (Dublin, 2007), p. 232.

23   Irish Trades Union Congress and Labour Party, *Annual Report of the Twenty-Second Irish Trades Union Congress and Labour Party, 1916*, p. 24.

24   Metscher, 'James Connolly, the Easter Rising and the First World War', p. 141.

25   Priscilla Metscher, *James Connolly and the Reconquest of Ireland* (Minneapolis, 2002), p. 179.

26   *Irish Worker*, 8 Aug. 1914.

27   Joll, *The Second International*, p. 109.

28   Emmet O'Connor, *A Labour History of Ireland 1824–1960* (Dublin, 1992), p. 90.

29   *Irish Worker*, 15 Aug. 1914.

30   Internationaler Sozialisten-Kongreß, *Stuttgart 1907* (Berlin, 1907).

31   Owen Dudley Edwards, 'Connolly and the Irish Tradition' in *The Furrow*, 7 (1979), p. 420.

32   Internationaler Sozialisten-Kongreß, *Stuttgart*, p. 66.

33   J.C. Kennedy, 'The Stuttgart Congress' in *Journal of Political Economy*, 8 (1907), p. 489.

34   Kennedy, 'The Stuttgart Congress', p. 489.

35   Joll, *The Second International*, p. 207.

36   *Workers' Republic*, 3 July 1915.

37   *Irish Worker*, 8 Aug. 1914.

38   R. Palme Dutt, *The Two Internationals* (London, 1920), p. 3.

39   Wayne Thorpe, 'The European Syndicalists and War, 1914–1918' in *Contemporary European History*, 1 (2001), p. 1.

40   Ibid. pp. 1–2; Ralph Darlington, 'Revolutionary Syndicalist Opposition to the First World War: A Comparative Reassessment' in *Revue Belge de Philologie et D'histoire*, 4 (2006), p. 983.

41   Darlington, 'Revolutionary Syndicalist Opposition to the First World War', p. 1002.

42   Ibid. p. 990.

43   Kevin Morgan, 'Militarism and Anti-Militarism: Socialists, Communists and Conscription in France and Britain 1900–1940' in *Past and Present*, 202 (2009), 219–20.

44   Martin Crick, *The History of the Social Democratic Federation* (Staffordshire, 1994), p. 232.

45   Douglas J. Newton, *British Labour, European Socialism and the Struggle for Peace 1889–1914* (Oxford, 1985), p. 310.

46   Ibid. p. 310.

47   Ransom, 'James Connolly and the Scottish Left', p. 309.

48   David Granville, 'The British Labour and Socialist Movement and the 1916 Rising' in Ruán O'Donnell (ed.), *The Impact of the 1916 Rising Among the Nations* (Dublin, 2008), p. 60; Ransom, 'James Connolly and the Scottish Left', p. 315.

49   *Workers' Republic*, 6 Nov. 1915.

50   Foster, *Vivid Faces*, p. 23.

51   Ann Matthews, *The Irish Citizen Army* (Cork, 2014), p. 13; R.M. Fox, *The History of the Irish Citizen Army* (Dublin, 1943), p. 16.

52   David Lynch, *Radical Politics in Modern Ireland: the Irish Socialist Republican Party 1896–1904* (Dublin, 2005), p. 1.

53   Adrian Grant, *Irish Socialist Republicanism 1909–36* (Dublin, 2012), p. 15.

54   James Connolly, *Collected Works Volume One* (Dublin, 1987), p. 466.

55   *Irish Worker*, 28 Mar. 1914.

56   *The Masses*, Jul. 1916.

57   Foster, *Vivid Faces*, p. 183.

58   Bill Moran, '1913, Jim Larkin and the British Labour Movement' in *Saothar*, 1 (1978), p. 36; Charles McCarthy, 'The Impact of Larkinism on the Irish Working Class' in *Saothar*, 1 (1978), p. 54.

59   Emmet O'Connor, *A Labour History of Ireland 1824–2000* (Dublin, 2011), p. 75.

60   Grant, *Irish Socialist Republicanism*, p. 28.

61   McCarthy, 'The Impact of Larkinism', p. 56.

62   Pádraig Yeates, *Lockout Dublin 1913* (Dublin, 2000), p. x; Emmet Larkin, 'James Larkin: Labour Leader' in Donal Nevin (ed.), *James Larkin: Lion of the Fold* (Dublin, 2006), p. 5.

63   Grant, *Irish Socialist Republicanism*, p. 30.

64   Diarmaid Ferriter, *A Nation and Not A Rabble: The Irish Revolution 1913–23* (London, 2015), p. 2.

65   Frank Robbins, *Under the Starry Plough: Recollections of the Irish Citizen Army* (Dublin, 1977), p. 15.

66   Emmet O'Connor, *James Larkin: Hero or Wrecker?* (Dublin, 2015), pp. 63–4.

67   Ibid. p. 64.

68   *The Masses*, Jul. 1916.

69   Foster, *Vivid Faces*, p. 8.

70   Ibid. pp. 9–10.

71   John Newsinger, '"A Lamp to Guide Your Feet": Jim Larkin, the Irish Worker and the Dublin Working Class' in *European History Quarterly*, 1 (1990), p. 65.

72   Newsinger, 'A Lamp to Guide Your Feet', p. 63.

73   Robbins, *Under the Starry Plough*, pp. 14–15.

74   *Irish Worker*, 25 Oct. 1913.

75   *Irish Worker*, 28 Mar. 1914; *Irish Worker*, 9 May 1914; *Irish Worker*, 22 Aug. 1914.

76   Foster, *Vivid Faces*, p. 147.

77   Population Distribution of ICA circa 1916, map.

78   Lecture on 'The Influence of James Fintan Lalor', undated, Old IRA Literary Society 1, Hanratty Papers, Kilmainham Gaol.

79   *Irish Times*, 30 Aug. 1913; William O'Brien, undated, notes on the Irish Citizen Army, William O'Brien papers (WOBP), MS 15673 (1), National Library of Ireland (NLI).

80   Matthews, *Irish Citizen Army*, p. 16.

81   Jack White, *Misfit* (London, 1930), p. 241.

82   Robbins, *Under the Starry Plough*, p. 43.

83   James Moran, *Four Irish Rebel Plays* (Dublin, 2007), p. 21.

84   Foster, *Vivid Faces*, p. 76.

85   Ibid. p. 81.

86   Declan Kiberd, *Inventing Ireland: The Literature of the Modern Nation* (London, 1996), pp. 202–3.

87   *Irish Worker*, 13 Nov. 1913; Nelson O'Ceallaigh Ritschel, 'Shaw, Connolly and the Irish Citizen Army' in *The Annual of Bernard Shaw Studies*, 27 (2007), p. 120.

88   R.M. Fox, *History of the Irish Citizen Army* (Dublin 1943), p. 45.

89   Foster, *Vivid Faces*, p. 78.

90   Pádraig Yeates, *A City in Wartime Dublin 1914–18* (Dublin, 2011), p. 74.

91   Foster, *Vivid Faces*, p. 78.

92   Senia Paseta, '1798 in 1898: The Politics of Commemoration' in *The Irish Review*, 22 (1998), p. 46.

93   Lynch, *Radical Politics in Modern Ireland*, pp. 41–5.

94   Metscher, *James Connolly*, pp. 41–2.

95   Foster, *Vivid Faces*, p. 166.

96   *Fianna*, June 1915.

97   *Irish Freedom*, Nov. 1913; *Irish Worker*, 31. Oct. 1914.

98   Foster, *Vivid Faces*, p. xvi.

Chapter 2

1   Seán O'Casey to Barney Conway, MS 22,961, NLI.

2   Judicial Division's Report on Year of 1913, CO 903 17, TNA.

3   O'Connor, *A Labour History of Ireland*, p. 14.

4   Uinseann Mac Eoinn, *Survivors* (Dublin, 1987), p. 194.

5   Dermot Keogh, *The Rise of the Irish Working Class* (Belfast, 1982), p. 40.

6   *Report on the Housing Conditions of the Working Class in the City of Dublin*, 1914 [Cd. 7273], p. 3.

7   Francis Devine, *Organising History: A Centenary of SIPTU* (Dublin, 2009), p. 49.

8   Kevin Morley, *A Descriptive History of the Irish Citizen Army* (Dublin, 2012), p. 6.

9   John W. Boyle, 'Connolly, the Citizen Army and the Rising' in K. Nowlan (ed.) *The Making of 1916 Studies in the History of the Rising* (Dublin, 1969), pp. 53–4.

10   Nevin, 'The Irish Citizen Army, 1913–1916' p. 257; O'Connor Lysaght, 'White, Connolly and Larkin', p. 17.

11   *Irish Worker*, 11 Oct. 1913.

12   Ibid. 19 Apr. 1924.

13   Ibid. 27 Dec. 1913.

14   Frank Henderson, BMH WS 249, p. 3.

15   Seán O'Casey, *The Story of the Irish Citizen Army* (London, 1980), p. 3.

16   Lecture by John Hanratty Entitled 'The Influence of James Fintan Lalor', undated, Old IRA Literary and Debating Society, Hanratty Papers, Kilmainham Gaol.

17   Seamus O'Brien, 'The Great Dublin Strike and Lockout, 1913' in *Dublin's Fighting Story 1916–21* (Dublin, 2009), p. 41.

18   Pamphlet by William O'Brien Entitled '1913 and its Significance', undated, Thomas McPartlin Papers (TMPP), P19/D/40, UCDA.

19   Anastasia Dukova, 'Policing the Lockout' in *History Ireland*, 4 (2003), p. 32.

20   *Irish Times*, 5 Sept. 1913; Dukova, 'Policing the Lockout', p. 32.

21   Irish Transport and General Workers' Union [ITGWU], *Fifty Years of Liberty Hall the Golden Jubilee of the Irish Transport and General Workers' Union 1909–59* (Dublin, 1959), p. 46.

22   *Irish Worker*, 23 Aug. 1913.

23   Ibid.

24   Dukova, 'Policing the Lockout', p. 33.

25   O'Connor, *A Labour History of Ireland*, p. 92; Jacqueline Van Voris, *Constance De Markievicz in the Cause of Ireland* (Vermont, 1967), p. 107.

26   Fox, *History*, pp. 6–7.

27   James Larkin Jr, BMH WS 906, p. 13.

28   Lecture by John Hanratty Entitled 'The Influence of James Fintan Lalor', undated, Old IRA Literary and Debating Society, Hanratty Papers, Kilmainham Gaol.

29   Arnold Wright, *Disturbed Dublin* (Dublin, 1914), p. 141.

30   *Report of the Dublin Disturbances Commission*, 1914 [Cd. 7269], p. 4.

31   Ibid.

32   *Appendix to Report of the Dublin Disturbances Commission Minutes of Evidence and Appendices*, 1914 [Cd. 7272], p. 420.

33   Ibid. p. 424.

34   John Newsinger, *Rebel City Larkin, Connolly and the Dublin Labour Movement* (London, 2004), p. 47.

35   *Irish Worker*, 13 Sept. 1913; *Irish Worker*, 4 Oct. 1913.

36   Dukova, 'Policing the Lockout', p. 32.

37   *Freeman's Journal*, 1 Sept. 1913.

38   *Irish Worker*, 6 Sept. 1913.

39   Ibid. 13 Nov. 1913.

40   Ibid. 11 Oct. 1913.

41   John Hanratty, BMH WS 96, p. 1.

42   Robbins, *Under the Starry Plough*, p. 16.

43   Dublin Metropolitan Police (DMP) Reports Relative to Secret Societies in DMP District Furnished During the Month of Nov. 1913 to Under-Secretary for Ireland, James Brown Dougherty, Dublin Metropolitan Police (hereafter DMP) Reports 1913–14, CO 904/14, TNA.

44   Nelson O'Ceallaigh Ritschel, 'Shaw, Connolly and the Irish Citizen Army', p. 120.

45   *The Times*, 8 Nov. 1913.

46   White, *Misfit*, p. 241.

47   T.M. Kettle, 'the Agony of Dublin' in *The Irish Review*, 3 (1913), p. 444.

48   Ibid.

49   Pádraig Yeates, *Lockout*, p. 399.

50   Resolution of Dublin Civic League Regarding the Asquith Commission, undated, Sheehy Skeffington Papers (SSP), MS 22,273, NLI.

51   Thomas O'Donoghue, BMH WS 1666, pp. 4–5.

52   Matthews, *Irish Citizen Army* (Cork, 2014), p. 20.

53   Lecture by John Hanratty Entitled 'The Influence of James Fintan Lalor', undated, Old IRA Literary and Debating Society, Hanratty Papers, Kilmainham Gaol.

54   Lorcan Collins, *James Connolly* (Dublin, 2012), p. 218.

55   Morley, *A Descriptive History*, p. 7; Newsinger, *Rebel City*, p. 81.

56   Matthews, *Irish Citizen Army*, p. 22.

57   Note by William O'Brien on the Irish Citizen Army, undated, WOBP, MS 15,673 (1), NLI.

58   *Irish Times*, 12 Nov. 1913.

59   Ibid. 19 Nov. 1913.

60   *Freeman's Journal*, 19 Nov. 1913; *Irish Times*, 19 Nov. 1913.

61   Leo Keohane, *Captain Jack White: Imperialism, Anarchism and the Irish Citizen Army* (Dublin, 2014), p. 116.

62   Fox, *History*, p. 45. The concept of the army as a tool for morale will be discussed anon.

63   White, *Misfit*, p. 258.

64   Keohane, *Jack White*, p. 102.

65   *Irish Times,* 19 Nov. 1913.

66   Fox, *History*, p. 45.

67   Morley, *A Descriptive History*, p. 16.

68   O'Casey, *Story of the Irish Citizen Army*, pp. 4–6.

69   Hanratty, BMH WS 96, pp. 1–2.

70   Collins, *Connolly*, p. 220.

71   *Freeman's Journal*, 24 Nov. 1913.

72   Collins, *Connolly*, p. 220.
73   Ibid. pp. 220–1.
74   *Irish Times*, 28 Nov. 1913.
75   White, *Misfit*, p. 263.
76   John Hanratty, BMH WS 96, p. 2.
77   White, *Misfit*, p. 262.

Chapter 3

1   Frank Robbins, 'Introducing Some Friends' in *Dublin Historical Record* 3 (1972), p. 93.
2   O'Casey, *Story of the Irish Citizen Army*, pp. 4–5.
3   Timothy Bowman, *Carson's Army: The Ulster Volunteer Force, 1910–22* (Manchester, 2007), p. 38.
4   *Irish Times*, 30 Aug. 1913.
5   *Evening Telegraph*, 14 Nov. 1913.
6   Alan Noonan, '"Real Irish Patriots Would Scorn to Recognise the Like of You": Larkin and Irish-America' in David Convery (ed.), *Locked Out: A Century of Irish Working Class Life* (Dublin, 2013), p. 58.
7   Fox, *History*, p. 7.
8   *Irish Worker*, 27 Dec. 1913.
9   O'Casey, *Story of the Irish Citizen Army*, p. 8.
10   Bowman, *Carson's Army*, p. 38.
11   *Irish Worker*, 6 Sept. 1913.
12   *New York Times*, 13 Nov. 1913.
13   Untitled Lecture by John Hanratty, undated, Old IRA Literary and Debating Society, Hanratty Papers, Kilmainham Gaol.
14   Recollection of William O'Brien, undated, Notes by William O'Brien on Irish Citizen Army, WOBP, MS 15,673 (1) (part 1), NLI.
15   C. Desmond Greaves, *The Life and Times of James Connolly* (Berlin, 1971), p. 328.
16   *The Christian Science Monitor*, 2 Dec. 1913.
17   White, *Misfit*, pp. 197–9.
18   Keohane, *Jack White*, p. 71.
19   Resolution Drafted by James Connolly for Submission to a Mass Meeting in St Mary's Hall After the Introduction of the Home Rule Bill, 1912, undated, Volume of letters from James Connolly, WOBP, MS 15,668, NLI.
20   *Irish Times*, 4 Oct. 1913.
21   *Weekly Irish Times*, 29 Nov. 1913.
22   Helena Molony, BMH WS 391, p. 19.
23   *Weekly Irish Times*, 29 Nov. 1913.
24   *Irish Times*, 17 Dec. 1913.
25   Morley, *A Descriptive History*, p. 14.

26   Helena Molony, BMH WS 391, p. 19.

27   White, *Misfit*, p. 277.

28   *Irish Times*, 19 Nov. 1913.

29   Ibid.

30   Ibid.

31   White, *Misfit*, p. 261.

32   Ibid. p. 260.

33   *Irish Worker*, 27 Dec. 1913.

34   White, *Misfit*, p. 256.

35   Keohane, *Jack White*, p. 94.

36   Conor McCabe, '"Your Only God is Profit": Irish Class Relations and the 1913 Lockout' in D. Convery (ed.), *Locked Out: A Century of Irish Working Class Life* (Dublin, 2013), p. 21.

37   White, *Misfit*, p. 250.

38   Ibid. p. 258.

39   Nevin, 'The Irish Citizen Army, 1913–1916', p. 258.

40   Ruan O'Donnell, 'New Introduction' in F.X. Martin (ed.), *The Irish Volunteer 1913–15: Recollections and Documents* (Dublin, 2013), p. 2.

41   Letter from Agnes Newman to Desmond Ryan, undated, COSP 80, ILHSMA.

42   David Lynch, *Radical Politics in Modern Ireland: the Irish Socialist Republican Party 1896–1904* (Dublin, 2005), p. 4.

43   James Connolly, *Collected Works Volume One*, pp. 369–70.

44   Newsinger, *Rebel City*, p. 37.

45   *Irish Worker, ad passim*.

46   Ibid. 27 May 1913.

47   Newsinger, 'A Lamp to Guide Your Feet', p. 65.

48   *Irish Worker*, 1 Feb. 1913.

49   Ibid. 22 Feb. 1913.

50   Ibid. 10 May 1913.

51   Grant, *Socialist Republicanism,* pp. 52–7.

52   *Irish Freedom*, Jan. 1913.

53   *Shan Van Vocht*, Jan. 1897.

54   *Irish Freedom*, Jan. 1913.

55   Ibid.

56   Owen McGee, *The IRB: the Irish Republican Brotherhood from Land League to Sinn Féin* (Dublin, 2005), p. 355.

57   Grant, *Socialist Republicanism*, p. 57.

58   *Irish Freedom*, Nov. 1913.

59   Grant, *Socialist Republicanism*, p. 56.

60   *Irish Worker*, 28 June 1913.

61   Pádraig Pearse, 'The Coming Revolution' in F.X. Martin (ed.), *The Irish Volunteer 1913–15: Recollections and Documents* (Dublin, 2013), p. 72.

62   Ibid.

63   White, *Misfit*, p. 254.

64   John Hanratty, BMH WS 96, p. 3; For information regarding the role of the IRB in the formation of the Irish Volunteers see: Bulmer Hobson, 'Ireland's Hour of Destiny' in Martin (ed.), *The Irish Volunteers*, pp. 37–44.

65   Roger McHugh, "'Always Complainin'': The Politics of Young Seán' in *Irish University Review* 1 (1980), p. 91.

66   Newsinger, *Rebel City*, p. 112.

67   O'Casey, *Drums Under the Windows* (London, 1972), p. 226.

68   Metscher, *James Connolly*, p. 166.

69   Yeates, *Lockout*, p. 439.

70   Emmet O'Connor, *Big Jim Larkin: Hero or Wrecker?* (Dublin, 2015), p. 134.

71   Bulmer Hobson, 'Ireland's Hour of Destiny' in F.X. Martin (ed.), *The Irish Volunteers 1913–15: Recollections and Documents* (Dublin, 2013), p. 43; Joseph O'Connor, BMH WS 157, p. 5.

72   Robbins, *Under the Starry Plough*, p. 24.

73   *Irish Worker*, 29 Nov. 1913.

74   William O'Brien, BMH WS 1766, p. 50.

75   *Irish Worker*, 7 Mar. 1914.

76   John Newsinger, "'In the Hunger-cry of the Nation's Poor is Heard the Voice of Ireland": Seán O'Casey and Politics 1908–1916' in *Journal of Contemporary History*, 2 (1985), p. 228.

77   Hobson, 'Ireland's Hour of Destiny', p. 43.

78   O'Casey, *Story of the Irish Citizen Army*, p. 69.

79   *Freeman's Journal*, 9 July 1910; Grant, *Socialist Republicanism*, p. 52.

80   *Irish Worker*, 27 Sept. 1913.

81   James McConnel, 'The Irish Parliamentary Party, Industrial Relations and the 1913 Dublin Lockout' in *Saothar, 28* (2003), p. 32.

82   McConnel, 'The Irish Parliamentary Party', p. 32; *Irish Worker*, 27 Sept. 1913.

83   Keohane, *Jack White*, p. 173.

84   ITGWU, *Fifty Years of Liberty Hall*, p. 49.

85   *Irish Worker*, 29 Nov. 1913.

86   John White, 'Bad, Sad Specimens of the Human Race' in *History Ireland* 4 (2013), p. 36.

87   Seán MacDermott to Joe McGarrity, 12 Dec. 1913, Memorandum of Detention of Trade Union Leaders, Thomas Johnson Papers (TJP), MS 17,118, NLI.

88   Thomas Clarke to Joe McGarrity, 14 May 1914, Handbill Advertising Lecture by John Hanratty, WOBP, MS 33,718 h (205–255), NLI.

89   Justin Dolan Stover, 'Delaying division, Eoin MacNeill, John Redmond and the Irish Volunteers' in *History Studies*, 8 (2007), p. 112.

90   O'Casey, *Story of the Irish Citizen Army*, p. 9.

91   *Irish Worker*, 24 Jan. 1914.

92 O'Casey, *Drums*, p. 230.

93 James O'Shea, BMH WS 733, p. 6.

94 Christopher Poole, undated, Irish Citizen Army MSPC RO 10A.

95 *Irish Worker*, 24 Jan. 1914.

96 Ibid. 7 Feb. 1914.

Chapter 4

1 O'Casey, *Story of the Irish Citizen Army*, p. 16.

2 Ibid.

3 Lecture by John Hanratty Entitled 'The Influence of James Fintan Lalor', undated, Old IRA Literary and Debating Society, Hanratty Papers, Kilmainham Gaol.

4 *Irish Times,* 15 Jan. 1914.

5 Yeates, *Lockout*, p. 522.

6 Ibid. pp. 520–2.

7 Newsinger, *Rebel City*, p. 105.

8 Fox, *History*, p. 62.

9 *Irish Times*, 18 June 1968.

10 Advertisement by the Labour Party, Drumcondra Branch, for a lecture by John Hanratty, 16 Apr. 1946, WOBP, MS 33,718h (205– 255), NLI.

11 Yeates, *City in Wartime*, p. 42.

12 Recollection of William O'Brien, undated, Notes on Irish Citizen Army, WOBP, MS 15,673 (1) (part one), NLI.

13 Matthews, *Irish Citizen Army*, p. 34; Newsinger, *Rebel City*, p. 114.

14 *Irish Worker*, 21 Mar. 1914.

15 C. Desmond Greaves, *Seán O'Casey: Politics and Art* (London, 1979), p. 72.

16 Matthews, *Irish Citizen Army*, p. 34.

17 O'Casey, *Story of the Irish Citizen Army,* pp. 11–12.

18 *Irish Worker*, 18 Apr. 1914.

19 Ibid. 28 Mar. 1914. Appendix 1: 'ICA Constitution, 22 March 1914'.

20 Ibid. *ad passim.*

21 Boyle, 'Connolly, the Citizen Army and the Rising', p. 57.

22 *Irish Worker*, 28 Mar. 1914.

23 Ibid.

24 Matthews, *Irish Citizen Army*, p. 34.

25 O'Connor Lysaght, 'White, Larkin, and Connolly', p. 18.

26 O'Connor, *A Labour History of Ireland*, p. 30.

27 *Forward*, 30 May 1914.

28 *Irish Times*, 19 Nov. 1913.

29 Ibid. 24 Nov. 1913.

30 *Irish Worker*, 4 Apr. 1914.

31 *Evening Telegraph*, 24 Nov. 1913.

32 *Irish Worker,* 13 Dec. 1913.

33 *Daily Herald,* 24 Jan. 1914; *Daily Herald,* 26 Jan. 1914.

34 Lecture by John Hanratty on the Irish Citizen Army, 1955, Old IRA Society II, Hanratty Papers, Kilmainham Gaol; *Irish Worker,* 28 Mar. 1914.

35 O'Connor, *A Labour History of Ireland* (1992), p. 91.

36 O'Casey, *Story of the Irish Citizen Army,* p. 23.

37 *Irish Worker,* 9 May 1914.

38 Ibid. Appendix 2: 'Revised ICA Constitution'.

39 Matthews, *Irish Citizen Army,* p. 44.

40 *Irish Worker,* 22 Aug. 1914.

41 Ibid. 9 May 1914.

42 Irish Citizen Army Constitution, undated, in James O'Neill, MSP, 34REF8368. Appendix 2: 'Revised ICA Constitution'.

43 *Irish Worker,* 4 Apr. 1914.

44 Ibid. 28 Mar. 1914; Matthews, *Irish Citizen Army,* p. 36; Morley, *A Descriptive History,* p. 30; Fox, *History,* p. 64.

45 *Irish Times,* 19 Nov. 1913.

46 John Hanratty, BMH WS 96, p. 2.

47 *Irish Times,* 19 Nov. 1913.

48 O'Casey, *Story of the Irish Citizen Army,* p. 14.

49 Michael Noyk, BMH WS 707, p. 8.

50 White, *Misfit,* p. 250.

51 Christopher Poole, undated, Irish Citizen Army MSPC RO 10A.

52 O'Connor Lysaght, 'White, Larkin and Connolly', p. 18.

53 Christopher Poole, undated, Irish Citizen Army MSPC RO 10A.

54 Scheme for a History of the Irish Citizen Army by John Hanratty, undated, 1913–23 Documents I, Hanratty Papers, Kilmainham Gaol.

55 Minutes of Committee Meetings of the ITGWU Feb. 1914–Feb. 1916, Together with Minutes of the Strike Committee Oct 1913, 8 July 1914, MS 7298, NLI.

56 O'Casey, *Drums,* p. 227.

57 Anne Marreco, *The Rebel Countess: the Life and Times of Constance Markievicz* (London, 2000), p. 171.

58 O'Casey, *Drums,* p. 227.

59 Ibid.

60 O'Casey, *Story of the Irish Citizen Army,* p. 17.

61 Kingstown Report, 16 July 1914, WOBP, MS 15,673, NLI.

62 Robbins, *Under the Starry Plough,* p. 35.

63 Seán Prendergast, BMH WS 755, p. 13.

64 Morley, *A Descriptive History,* p. 23.

65 *Irish Worker,* 11 Apr. 1914.

66 Greaves, *O'Casey,* p. 74.

67   Irish Citizen Army Membership Card, undated, in Irish Citizen Army, MSPC RO 10A; Greaves, *O'Casey*, p. 74; Collins, *Connolly*, p. 228.

68   Greaves, *O'Casey*, p. 74.

69   O'Casey, *Drums*, p. 231.

70   *Irish Worker*, 4 Apr. 1914.

71   O'Casey, *Story of the Irish Citizen Army*, p. 17.

72   Brian Hughes, *Michael Mallin* (Dublin, 2012), p. 90.

73   Population Distribution of ICA circa 1916, map.

74   *Irish Worker*, 11 Apr. 1914.

75   *Christian Science Monitor*, 16 June 1914.

76   *Irish Worker*, 29 Aug. 1914.

77   O'Casey, *Story of the Irish Citizen Army*, p. 31.

78   Irish Citizen Army Notebook, 1914–1915, WOBP, MS 34,937, NLI.

79   *Irish Times*, 16 Mar. 1914.

80   Kingstown Report, 16 July 1914, WOBP, MS 15,673, NLI.

81   Fox, *History*, p. 69.

82   Ibid.; Grant, *Socialist Republicanism*, p. 60; 'Manifesto Sent to Irish Trades Bodies', Appendix in O'Casey, *Story of the Irish Citizen Army*, pp. 68–9.

83   O'Casey, *Story of the Irish Citizen Army*, p. 43.

84   Fox, *History*, p. 69.

85   *Irish Worker*, 4 Apr. 1914.

86   O'Casey, *Drums*, p. 227.

87   Ibid. p. 226.

88   Irish Citizen Army Notebook, 1914–1915, WOBP, MS 34,937, NLI.

89   ITGWU Committee Meeting Minutes, 8 July 1914, MS 7298, NLI.

90   Frank Robbins, BMH WS 585, p. 3.

91   O'Casey, *Story of the Irish Citizen Army*, p. 18.

92   ITGWU Committee Meeting Minutes, 22 Apr. 1914 MS 7298, NLI.

93   Ibid. 8 July 1914, MS 7298, NLI.

94   ITGWU Committee Meeting Minutes, 20 Aug. 1914, MS 7298, NLI.

95   Robbins, *Under the Starry Plough*, p. 43.

96   Ibid.

97   Robbins, *Under the Starry Plough*, p. 39.

98   *Irish Times*, 16 Mar. 1914.

99   DMP Reports Relative to Secret Societies in DMP District Furnished During the Month of Oct. 1914 to Under-Secretary for Ireland, Matthew Nathan, DMP Reports 1913–14, CO 904/14, TNA. It should be recognised that White was mentioned in May 1914 but this was through his association with the Irish Volunteers.

100 DMP Reports Relative to Secret Societies in DMP District Furnished During the Month of May 1914 to Under-Secretary for Ireland, James Brown Dougherty, DMP Reports 1913–14, CO 904/14, TNA.

101   ITGWU, *Fifty Years of Liberty Hall*, pp. 51–2.
102   David George Boyce, 'The Ulster crisis: Prelude to 1916?' in Gabriel Doherty and Dermot Keogh (eds), *1916 the Long Revolution* (Cork, 2007), p. 45.
103   *Forward*, 21 Mar. 1914.
104   *Irish Worker*, 28 Mar. 1914.
105   *Irish Worker*, 11 Apr. 1914.
106   *House of Commons Debate*, 9 March 1914, volume 59, cc. 907–948.
107   *Irish Worker*, 4 Apr. 1914.
108   Memorandum Entitled 'Ireland and the Anglo-German War' Signed by S.T. O'Kelly and S. Milroy on Behalf of the Irish Neutrality League, September 1914, Irish Neutrality League 1914; Anti-Conscription Committee 1915, WOBP, MS 13,954, NLI.
109   Irish Trades Union Congress, *Annual Report of the Twenty-First Irish Trades Union Congress, 1914*, p. 12.
110   Grant, *Socialist Republicanism*, pp. 61–2.
111   *Irish Worker*, 14 Mar. 1914; *Forward*, 21 Mar. 1914; *Forward*, 11 Apr. 1914.
112   *Irish Worker*, 14 Mar. 1914.
113   Ibid.
114   *Irish Times*, 16 Mar. 1914.
115   *Forward*, 11 Apr. 1914.
116   Ibid. 21 Mar. 1914.
117   *Irish Worker*, 4 Apr. 1914.
118   Ibid.
119   Yeates, *Lockout*, p. 565.
120   C. Desmond Greaves, *The Irish Transport Union and General Workers' Union* (Dublin, 1982), pp. 127–8.
121   *Irish Worker*, 28 Mar. 1914.
122   Ibid.
123   Ibid.
124   Ibid.
125   Fox, *History*, p. 66.
126   Ibid.
127   *Irish Worker*, 21 Mar. 1914.
128   Ibid. 28 Mar. 1914.
129   Metscher, *James Connolly*, p. 170.
130   O'Connor, *A Labour History of Ireland*, p. 89.
131   *Irish Worker*, 28 Mar. 1914.
132   Ibid. 11 Apr. 1914.
133   Matthews, *Irish Citizen Army*, p. 19.
134   Ibid.
135   *Irish Worker*, 4 Apr. 1914.
136   'Manifesto Sent to Irish Trades Bodies', Appendix in O'Casey, *Story of the Irish Citizen Army*, p. 69.

137   Fox, *History*, p. 69; Grant, *Socialist Republicanism*, p. 60.

138   'Manifesto Sent to Irish Trades Bodies', Appendix in O'Casey, *Story of the Irish Citizen Army*, pp. 68–9.

Chapter 5

1   *Irish Freedom*, Feb. 1914.

2   Ibid. Jan. 1914.

3   Ibid. Feb. 1914.

4   Newsinger, 'In the Hunger-cry of the Nation's Poor is Heard the Voice of Ireland', pp. 233–4.

5   Fox, *History*, p. 9; p. 67.

6   *Irish Worker*, 21 Feb. 1914.

7   Ibid. 21 Feb. 1914.

8   Ibid. 28 Feb. 1914.

9   Ibid.

10   Ibid. 11 Apr. 1914.

11   Ibid.

12   O'Casey, *Story of the Irish Citizen Army*, p. 18.

13   *Irish Worker*, 7 Mar. 1914.

14   Ibid. 25 Apr. 1914.

15   Ibid.

16   *Irish Freedom*, Jan. 1914.

17   *Irish Worker*, 21 Feb. 1914.

18   *Irish Freedom*, Mar. 1914.

19   Ibid.

20   *Irish Worker*, 16 May 1914.

21   *The Masses*, July 1916.

22   Fox, *History*, p. 70.

23   O'Connor, *Big Jim Larkin*, p. 151.

24   O'Connor Lysaght, 'White, Larkin, and Connolly', p. 18.

25   White, *Misfit*, p. 304.

26   Fox, *History*, p. 71.

27   O'Casey, *Story of the Irish Citizen Army*, p. 26.

28   *Irish Times*, 4 May 1914.

29   Bulmer Hobson, 'John Redmond and the Volunteer' in F.X. Martin (ed.), *The Irish Volunteers 1913–15: Recollections and Documents* (Dublin, 2013), p. 56.

30   *Irish Times*, 5 May 1914.

31   Keohane, *Jack White*, p. 154.

32   Ibid. p. 165.

33   White, *Misfit*, p. 272.

34   Keohane, *Jack White*, p. 141.

35   Frank Robbins, BMH WS 586, p. 6.

36   Keohane, *Jack White*, p. 141.

37   White, *Misfit*, p. 301.

38   O'Casey, *Story of the Irish Citizen Army*, p. 45.

39   Robbins, *Under the Starry Plough*, p. 20.

40   Greaves, *O'Casey*, p. 76.

41   *Irish Worker*, 21 Feb. 1914.

42   Untitled Lecture by John Hanratty, undated, Old IRA Literary Society I, Hanratty Papers, Kilmainham Gaol.

43   O'Casey, *Story of the Irish Citizen Army*, p. 35.

44   Seán Prendergast, BMH WS 755, p. 21; Marreco, *Rebel Countess*, p. 172.

45   Ferghal McGarry, *The Rising Ireland: Easter 1916* (New York, 2011), p. 20; Greaves, *O'Casey*, p. 75.

46   Bulmer Hobson, 'John Redmond and the Volunteers – Negotiations with MacNeill' in F.X. Martin (ed.), *The Irish Volunteers 1913–15: Recollections and Documents* (Dublin, 2013), p. 58.

47   Van Voris, *Constance de Markievicz*, p. 134.

48   Diarmaid Ferriter, 'Introduction' in Brian Ó Conchubhair (ed.), *Dublin's Fighting Story 1916–21 Told by the Men Who Made It* (Dublin, 2009), pp. 27–8.

49   Newsinger, 'In the Hunger-cry of the Nation's Poor is Heard the Voice of Ireland', p. 235.

50   O'Connor Lysaght, 'White, Larkin and Connolly', p. 19.

51   *Irish Worker*, 27 June 1914.

52   Newsinger, 'Seán O'Casey and Politics', p. 234.

53   Ibid.

54   Frank Henderson, BMH WS 249, p. 8.

55   Charles Shelley, BMH WS 870, p. 1.

56   James Carrigan, BMH WS 613, p. 1.

57   Bulmer Hobson, BMH WS 53, p. 12.

58   *Royal Commission into the Circumstances Connected with the Landing of Arms at Howth on July 26th*, 1914 [Cd. 7631], p. 5.

59   Ibid.

60   Fox, *History*, p. 74.

61   Greaves, *O'Casey*, p. 76.

62   Marreco, *Rebel Countess*, pp. 178–9.

63   Statement of Christopher Poole Recorded by John Hanratty, undated, 1913–23 Documents I, Hanratty Papers, Kilmainham Gaol.

64   *Royal Commission into the Circumstances Connected with the Landing of Arms at Howth on July 26th*, 1914 [Cd. 7631], p. 5.

65   Fox, *History*, p. 75.

66   Statement of Christopher Poole Recorded by John Hanratty, undated, 1913–23 Documents I, Hanratty Papers, Kilmainham Gaol.

67   Ibid.

68   Fox, *History*, p. 75.

69   Yeates, *City in Wartime*, p. 5.

70   Ibid. p. 7.

71   Nevin, 'The Irish Citizen Army, 1913–1916', p. 260.

72   Greaves, *O'Casey*, p. 76.

73   O'Casey, *Story of the Irish Citizen Army*, p. 43.

74   Bulmer Hobson, 'Foundation and Growth of the Irish Volunteers 1913–14' in F.X. Martin (ed.), *The Irish Volunteers 1913–15: Recollections and Documents* (Dublin, 2013), p. 49.

75   Thomas J. Morrissey SJ, *Willliam O'Brien 1881–1968: Socialist, Republican, Dáil Deputy, Editor and Trade Union Leader* (Dublin, 2007), p. 90.

76   *Irish Worker*, 1 Aug. 1914.

77   Boyle, 'Connolly, the Citizen Army and the Rising', p. 61.

78   Mac Eoinn, *Survivors*, p. 196.

79   Patricia Jalland and John Stubbs, 'The Irish Question after the Outbreak of War in 1914: Some Unfinished Party Business' in *The English Historical Review*, 96 (1981), p. 782; Stephen Collins, 'John Redmond: Discarded Leader' in *An Irish Quarterly Review*, 98 (200), p. 128.

80   Collins, 'John Redmond', p. 129.

81   Kevin O'Sheil, BMH WS 1170, pp. 478–9.

82   Laurence Nugent, BMH WS 907, p. 14.

83   *The Masses*, July 1916.

84   Fox, *History*, p. 84.

85   David George Boyce, *Nationalism in Ireland* (London, 1982), p. 307.

86   Boyle, 'Connolly, the Citizen Army and the Rising', p. 62.

87   O'Connor, *A Labour History of Ireland*, p. 96.

88   Lecture by John Hanratty on the Irish Citizen Army, 1955, Old IRA Society II, Hanratty Papers, Kilmainham Gaol.

89   Robbins, *Under the Starry Plough*, p. 21.

90   *Workers' Republic*, 30 Oct. 1915.

91   The ITGWU's golden jubilee issue estimated that eighty Volunteers and forty ICA were organised for this. See ITGWU, *Fifty years of Liberty Hall*, p. 54.

92   Fox, *History*, p. 80.

93   Seán T. O'Kelly, BMH WS 1765, pp. 160–1.

94   Robbins, *Under the Starry Plough*, pp. 21–2.

95   Fionan Lynch, BMH WS 192, p. 6.

96   Notes by William O'Brien, undated, 6 notebooks of William O'Brien, WOBP, MS 15,704, NLI.

97   Fox, *History*, p. 81.

98   Robbins, *Under the Starry Plough*, p. 23.

99 Note from James Connolly, Belfast, to William O'Brien, Dublin, Written on a Draft Circular Calling for a Conference Which Established the Irish Neutrality League, Sept. 1914, Irish Neutrality League 1914; Anti-Conscription Committee 1915, WOBP, MS 13,954, NLI.

100 Fionan Lynch, BMH WS 192, p. 6.

101 Piaras Béaslaí, 'How the Fight Began' in Brian Ó Conchubhair (ed.), *Dublin's Fighting Story 1916–21 Told by the Men Who Made It* (Dublin, 2009), p. 30.

102 Fox, *History*, p. 81.

103 Robbins, *Under the Starry Plough*, p. 22.

104 Yeates, *City in Wartime*, p. 43.

105 Robbins, *Under the Starry Plough*, pp. 22–3.

106 Statement of Christopher Poole Recorded by John Hanratty, undated, 1913–23 Documents I, Hanratty Papers, Kilmainham Gaol.

107 Fox, *History*, pp. 82–3.

108 Robbins, *Under the Starry Plough*, p. 23.

109 Ibid.

110 Fox, *History*, p. 83; Robbins, *Under the Starry Plough*, p. 23.

111 Fox, *History*, p. 88.

112 Robbins, *Under the Starry Plough*, p. 23.

113 Fox, *History*, p. 88.

114 *Irish Worker*, 3 Oct. 1914.

Chapter 6

1 Matthews, *Irish Citizen Army*, p. 39.

2 Ibid. p. 47.

3 Manus O'Riordan, 'Larkin in America: the Road to Sing Sing' in Donal Nevin (ed.), *James Larkin: Lion to the Fold* (Dublin, 2006), p. 64.

4 Pamphlet Entitled 'Some Pages From Union History The Facts Concerning Larkin's Departure to America', 12 Apr. 1924, WOBP, MS 33,718 h (205–255), NLI.

5 Robbins, *Under the Starry Plough*, p. 15.

6 Christopher Poole, 14 February 1936, MSP, 34REF10145.

7 Robbins, *Under the Starry Plough*, p. 27.

8 James Connolly, Belfast, to William O'Brien, Dublin, 15 June 1914, Volume of Letters from James Connolly, WOBP, MS 15,668, NLI.

9 Newsinger, *Rebel City*, p. 123.

10 O'Connor, *A Labour History of Ireland*, p. 98.

11 Letter from DMP Superintendent John Lowe to Chief Secretary for Ireland Augustine Birrell, 26 Oct. 1914, Lar files 232–234, CO 904 206, TNA.

12 O'Connor, *Big Jim Larkin*, p. 165.

13 Letter from DMP Superintendent John Lowe to Chief Secretary for Ireland Augustine Birrell, 26 Oct. 1914, Lar files 232–234, CO 904 206, TNA.

14 O'Connor, *A Labour History of Ireland*, p. 98.

15 *The Masses*, July 1916.

16 John J. Lyng to William O'Brien, 14 Apr. 1924, WOBP, MS 33,718 h (205–255), NLI.

17 O'Connor, *A Labour History of Ireland*, p. 98; *Irish Worker*, 10 Oct. 1914.

18 *Irish Worker*, 24 Oct. 1914.

19 O'Riordan, 'Larkin in America', p. 64.

20 Cecil Spring Rice, British Ambassador to the United States, to Edward Grey, British Secretary of State for Foreign Affairs, 28 Nov. 1914, Lar files 232–234, CO 904 206, TNA.

21 *The Public Ledger*, 25 Nov. 1914; *The Philadelphia Press*, 25 Nov. 1914.

22 *The Gaelic American*, 26 Dec. 1914.

23 Ibid.

24 British Consul-General, Courtenay Bennett, to the British Secretary of the State for Foreign Affairs, Edward Grey, 11 Dec. 1914, Lar files 232–234, CO 904 206, TNA.

25 *New York American*, 7 Dec. 1914.

26 O'Connor, *Big Jim Larkin*, p. 171.

27 *Irish Worker*, 24 Oct. 1914.

28 Ibid.

29 Matthews, *Irish Citizen Army*, p. 39.

30 Seán T. O'Kelly, BMH WS 1765, p. 155.

31 Ibid. pp. 156–9.

32 Florence O'Donoghue, 'Plans for the 1916 Rising' in *University Review*, 1 (1963), p. 8.

33 Ibid.

34 Seán T. O'Kelly, BMH WS 1765, pp. 156–9.

35 *Irish Worker*, 24 Oct. 1914.

36 R.M. Fox, *James Connolly the Forerunner* (Tralee, 1946), p. 175.

37 William Delany, *The Green and the Red: Revolutionary Republicanism and Socialism in Irish History: 1848–1923* (Lincoln, 2011), p. 376.

38 Greaves, *Life and Times*, p. 365.

39 *Irish Worker*, 31 Oct. 1914; *Irish Worker*, 9 May 1914.

40 Ibid. 28 Mar. 1914; ibid. 9 May 1914.

41 Ibid. 31. Oct. 1914; Nellie Donnelly, BMH WS 256, pp. 1–3.

42 *Irish Worker*, 9 May 1914.

43 Ibid. 31. Oct. 1914.

44 White, *Misfit*, p. 248.

45 *Irish Worker*, 31. Oct. 1914.

46 Advertising Bill of the Irish Citizen Army, undated, WOBP, Documents on Irish Citizen Army, MS 15,673 (1), NLI.

47 Greaves, *Life and Times*, p. 366.

48   Fox, *History*, pp. 92–4.
49   Recollection of William O'Brien, undated, Notes by William O'Brien on the Irish Citizen Army, WOBP, MS 15,673 (1) (part 3), NLI.
50   Robbins, *Under the Starry Plough*, p. 24.
51   Robbins, BMH WS 585, p. 39.
52   Ibid.
53   *Irish Worker*, 21 Nov. 1914; *Irish Worker*, 14 Nov. 1914.
54   Fox, *History*, p. 94.
55   Van Voris, *Constance de Markievicz*, p. 148.
56   James O'Shea, BMH WS 733, p. 15.
57   Robbins, *Under the Starry Plough*, p. 68.
58   Fox, *Connolly*, p. 178.
59   Robbins, *Under the Starry Plough*, p. 68.
60   *Royal Commission on the Rebellion in Ireland. Minutes of Evidence and Appendix of Documents*, 1916 [Cd. 8311], p. 5.
61   James O'Shea, BMH WS 733, p. 15.
62   William Mulligan, 'Forging a Better World: Socialists and International Politics in the Early Twentieth Century' in Paul Daly, Rónán O'Brien and Paul Rouse (eds), *Making the Difference? The Irish Labour Party 1912–2012*, p. 57.
63   Newsinger, *Rebel City*, p. 123.
64   Greaves, *Life and Times*, p. 283.
65   Metscher, 'James Connolly, the Easter Rising and the First World War', p. 149.
66   Memorandum Entitled 'Ireland and the Anglo-German War' Signed by S.T. O'Kelly and S. Milroy on Behalf of the Irish Neutrality League, September 1914, Irish Neutrality League 1914; Anti-Conscription Committee 1915, WOBP, MS 13,954, NLI.
67   Ibid.
68   Ibid.
69   Notes by Cathal O'Shannon on James Connolly, undated, MS 18,775 (2), NLI.
70   Seán T. O'Kelly, BMH WS 1765, p. 164.
71   Invitation for an Irish Neutrality League Public Meeting to be Held on 12 Oct. 1914, 5 Oct. 1914, Irish Neutrality League 1914; Anti-Conscription Committee 1915, WOBP, MS 13,954, NLI.
72   Greaves, *Life and Times*, pp. 285–6.
73   Emmet O'Connor, 'War and Syndicalism 1914–23' in Donal Nevin (ed.), *Trade Union Century* (Dublin, 1994), pp. 54–5.
74   Yeates, *City in Wartime*, p. 48.
75   Ibid. pp. 28–9.
76   O'Connor Lysaght, 'White, Larkin and Connolly', p. 20.
77   Matthews, *Irish Citizen Army*, p. 45.
78   *Cork Free Press*, 22 Oct. 1914.
79   Greaves, *Life and Times*, p. 358.

80   *Workers' Republic*, 18 Dec. 1915.

81   Nellie Donnelly, BMH WS 256, p. 1.

82   Ibid.

83   *The Masses*, July 1916.

84   *Workers' Republic*, 18 Dec. 1915.

85   A.W. Zurbrugg, 'Introduction' in A.W. Zurbrugg (ed.), *Not Our War Writing Against the First World War* (London, 2014), p. 1.

86   Ralph Darlington, 'Revolutionary Syndicalist Opposition to the First World War', p. 983.

87   Internationaler Sozialisten-Kongreß, *Stuttgart 1907* (Berlin, 1907), p. 66; Original script reads: 'Droht der Ausbruch eines Krieges, so sind die arbeitenden Klassen und deren parlamentarische Vertretungen in den beteiligten Laendern verpflichtet, unterstuetzt durch die zusammenfassende Taetigkeit des Internationalen Bureaus alles aufzubieten, um durch die Anwendung der ihnen am wirksamsten erscheinenden Mittel den Ausbruch des Krieges zu verhindern, die sich je nach der Verschaerfung des Klassenkampfes und der Verschaerfung der allgemeinen politischen Situation naturgemaess aendern.'

88   Metscher, 'James Connolly, the Easter Rising and the First World War', p. 150.

89   Joll, *The Second International*, p. 139.

90   Greaves, *Life and Times*, p. 353.

91   Michael T. Foy and Brian Barton, *The Easter Rising* (Gloucestershire, 2011), p. 34.

92   *Irish Worker*, 8 Aug. 1914.

93   Ibid. 15 Aug. 1914.

94   *Workers' Republic*, 30 Oct. 1915.

95   *Irish Worker*, 3 Oct. 1914.

96   Greaves, *Life and Times*, pp. 351–3.

97   *Irish Worker*, 10 Oct. 1914. Here the ICA was referring to Emmet's speech before being sentenced to execution when he stated 'when my country takes her place among the nation of earth, then and not till then, let my epitaph be written'.

98   Ibid. 8 Aug. 1914.

99   Fox, *History*, pp. 4–5.

100   Internationaler Sozialisten-Kongreß, *Stuttgart 1907*, p. 66. Original script reads: 'Falls der Krieg dennoch ausbrechen sollte, ist es die Pflicht, fuer dessen rasche Beendigung einzutreten und mit allen Kraeften dahin zu streben, die durch den Krieg harbeigefuehrte wirtschaftliche und politische Krise zur Aufruettelung des Volkes auszunutzen und dadurch die Beseitigung der kapitalistischen Klassenherrschaft zu beschleunigen.'

101   *Irish Worker*, 32 Oct. 1914.

102   *International Socialist Review*, 8 (1915), p. 450.

103   James Connolly, 'Revolutionary Unionism and the War' in *International Socialist Review*, 9 (1915), pp. 523–6.

104   Ibid. pp. 525–6.

105   *Forward*, 15 Aug. 1914.

106   Ibid.

107   Mark Schafer, Sam Robinson and Bradley Aldrich, 'Operational Codes and the 1916 Easter Rising in Ireland: A Test of the Frustration–Aggression Hypothesis' in *Foreign Policy Analysis*, 2 (2006), p. 67; ibid. p. 70.

108   Schafer *et al.*, 'Operational codes', p. 72.

109   Collins, *Connolly*, p. 257.

110   James Connolly to Winifred Carney, 2 Dec. 1915, Letters from James Connolly to Winifred Carney, COS 93 12 90, ILHMA.

111   Yeates, *City in Wartime*, pp. 55–6.

112   Handbill on the Subject of Conscription Published by the Dublin United Trades Council and Signed by William O'Brien, 25 Oct. 1915, Documents on the Citizen Army, WOBP, MS 15,673 (1) (part 8), NLI.

113   Dublin Metropolitan Police Report on the Movement of Extremists, 19 July 1915, CSO/JD/2/39, NAI.

114   *Irish Worker*, 24 Oct. 1914.

115   Ibid.

116   *Fianna*, June 1915.

117   Collins, *Connolly*, pp. 246–7.

118   *Workers' Republic*, 5 June 1915.

119   Ibid. 24 July 1915.

120   Patrick Casey, BMW WS 1148, p. 3.

121   *Irish Worker*, 21 Nov. 1914.

122   DMP Reports Relative to Secret Societies in DMP District Furnished During the Month of Nov. 1914 to Under-Secretary for Ireland, Matthew Nathan, DMP Reports 1913–14, CO 904/14.

123   Ibid.

124   *Irish Worker*, 28 Nov. 1914.

125   McGarry, *Easter 1916*, p. 20.

126   *Workers' Republic*, 26 June 1915.

127   Dublin Metropolitan Police Report on the Movement of Extremists, 21 June 1915, CSO/JD/2/16 (2), NAI.

128   *Workers' Republic*, 26 June 1915.

129   Matthews, *Irish Citizen Army*, p. 59.

130   Foy and Barton, *The Easter Rising*, p. 32; Matthews, *Irish Citizen Army*, p. 60; Foy and Barton, *op. cit.*

131   Donal Nevin, *James Connolly: a Full Life* (Dublin, 2006), p. 600.

132   *Workers' Republic*, 31 July 1915.

133   Yeates, *City in Wartime*, pp. 72–3.

134   Matthews, *Irish Citizen Army*, p. 60.

135   *Workers' Republic*, 10 July 1915.

136   James Connolly, *Collected Works Volume Two* (Dublin, 1988), p. 69.

137 Robbins, *Under the Starry Plough*, p. 54.

138 Recollection of William O'Brien, undated, Documents Relating to William O'Brien, WOBP, MS 15,704 (2), NLI.

139 Yeates, *City in Wartime*, p. 74.

140 Lynch, *The Irish Socialist Republican Party*, pp. 42–3.

141 Connolly, *Collected Works Volume Two*, p. 70.

142 *Workers' Republic*, 7 Aug. 1915.

143 Helga Woggon, 'Not Merely a Labour Organisation: the ITGWU and the Dublin Dock Strike, 1915–6' in *Saothar*, 27 (2002), p. 43.

144 Helga Woggon, 'Interpreting James Connolly' in Fintan Land and Donal Ó Drisceoil (eds), *Politics and the Irish Working Class* (New York, 2005), p. 173.

145 *Workers' Republic*, 3 July 1915.

146 Ibid. 31 July 1915.

147 Collins, *Connolly*, p. 248.

148 C. Desmond Greaves, *ITGWU*, p. 137.

149 Dublin Metropolitan Police Report on the Movement of Extremists, 9 June 1915, CSO/JD/2/8, NAI.

150 Greaves, *ITGWU*, p. 138.

151 Woggon, 'Interpreting James Connolly', p. 47.

152 Robbins, *Under the Starry Plough*, p. 32; Fox, *Connolly*, p. 181.

153 Frank Robbins, BMH WS 585, p. 43.

154 *Workers' Republic*, 30 Oct. 1915.

155 Grant, *Socialist Republicanism*, p. 69.

156 ITGWU Branch No. 1. Minutes, 13 Jan. 1914, Minutes of Committee Meetings of the ITGWU Feb. 1914–Feb. 1916, Together with Minutes of the Strike Committee Oct. 1913, MS 7298, NLI. ITGWU Branch No. 1. Minutes, 10 Mar. 1914, Minutes of Committee Meetings of the ITGWU Feb. 1914–Feb. 1916, Together with Minutes of the Strike Committee Oct. 1913, MS 7298, NLI. ITGWU Branch No. 1. Minutes, 24 Mar. 1914, Minutes of Committee Meetings of the ITGWU Feb. 1914–Feb. 1916, Together with Minutes of the Strike Committee Oct. 1913, MS 7298, NLI. ITGWU Branch No. 1. Minutes, 4 Aug. 1914, Minutes of Committee Meetings of the ITGWU Feb. 1914–Feb. 1916, Together with Minutes of the Strike Committee Oct. 1913, MS 7298, NLI.

157 Frank Robbins, BMH WS 585, p. 28.

158 ITGWU Branch No. 1. Minutes, 27 Jan. 1914, Minutes of Committee Meetings of the ITGWU Feb. 1914–Feb. 1916, Together with Minutes of the Strike Committee Oct. 1913, MS 7298, NLI. ITGWU Branch No. 1. Minutes, 2 June 1914, Minutes of Committee Meetings of the ITGWU Feb. 1914–Feb. 1916, Together with Minutes of the Strike Committee Oct. 1913, MS 7298, NLI.

159 Fox, *Connolly*, p. 181.

160 Woggon, 'Not Merely a Labour Organisation', p. 47.

161 *Workers' Republic*, 6 Nov. 1915.

162   Woggon, 'Not Merely a Labour Organisation', p. 47.
163   *Workers' Republic*, 30 Oct. 1915.

Chapter 7

1   ITGWU, *Fifty Years of Liberty*, p. 26.
2   Metscher, *The Reconquest of Ireland*, p. 172.
3   James O'Shea, BMH WS 733, p. 8.
4   Hughes, *Mallin*, p. 90.
5   James O'Shea, BMH WS 733, p. 8.
6   Thomas Mallin, BMH WS 382, p. 1.
7   Hughes, *Mallin*, p. 23.
8   Ibid. p. 91.
9   Robbins, *Under the Starry Plough*, p. 27.
10   *Irish Worker*, 24 Oct. 1914.
11   Matthews, *Irish Citizen Army*, p. 47.
12   *Irish Worker*, 7 Nov. 1914.
13   Ibid. 14 Nov. 1914.
14   *Royal Commission on the Rebellion in Ireland. Minutes of Evidence and Appendix of Documents*, 1916 [Cd. 8311], p. 4.
15   *Workers' Republic*, 9 Oct. 1915. Interestingly, Williams does not appear on Poole's list of ICA officers during the Rising.
16   Matthews, *Irish Citizen Army*, p. 48.
17   *Irish Worker*, 17 Oct. 1914.
18   Ibid. 31 Oct. 1914.
19   Ibid. 31 Oct. 1914.
20   Ibid. 14 Nov. 1914.
21   Ibid. 21 Nov. 1914.
22   Ibid. 7 Nov. 1914.
23   Máirtín Seán Ó Catháin, 'A Land Beyond the Sea: Irish and Scottish Republicans in Dublin 1916' in Ruán O'Donnell (ed.), *The Impact of the 1916 Rising Among the Nations* (Dublin, 2008), pp. 38–41.
24   Seamus Reader, BMH WS 627, p. 12.
25   *Irish Worker*, 28 Nov. 1914.
26   Hughes, *Mallin*, p. 89.
27   Helena Molony, BMH WS 391, p. 27.
28   ITGWU Branch No. 1. Minutes, 27 Oct. 1914, Minutes of Committee Meetings of the ITGWU Feb. 1914–Feb. 1916, Together with Minutes of the Strike Committee Oct. 1913, MS 7298, NLI.
29   *Irish Worker*, 31 Oct. 1914.
30   Ibid.
31   Robbins, *Under the Starry Plough*, p. 50.

32   *Workers' Republic*, 11 Sept. 1915.

33   *Royal Commission on the Rebellion in Ireland. Minutes of Evidence and Appendix of Documents*, 1916 [Cd. 8311], p. 13.

34   Robbins, *Under the Starry Plough*, p. 45.

35   Ibid. p. 27.

36   Fox, *History*, p. 97.

37   Frank Robbins, BMH WS 585, p. 12.

38   Helena Molony, BMH WS 391, p. 27.

39   Frank Robbins, BMH WS 585, p. 12.

40   *Irish Worker*, 19 Sept. 1914; *Irish Worker*, 3 Oct. 1914; *Irish Worker*, 28 Nov. 1914; *Irish Worker*, 5 Dec. 1914.

41   White, *Misfit*, p. 262.

42   Three Notebooks Containing Names of ICA Members, 1915–1916, WOBP, MS 15,672, NLI.

43   Ibid.; Matthews, *Irish Citizen Army*, p. 46.

44   Dublin Metropolitan Police Report on the Movement of Extremists, Special Report on the Irish Citizen Army, 22 Sept. 1915, CSO/JD/2/94, NAI.

45   James O'Shea, BMH WS 733, p. 16.

46   Robbins, *Under the Starry Plough*, p. 45; Irish Citizen Army Notebook, 1914–15, WOBP, MS 34,937, NLI.

47   James O'Shea, BMH WS 733, p. 8.

48   White, *Misfit*, pp. 258–60.

49   James O'Shea, BMH WS 733, p. 22.

50   *Workers' Republic*, 29 May 1915.

51   Ibid. 5 June 1915.

52   Ibid.

53   Collins, *Connolly*, p. 255.

54   *Workers' Republic*, 24 Jul. 1915.

55   Ibid. 24 Jul. 1915.

56   Robbins, *Under the Starry Plough*, p. 45.

57   *Irish Worker*, 12 Sept. 1914.

58   Ibid. 26 Sept. 1914.

59   Ibid. 17 Oct. 1914.

60   White, *Misfit*, p. 259.

61   Three Notebooks Containing Names of ICA Members, 1915–1916, WOBP, MS 15,672, NLI; Matthews, *Irish Citizen Army*, p. 46.

62   ICA Drill circa 1915, map.

63   Irish Citizen Army Notebook, 1914–15, WOBP, MS 34,937, NLI.

64   James O'Shea, BMH WS 733, p. 31.

65   *Royal Commission on the Rebellion in Ireland. Minutes of Evidence and Appendix of Documents*, 1916 [Cd. 8311], p. 13.

66   *Workers' Republic*, 23 Oct. 1914.

67   Robbins, *Under the Starry Plough*, p. 45.

68   James O'Shea, BMH WS 733, p. 31; Robbins, *Under the Starry Plough*, p. 46; *Workers' Republic*, 23 Oct. 1914.

69   Robbins, *Under the Starry Plough*, p. 46.

70   William Oman, BMH WS 421, p. 3.

71   James O'Shea, BMH WS 733, p. 31.

72   *Workers' Republic*, 30 Oct. 1915; James O'Shea, BMH WS 733, p. 31.

73   *Workers' Republic*, 30 Oct. 1915.

74   James O'Shea, BMH WS 733, p. 31.

75   Robbins, *Under the Starry Plough*, p. 51.

76   Robbins, BMH WS 585, pp. 14–15.

77   James O'Shea, BMH WS 733, p. 9.

78   Dublin Metropolitan Police Report on the Movement of Extremists, 28 June 1915, CSO/JD/2/20, NAI.

79   James O'Shea, BMH WS 733, p. 10; Robbins, *Under the Starry Plough*, p. 51.

80   *Workers' Republic*, 3 July 1915.

81   James O'Shea, BMH WS 733, p. 9.

82   Robbins, *Under the Starry Plough*, p. 39.

83   Fox, *History*, p. 95.

84   Robbins, BMH WS 545, p. 13.

85   James O'Shea, BMH WS 733, p. 30.

86   Boyle, 'Connolly, the Citizen Army and the Rising', p. 63.

87   Matthews, *Irish Citizen Army*, p. 66.

88   Fox, *History*, p. 95.

89   Richard Corbally, 11 February 1935, MSP, 34REF208.

90   James O'Shea, BMH WS 733, p. 28.

91   Robbins, BMH WS 545, p. 22.

92   Robbins, *Under the Starry Plough*, p. 44.

93   Fox, *History*, p. 96.

94   James O'Shea, BMH WS 733, p. 14.

95   Ibid.; James O'Shea, BMH WS 733, p. 30.

96   Richard Corbally, 11 Feb. 1935, MSP, 34REF208.

97   James O'Shea, BMH WS 733, p. 30.

98   *Irish Worker*, 14 Nov. 1914.

99   'List of Premises Searched by Police for Arms' Attached to Memorandum from DMP Chief Superintendent Owen Brien, 12 May 1916, Arms Importation and Distribution, CO 904/28, TNA.

100 'List of Premises Searched by Police for Arms' Attached to Memorandum from DMP Chief Superintendent Owen Brien, 12 May 1916, Arms Importation and Distribution, CO 904/28, TNA.

101 William Oman, BMH WS 421, p. 1.

102 Seamus Reader, BMH WS 627, pp. 3–4.

103   Ibid. pp. 7–8.

104   Seamus Reader, 10 May 1938, in Frank Murray, MSP, 34REF21493.

105   Memorandum from DMP Chief Superintendent Owen Brien, 12 May 1916, Arms Importation and Distribution, CO 904/28, TNA.

106   Fox, *History*, p. 92; Greaves, *Life and Times*, p. 369; James O'Neill, undated, in Seamus McGowan, MSP, 4289.

107   Memorandum from DMP Chief Superintendent Owen Brien, 12 May 1916, Arms Importation and Distribution, CO 904/28, TNA.

108   William Omen, BMW WS 421, p. 2.

109   *San Francisco Chronicle*, 22 May 1916.

110   Christopher Poole, 14 Feb. 1936, MSP, 34REF10145.

111   James O'Shea, BMH WS 733, p. 13.

112   Ibid. p. 14.

113   Ibid.

114   Lecture by John Hanratty on the Irish Citizen Army, 1955, Old IRA Society II, Hanratty Papers, Kilmainham Gaol.

Chapter 8

1   Eamon Dore, BMH WS 392, p. 1.

2   Elliot Elmes, 27 June 1935, MSP, 34REF866; Christopher Crothers, 27 June 1935, MSP, 34REF210; Thomas Kain, 30 November 1937, MSP, 34REF13912.

3   Greaves, *ITGWU*, p. 162.

4   Dublin Metropolitan Police Report on the Movement of Extremists, 16 July 1915, CSO/JD/2/37, NAI.

5   Robbins, *Under the Starry Plough*, p. 55.

6   Frank Robbins, BMH WS 585, p. 28.

7   *Royal Commission on the Rebellion in Ireland. Minutes of Evidence and Appendix of Documents*, 1916 [Cd. 8311], p. 3.

8   *Irish Worker*, 10 Oct. 1914.

9   Recollection of William O'Brien, undated, 6 Notebooks of William O'Brien, WOBP, MS 15,704 (4), NLI.

10   Robbins, *Under the Starry Plough*, p. 66.

11   T.A. Jackson, *Ireland Her Own: an Outline History of the Struggle* (Berlin, 1971), p. 391.

12   Foy and Barton, *The Easter Rising*, pp. 33–4.

13   Collins, *Connolly*, p. 259.

14   Note by William O'Brien, undated, O'Brien's 'Reminiscences', WOBP, MS 15,704 (1), NLI.

15   Recollection by William O'Brien, undated, William O'Brien's Notes on ICA, WOBP, MS 15,673 (1) (2), NLI.

16   Statement by Richard McCormick Given to John Hanratty, undated, 1913–23 Documents I, Hanratty Papers, Kilmainham Gaol.
17   Morrissey SJ, *William O'Brien*, p. 96.
18   Collins, *Connolly*, p. 260.
19   William O'Brien, BMH WS 1,766, p. 64.
20   Recollection of William O'Brien, undated, 6 Notebooks of William O'Brien, WOBP, MS 15,704 (4), NLI.
21   Note by William O'Brien, undated, O'Brien's 'Reminiscences', WOBP, MS 15,704 (1), NLI.
22   Eamon Dore, BMH WS 392, p. 1.
23   Fox, *History*, p. 119.
24   Eamon Dore, BMH WS 392, p. 1.
25   Ibid. pp. 1–2.
26   Hughes, *Mallin*, p. 108.
27   Geraldine Dillon, BMH WS 358, p. 8.
28   Statement by Richard McCormick Given to John Hanratty, undated, 1913–23 Documents I, Hanratty Papers, Kilmainham Gaol.
29   Robbins, *Under the Starry Plough*, p. 74.
30   Collins, *Connolly*, p. 261.
31   *Workers' Republic*, 29 Jan. 1916.
32   Charles Townshend, *Easter 1916: The Irish Rebellion* (London, 2006), p. 109.
33   Foy and Barton, *The Easter Rising*, p. 36.
34   Florence O'Donoghue, 'Plans for the 1916 Rising', p. 5.
35   Statement by Richard McCormick Given to John Hanratty, undated, 1913–23 Documents I, Hanratty Papers, Kilmainham Gaol.
36   Matthews, 'Vanguard of the Revolution', p. 35.
37   Marie Mulholland, *The Politics and Relationships of Kathleen Lynn* (Cork, 2002), p. 35.
38   James O'Shea, BMH WS 733, p. 22.
39   Fox, *History*, p. 121.
40   Matthews, *Irish Citizen Army*, p. 64; Aine Ceannt, BMH WS 264, p. 14. This indicates that the decision to take Dublin Castle pre-dates the settlement on a general rising plan between Connolly and other IRB military council members which highlights the seriousness of the mimic attack in 1915.
41   Note by William O'Brien, undated, O'Brien's 'Reminiscences', WOBP, MS 15,704 (1), NLI.
42   Ibid.
43   Ibid.
44   Aine Ceannt, BMH WS 264, p. 14.
45   Robbins, *Under the Starry Plough*, p. 71.
46   Hughes, *Mallin*, p. 111.
47   Ibid.

48   James O'Neill, 30 March 1936, in Seamus McGowan, MSP, 34REF4289.

49   Matthews, *Irish Citizen Army*, pp. 67–8.

50   Ibid. p. 66.

51   Matthew Connolly, BMH WS 1746, pp. 2–3.

52   Seamus Reader, BMH WS 1767, p. 18.

53   Robbins, *Under the Starry Plough*, p. 64.

54   Ibid.

55   Frank Robbins, BMH WS 585, p. 34.

56   James O'Shea, BMH WS 733, p. 15.

57   James O'Neill, 22 July 1935, MSP, 34REF836.

58   John Hanratty, 19 December 1938, in John White, MSP, 34REF28572.

59   James O'Neill, undated, in Irish Citizen Army, MSPC, RO 10A.

60   James O'Neill, 30 March 1936, in Seamus McGowan, MSP, 34REF4289.

61   Fox, *History*, pp. 111–12.

62   Frank Robbins, BMH WS 585, pp. 13–14.

63   Fox, *History*, pp. 110–11.

64   James O'Shea, BMH WS 733, p. 17.

65   Certificate Under Order in Council No. 12 Explosives Act, 1875 (38 Vict, c. 17),
     26 Feb. 1916, in James O'Neill, MSP, 34REF8368; James O'Neill, undated, MSP,
     34REF8368.

66   Fox, *History*, p. 110.

67   Ibid. p. 110; James O'Neill, undated, MSP, 34REF8368.

68   James O'Neill, undated, MSP, 34REF8368.

69   Christopher Crothers, 16 July 1935, in Seamus McGowan, MSP, 34REF4289.

70   James O'Neill, undated, MSP, 34REF8368.

71   Ibid.

72   Ibid.

73   Frank Robbins, BMH WS 585, p. 34.

74   Ibid.

75   James O'Neill, 18 July 1935, in Seamus McGowan, MSP, 34REF4289.

76   Frank Robbins, BMH WS 585, p. 35.

77   John Hanratty, 21 June 1935, MSP, 34REF1362.

78   James O'Neill, undated, MSP, 34REF8368.

79   James O'Shea, BMH WS 733, p. 18.

80   Ibid. pp. 19–21.

81   Collins, *Connolly*, p. 263.

82   Minutes of Committee Meetings of the ITGWU June 1915–Apr. 1916, MS 7303,
     NLI, *ad passim*.

83   *Royal Commission on the rebellion in Ireland. Minutes of Evidence and Appendix of
     Documents*, 1916 [Cd. 8311], p. 36.

84   James O'Shea, BMH WS 733, p. 34.

85   Matthews, *Irish Citizen Army*, p. 68.

86 James O'Shea, BMH WS 733, p. 28.

87 *Defence of the Realm. A Bill to Confer on his Majesty in Council Power to Make Regulations during the Present War for the Defence of the Realm*, 1914 (359), p. 1.

88 *Defence of the Realm (no. 2). A Bill to Amend the Defence of the Realm Act, 1914*, 1914 (383), p. 1.

89 *Royal Commission on the Rebellion in Ireland. Minutes of Evidence and Appendix of Documents*, 1916 [Cd. 8311], p. 5.

90 Matthews, *Irish Citizen Army*, p. 70; Rose Hackett, BMH WS 546, p. 2.

91 Dublin Metropolitan Police Report on the Movement of Extremists, 5 June 1915, CSO/JD/2/5, NAI; Dublin Metropolitan Police Report on the Movement of Extremists, 25 June 1915, CSO/JD/2/19, NAI; Dublin Metropolitan Police Report on the Movement of Extremists, 3 July 1915, CSO/JD/2/25, NAI; Dublin Metropolitan Police Report on the Movement of Extremists, 9 July 1915, CSO/JD/2/30, NAI; Dublin Metropolitan Police Report on the Movement of Extremists, 16 July 1915, CSO/JD/2/37, NAI; Dublin Metropolitan Police Report on the Movement of Extremists, 30 July, CSO/JD/2/48, NAI; Dublin Metropolitan Police Report on the Movement of Extremists, 6 August 1915, CSO/JD/2/54, NAI; Dublin Metropolitan Police Report on the Movement of Extremists, 13 August 1915, CSO/JD/2/60, NAI; Dublin Metropolitan Police Report on the Movement of Extremists, 27 August 1915, CSO/JD/2/72, NAI; Dublin Metropolitan Police Report on the Movement of Extremists, 3 Sept. 1915, CSO/JD/2/78, NAI.

92 Dublin Metropolitan Police Report on the Movement of Extremists, 5 Nov. 1915, CSO/JD/2/129, NAI.

93 Matthews, *Irish Citizen Army*, p. 69; *Royal Commission on the Rebellion in Ireland. Minutes of Evidence and Appendix of Documents*, 1916 [Cd. 8311], p. 5.

94 Joseph Brady, BMH WS 705, p. 1.

95 Frank Robbins, BMH WS 585, p. 36.

96 Joseph Brady, BMH WS 705, p. 2.

97 Rose Hackett, BMH WS 546, p. 1.

98 Collins, *Connolly*, p. 262.

99 Michael J. Molloy, BMH WS 716, p. 2.

100 Joseph Brady, BMH WS 705, p. 2.

101 Rose Hackett, BMH WS 546, pp. 1–2; Joseph Brady, BMH WS 705, p. 2.

102 Rose Hackett, BMH WS 546, p. 2; Joseph Brady, BMH WS 705, p. 2.

103 Matthews, *Irish Citizen Army*, p. 70; *Workers' Republic*, 1 Apr. 1916.

104 Collins, *Connolly*, p. 262.

105 James O'Shea, BMH WS 733, p. 24.

106 Joseph Brady, BMH WS 705, p. 3. There is no Tom Keane in the ICA record books so it is likely that this is Thomas Kain.

107 Thomas Kain, 30 November 1937, MSP, 34REF13912.

108 Frank Robbins, BMH WS 585, p. 30.

109 James O'Shea, BMH WS 733, p. 26.

110   Frank Robbins, BMH WS 585, p. 30.
111   *Workers' Republic*, 8 Apr. 1916.
112   Ibid. 1 Apr. 1916.
113   Frank Robbins, BMH WS 585, p. 32.
114   Matthews, *Irish Citizen Army*, p. 72.
115   Helena Molony, BMH WS 391, p. 29.
116   William Oman, BMH WS 421, p. 2.
117   Elliot Elmes, 27 June 1935, MSP, 34REF866.
118   Christopher Crothers, 27 June 1935, MSP, 34REF210.
119   Thomas Kain, 30 Nov. 1937, MSP, 34REF13912.
120   James O'Shea, 20 June 1935, MSP, 34REF150.
121   Grant, *Socialist Republicanism*, p. 70.
122   Matthew Connolly, BMH WS 1746, p. 2.
123   Christopher Crothers, 27 June 1935, MSP, 34REF210.
124   Robbins, *Under the Starry Plough*, p. 65.
125   Statement by Seamus McGowan given to John Hanratty, undated, 1913–23 Documents I, Hanratty Papers, Kilmainham Gaol.
126   Rose Hackett, BMH WS 546, p. 3.
127   Mary Allen, 23 Nov. 1937, MSP, 34REF8867.
128   *Workers' Republic*, 29 Jan. 1916.
129   Ibid. 5 Feb. 1916.
130   Helena Molony, BMH WS 391, p. 32.
131   Joseph Brady, BMH WS 705, p. 4; Michael J. Molloy, BMH WS 716, pp. 2–3.
132   Joseph Brady, BMH WS 705, p. 4.
133   Michael J. Molloy, BMH WS 716, p. 4; Joseph Brady, BMH WS 705, p. 6.
134   Joseph Brady, BMH WS 705, p. 6.
135   Greaves, *ITGWU*, pp. 162–3.
136   Frank Robbins, BMH WS 585, p. 38.
137   Greaves, *ITGWU*, pp. 162–3; *Workers' Republic*, 8 Apr. 1916.
138   *Workers' Republic*, 8 Apr. 1916.
139   Greaves, *ITGWU*, p. 163.
140   ITGWU Branch No. 1 Minutes, 12 Apr. 1915, Minutes of Committee Meetings of the ITGWU June 1915–Apr. 1916, MS 7303, NLI.
141   ITGWU Branch No. 1 Minutes, 13 Apr. 1915, Minutes of Committee Meetings of the ITGWU June 1915–Apr. 1916, MS 7303, NLI; Greaves, *ITGWU*, pp. 163–4; Matthews, *Irish Citizen Army*, p. 74.
142   Frank Robbins, BMH WS 585, pp. 28–30.
143   Greaves, *ITGWU*, p. 164.
144   Untitled Lecture by John Hanratty, undated, Old IRA Literary and Debating Society, Hanratty Papers, Kilmainham Gaol.
145   Foy and Barton, *The Easter Rising*, p. 62.
146   Robbins, *Under the Starry Plough*, p. 79.

147 Collins, *Connolly*, p. 275.
148 Emily Norgrove's Recollection of the Easter Rising, undated, Emily Norgrove's Account of 1916, Hanratty Papers, Kilmainham Gaol.
149 Ibid.
150 Statement by Seamus McGowan given to John Hanratty, undated, 1913–23 Documents I, Hanratty Papers, Kilmainham Gaol. It should be noted that McGowan recorded this as happening before the route march but Norgrove remembers this as having taken place after it. Robbins also remembers this as preceding the march.
151 Robbins, *Under the Starry Plough*, p. 79.
152 Ruán O'Donnell, *Patrick Pearse* (Dublin, 2016), pp. 182–4.
153 Seamus McGowan, 19 Dec. 1935, MSP, 34REF4289.
154 Thomas Kain, 30 Nov. 1937, MSP, 34REF13912.
155 James O'Neill, undated, in Seamus McGowan, MSP, 34REF4289.
156 Christopher Poole, undated, in Irish Citizen Army, MSPC, RO 10A; James O'Shea, BMH WS 733, p. 39. Not all of these men were promoted over the course of that weekend; for instance, Thomas O'Donoghue was given his commission three weeks before the Easter Rising.
157 Christopher Crothers, 16 July 1935, in Richard McCormick, MSP, 34REF2186.
158 Greaves, *Life and Times*, p. 403.
159 William Oman, BMH WS 421, p. 5.
160 Ibid.; Rose Hackett, BMH WS 546, p. 4.
161 *Workers' Voice*, 14 May 1932.
162 Fox, *History*, p. 144.
163 George Oman, 28 Sept. 1936, MSP, 34REF14740.
164 James O'Neill, 22 July 1935, MSP, 34REF8368.
165 Lecture by John Hanratty on the Irish Citizen Army, 1955, Old IRA Society II, Hanratty Papers, Kilmainham Gaol.

Chapter 9

1   Matthews, 'Vanguard of the Revolution', p. 31.
2   James O'Shea, BMH WS 733, p. 40.
3   Ibid. pp. 40–1.
4   William Oman, BMH WS 421, p. 6.
5   Robbins, *Under the Starry Plough* p. 84.
6   Foy and Barton, *The Easter Rising*, p. 77.
7   McGarry, *Easter 1916*, p. 120.
8   Paul O'Brien, *1916 in Focus: Shootout – the Battle for St. Stephen's Green 1916* (Dublin, 2013), p. 94.
9   Fox, *History*, p. 157.
10 Townshend, *Easter 1916*, p. 166.

11   Statement by Richard McCormick Given to John Hanratty, undated, 1913–23 Documents I, Hanratty Papers, Kilmainham Gaol.

12   Irish Citizen Army Notebook, 1914–15, WOBP, MS 34,937, NLI.

13   Statement by Richard McCormick Given to John Hanratty, undated, 1913–23 Documents I, Hanratty Papers, Kilmainham Gaol.

14   Robbins, *Under the Starry Plough*, pp. 75–6; Richard McCormick, 21 February 1935, MSP, 34REF2186.

15   Christopher Crothers, 16 July 1935, in Richard McCormick, MSP, 34REF2186.

16   Christopher Poole, undated, MSP, 34REF10145; Richard McCormick, 21 June 1935, MSP, 34REF2186.

17   Robbins, *Under the Starry Plough*, pp. 75–6.

18   Statement by Richard McCormick Given to John Hanratty, undated, 1913–23 Documents I, Hanratty Papers, Kilmainham Gaol.

19   Townshend, *Easter 1916*, p. 168.

20   Irish Citizen Army Notebook, 1914–15, WOBP, MS 34,937, NLI.

21   R. Henderson, BMH WS 1686, p. 11. (tabulated history).

22   Robbins, *Under the Starry Plough*, p. 92.

23   Hughes, *Mallin*, p. 108.

24   *Workers' Republic*, 7 Aug. 1915.

25   Statement by Richard McCormick given to John Hanratty, undated, 1913–23 Documents I, Hanratty Papers, Kilmainham Gaol.

26   *Royal Commission on the Rebellion in Ireland. Minutes of Evidence and Appendix of Documents*, 1916 [Cd. 8311], p. 80.

27   James O'Shea, BMH WS 733, p. 44.

28   Fox, *History*, p. 156.

29   James Stephens, *The Insurrection in Dublin* (Dublin, 1916), p. 8.

30   James O'Shea, BMH WS 733, p. 45.

31   F.X. Martin, 'The 1916 Rising: a "Coup D'état" or a "Bloody Protest"?' in *Studia Hibernica*, 8 (1968), p. 113.

32   Hughes, *Mallin*, p. 104.

33   Fox, *History*, p. 156.

34   Thomas O'Donoghue, BMH WS 1666, p. 19; *Workers' Republic*, 9 Oct. 1915.

35   Thomas O'Donoghue, BMH WS 1666, p. 19.

36   Seamus Kavanagh, BMH WS 1670, p. 35.

37   Thomas O'Donoghue, BMH WS 1666, p. 16.

38   Hughes, *Mallin*, p. 128.

39   Thomas O'Donoghue, BMH WS 1666, p. 16.

40   Hughes, *Mallin*, p. 129.

41   Ibid. p. 194.

42   Thomas O'Donoghue, BMH WS 1666, p. 19.

43   James O'Shea, BMH WS 733, p. 48.

44   Robbins, *Under the Starry Plough*, pp. 94–5.

45   Frank Robbins, BMH WS 585, p. 75; Lecture by Frank Robbins Entitled 'The Irish Citizen Army's Part in the Easter Week Rising St. Stephen's Green Area', undated, The Old IRA Literary Society 1, Hanratty Papers, Kilmainham Gaol.

46   June Shannon, 'Remembering RCSI and the 1916 Rising' in *Irish Journal of Medical Science*, 2 (2006), p. 8.

47   Harry Nicholls, BMH WS 296, p. 8.

48   James O'Shea, BMH WS 733, pp. 47–8.

49   Foy and Barton, *The Easter Rising*, p. 87.

50   Stephens, *Insurrection*, p. 26.

51   Robbins, *Under the Starry Plough*, p. 103.

52   James O'Shea, BMH WS 733, pp. 47–8.

53   Lecture by Frank Robbins Entitled 'The Irish Citizen Army's Part in the Easter Week Rising St. Stephen's Green Area', undated, The Old IRA Literary Society 1, Hanratty Papers, Kilmainham Gaol.

54   Christopher Crothers, 27 June 1935, MSP, 34REF210.

55   Peter Bermingham, 18 Dec. 1936, MSP, 34REF1965; Christopher Crothers, 27 June 1935, MSP, 34REF210.

56   Robbins, *Under the Starry Plough*, p. 95; James O'Shea, BMH WS 733, p. 48.

57   Matthews, *Irish Citizen Army*, p. 101.

58   Thomas O'Donoghue, BMH WS 1666, p. 20.

59   Lecture by Frank Robbins Entitled 'The Irish Citizen Army's Part in the Easter Week Rising St. Stephen's Green Area', undated, The Old IRA Literary Society 1, Hanratty Papers, Kilmainham Gaol.

60   James O'Shea, BMH WS 733, p. 49.

61   Statement by Richard McCormick Given to John Hanratty, undated, 1913–23 Documents I, Hanratty Papers, Kilmainham Gaol.

62   Robbins, *Under the Starry Plough*, pp. 105–6.

63   Stephens, *Insurrection*, pp. 35–6.

64   Thomas O'Donoghue, BMH WS 1666, p. 21.

65   Ibid.; Robbins, *Under the Starry Plough*, p. 96.

66   James O'Shea, BMH WS 733, p. 49.

67   Robbins, *Under the Starry Plough*, p. 103.

68   Lecture by Frank Robbins Entitled 'The Irish Citizen Army's Part in the Easter Week Rising St. Stephen's Green Area', undated, The Old IRA Literary Society 1, Hanratty Papers, Kilmainham Gaol.

69   Hughes, *Mallin*, p. 141.

70   Lecture by Frank Robbins Entitled 'The Irish Citizen Army's Part in the Easter Week Rising St. Stephen's Green Area', undated, The Old IRA Literary Society 1, Hanratty Papers, Kilmainham Gaol.

71   James O'Shea, BMH WS 733, p. 50.

72   Stephens, *Insurrection*, p. 33.

73   Margaret Skinnider, 13 Nov. 1936, MSP, 34REF1991.

74   James O'Shea, BMH WS 733, p. 50.

75   Shannon, 'Remembering RCSI', pp. 5–7.

76   James O'Shea, BMH WS 733, p. 50.

77   Hughes, *Mallin*, pp. 141–2.

78   William Oman, BMH WS 421, p. 11.

79   Thomas O'Donoghue, BMH WS 1666, p. 21.

80   Shannon, 'Remembering RCSI', p. 5.

81   W.J. Brennan-Whitmore, *Dublin Burning: the Easter Rising from Behind the Barricades* (Dublin, 2013), p. 21.

82   Shannon, 'Remembering RCSI', p. 7.

83   Foy and Barton, *The Easter Rising*, p. 77.

84   James O'Shea, BMH WS 733, p. 51.

85   Robbins, *Under the Starry Plough*, p. 50.

86   Fox, *History*, p. 159.

87   Lecture by John Hanratty on the Irish Citizen Army, 1955, Old IRA Society II, Hanratty Papers, Kilmainham Gaol.

88   James O'Shea, BMH WS 733, p. 51.

89   Ibid. p. 53.

90   Lecture by Frank Robbins Entitled 'The Irish Citizen Army's Part in the Easter Week Rising St. Stephen's Green Area', undated, The Old IRA Literary Society 1, Hanratty Papers, Kilmainham Gaol.

91   James O'Shea, BMH WS 733, p. 54.

92   Lecture by Frank Robbins Entitled 'The Irish Citizen Army's Part in the Easter Week Rising St. Stephen's Green Area', undated, The Old IRA Literary Society 1, Hanratty Papers, Kilmainham Gaol.

93   Robert de Coeur, 1 Feb. 1935, MSP, 34REF1658.

94   Robbins, *Under the Starry Plough*, p. 114.

95   Thomas O'Donoghue, BMH WS 1666, p. 23.

96   Margaret Skinnider, 13 Nov. 1936, MSP, 34REF1991.

97   Thomas O'Donoghue, BMH WS 1666, p. 23.

98   Margaret Skinnider, 13 Nov. 1936, MSP, 34REF1991; Thomas O'Donoghue, BMH WS 1666, p. 23.

99   Hughes, *Mallin*, p. 147.

100   Lecture by Frank Robbins Entitled 'The Irish Citizen Army's Part in the Easter Week Rising St. Stephen's Green Area', undated, The Old IRA Literary Society 1, Hanratty Papers, Kilmainham Gaol.

101   Matthews, *Irish Citizen Army*, p. 103.

102   Robbins, *Under the Starry Plough*, pp. 114–19; James O'Shea, BMH WS 733, p. 54.

103   Robbins, *Under the Starry Plough*, p. 117.

104   Thomas O'Donoghue, BMH WS 1666, p. 26.

105   Ibid. p. 27.

106   Frank Robbins, BMH WS 585, p. 80.

107   James O'Shea, BMH WS 733, p. 54.
108   Frank Robbins, BMH WS 585, p. 80.
109   Thomas O'Donoghue, BMH WS 1666, p. 27.
110   James O'Shea, BMH WS 733, p. 55.
111   Robbins, *Under the Starry Plough*, p. 122.
112   James O'Shea, BMH WS 733, p. 55; Thomas O'Donoghue, BMH WS 1666, p. 27.
113   Thomas O'Donoghue, BMH WS 1666, p. 28.
114   Rose Hackett, BMH WS 546, pp. 7–8.
115   R. Henderson, BMH WS 1686, p. 12. (tabulated history); Shannon, 'Remembering RCSI', p. 8.
116   Joseph E.A. Connell Jnr, *Dublin in Rebellion* (Dublin, 2006), p. 329.
117   Frank Robbins, BMH WS 585, p. 80.
118   Emily Norgrove's Recollection of the Easter Rising, undated, Emily Norgrove's Account of 1916, Hanratty Papers, Kilmainham Gaol.

Chapter 10

1   William Oman, BMH WS 421, p. 3.
2   Peter Folan, BMH WS 316, p. 4.
3   William Oman, BMH WS 421, p. 3; Robbins, *Under the Starry Plough*, p. 98; R. Henderson, BMH WS 1686, p. 18. (tabulated history); William Oman, BMH WS 421, *op. cit.*
4   Robbins, *Under the Starry Plough*, pp. 98–9.
5   William Oman, BMH WS 421, p. 3.
6   Matthews, *Irish Citizen Army*, p. 87; Robbins, *Under the Starry Plough*, pp. 99; Transcript List of ICA Members, undated, ICA Members 1916–23, Hanratty Papers, Kilmainham Gaol.
7   William Oman, BMH WS 421, p. 3; Robbins, *Under the Starry Plough*, pp. 99–100.
8   R. Henderson, BMH WS 1686, p. 3.
9   Martin King, BMH WS 543, p. 2.
10   Dublin Castle Bases, Easter 1916, map; ICA Drill circa 1915, map.
11   Seamus Pounch, BMH WS 267, p. 9.
12   William Oman, BMH WS 421, p. 7.
13   Townshend, *Easter 1916*, p. 109.
14   Fox, *History*, p. 148.
15   George Connolly, 21 Sept. 1936, MSP, 34REF1284.
16   Helena Molony, BMH WS 391, p. 34.
17   William Oman, BMH WS 421, p. 7.
18   Foy and Barton, *The Easter Rising*, p. 74.
19   Fox, *History*, p. 147.

20 Thomas Kain, 30 Nov. 1937, MSP, 34REF13912.

21 Helena Molony, BMH WS 391, p. 35.

22 Ibid.

23 Jane Shanahan, 13 Nov. 1936, MSP, 34REF1015.

24 Helena Molony, BMH WS 391, p. 36.

25 Ibid. p. 37; Kathleen Lynn, BMH WS 357, p. 5.

26 Kathleen Lynn, BMH WS 357, p. 5; Jane Shanahan, 13 Nov. 1936, MSP, 34REF1015.

27 George Norgrove, 21 June 1935, MSP, 34REF1764.

28 Frank Robbins, BMH WS 585, p. 87.

29 Matthews, *Irish Citizen Army*, p. 91.

30 John Hanratty, BMH WS 96, p. 5.

31 Robbins, *Under the Starry Plough*, p. 100.

32 Helena Molony, BMH WS 391, p. 37; Foy and Barton, *The Easter Rising*, p. 74.

33 Peter Folan, BMH WS 316, p. 4.

34 Transcript List of ICA Members, undated, ICA Members 1916–23, Hanratty Papers, Kilmainham Gaol.

35 Thomas Kain, 30 Nov. 1937, MSP, 34REF13912.

36 Ibid.

37 Philip O'Leary, 20 June 1935, MSP, 34REF970.

38 George Connolly, 21 Nov. 1936, MSP, 34REF1284.

39 Ibid.; Matthews, *Irish Citizen Army*, p. 91; George Connolly, *op. cit.*

40 Thomas Kain, 30 Nov. 1937, MSP, 34REF13912. Incidentally, Lahiff's was the location where Kain hid his membership roll that historians use today.

41 Matthews, *Irish Citizen Army*, p. 87.

42 Foy and Barton, *The Easter Rising*, p. 75.

43 Jane Shanahan, 13 Nov. 1936, M1SP, 34REF1015.

44 Fox, *History*, p. 147.

45 John Hanratty, BMH WS 96, p. 5.

46 Matthews, *Irish Citizen Army*, pp. 108–9.

47 Foy and Barton, *The Easter Rising*, p. 75.

48 Matthews, *Irish Citizen Army*, p. 108.

49 Fox, *History*, p. 147; Kathleen Lynn, BMH WS 357, p. 6.

50 Kathleen Lynn, BMH WS 357, p. 6; Fox, *History*, p. 147; Kathleen Lynn, *op. cit.*

51 Jane Shanahan, 13 Nov. 1936, MSP, 34REF1015.

52 John Hanratty, BMH WS 96, pp. 4–5.

53 William Oman, BMH WS 421, p. 7.

54 Ibid.

55 William Oman, BMH WS 421, pp. 7–8.

56 Emily Norgrove's Recollection of the Easter Rising, undated, Emily Norgrove's Account of 1916, Hanratty Papers, Kilmainham Gaol.

57 Robbins, *Under the Starry Plough*, p. 98.

Chapter 11

1 Foy and Barton, *The Easter Rising*, p. 171.
2 Fox, *History*, p. 156.
3 Robert de Coeur, 11 Feb. 1935, in Frederick Norgrove, MSP, 34REF204.
4 Transcript List of ICA Members, undated, ICA Members 1916–23, Hanratty Papers, Kilmainham Gaol.
5 R. Henderson, BMH WS 1686, p. 1.
6 Ibid.
7 Foy and Barton, *The Easter Rising*, pp. 172–3.
8 R. Henderson, BMH WS 1686, p. 1.
9 Paul O'Brien, *Battleground: the Battle for the General Post Office, 1916* (Dublin, 2015), pp. 16–17.
10 Michael Staines, BMH WS 284, p. 11.
11 Ibid.
12 R. Henderson, BMH WS 1686, p. 2.
13 Michael Cremen, BMH WS 563, p. 6.
14 James O'Neill, 30 March 1936, in Seamus McGowan, MSP, 34REF4289.
15 R. Henderson, BMH WS 1686, p. 4.
16 Ibid. p. 19; James O'Neill, undated, MSP, 34REF8368.
17 Frank Thornton, 13 Feb. 1935, in Patrick Colman Tuohy, MSP, 34REF222.
18 R. Henderson, BMH WS 1686, p. 19.
19 Michael Staines, BMH WS 284, p. 14.
20 James O'Neill, 30 March 1936, in Seamus McGowan, MSP, 34REF4289.
21 James O'Neill, undated, MSP, 34REF8368.
22 Oscar Traynor, 24 Jan. 1936, in James O'Neill, MSP, 34REF8368.
23 Ibid.
24 Seamus Ua Caomhanaigh, BMH WS 889, p. 56.
25 Michael Staines, BMH WS 284, p. 1.
26 Oscar Traynor, 24 Jan. 1936, in James O'Neill, MSP, 34REF8368.
27 Diarmuid Lynch, BMH WS 4, p. 5.
28 Foy and Barton, *The Easter Rising*, p. 182.
29 Seamus Robinson, BMH WS 156, p. 16; Three Notebooks Containing Names of ICA Members, 1915–1916, WOBP, MS 15,672, NLI; Transcript List of ICA Members, undated, ICA Members 1916–23, Hanratty Papers, Kilmainham Gaol.
30 Foy and Barton, *The Easter Rising*, p. 175.
31 Cormac Turner, 'The Defence of Messrs Hopkins and Hopkins, O'Connell Street, Dublin' in *An tÓglác*, 1 (June, 1926), p. 3.
32 Seamus Robinson, BMH WS 156, p. 15.
33 Turner, 'Hopkins and Hopkins', p. 3; Seamus Robinson, BMH WS 156, p. 15.
34 Turner, 'Hopkins and Hopkins', p. 3.
35 Ibid.; Seamus Robinson, BMH WS 156, p. 16.
36 Seamus Robinson, BMH WS 156, p. 16.

ENDNOTES

37   Frank Henderson, BMH WS 249, p. 39.

38   Connell Jnr, *Dublin in Rebellion*, p. 114; Frank Henderson, BMH WS 249, pp. 32–5.

39   R. Henderson, BMH WS 1686, p. 4.

40   Note by John Saunders, Member of 1 Company 1 Battalion IRA, 8 Mar. 1938, 1913–23 Documents I, Hanratty Papers, Kilmainham Gaol.

41   Christopher Crothers, 16 July 1935, in Vincent Poole, MSP, 34REF460.

42   Sceilg, 'The GPO' in Brian Ó Conchubhair (ed.), *Dublin's Fighting Story 1916–21 Told by the Men Who Made It* (Cork, 2009), p. 136.

43   R. Henderson, BMH WS 1686, p. 6.

44   Ibid. p. 20.

45   George Oman, 28 Sept. 1936, MSP, 34REF14740.

46   Michael Finegan, 23 Nov. 1937, MSP, 34REF14715.

47   Charles Smith, undated, MSP, 34REF188.

48   Transcript List of ICA Members, undated, ICA Members 1916–23, Hanratty Papers, Kilmainham Gaol; Andrew Redmond, 20 June 1935, MSP, 34REF3719; Frank Thornton, BMH WS 510, p. 16.

49   Frank Thornton, BMH WS 510, p. 16.

50   Seamus Daly, BMH WS 360, p. 36.

51   Diarmuid Lynch, BMH WS 120, p. 6.

52   Frank Thornton, BMH WS 510, p. 16.

53   Foy and Barton, *The Easter Rising*, p. 181.

54   Patrick Devereux, 9 Dec. 1938, MSP, 34REF1356.

55   Letter from James Connolly to the Dublin Bread Company Garrison, 25 Apr. 1916, Communist Party of Ireland Papers (CPIP) 12/070, Dublin City Library (DCL).

56   Seamus Robinson, BMH WS 156, p. 17.

57   Turner, 'Hopkins and Hopkins', p. 4.

58   Seamus Robinson, BMH WS 156, p. 17.

59   Turner, 'Hopkins and Hopkins', p. 4.

60   Seamus Robinson, BMH WS 156, p. 17.

61   Sinn Féin, *Sinn Féin Rebellion Handbook Easter 1916*, p. 23.

62   Townshend, *Easter 1916*, p. 191.

63   Seamus Robinson, BMH WS 156, p. 17.

64   Frank Robbins, BMH WS 585, p. 89.

65   Townshend, *Easter 1916*, p. 191.

66   Sinn Féin, *Rebellion Handbook*, p. 23.

67   Brennan-Whitmore, *Dublin Burning*, p. 96.

68   R. Henderson, BMH WS 1686, p. 10; Lar Joye, 'TSS Helga II' in *History Ireland*, 2 (2010), p. 39.

69   Foy and Barton, *The Easter Rising*, p. 183.

70   Turner, 'Hopkins and Hopkins', p. 4.

71   Foy and Barton, *The Easter Rising*, p. 183.

72   Liam Tannam, BMH WS 242, p. 28.
73   R. Henderson, BMH WS 1686, p. 11.
74   Foy and Barton, *The Easter Rising*, p. 184.
75   Seamus Robinson, BMH WS 156, p. 18.
76   Turner, 'Hopkins and Hopkins', p. 4.
77   Liam Tannam, BMH WS 242, p. 32.
78   Seamus Daly, BMH WS 360, p. 38.
79   Liam Tannam, BMH WS 242, pp. 32–4.
80   Seamus Daly, BMH WS 360, p. 39.
81   Frank Thornton, 13 Feb. 1935, in Patrick Colman Tuohy, MSP, 34REF222.
82   Charles Smith, undated, MSP, 34REF188.
83   Patrick Devereux, 9 Dec. 1938, MSP, 34REF1356.
84   Seamus Daly, BMH WS 360, p. 38.
85   Frank Thornton, BMH WS 510, p. 16.
86   Charles Smith, 20 June 1935, MSP, 34REF188.
87   Andrew Conroy, 21 Sept. 1936, MSP, 34REF20076.
88   Seamus Robinson, 13 Feb. 1935, in Andrew Conroy, MSP, 34REF20076.
89   Seamus Robinson, BMH WS 156, p. 18.
90   Andrew Conroy, 21 Sept. 1936, MSP, 34REF20076; Seamus Robinson, 13 Feb. 1935, in Andrew Conroy, MSP, 34REF20076; Seamus Robinson, BMH WS 156, p. 18.
91   Collins, *Connolly*, p. 286; Foy and Barton, *The Easter Rising*, p. 187.
92   J.C. Ridgway, BMH WS 1431, p. 3.
93   Molly Reynolds, BMH WS 195, p. 6.
94   Sinn Féin, *Rebellion Handbook*, p. 50.
95   Foy and Barton, *The Easter Rising*, pp. 187–8.
96   Ibid. p. 193.
97   Sinn Féin, *Rebellion Handbook*, p. 13.
98   Liam Tannam, BMH WS 242, p. 34.

Chapter 12

1   Alfred Bucknill, BMH WS 1019, p. 2; Foy and Barton, *The Easter Rising*, p. 294; Matthews, *Irish Citizen Army*, pp. 135–6.
2   Seán Enright, *Easter Rising: the Trials* (Dublin, 2014), p. 43.
3   Report by General Commanding the Forces in Ireland, L.B. Friend, on the Subject of 'Assembly and Proceedings Of Field General Court Martial on Active Service, 5 May 1916, Court Martial of Michael Mallin', WO 71 353, TNA.
4   Foy and Barton, *The Easter Rising*, p. 294.
5   Enright, *Trials*, pp. 45–6.
6   Report by the British Major General of the 59th Division, Arthur Sandbach, on the Executions of P.H. Pearse, Thomas MacDonagh and Thomas Clarke, 3 May 1916, Execution of Rebel Prisoners, WO 35 67, TNA.

7   Matthews, *Irish Citizen Army*, p. 134.

8   Connell Jnr, *Dublin in Rebellion*, pp. 405–6.

9   Townshend, *Easter 1916*, p. 283.

10 Confidential Note by British Brigadier General Joseph Byrne on the Executions of P.H. Pearse, Thomas MacDonagh and Thomas Clarke, 2 May 1916, Execution of Rebel Prisoners, WO 35 67, TNA.

11 Ibid.

12 Hughes, *Mallin*, p. 164.

13 Report by General Commanding the Forces in Ireland, L.B. Friend, on the Subject of 'Assembly and Proceedings of Field General Court Martial on Active Service, 5 May 1916, Court Martial of Michael Mallin', WO 71 353, TNA.

14 Hughes, *Mallin*, p. 165.

15 Enright, *Trials*, p. 58.

16 Collins, *Connolly*, p. 256; Dublin Metropolitan Police Report on the Movement of Extremists, 26 July 1915, CSO/JD/2/44, NAI.

17 Enright, *Trials*, pp. 191–2.

18 Ibid. pp. 190–1.

19 Alfred Bucknill, BMH WS 1019, p. 7.

20 Report by General Commanding the Forces in Ireland, L.B. Friend, on the Subject of the Sentencing of Michael Mallin, 6 May 1916, Court Martial of Michael Mallin, WO 71 353, TNA.

21 Enright, *Trials*, p. 185.

22 Alfred Bucknill, BMH WS 1019, p. 5.

23 Report on the Court Martial of Countess Markievicz by the Convening Officer General John Maxwell, 6 May 1916, Activities of Countess Markievicz, HO 144 1580 316818, TNA.

24 Enright, *Trials*, p. 186.

25 Report by DMP Chief Superintendent Owen Brien, on the Subject of Property Found on Prisoner James Connolly, 21 May 1916, Personalities, CO 904 197, TNA.

26 Enright, *Trials*, p. 119.

27 Ibid. pp. 117–18.

28 Francis Costello, *The Irish Revolution and its Aftermath 1916–23, Years of Revolt* (Dublin, 2011), p. 19.

29 Appendix 5: 'Deportation of ICA Members, 1916 to British Prisons'.

30 Ibid.

31 Robbins, *Under the Starry Plough*, pp. 133–4.

32 James O'Connor, BMH WS 142, p. 6.

33 Charles Browne, BMH WS 873, pp. 4–5.

34 Seán M. O'Duffy, BMH WS 618, p. 4.

35 Ibid. pp. 10–11.

36 James O'Connor, BMH WS 142, p. 6.

37 William O'Brien, BMH WS 1766, p. 28.

38 Frank Henderson, BMH WS 249, p. 67.

39 W.J. Brennan-Whitmore, *With the Irish in Frongoch* (Cork, 2013), pp. 9–11.

40 Joseph Good, BMH WS 388, p. 23.

41 Note by William O'Brien, undated, O'Brien's 'Reminiscences', WOBP, MS 15,704 (1), NLI.

42 Matthew Connolly, BMH WS1746, p. 3.

43 Andrew Conroy, 28 Nov. 1936, MSP, 34REF20076.

44 James O'Neill, 26 Aug. 1916, Reading Gaol and Frongoch Internment Camp Autograph Book 1916–17, MS 46,586, NLI.

45 Richard McCormick, 22 Dec. 1916, Reading Gaol and Frongoch Internment Camp Autograph Book 1916–17, MS 46,586, NLI.

46 Seamus McGowan, 22 Dec. 1916, Reading Gaol and Frongoch Internment Camp Autograph Book 1916–17, MS 46,586, NLI.

47 O'Donnell, *Pearse*, p. 197.

48 Joseph Reader Robinson, 22 Dec. 1916, Reading Gaol and Frongoch Internment Camp Autograph Book 1916–17, MS 46,586, NLI; Seajan Ó Callaig, 22 Dec. 1916, Reading Gaol and Frongoch Internment Camp Autograph Book 1916–17, MS 46,586, NLI; Tomás MacCurtain, Christmas, Reading Gaol and Frongoch Internment Camp Autograph Book 1916–17, MS 46,586, NLI; Tomás Ó Grabám, undated, Reading Gaol and Frongoch Internment Camp Autograph Book 1916–17, MS 46,586, NLI.

49 Brennan-Whitmore, *With the Irish in Frongoch*, p. 39.

50 Lyn Ebenezer, *Frongoch Camp 1916 and the Birth of the IRA* (Llanrwst, 2012), p. 118.

51 Brennan-Whitmore, *With the Irish in Frongoch*, p. 39.

52 Robbins, BMH WS 585, p. 104.

53 Ibid. p. 105.

54 Brennan-Whitmore, *With the Irish in Frongoch*, p. 41.

55 Ibid. p. 45.

56 Ibid. p. 46; Robbins, BMH WS 585, p. 106.

57 Joseph V. Lawless, BMH WS 1043, p. 176.

58 Liam O'Maguire, 15 July 1916, Reading Gaol and Frongoch Internment Camp Autograph Book 1916–17, MS 46,586, NLI.

59 Seán MacGarigal, 18 July 1916, Reading Gaol and Frongoch Internment Camp Autograph Book 1916–17, MS 46,586, NLI.

60 Ebenezer, *Frongoch*, p. 116.

61 Brennan-Whitmore, *With the Irish in Frongoch*, p. 47; Ruán O'Donnell, 'Forward' in Brennan-Whitmore, *With the Irish in Frongoch*, p. 6.

Chapter 13

1 Michael Laffan, *The Resurrection of Ireland: the Sinn Féin Party, 1916–1923* (Cambridge, 2004), p. 77; Fox, *History*, p. 189.

2 Joost Augusteijn, *From Public Defiance to Guerrilla Warfare: the Experience of Ordinary Volunteers in the Irish War of Independence 1916–21* (London, 1998), pp. 56–9; p. 252.

3 Seamus McGowan, 19 Dec. 1935, MSP, 34REF4289.

4 Christopher Crothers, 27 June 1935, MSP, 34REF210.

5 John Hanratty, 22 Oct. 1936, in Christopher Poole, MSP, 34REF10145.

6 Greaves, *ITGWU*, p. 182.

7 Matthews, *Irish Citizen Army*, p. 160.

8 James O'Neill, undated, MSP, 34REF8368.

9 Fox, *History*, p. 205.

10 James O'Neill, undated, MSP, 34REF8368.

11 Oscar Traynor, 24 Jan. 1936, in James O'Neill, MSP, 34REF8368.

12 James O'Neill, 29 March 1935, in Irish Citizen Army, MSPC, RO 10A.

13 Hanley, 'The Irish Citizen Army After 1916', p. 39.

14 James O'Neill, 29 March 1935, in Irish Citizen Army, MSPC, RO 10A.

15 Ibid.; James O'Neill, 22 July 1935, MSP, 34REF8368.

16 Christopher Poole, 14 Feb. 1936, MSP, 34REF10145.

17 John Hanratty, 22 Oct. 1936, in Christopher Poole, MSP, 34REF10145.

18 Christopher Poole, 14 Feb. 1936, MSP, 34REF10145.

19 James O'Neill, undated, in Irish Citizen Army, MSPC, RO 10A.

20 Matthews, *Irish Citizen Army*, pp. 162–3.

21 James O'Neill, 18 July 1935, in John Hanratty, MSP, 34REF1362.

22 Christopher Poole, 14 Feb. 1936, MSP, 34REF10145.

23 Seamus McGowan, 19 Dec. 1935, MSP, 34REF4289.

24 Outline History of the 1917–23 Period by O/C John Hanratty, undated, 1913–23 Documents I, Hanratty Papers, Kilmainham Gaol.

25 Augusteijn, *From Public Defiance to Guerrilla Warfare*, p. 335.

26 Irish Citizen Army, MSPC, RO 10A.

27 Matthews, *Irish Citizen Army*, p. 160.

28 Fox, *History*, p. 194.

29 Jane Shanahan, 13 Nov. 1936, MSP, 34REF1015.

30 Helena Molony, BMH WS 391, p. 48.

31 Greaves, *ITGWU*, p. 168.

32 Irish Trades Union Congress and Labour Party, *Annual Report of the Twenty-Second Irish Trades Union Congress and Labour Party, 1916*, p. 6.

33 Ibid. p. 21.

34 Helena Molony, BMH WS 391, p. 48.

35 Fox, *History*, p. 198.

36 Greaves, *ITGWU*, p. 181.

37   Irish Trades Union Congress and Labour Party, *Annual Report of the Twenty-Third Irish Trades Union Congress and Labour Party, 1917*, p. 29.

38   Helena Molony, BMH WS 391, p. 48.

39   Greaves, *ITGWU*, p. 173.

40   Irish Citizen Army Memorandum, 1 June 1922, WOBP, MS 15,673, NLI.

41   Frank Robbins, BMH WS 585, p. 157.

42   Metscher, 'James Connolly', p. 147; Costello, *The Irish Revolution and its Aftermath*, p. 29.

43   Metscher, 'James Connolly', p. 147.

44   Andrew Conroy, 28 Nov. 1936, MSP, 34REF20076.

45   Jane Shanahan, 13 Nov. 1936, MSP, 34REF1015.

46   Untitled Royal Irish Constabulary Report, 1916, Gunrunning, CO 904 29, TNA. Robbins, *Under the Starry Plough*, p. 153.

47   Ibid.

48   Seamus McGowan, 19 Dec. 1935, MSP, 34REF4289.

49   Memorandum from DMP Chief Superintendent Owen Brien, 17 May 1916, Arms Importation and Distribution, CO 904/28, TNA.

50   John Byrne, undated, in Seamus McGowan, MSP, 34REF4289.

51   Helena Molony, 3 July 1936, MSP, 34REF11739.

52   Ibid.

53   Ibid.

54   Dennis Farrell, 27 June 1935, MSP, 34REF229.

55   Seamus Reader, BMH WS 933, p. 3.

56   Richard McCormick, 21 June 1935, MSP, 34REF2186.

57   James O'Shea, BMH WS 733, pp. 59–60.

58   Christopher Crothers, 20 June 1935, in James O'Shea, MSP, 34REF150.

59   James Keogh, 11 Feb. 1935, in Richard Corbally, MSP, 34REF208.

60   Richard McCormick, 20 June 1935, in James Keogh, MSP, 34REF1314.

61   Richard Corbally, 11 February 1935, MSP, 34REF208.

62   James Keogh, 11 Feb. 1935, in Richard Corbally, MSP, 34REF208; Richard McCormick, 21 June 1935, MSP, 34REF2186.

63   Richard McCormick, 21 June 1935, MSP, 34REF2186.

64   James O'Shea, BMH WS 733, p. 60.

65   Edward Handley, BMH WS 625, p. 1; James O'Shea, BMH WS 733, p. 60.

66   Edward Handley, BMH WS 625, p. 1.

67   Ibid. pp. 1–2.

68   James O'Shea, BMH WS 733, p. 6; p. 60.

69   Edward Handley, BMH WS 625, p. 2.

70   James O'Shea, BMH WS 733, pp. 61–2.

71   Outline History of the 1917–23 Period by O/C John Hanratty, undated, 1913–23 Documents I, Hanratty Papers, Kilmainham Gaol.

72   Fox, *History*, p. 206.

73   James O'Dwyer, 28 June 1935, MSP, 34REF1604.

74   Christopher Crothers, 22 Feb. 1935, in Robert de Coeur, MSP, 34REF158.

75   Christopher Poole, 14 Feb. 1936, MSP, 34REF10145; Peter Coates, undated, MSP, 34REF615; George Connolly, 21 Sept. 1936, MSP, 34REF1284; Laurence Corbally, 28 June 1935, MSP, 34REF1390; Richard Corbally, 11 Feb. 1935, MSP, 34REF208; James O'Shea, 20 June 1935, MSP, 34REF150.

76   Fox, *History*, p. 206.

77   George Connolly, 21 Sept. 1936, MSP, 34REF1284.

78   Fox, *History*, p. 207.

79   Seamus McGowan, 19 Dec. 1935, MSP, 34REF4289.

80   John Hanratty, 21 June 1935, MSP, 34REF1362.

81   Fox, *History*, pp. 207–8.

82   Richard Corbally, 11 Feb. 1935, MSP, 34REF208.

83   Intelligence Report of the Judicial Division, Chief Secretary's Office, 1919, Intelligence Notes, CO 903 19, TNA.

84   Matthews, *Irish Citizen Army*, p. 162.

85   Mary Allen, 23 November 1937, MSP, 34REF8867.

86   Greaves, *ITGWU*, p. 225.

Chapter 14

1   James O'Neill, undated, MSP, 34REF8368.

2   Obituary of Michael O'Doherty by Countess Markievicz, undated, Letters from Countess Markievicz, Joseph McGarrity Papers (JMP), MS 17,463, NLI; Countess Markievicz to Joseph McGarrity, undated, Letters from Countess Markievicz, JMP, MS 17,463, NLI; Essay on 'The Police' by Countess Markievicz, undated, Letters from Countess Markievicz, JMP, MS 17,463, NLI.

3   Army Pensions Board, 7 April 1941, in James O'Dwyer, MSP, 34REF1604.

4   Matthews, *Irish Citizen Army*, p. 167; Mulholland, *Kathleen Lynn*, p. 69.

5   Hanley, 'The Irish Citizen Army After 1916', p. 37.

6   Robbins, BMH WS 585, p. 158.

7   Fox, *History*, p. 205.

8   James O'Neill, 22 July 1935, MSP, 34REF8368.

9   Hanley, 'The Irish Citizen Army After 1916', p. 38.

10   W.H. Kautt, *Ambushes and Armour: the Irish rebellion 1919–1921* (Dublin, 2010), p. 185.

11   Andrew Conroy, undated, MSP, 34REF2007; Robbins, *Under the Starry Plough*, p. 215. Controversy over this event led to the dismissal of O'Neill and is discussed later in the chapter.

12   John Hanratty, 21 June 1935, MSP, 34REF1362.

13   Seamus McGowan, 21 June 1935, MSP, 34REF4289.

14   Hanley, 'The Irish Citizen Army After 1916', pp. 38–9.

15 James O'Neill, 22 July 1935, MSP, 34REF8368; Oscar Traynor, 24 Jan. 1936, in James O'Neill, MSP, 34REF8368.

16 Frank Murray, 13 May 1938, MSP, 34REF21493.

17 James O'Neill, 29 March 1935, in Irish Citizen Army, MSPC, RO 10A.

18 Frank Robbins, BMH WS 585, p. 160.

19 Edmond O'Brien, 1 April 1936, in Seamus McGowan, MSP, 34REF4289.

20 Christopher Crothers, 9 July 1935, in James Keogh, MSP, 34REF1314.

21 Ibid.

22 James O'Neill, 29 March 1935, in Irish Citizen Army, MSPC, RO 10A.

23 Robert de Coeur, 22 Feb. 1935, MSP, 34REF1658.

24 Oscar Traynor, 24 Jan. 1936, in James O'Neill, MSP, 34REF8368.

25 James O'Shea, 20 June 1935, MSP, 34REF150.

26 Martin Shannon, 21 Jan. 1935, MSP, 34REF1397.

27 Thomas Shiel, 20 June 1935, MSP, 34REF903.

28 Andrew Redmond, 28 Feb. 1935, MSP, 34REF3719; William Scott, 1 Feb. 1935, MSP, 34REF1644; Peter Bermingham, 13 Feb. 1935, MSP, 34REF1965.

29 Joseph Doolan, 4 June 1951, MSP, 34REF62059.

30 Matthews, *Irish Citizen Army*, p. 168.

31 South County Dublin Unit, in Irish Citizen Army, MSPC, RO 10A.

32 Pádraig Ó Broin, 20 Feb. 1937, in Dennis Dunne, MSP, 34REF1028.

33 Memorandum by Pádraig Ó Broin on the Subject of the South County Dublin ICA Unit's Active and General Service Between 1921–23, 1 June 1935, 1913–23 Documents I, Hanratty Papers, Kilmainham Gaol; Memorandum by Pádraig Ó Broin on the Subject of the South County Dublin ICA Unit's Active and General Service Between 1921–23, 1 June 1935, in Irish Citizen Army, MSPC, RO 10A.

34 Humphrey Murray, undated, in Pádraig Ó Broin, MSP, 34REF981.

35 Pádraig Ó Broin, 11 Dec. 1936, MSP, 34REF981.

36 Fox, *History*, pp. 205–6.

37 John Kearny, undated, in Q Company, MSP RO 611. The Hibernian Rifles was a splinter group of the AOH. Between twenty and thirty of its members had active service in the Easter Rising.

38 Oscar Traynor, 24 Jan. 1936, in James O'Neill, MSP, 34REF8368.

39 John Kearny, undated, in Q Company, MSP RO 611.

40 Christina Caffrey, 6 July 1937, MSP, 34REF9970.

41 Charles Diamond, 21 Nov. 1937, in Roderick Connolly, MSP, 34REF38900.

42 James Corbett, 10 Oct. 1938, in Frank Murray, MSP, 34REF21493.

43 James FitzGerald, 7 Oct. 1939, in Frank Murray, MSP, 34REF21493.

44 Christina Caffrey, 6 July 1937, MSP, 34REF9970.

45 Frank Murray, 22 Feb. 1935, in Robert de Coeur, MSP, 34REF1658.

46 Old IRA Scottish Division, 11 Nov. 1939, in Frank Murray, MSP, 34REF21493.

47 Seán MacMahon, 14 Oct. 1939, in Frank Murray, MSP, 34REF21493; James Corbett, 10 Oct. 1938, in Frank Murray, MSP, 34REF21493.

48   Joe Vize to Michael Collins, 5 Sept. 1919, RMP, P7/A/11, UCDA.

49   Michael Collins to Joe Vize, 11 Sept. 1919, RMP, P7/A/11, UCDA.

50   Gerard Noonan, *The IRA in Britain, 1919–23 in the Heart of Enemy Lines* (Liverpool, 2014), p. 310.

51   Report by the Home Office's Director of Intelligence, Basil H. Thompson, on Revolutionary Organisations in the United Kingdom, 10 July 1919, CAB 24/80/5, TNA.

52   Noonan, *The IRA in Britain*, p. 272.

53   Frank Murray, 13 May 1938, MSP, 34REF21493.

54   Seamus Reader, BMH WS 933, p. 9.

55   Frank Murray, 22 Feb. 1935, in Robert de Coeur, MSP, 34REF1658.

56   John Byrne, undated, in Seamus McGowan, MSP, 34REF4289.

57   John Hanratty, 21 June 1935, MSP, 34REF1362.

58   Pádraig Ó Broin, 11 Dec. 1936, MSP, 34REF981.

59   Oscar Traynor, 24 Jan. 1936, in James O'Neill, MSP, 34REF8368.

60   Ibid.

61   James Fitzgerald, 14 Jan. 1922, in John Byrne, MSP, 34REF17897; Seán McMahon, 14 Jan. 1922, in John Byrne, MSP, 34REF17897.

62   Seamus McGowan, 19 Dec. 1935, MSP, 34REF4289.

63   Gerry Golden, 20 April 1936, in Seamus McGowan, MSP, 34REF4289.

64   Michael Collins to Joe Vize, 29 May 1919, RMP, P7/A/11, UCDA; Michael Collins to Joe Vize, 19 June 1919, P7/A/11, UCDA.

65   Memorandum by Pádraig Ó Broin on the Subject of the South County Dublin ICA Unit's Active and General Service Between 1921–23, 1 June 1935, in Irish Citizen Army, MSPC, RO 10A.

66   Pádraig Ó Broin, 11 Dec. 1936, MSP, 34REF981.

67   Memorandum by Pádraig Ó Broin on the Subject of the South County Dublin ICA Unit's Active and General Service Between 1921–23, 1 June 1935, in Irish Citizen Army, MSPC, RO 10A.

68   Pádraig Ó Broin, 11 Dec. 1936, MSP, 34REF981.

69   Richard McCormick, 20 June 1935, in James Keogh, MSP, 34REF1314.

70   Edward Handley, BMH WS 625, p. 2.

71   Ibid. pp. 2–3.

72   Ibid. pp. 3–4.

73   Ibid. pp. 4–5.

74   Pádraig Ó Broin, 11 Dec. 1936, MSP, 34REF981.

75   Frank Robbins, 24 Nov. 1937, MSP, 34REF17899.

76   Helena Molony, 3 July 1936, MSP, 34REF11739.

77   Seamus McGowan, 19 Dec. 1935, MSP, 34REF4289.

78   William Carn, 7 Dec. 1936, in Kathleen Barrett, MSP, 34REF2198.

79   James O'Shea, 28 June 1935, in Edward Burke, MSP, 34REF1199.

80   Patrick Kiernan, 9 Dec. 1936, in Pádraig Ó Broin, MSP, 34REF981.

81   Christina Caffrey, 6 July 1937, MSP, 34REF9970.
82   John Hanratty, 11 Feb. 1935, in Frederick Norgrove, MSP, 34REF204.
83   Memorandum by Pádraig Ó Broin on the Subject of the South County Dublin ICA Unit's Active and General Service Between 1921–23, 1 June 1935, in Irish Citizen Army, MSPC, RO 10A.
84   Fox, *History*, p. 202.
85   James O'Neill, undated, MSP, 34REF8368.
86   Fox, *History*, p. 202.
87   James O'Shea, 20 June 1935, MSP, 34REF150.
88   Outline History of the 1917–23 Period by O/C John Hanratty, undated, 1913–23 Documents I, Hanratty Papers, Kilmainham Gaol.
89   Kautt, *Ambushes*, p. 187.
90   James O'Neill, 29 March 1935, in Irish Citizen Army, MSPC, RO 10A.
91   Kautt, *Ambushes*, p. 186.
92   Memorandum by Pádraig Ó Broin on the Subject of the South County Dublin ICA Unit's Active and General Service Between 1921–23, 1 June 1935, in Irish Citizen Army, MSPC, RO 10A.
93   Pádraig Ó Broin, 11 Dec. 1936, MSP, 34REF981.
94   Ibid.
95   James O'Neill, undated, MSP, 34REF8368.
96   Fox, *History*, p. 206.
97   Christopher Crothers, 9 July 1935, in Laurence Corbally, MSP, 34REF1390.
98   Laurence Corbally, 28 June 1935, MSP, 34REF1390.
99   James O'Neill, undated, MSP, 34REF8368; Philip O'Leary, 20 June 1935, MSP, 34REF970.
100 Pádraig Ó Broin, 11 Dec. 1936, MSP, 34REF981; James O'Neill, undated, MSP, 34REF8368.
101 Gerry Golden, 20 April 1936, in Seamus McGowan, MSP, 34REF4289.
102 William Oman, 11 Feb. 1935, MSP, 34REF37; Pádraig Yeates, *A City in Turmoil Dublin 1919–21* (Dublin, 2012), p. 47.
103 Thomas Kain, 30 Nov. 1937, MSP, 34REF12912; Laurence Corbally, 28 June 1935, MSP, 34REF1390; Christopher Crothers, 9 July 1935, in James O'Shea, MSP, 34REF150; William Oman, 11 Feb. 1935, MSP, 34REF37; Philip O'Leary, 20 June 1935, MSP, 34REF970.
104 William Oman, 11 Feb. 1935, MSP, 34REF37; Thomas Kain, 30 Nov. 1937, MSP, 34REF12912; Yeates, *City in Turmoil*, p. 47.
105 Charles Townshend, 'The Irish Railway Strike of 1920: Industrial Action and Civil Resistance in the Struggle for Independence' in *Irish Historical Studies*, 22 (1979), p. 265.
106 D.R. O'Connor Lysaght, *The Story of the Limerick Soviet: The 1919 General Strike Against British Militarism* (Limerick, 2003), pp. 7–9.
107 Grant, *Socialist Republicanism*, pp. 93–4.

108   Kostick, 'Labour Militancy', p. 197.
109   O'Connor Lysaght, *The Story of the Limerick Soviet*, pp. 9–10.
110   Kostick, 'Labour Militancy', p. 197.
111   Ibid.
112   Irish Labour Party and Trades Union Congress, *Annual Report of the Twenty-Fifth Irish Labour Party and Trades Union Congress, 1919*, p. 76.
113   Grant, *Socialist Republicanism*, p. 95.
114   O'Connor Lysaght, *The Story of the Limerick Soviet*, p. 20.
115   Irish Labour Party and Trades Union Congress, *Annual Report of the Twenty-Fifth Irish Labour Party and Trades Union Congress, 1919*, pp. 74–5.
116   Ibid. p. 77.
117   Lysaght, *The Story of the Limerick Soviet*, p. 5.
118   D.R. O'Connor Lysaght, *Syndicalism in Ireland 1917–23* (Limerick, 2003), p. 88.
119   Townshend, 'The Irish Railway Strike of 1920', p. 266.
120   Irish Labour Party and Trades Union Congress, *Annual Report of the Twenty-Sixth Irish Labour Party and Trades Union Congress, 1920*, p. 3.
121   Grant, *Socialist Republicanism*, p. 101; Costello, *The Irish Revolution and its Aftermath*, p. 171.
122   Irish Labour Party and Trades Union Congress, *Annual Report of the Twenty-Sixth Irish Labour Party and Trades Union Congress, 1920*, p. 41.
123   Kostick, 'Labour Militancy', p. 203.
124   Costello, *The Irish Revolution and its Aftermath*, pp. 173–4.
125   Ibid. p. 174.
126   Townshend, 'The Irish Railway Strike of 1920', p. 266.
127   Ibid. p. 273.
128   Costello, *The Irish Revolution and its Aftermath*, pp. 176–7.
129   Irish Labour Party and Trades Union Congress, *Annual Report of the Twenty-Seventh Irish Labour Party and Trades Union Congress, 1921*, p. 10.
130   Ibid. p. 11.
131   Costello, *The Irish Revolution and its Aftermath*, p. 179.
132   James O'Neill, 29 March 1935, in Irish Citizen Army, MSPC, RO 10A.
133   Oscar Traynor, 24 Jan. 1936, in James O'Neill, MSP, 34REF8368.
134   James O'Neill, 29 March 1935, in Irish Citizen Army, MSPC, RO 10A.
135   James O'Neill, 18 July 1935, in Christopher Crothers, MSP, 34REF210; James O'Neill, 28 June 193[undated], in Christopher Crothers, MSP, 34REF210.
136   Christopher Crothers, 27 June 1935, MSP, 34REF210; Christopher Crothers, BMH WS 1759, p. 1.
137   Christopher Crothers, 27 June 1935, MSP, 34REF210.
138   Ibid.
139   James O'Neill, 18 July 1935, in Christopher Crothers.
140   Christopher Crothers, BMH WS 1759, pp. 3–4.

141 Robert de Coeur, 22 Feb. 1935, MSP, 34REF1658; Christopher Crothers, BMH WS 1759, p. 2.

142 James O'Neill, 29 March 1935, in Irish Citizen Army, MSPC, RO 10A; Christopher Crothers, 27 June 1935, MSP, 34REF210.

143 James O'Neill, 29 March 1935, in Irish Citizen Army, MSPC, RO 10A.

144 ITGWU Branch No. 1 Minutes, 30 May 1917, Minutes of Committee Meetings of the ITGWU June 1916–June 1919, MS 7299300, NLI.

145 James O'Neill, 29 March 1935, in Irish Citizen Army, MSPC, RO 10A.

146 ICA Council Minutes, 10 Feb. 1919, ICA 1919–20 Minute book, IHLSM.

147 'Proceedings of a District Court Martial for the Trial of Peter Ennis, Civilian', 31 Oct. 1920, Raid on Liberty Hall, WO 35/106, TNA; 'Proceedings of a District Court Martial for the Trial of Christopher Quigley, Civilian', 24 Sept. 1919, Raid on Liberty Hall, WO 35/106, TNA.

148 Matthews, *Irish Citizen Army*, p. 168.

149 Greaves, *ITGWU*, p. 251.

150 Report by the Home Office's Director of Intelligence, Basil H. Thompson, on Revolutionary Organisations in the United Kingdom, 25 Sept. 1919, CAB 24/80/5, TNA.

151 ITGWU Branch No. 1 Minutes, 20 May 1917, Minutes of Committee Meetings of the ITGWU June 1916–June 1919, MS 7299-300, NLI.

152 Ibid.

153 Appendix 6: 'Irish Transport Union and General Workers' Union Branch No. 1 Minutes Relating to the Irish Citizen Army'.

154 Matthews, *Irish Citizen Army*, p. 168.

155 Frank Robbins, 24 Nov. 1937, MSP, 34REF17899.

156 *Watchword of Labour*, 15 Nov. 1919.

157 Report by the Home Office's Director of Intelligence, Basil H. Thompson, on Revolutionary Organisations in the United Kingdom, 4 June 1919, CAB 24/80/5, TNA.

158 Summary of the Argument of the Socialist Party of Ireland in Support of the Irish Claim at the International Socialist Conference Stockholm 1917, undated, COS 93/12/69(1), ILHSMA.

159 Roddy Connolly's Notes on Organisation of the SPI, 16 Sept. 1921, CPIP 1/001, DCL.

Chapter 15

1 ITGWU Branch No. 1 Minutes, 6 Oct. 1921, Minutes of Committee Meetings of the ITGWU Sept. 1920–May 1925, MS 7304-7308, NLI.

2 ITGWU Branch No. 1 Minutes, 5 Jan. 1922, Minutes of Committee Meetings of the ITGWU Sept. 1920–May 1925, MS 7304-7308, NLI; ITGWU Branch No. 1 Minutes, 26 Jan. 1922, Minutes of Committee Meetings of the ITGWU Sept. 1920–May 1925, MS 7304-7308, NLI.

3   James O'Neill, 29 March 1935, in Irish Citizen Army, MSPC, RO 10A.

4   Membership Form for an Irish Workers' Army, undated, Irish Citizen Army Documents, WOBP, MS 15,673 (1), NLI.

5   Ibid.

6   Letter sent from Unnamed Person to ITGWU Organisers Concerning the Advisability of Forming a Workers' Army, undated, WOBP, MS 27,044, NLI.

7   Ibid.

8   Matthews, *Irish Citizen Army*, p. 174.

9   Hanley, 'The Irish Citizen Army After 1916', p. 37; Letter from William O'Brien to Unnamed Persons Concerning the Advisability of Forming a Workers' Army, 2 Mar. 1922, Irish Citizen Army Documents, WOBP, MS 15,673 (1), NLI.

10 Andrew Conroy, 28 Nov. 1936, MSP, 34REF20076; Robbins, *Under the Starry Plough*, pp. 214–16.

11 Irish Citizen Army Memorandum, 1 June 1922, WOBP, MS 15,673, NLI.

12 John Hanratty, 21 June 1935, MSP, 34REF1362.

13 Fox, *History*, p. 216.

14 Ibid. pp. 216–17.

15 Pádraig Yeates, *A City in Civil War Dublin 1919–21* (Dublin, 2015), p. 52.

16 Fox, *History*, pp. 215–16; Matthews, *Irish Citizen Army*, pp. 173–4.

17 Irish Citizen Army Memorandum, 1 June 1922, WOBP, MS 15,673, NLI.

18 Ibid.

19 Irish Citizen Army Circular, 13 June 1922, WOBP, MS 15,673, NLI.

20 Ibid.

21 Fox, *History*, pp. 214–15.

22 Pádraig Ó Broin, 11 Dec. 1936, MSP, 34REF981.

23 P. Corrigan, 1 Aug. 1925, in Luke Bradley, MSP, 23SP5856.

24 Joseph Kearns, 2 June 1926, in George Campbell, MSP, 24SP6503; J.J. Lestor, 16 April 1925, in John Conroy, MSP, 24SP3406; William Egan, 11 April 1924, MSP, 24SP859.

25 Francis Fitzpatrick, 13 Nov. 1924, MSP, 24SP3651; Martin Foy, 2 Feb. 1926, MSP, 24SP1285; John Hendrick, 26 Jan. 1925, MSP, 24SP8147; Peter Jackson, undated, MSP, 24SP735; Thomas Michael Jennings, 8 Jan. 1925, MSP, 24SP4257; Patrick Joseph Drury; 25 Nov. 1924, MSP, 24SP1303; Edward Tuke, 22 December 1924, MSP, 24SP3528; Michael Dwyer, 6 Nov. 1924, MSP, 24SP219; James Donnelly, 3 Feb. 1926, MSP, 24SP9180.

26 Letter from D Organisation to the Irish Citizen Army, 15 May 1922, 1913–23 Documents I, Hanratty Papers, Kilmainham Gaol.

27 Fox, *History*, p. 218.

28 Michael Hopkinson, *Green against Green: the Irish Civil War* (Dublin, 2004), p. 117.

29 Fox, *History*, p. 218.

30 John Hanratty, 22 Oct. 1926, in Seamus McGowan, MSP, 34REF4289.

31 Hopkinson, *Green against Green*, p. 123.

32 Christopher Crothers, 9 July 1935, in Richard McCormick, MSP, 34REF2186; Richard McCormick, 21 June 1935, MSP, 34REF2186.
33 Seamus McGowan, 19 Dec. 1935, MSP, 34REF4289.
34 James Maguire, 14 Feb. 1936, MSP, 34REF9992.
35 Hopkinson, *Green against Green*, p. 124.
36 Report of Activity from South County Dublin ICA Unit, 31 June 1922, 1913–23 Documents I, Hanratty Papers, Kilmainham Gaol.
37 Pádraig Ó Broin, 11 Dec. 1936, MSP, 34REF981.
38 Letter from IRA O/C Dublin, Oscar Traynor, to ICA O/C, John Hanratty, 26 July 1922, 1913–23 Documents I, Hanratty Papers, Kilmainham Gaol.
39 Hopkinson, *Green against Green*, p. 145.
40 Richard McCormick, 28 June 1935, in Edward Burke, MSP, 34REF1199; Patrick Buttner, 20 July 1936, MSP, 34REF980; Elliot Elmes, 9 Dec. 1935, MSP, 34REF866; Fox, *History*, pp. 223–4.
41 Seamus McGowan, 21 June 1935, MSP, 34REF4289; Christopher Crothers, 16 July 1935, in Seamus McGowan, MSP, 34REF4289; James O'Neill, 18 July 1935, in Seamus McGowan, MSP, 34REF4289.
42 Robert de Coeur, 22 Feb. 1935, MSP, 34REF1658; Pádraig Ó Broin, 11 Dec. 1936, MSP, 34REF981.
43 James Keogh, 20 June 1935, MSP, 34REF1314.
44 Patrick Carroll, 21 June 1938, MSP, 34REF32621.
45 Richard McCormick, 21 June 1935, MSP, 34REF2186; Christopher Crothers, 27 June 1935, MSP, 34REF210.
46 Alfred Norgrove, 21 June 1935, MSP, 34REF1764.
47 Outline History of the 1917–23 Period by O/C John Hanratty, undated, 1913–23 Documents I, Hanratty Papers, Kilmainham Gaol.

Chapter 16

1 Hanley, 'The Irish Citizen Army After 1916', p. 41.
2 Patrick Byrne, *The Irish Republican Congress Revisited* (London, 1994), p. 15.
3 Hanley, 'The Irish Citizen Army After 1916', p. 42.
4 Unsigned ICA Memorandum, 3 Jan. 1935, Miscellaneous Leaflets and Pamphlets, Hanratty papers, Kilmainham Gaol.
5 Hanley, 'The Irish Citizen Army After 1916', p. 42.
6 Matthews, *Irish Citizen Army*, pp. 179–80.
7 Ibid. p. 80; Hanley, 'The Irish Citizen Army After 1916', p. 43.
8 Matthews, *Irish Citizen Army*, p. 83.
9 Big Flame, *Ireland Rising in the North* (Birmingham, 1981), p. 16.
10 Brian Hanley and Scott Millar, *The Lost Revolution: the Story of the Official IRA and the Workers' Party* (London, 2010), p. 146.
11 Judy Vannais, 'Postcards from the Edge: Reading Political Murals in the North of Ireland' in *Irish Political Studies*, 1(2001), p. 145.

12   Dominic Bryan, Clifford Stevenson, Gordon Gillespie and John Bell, *Public Displays of Flags and Emblems in Northern Ireland Survey 2006–2009* (Belfast, 2010), p. 34.

13   Connolly Association, *What is the Connolly Association? Constitution and Explanation* (Derby, 1963), p. 1.

14   Ibid. p. 7.

15   Connolly Association, 'Aims, Objects, and Methods' (http://www.connollyassociation.org.uk/aims-objects-methods/) (23 Aug. 2016)

16   Seán Murray, *The Irish Revolt: 1916 and After* (London, 1966), p. 3.

17   Ibid. p. 2.

18   Ibid. p. 3.

19   *Irish Times*, 24 Jan. 1991.

20   Joan Burton, 'Connolly Lit the Flame For Independence' (https://www.labour.ie/news/2016/05/15/connolly-lit-the-flame-for-independence/) (24 Aug. 2016).

21   Burton, 'Connolly Lit the Flame For Independence'.

22   Ibid.

23   Gerry Adams, 'Launch of Sinn Féin's National Programme of Events to Mark the Centenary of the 1916 Rising' (http://www.sinnfein.ie/contents/33261) (25 Aug. 2016).

24   Adams, 'Launch of Sinn Féin's National Programme'.

25   Ibid.

26   Lecture by Paul Murphy, entitled 'James Connolly: His Life and Ideas', 11 May 2016, Pery's Hotel, Limerick. Personal Recording.

27   Cian Prendiville to Author, 24 Aug. 2016.

28   Murphy, 'James Connolly'.

29   Ibid.

30   Ibid.

31   (http://eastwallforall.ie/?m=201403) (26 Aug. 2016)

32   East Wall for All, '"The Fighting Old Guard": The O'Doherty family in the North Dock' (http://eastwallforall.ie/?p=3108) (26 Aug. 2016); East Wall for All, '"He Was Buried From Stephen's Green" The Life and Death of James Corcoran – North Dock Resident, Trade Unionist and Citizen Army Volunteer' (http://eastwallforall.ie/?p=2817) (26 Aug. 2016); East Wall for All, '"Fighting and Hoping" – James Connolly to Chris Caffrey, Mar. 1916.' (hhttp://eastwallforall.ie/?p=3285) (26 Aug. 2016).

33   Michael D. Higgins, 'A Celebration of James Connolly & the Irish Citizen Army' in *Saothar*, 41 (2016), p. 26.

34   *New York Times*, 16 Mar. 2016. The other four women mentioned were Winifred Carney, Elizabeth O'Farrell, Kathleen Clarke and Mary Josephine Mulcahy.

35   *Irish Worker*, 9 May 1914; *Irish Worker*, 22 Aug. 1914; Irish Citizen Army Constitution, undated, in James O'Neill, MSP, 34REF8368.

36   Ibid.

37   Higgins, 'A Celebration of James Connolly & the Irish Citizen Army', p. 28.

BIBLIOGRAPHY

PRIMARY SOURCES

Archives
Ireland
Dublin City Library
Communist Party of Ireland Papers

Irish Labour History Society Museum and Archives, Dublin
Cathal O'Shannon Papers
Irish Citizen Army Minute Book 1919–20

Kilmainham Gaol, Dublin
Hanratty Papers

Military Archives, Dublin
Bureau of Military History Witness Statements
Military Service Pension Collection

National Archives of Ireland, Dublin
Dublin Metropolitan Police Movement of Extremists

National Library of Ireland, Dublin
Branch No. 1, Irish Transport and General Workers' Union Minutes, 1913–23
Joseph McGarrity Papers
Sheehy Skeffington Papers
Thomas Johnson Papers
William O'Brien Papers

University College Dublin
Richard Mulcahy Papers

Thomas McPartlin Papers

United Kingdom
The National Archives, London
Cabinet Papers
Colonial Office
War Office
Home Office

Newspapers and Periodicals
Advocate of Peace
An tÓglách
Cork Free Press
Daily Herald
Evening Telegraph
Fianna
Fortnightly Review
Forward
Freeman's Journal
International Socialist Review
Irish Freedom
The Irish Times
Irish Worker
New York American
New York Times
San Francisco Chronicle
Shan Van Vocht
The Christian Science Monitor
The Gaelic American
The Masses
The Philadelphia Press
The Public Ledger
The Times
Watchword of Labour
Weekly Irish Times
Workers' Republic
Workers' Voice

Command Papers and Reports

Appendix to Report of the Dublin Disturbances Commission Minutes of Evidence and Appendices, 1914 [Cd. 7272].

Army. Increased Rates of Separation Allowance for the Wives and Children of Soldiers, 1914–16 [Cd. 7623].

Defence of the Realm (no. 2). A Bill to Amend the Defence of the Realm Act, 1914, 1914 (383).

Defence of the Realm. A Bill to Confer on his Majesty in Council Power to Make Regulations During the Present War for the Defence of the Realm, 1914 (359).

International Workingman's Association, *Documents of the First International* (London, 1964).

International Working Men's Association, *Resolutions of the Congress 1866 and the Congress of Brussels, 1868* (London, 1868).

International Socialist Congress, *Full Report of the Proceedings of the International Workers Congress London July and August 1896* (London, 1896).

Internationaler Sozialisten-Kongreß, *Stuttgart 1907* (Berlin, 1907).

Irish Labour Party and Trades Union Congress, *Annual Report of the Twenty-Fourth Irish Labour Party and Trades Union Congress, 1918, and Special Congress,1 Nov. to 2 Nov. 1918.*

Irish Labour Party and Trades Union Congress, *Annual Report of the Twenty-Fifth Irish Labour Party and Trades Union Congress, 1919.*

Irish Labour Party and Trades Union Congress, *Annual Report of the Twenty-Sixth Irish Labour Party and Trades Union Congress, 1920.*

Irish Labour Party and Trades Union Congress, *Annual Report of the Twenty-Seventh Irish Labour Party and Trades Union Congress, 1921.*

Irish Trades Union Congress, *Twenty-first Annual Report of the Irish Trades Union Congress, 1914.*

Irish Trades Union Congress and Labour Party, *Twenty-second Annual Report of the Irish Trades Union Congress and Labour Party, 1916.*

Irish Trades Union Congress and Labour Party, *Twenty-third Annual Report of the Irish Trades Union Congress and Labour Party, 1917.*

Report of the Dublin Disturbances Commission, 1914 [Cd. 7269].

Report of the Royal Commission on the Rebellion in Ireland, 1916[Cd. 8279].

Report to Inquire into the Housing Conditions of the Working Classes in the City of Dublin, 1914 [Cd. 7273].

Royal Commission into the Circumstances Connected with the Landing of Arms at Howth on July 26th, 1914 [Cd. 7631].

Royal Commission on the Rebellion in Ireland. Minutes of Evidence and Appendix of Documents, 1916 [Cd. 8311].

Sinn Féin, *Sinn Féin Rebellion Handbook Easter 1916* (Dublin, 1917).

Memoirs, Lectures and Contemporary Journals and Publications

Brennan-Whitmore, W.J., *Dublin Burning: the Easter Rising from Behind the Barricades* (Dublin, 2013).

—, *With the Irish in Frongoch* (Cork, 2013).

Connolly Association, *What is the Connolly Association? Constitution and Explanation* (Derby, 1963).

Connolly, James, *Collected Works Volume One* (Dublin, 1987).

—, *Collected Works Volume Two* (Dublin, 1988).

Fortescue, Granville, *Fore-Armed: How to Build a Citizen Army* (Philadelphia, 1916).

Irish Transport and General Workers' Union, *Fifty Years of Liberty Hall the Golden Jubilee of the Irish Transport and General Workers' Union 1909–59* (Dublin, 1959).

Jaurés, Jean, *Democracy and Military Service* (Kent, 1916).

Kennedy, J.C., 'The Stuttgart Congress' in *Journal of Political Economy*, 8 (1907), pp. 489–91.

Kettle, T.M., 'The Agony of Dublin' in *The Irish Review*, 3 (1913), pp. 441–9.

MacEoinn, Uinseann, *Survivors* (Dublin, 1987).

Martin, F.X. (ed.), *Irish Volunteers 1913–1915: Recollections and Documents* (Dublin, 2013).

O'Brien, Seamus, 'The Great Dublin Strike and Lockout, 1913' in *Dublin's Fighting Story 1916–21* (Dublin, 2009), pp. 35–51.

O'Casey, Seán, *Drums Under the Windows* (London, 1972).

—, *The Story of the Irish Citizen Army* (London, 1980).

O'Donovan Rossa Funeral Committee, *Diarmuid Ó Donnabáin Rosa 1831–1915 Souvenir of Public Funeral to Glasnevin Cemetery Dublin, August 1st 1915* (Dublin, 1915).

Quelch, Harry, *Social Democracy and the Armed Nation* (Clerkenwell Green, 1900).

Robbins, Frank, 'Introducing Some Friends' in *Dublin Historical Record* 3 (1972), pp. 93–101.

—, *Under the Starry Plough: Recollections of the Irish Citizen Army* (Dublin, 1977).

Stephens, James, *The Insurrection in Dublin* (Dublin, 1916).

White, Jack, *Misfit* (London, 1930).

Wright, Arnold, *Disturbed Dublin* (Dublin, 1914).

Lectures

Paul Murphy, *Teachta Dála* for the Anti-Austerity Alliance, entitled 'James Connolly: His Life and Ideas', 11 May 2016, Pery's Hotel, Limerick.

Correspondence

Cian Prendiville to author, 24 August 2016.

SECONDARY SOURCES
Books

Augusteijn, Joost, *From Public Defiance to Guerrilla Warfare: the Experience of Ordinary Volunteers in the Irish War of Independence 1916–21* (London, 1998).

Bowman, Timothy, *Carson's Army: the Ulster Volunteer Force, 1910–22* (Manchester, 2007).

Boyce, David George, *Nationalism in Ireland* (London, 1982).

Bryan, Dominic, Stevenson, Clifford, Gillespie, Gordon, and Bell, John, *Public Displays of Flags and Emblems in Northern Ireland Survey 2006–2009* (Belfast, 2010).

Byrne, Patrick, *The Irish Republican Congress Revisited* (London, 1994).

Clarkson, J.D., *Labour and Nationalism in Ireland* (New York, 1925).

Collins, Lorcan, *James Connolly* (Dublin, 2012).

Connell jnr, Joseph E.A., *Dublin in Rebellion: A Directory 1913–23* (Dublin, 2009).

Costello, Francis, *The Irish Revolution and its Aftermath 1916–23, Years of Revolt* (Dublin, 2011).

Crick, Martin, *The History of the Social Democratic Federation* (Staffordshire, 1994).

Delany, William, *The Green and the Red: Revolutionary Republicanism and Socialism in Irish History: 1848–1923* (Lincoln, 2011).

Devine, Francis, *Organising History: a Centenary of SIPTU* (Dublin, 2009).

Douglas, J. Newton, *British Labour, European Socialism and the Struggle for Peace 1889–1914* (Oxford, 1985).

Dutt, Rajani Palme, *The Two Internationals* (London, 1920).

Ebenezer, Lyn, *Frongoch Camp 1916 and the Birth of the IRA* (Llanrwst, 2012).

Enright, Seán, *Easter Rising: the Trials* (Dublin, 2014).

Ferriter, Diarmaid, *A Nation and not a Rabble: the Irish Revolution 1913–1923* (London, 2015).

Foster, R.F., *Vivid Faces: the Revolutionary Generation in Ireland 1890–1923* (Milton Keynes, 2015).

Fox, R.M., *James Connolly the Forerunner* (Tralee, 1946).

—, *The History of the Irish Citizen Army* (Dublin, 1943).

Foy, Michael T., and Barton, Brian, *The Easter Rising* (Gloucestershire, 2011).

Grant, Adrian, *Irish Socialist Republicanism 1909–36* (Dublin, 2012).

Greaves, C. Desmond, *Seán O'Casey: Politics and Art* (London, 1979).

—, *The Irish Transport and General Workers' Union* (Dublin, 1982).

—, *The Life and Times of James Connolly* (Berlin, 1971).

Hanley, Brian, and Millar, Scott, *The Lost Revolution: the Story of the Official IRA and the Workers' Party* (London, 2010).

Hopkinson, Michael, *Green Against Green: the Irish Civil War* (Dublin, 2004).

Hughes, Brian, *Michael Mallin* (Dublin, 2012).

Jackson, T.A., *Ireland Her Own: an Outline History of the Struggle* (Berlin, 1971).

Joll, James, *The Second International* (Boston, 1974).

Kautt, W.H., *Ambushes and Armour: the Irish Rebellion 1919–1921* (Dublin, 2010).

Keogh, Dermot, *The Rise of the Irish Working Class* (Belfast, 1982).

Keohane, Leo, *Captain Jack White: Imperialism, Anarchism and the Irish Citizen Army* (Dublin, 2014).

Kiberd, Declan, *Inventing Ireland: The Literature of the Modern Nation* (London, 1996).

Laffan, Michael, *The Resurrection of Ireland: the Sinn Féin Party, 1916–1923* (Cambridge, 2004).

Lynch, David, *Radical Politics in Modern Ireland: the Irish Socialist Republican Party 1896–1904* (Dublin, 2005).

Marreco, Anne, *The Rebel Countess: the Life and Times of Constance Markievicz* (London, 2000).

Matthews, Ann, *The Irish Citizen Army* (Cork, 2014).

McGarry, Ferghal, *The Rising Ireland: Easter 1916* (New York, 2011).

McGee, Owen, *The IRB The Irish Republican Brotherhood from Land League to Sinn Féin* (Dublin, 2005).

Metscher, Priscilla, *James Connolly and the Reconquest of Ireland* (Minneapolis, 2002).

Moran, James, *Four Irish Rebel Plays* (Dublin, 2007).

Morley, Kevin, *A Descriptive History of the Irish Citizen Army* (Dublin, 2012).

Morrissey SJ, Thomas J., *Willliam O'Brien 1881–1968: Socialist, Republican, Dáil Deputy, Editor and Trade Union Leader* (Dublin, 2007).

Mulholland, Marie, *The Politics and Relationships of Kathleen Lynn* (Cork, 2002).

Murray, Seán, *The Irish Revolt: 1916 and After* (London, 1966).

Nevin, Donal, *James Connolly: a Full Life* (Dublin, 2006).

Newsinger, John, *Rebel City Larkin, Connolly and the Dublin Labour Movement* (London, 2004).

Noonan, Gerard, *The IRA in Britain, 1919–23 in the Heart of Enemy Lines* (Liverpool, 2014).

O'Brien, Paul, *1916 In Focus Shootout: the Battle for St. Stephen's Green, 1916* (Dublin, 2013).

Ó Catháin, Máirtin Seán, *Irish Republicanism in Scotland 1858–1916 Fenians in Exile* (Dublin, 2007).

Ó Conchubhair Brian (ed.), *Dublin's Fighting Story 1916–21: Told by the Men Who Made It* (Dublin, 2009).

O'Connor, Emmet, *A Labour History of Ireland 1824–1960* (Dublin, 1992).

—, *A Labour History of Ireland 1824–2000* (Dublin, 2011).

—, *Big Jim Larkin: Hero or Wrecker?* (Dublin, 2015).

—, *Syndicalism in Ireland 1917–23* (Cork, 1988).

O'Connor Lysaght, D.R., *The Story of the Limerick Soviet: the 1919 General Strike Against British Militarism* (Limerick, 2003).

O'Donnell, Ruán, *Patrick Pearse* (Dublin, 2016).

Townshend, Charles, *Easter 1916: the Irish Rebellion* (London, 2006).

Van Voris, Jacqueline, *Constance De Markievicz* (Vermont, 1967).

Yeates, Pádraig, *A City in Civil War Dublin 1919–21* (Dublin, 2015).

—, *A City in Turmoil Dublin 1919-21* (Dublin, 2012).

—, *A City in Wartime Dublin 1914-18* (Dublin, 2011).

—, *Lockout Dublin 1913* (New York, 2001).

Articles

Collins, Stephen, 'John Redmond: Discarded Leader' in *An Irish Quarterly Review*, 98 (200), pp. 123–33.

Darlington, Ralph, 'Revolutionary Syndicalist Opposition to the First World War: A Comparative Reassessment' in *Revue Belge de Philologie et D'histoire*, 4 (2006), pp. 983–1003.

Dolan Stover, Justin, 'Delaying Division, Eoin MacNeill, John Redmond and the Irish Volunteers' in *History Studies*, 8 (2007), pp. 111–23.

Dukova, Anastasia, 'Policing the Lockout' in *History Ireland*, 4 (2003), pp. 32–3.

Fearon, James D., and Laitin, David D., 'Ethnicity, Insurgency, and Civil War' in *The American Political Science Review*, 1 (2003), pp. 75–90.

Hanley, Brian, 'The Irish Citizen Army After 1916' in *Saothar*, 28 (2003), pp. 37–47.

Higgins, Michael D., 'A Celebration of James Connolly & the Irish Citizen Army' in *Saothar*, 41 (2016), pp. 25–30.

Jalland, Patricia, and Stubbs, John, 'The Irish Question after the Outbreak of War in 1914: Some Unfinished Party Business' in *The English Historical Review*, 96 (1981), pp. 778–807.

Joye, Lar, 'TSS Helga II' in *History Ireland*, 2 (2010), p. 39.

Martin, F. X., 'The 1916 Rising: a "Coup D'état" or a "Bloody Protest"?' in *Studia Hibernica*, 8 (1968), pp. 106–37.

McCarthy, Charles, 'The Impact of Larkinism on the Irish Working Class' in *Saothar*, 1 (1978), pp. 54–6.

McConnel, James, 'The Irish Parliamentary Party, Industrial Relations and the 1913 Dublin Lockout' in *Saothar, 28* (2003), pp. 25–36.

McHugh, Roger, '"Always Complainin": The Politics of Young Seán' in *Irish University Review* 1 (1980), pp. 91–7.

Moran, Bill, '1913, Jim Larkin and the British Labour Movement' in *Saothar*, 1 (1978), pp. 35–49.

Morgan, Kevin, 'Militarism and Anti-Militarism: Socialists, Communists and Conscription in France and Britain 1900–1940' in *Past and Present*, 202 (2009), pp. 207–44.

Newsinger, John, '"A Lamp to Guide Your Feet": Jim Larkin, the Irish Worker and the Dublin Working Class' in *European History Quarterly*, 1 (1990), pp. 63–99.

—, 'Seán O'Casey and Politics' in *Journal of Contemporary History*, 2 (1985), pp. 221–40.

O'Ceallaigh Ritschel, Nelson, 'Shaw, Connolly and the Irish Citizen Army' in *The Annual of Bernard Shaw Studies*, 27 (2007), pp. 118–34.

O'Connor Lysaght, D.R., 'The Irish Citizen Army 1913–16: White, Larkin, and Connolly' in *History Ireland*, 2 (2006), pp. 16–21.

O'Donoghue, Florence, 'Plans for the 1916 Rising' in *University Review*, 1 (1963), pp. 3–21.

Paseta, Senia, '1798 in 1898: The Politics of Commemoration' in *The Irish Review*, 22 (1998), pp. 46–53.

Ron, James, 'Paradigm in Distress? Primary Commodities and Civil War' in *The Journal of Conflict Resolution*, 4 (2005), pp. 443–50.

Schafer, Mark, Robinson, Sam, and Aldrich, Bradley, 'Operational Codes and the 1916 Easter Rising in Ireland: a Test of the Frustration–Aggression Hypothesis' in *Foreign Policy Analysis*, 2 (2006), pp. 63–82.

Shannon, June, 'Remembering RCSI and the 1916 Rising' in *Irish Journal of Medical Science*, 2 (2006), pp. 5–9.

Thorpe, Wayne, 'The European Syndicalists and War, 1914–1918' in *Contemporary European History*, 1 (2001), pp. 1–24.

Townshend, Charles, 'The Irish Railway Strike of 1920: Industrial Action and Civil Resistance in the Struggle for Independence' in *Irish Historical Studies*, 22 (1979), pp. 265–82.

Vannais, Judy, 'Postcards from the Edge: Reading Political Murals in the North of Ireland' in *Irish Political Studies*, 1(2001), pp. 133–60.

White, John, 'Bad, Sad Specimens of the Human Race' in *History Ireland* 4 (2013), pp. 34–6.

Woggon, Helga, 'Not Merely a Labour Organisation: the ITGWU and the Dublin Dock Strike, 1915–6' in *Saothar*, 27 (2002), pp. 43–54.

Chapters in Edited Books

Beiner, Guy, 'Making Sense of Memory: Coming to Terms With Conceptualisation of Historical Remembrance' in Richard Grayson and Fearghal McGarry (eds), *Remembering 1916 The Easter Rising, The Somme and The Politics of Memory in Ireland* (Cambridge, 2016), pp. 13–23.

Boyce, David George, 'The Ulster Crisis: Prelude to 1916?' in Gabriel Doherty and Dermot Keogh (eds), *1916: the Long Revolution* (Cork, 2007), pp. 45–60.

Boyle, John W., 'Connolly, the Citizen Army and the Rising' in K. Nowlan (ed.) *The Making of 1916 Studies in the History of the Rising* (Dublin, 1969), pp. 51–68.

Granville, David, 'The British Labour and Socialist Movement and the 1916 Rising' in Ruán O'Donnell (ed.), *The Impact of the 1916 Rising Among the Nations* (Dublin, 2008), pp. 49–70.

Hart, Peter, 'Definition: Defining the Irish Revolution' in Joost Augusteijn (ed.), *The Irish Revolution, 1913–23* (London, 2002), pp. 17–33.

Kostick, Conor, 'Labour Militancy during the Irish War of Independence' in F. Lane and D. O'Drisceoil (eds), *Politics and the Irish Working Class 1830–1945* (New York, 2005), pp. 187–206.

Matthews, Ann, 'Vanguard of the Revolution? The Irish Citizen Army, 1916' in Ruán O'Donnell (ed.), *The Easter Rising Among the Nations* (Dublin, 2008), pp. 24–36.

McCabe Conor, '"Your Only God is Profit": Irish Class Relations and the 1913 Lockout' in David Convery (ed.), *Locked Out: A Century of Irish Working Class Life* (Dublin, 2013), pp. 9–22.

Metscher, Priscilla, 'James Connolly, the Easter Rising and the First World War: A Contextual Study' in Ruan O'Donnell (ed.), *The Impact of the 1916 Rising Among the Nations* (Dublin, 2008), pp. 141–60.

Mulligan, William, 'Forging a Better World: Socialists and International Politics in the Early Twentieth Century' in Paul Daly, Rónán O'Brien and Paul Rouse (eds), *Making the Difference? The Irish Labour Party 1912–2012*, pp. 54–6.

Nevin, Donal, 'The Irish Citizen Army' in Donal Nevin (ed.), *James Larkin: Lion to the Fold* (Dublin, 2006), pp. 253–6.

Noonan, Alan, '"Real Irish Patriots Would Scorn to Recognise the Like of You": Larkin and Irish-America' in David Convery (ed.), *Locked Out: A Century of Irish Working Class Life* (Dublin, 2013), pp. 57–74.

Ó Catháin, Máirtín Seán, 'A Land Beyond the Sea: Irish and Scottish Republicans in Dublin 1916' in R. O'Donnell (ed.), *The Impact of the 1916 Rising Among the Nations* (Dublin, 2008), pp. 37–48.

O'Connor, Emmet, 'War and Syndicalism 1914–23' in Donal Nevin (ed.), *Trade Union Century* (Dublin, 1994), pp. 54–65.

O'Donnell, Ruán, 'Forward' in Brennan-Whitmore, *With the Irish in Frongoch* (Cork, 2013), pp. 5–6.

—, 'New Introduction' in F.X. Martin (ed.), *The Irish Volunteer 1913–15: Recollections and Documents* (Dublin, 2013), pp. 1–4.

O'Riordan, Manus, 'Larkin in America: the Road to Sing Sing' in Donal Nevin (ed.), *James Larkin: Lion to the Fold* (Dublin, 2006), pp. 64–73.

Townshend, Charles, 'Historiography: Telling the Irish Revolution' in Joost Augusteijn (ed.), *The Irish Revolution, 1913–23* (London, 2002), pp. 1–16.

Woggon, Helga, 'Interpreting James Connolly' in Fintan Land and Donal Ó Drisceoil (eds), *Politics and the Irish Working Class* (New York, 2005), pp.172–86.

Zurbrugg, A.W., 'Introduction' in A.W. Zurbrugg (ed.), *Not Our War Writing Against the First World War* (London, 2014), pp. 1–4.

Theses

Campbell Ransom, Bernard, 'James Connolly and the Scottish Left' (unpublished PhD thesis, University of Edinburgh, 1975).

Online Resources

Connolly Association, 'Aims, Objects, and Methods' (http://www. connollyassociation.org.uk/aims-objects-methods/) (23 Aug. 2016).

INDEX

Note: Page locators in bold refer to tables.